TEACHING STRATEGIES FOR THE SOCIAL STUDIES

FOURTH EDITION

TEACHING STRATEGIES FOR THE SOCIAL STUDIES

Inquiry, Valuing, and Decision-Making

James A. Banks
University of Washington, Seattle

With contributions by
Ambrose A. Clegg, Jr.
Kent State University, Ohio

Longman
New York & London

Teaching Strategies for the Social Studies:
Inquiry, Valuing, and Decision-Making, fourth edition

Longman, 95 Church Street, White Plains, N.Y. 10601

Associated companies:
Longman Group Ltd., London
Longman Cheshire Pty., Melbourne
Longman Paul Pty., Auckland
Copp Clark Pitman, Toronto

Executive editor: Raymond T. O'Connell
Production editor: Dee Amir Josephson
Text design: Kevin Kall
Cover design: Anne M. Pompeo
Production supervisor: Joanne Jay

Library of Congress Cataloging-in-Publication Data

Banks, James A.
    Teaching strategies for the social studies: inquiry, valuing, and
decision-making / James A. Banks ; with contributions by Ambrose A.
Clegg, Jr. — 4th ed.
        p.   cm.
    Includes bibliographical references.
    1. Social sciences—Study and teaching (Higher)   I. Clegg,
Ambrose A.   II. Title.
H62.B325   1990
300′.71′173—dc20   89-13029
                                                                CIP

CDEFGHIJ-DO-99   98 97 96 95 94 93 92 91 90

To Cherry
Compassionate critic, respected colleague and best friend,
And to Angela and Patricia,
With the hope that their generation will create a better world

Contents

Preface

The torrid weather in the U. S. Midwestern states during the spring and summer of 1988 and the resulting drought dramatized U.S. Iinks with the world and the extent to which humans everywhere on the earth share a common fate and destiny. Some scientists believe that the high temperatures and drought indicated that the greenhouse effect is taking place and that human pollutants are depleting the ozone layer of the atmosphere. Other scientists are reluctant to link the high temperatures and destructive drought of 1988 to the greenhouse effect. However, scientists agree that human pollutants, which have global origins, are depleting the stratospheric ozone and that the earth's temperature is rising.

The depletion of the ozone layer illustrates that the world is a global system and that all of earth's inhabitants share intractable problems, which cannot be solved unless citizens from many different nations and cultures participate in the shaping of public policies to ensure the survival of planet earth and humankind. Despite the growing interdependence of the world and its problems, nationalism is as strong as ever. The challenge to the social studies on the eve of the twenty-first century is to help students develop reflective attachments to their nation-states *and* a sense of kinship with citizens in all parts of the world.

We also need to help students develop the ability and commitment to influence public policy. As in the previous editions, our central thesis is that the main goal of the social studies should be to help students develop the ability to make reflective decisions. This goal remains essential despite the call by many popular writers for a social studies curriculum that emphasizes the mastery of factual knowledge. To make reflective decisions and to act to make the U.S. and the world more humane, students need to master important outcomes in addition to facts. They need to understand how knowledge is constructed, what purposes it serves, and how it reflects the values and goals of the people who formulate the knowledge categories. Understanding how knowledge is socially constructed will help students to become reflective citizen actors.

Our belief about the proper goal of the social studies is based on the assumption that humans will always face personal and social problems, and that all citizens should participate in the making of civic and public policy. The theory of social studies education presented in this book is grounded in democratic beliefs. One of its basic assumptions is that citizen participation in the making of public policy is essential for the creation and perpetuation of a free, humane, and civic community. This theory also assumes that individuals are not born with the ability to make reflective decisions, but that decision-making consists of a set of interrelated skills that can be identified and systematically taught. It also assumes that people can identify and clarify their values, and that they can be taught to reflect on problems before taking actions to solve them. The main components of decision-making are scientific knowledge, value analysis and clarification, and the synthesis of knowledge and values. Reflective citizens act on many of their decisions.

The organization of this text reflects the basic components of the decision-making and citizen action theory presented within it. Part I describes the rationale for a social studies curriculum focused on decision-making and citizen action, along with the knowledge and inquiry components of such a curriculum. Social studies skills, issues, and materials are described in Part II. Part III describes the social science disciplines and activities and strategies that can be used to teach important social science concepts and generalizations. Each of the social science disciplines provides students with a unique way to view human behavior, one that is essential for reflective decision-making. Exemplary strategies for teaching the key ideas of the disciplines and for helping students to view public issues from an interdisciplinary perspective constitute a major section of Part III. The final section of the book, Part IV, focuses on value inquiry, decision-making, citizen action, and evaluation.

This fourth edition has been revised throughout to reflect current developments, research, and discussions in social studies education. A new feature of this edition, inquiry strategies are interspersed within the chapters to illustrate concrete ways to teach the major concepts and skills discussed. More profiles of social scientists working on the cutting edges of their disciplines have been added to this edition. The profiles are designed to add to the reading appeal of the book as well as to acquaint readers with some of the important work that social scientists are doing to help solve human problems.

When undertaking a revision of this scope and magnitude, an author becomes indebted to many friends and colleagues. Professor Ambrose A. Clegg, Jr. provided thoughtful and helpful comments on Chapters 1, 2, 3, 5 and 7, many of which I incorporated into the text. He also revised Chapters 4, 14, and 16. Christine C. Schaefer contributed and revised Chapter 6. Cherry A. McGee Banks is the original author of Chapter 7, which I revised for this fourth edition. I wish to thank Patricia Avery, John Degutis, and Patricia Van Decar for reviewing the third edition and making helpful suggestions for this revision. I am grateful to Professor Walter C. Parker for commenting on a draft of this preface.

I wish to thank several individuals for helping me to identify and obtain photographs to illustrate the text: Edna Kellman, Seattle Public Schools; Terri Malinowski, Northshore School District, Bothell Washington, and Judy Mix, Lake Washington School District, Kirkland, Washington. I am also grateful to the staff of the Photograph Division of the National Archives, Washington, D.C. for helping me to identify and secure photographs for use in this fourth edition.

I am indebted to Cherry A. McGee Banks for being a caring and reflective colleague for over two decades and for preparing the index. I am grateful to Angela and Patricia, my daughters who are public school students, for sharing their views about effective social studies teaching.

James A. Banks

PART _____ I

The Goal of Social Studies Education

(*Source:* Robb Mitchell, Lake Washington School District, Seattle.)

Part I describes the goals of social studies education in a post-industrial world society and sets forth the essential components of an effective social studies curriculum. Chapter 1 describes some of the characteristics of the post-industrial world and the kind of social studies curriculum needed to help students acquire the knowledge, skills, and attitudes needed to become effective citizen actors in our nation and world. It presents a rationale for a social studies curriculum focused on decision-making and reflective citizen action. The essential components of decision-making are discussed and illustrated. They include scientific, interdisciplinary, and higher-level knowledge, value analysis and clarification, and the synthesis of knowledge and values.

Sound decisions must be derived from scientific and interdisciplinary knowledge. Knowledge from any one discipline is too limited to enable the citizen actor to fully understand the complexity of human behavior and to make reflective decisions on personal and public issues. Because each of the social science disciplines provides us with a unique lens with which to view the human drama, the reflective citizen actor must be able to see human behavior from diverse disciplinary perspectives. Chapter 2 illustrates ways in which teachers can conceptualize, plan, and teach interdisciplinary social studies units that are based on higher-level concepts and generalizations and that focus on important topics and social issues.

Reflective citizen actors must not only be able to use interdisciplinary knowledge derived from several disciplines, they must also understand the nature of social inquiry, be aware of its assumptions, and be able to use the method themselves when it is necessary and appropriate. The first part of Chapter 3 describes the nature of social inquiry and illustrates ways in which teachers can help students to develop social inquiry skills. The second part of the chapter discusses the nature of social knowledge—facts, concepts, generalizations, and theories—and ways to help students derive this knowledge. Chapter 4 focuses on questioning strategies, which are an integral and important part of social inquiry and the decision-making process.

1

The Social Studies:
Nature and Goals

THE SOCIAL STUDIES
IN A POST-INDUSTRIAL WORLD SOCIETY

The social studies is that part of the elementary and high school curriculum which has the primary responsibility for helping students to develop the knowledge, skills, attitudes, and values needed to participate in the civic life of their local communities, the nation, and the world. While the other curriculum areas also help students to attain some skills needed to participate in a democratic society, the social studies is the only area that has the development of civic competencies and skills as its primary goal.

Helping students become effective citizens in today's world is a tremendous challenge because of the enormous changes in our global society. Futurists agree that we are living in a world society characterized by rapid and tumultuous changes. The unprecedented changes sweeping our world society are neither temporary nor fleeting, but are signs that we are entering a new society and age in which many of our traditional values, assumptions, and behaviors will be challenged. New value problems and issues will also arise, as problems related to such developments as the eroding of the ozone layer of the atmosphere, biogenetic engineering, the nuclear challenge, and the aging of the population in Western societies become increasingly important.

Futurists use different words to describe the emerging world society. Alvin Toffler calls it the "Third Wave" society. John Naisbitt refers to it as the "information society." Daniel Bell prefers the term "post-industrial society."[1] These writers agree that the emerging world society will differ markedly from the industrial age that dominated Western democratic societies during the nineteenth and the first half of the twentieth centuries. While the indus-

3

trial age was characterized by the production of goods, the post-industrial society will be increasingly characterized by services and the production of knowledge. Bell believes that a knowledge or information class will emerge.

The post-industrial society will also be characterized by global rather than national economies, international problems that will require global rather than national solutions, and diversity in life-styles, values, beliefs, cultures, and political sentiments. Toffler writes, ". . . we begin to glimpse a new kind of social order—no longer a mass society, but a high-change, high-diversity, de-massified civilization."[2] Toffler believes that almost everyone will be a member of some kind of minority group in the post-industrial society, whether cultural, social, religious, or political.

The futurists also point out that participatory democracy will increasingly characterize post-industrial societies. More people will want to participate in the decisions affecting their lives—not only in politics, but on their jobs.[3] Much political activity will occur at the local and regional rather than at the national level. Decentralization, or the dispersal of power and decision-making, will be one of the characteristics of post-industrial society.

A social studies curriculum designed to help students develop the knowledge, skills, and values needed to effectively participate in a post-industrial world society must have characteristics different from traditional social studies curricula. Traditional social studies curricula emphasize the mastery of low-level facts, such as the names of rivers, capital cities, and important dates. Traditional social studies is also characterized by a focus on the Western world, the development of a tenacious and nonreflective nationalism, textbook-centered teaching, and scant attention to citizen action.

A social studies curriculum consistent with the changing world society in which we live must focus on higher levels of knowledge rather than on facts, teach about developing as well as Westernized nations, use a variety of teaching materials, and help students to develop clarified, reflective, and positive identifications with their local cultures, nation-state, and the world.[4]

Helping students to develop a reflective identification with their nation-state is necessary but not sufficient in today's world society. Solutions to many of the most pressing world problems require cooperation by citizens in many different parts of the world. Citizens who have a clarified and reflective identification with the world community are needed to help solve the most pressing problems that face humankind. A modernized social studies curriculum should also help students to develop the knowledge, skills and commitment needed to participate in action to shape public policy in their communities, nation, and the world.

THE GOALS OF THE SOCIAL STUDIES

The major goal of the social studies is to prepare citizens who can make reflective decisions and participate successfully in the civic life of their communities, nation, and the world. Goals in four categories contribute to this major goal: (1) *knowledge*, (2) *skills*, (3) *attitudes and values*, and (4) *citizen action*.

PROFILE

Lester R. Brown

Analyzing Global Trends and Urging Action

Lester R. Brown is President and Senior Researcher with Worldwatch Institute, a nonprofit Washington-based research institute devoted to the analysis of emerging global trends. In a series of annually published books called *State of the World*, Brown and his colleagues at the Worldwatch Institute describe the changing physical characteristics of the planet earth. A recent edition indicates that "the earth's forests are shrinking, its deserts expanding, and its soils eroding—all at record rates. Each year thousands of plants and animal species disappear, many before they are named or catalogued. The very temperature of the earth appears to be rising, posing a threat of unknown dimensions to virtually all the life-support systems on which humanity depends."

Brown does not describe the deteriorating state of the earth to counsel despair. Rather, he presents facts about the physical condition of the earth to urge world leaders and citizens to take decisive actions to save endangered earth and human life. Increasing public concern about the eroding of the ozone layer of the atmosphere has given his work a growing audience. He recommends specific actions to protect the earth, such as "reforesting the earth, avoiding a mass extinction of species, redesigning farming and industry to curtail toxic chemicals, and renewing the global commitment to family planning." [Lester Brown et al., *State of the World 1988* (New York: W. W. Norton, 1988).]

Knowledge

Students must master knowledge in order to make reflective decisions and to participate effectively in their civic communities. Knowledge in the social studies curriculum is usually drawn from the social science disciplines and from history. However, it may also be drawn from the humanities, as well as from other sources if it is needed by the citizen actor to make decisions and to take actions. Philosophy is frequently drawn upon in the social studies to help students identify and clarify their values. To make reflective decisions, citizen actors must use higher levels of knowledge, such as concepts, generalizations, and theories. The social science disciplines are discussed in Part III.

Skills

Skill goals are very important in the social studies. They can be categorized as follows:

> *Thinking Skills:* These skills include the ability to conceptualize, to interpret, to analyze, to generalize, to apply knowledge, and to evaluate knowledge.[5]
>
> *Social Science Inquiry Skills:* These skills include the ability to formulate scientific questions and hypotheses, to collect pertinent data, and to use the data to test hypotheses and to derive generalizations. Social science inquiry skills are discussed in Chapter 3.
>
> *Academic or Study Skills:* These skills include the ability to locate, organize, and acquire information through reading, to acquire information through listening and observing, to communicate orally and in writing, to interpret pictures, charts, graphs, and tables, to construct time lines, to take notes, to make charts, and to read and interpret maps.[6]
>
> *Group Skills:* These skills include the ability to perform effectively both as a leader and as a follower in solving group problems, to participate in group research projects, to help set group goals, to use power effectively and fairly in group situations, to make useful contributions to group projects, to communicate effectively in a group, and to help resolve controversy in groups.[7] Skills are discussed in Chapters 3, 4, 5, and 6.

Attitudes and Value Goals

Citizens must develop a commitment to democratic and humane values, such as human dignity and equality, in order to make reflective decisions and to take action consistent with the idealized values of the nation-state. However, it is inconsistent to try to develop commitments to democratic values by using indoctrination approaches. Modern social studies curricula try to help students develop a commitment to democratic values by teaching them a process for identifying the sources of their values, analyzing and clarifying their values, and justifying their values. The social studies should also help students to state the possible consequences of their value choices. A value inquiry model is presented and discussed in Chapter 15.

what if they want to become totalitarian fascists

Citizen Action Goals

The social studies curriculum should provide opportunities for students to participate in projects and activities that will develop a greater sense of political efficacy and teach skills useful in influencing social and civic institutions. The National Council for the Social Studies Curriculum Guidelines emphasizes the importance of citizen action in the social studies:

> Extensive involvement by students of all ages in the activities of their community is essential. Many of these activities may be in problem areas held, at least by some, to be controversial. The involvement may take the form of observation or information-seeking, attending meetings, and interviews. It may take the form of political campaigning, community service or improvement, or even responsible demonstrations. The school should not only provide channels for such activities, but build them into the design of its K–12 social studies program.[8]

The primary goal of citizen action projects undertaken in the social studies should be to provide experiences whereby students can attain a sense of personal, social, and civic efficacy, and not simply serve the community. However, the most effective projects contribute to each of these goals. Citizen action is discussed in detail in Chapter 15.

CHARACTERISTICS OF A MODERN SOCIAL STUDIES CURRICULUM

We stated that a modern social studies curriculum helps students develop the ability to make reflective decisions and to successfully participate in the civic life of their communities. We have also noted that it helps students develop mastery in four goal areas: (1) knowledge, (2) skills, (3) attitudes and values, and (4) citizen action. The effective social studies curriculum also has other characteristics.

It helps students develop the knowledge, attitudes, values, and skills needed to deal reflectively with the major social issues and problems in our nation and world. The rights of the handicapped, the problems of women, ethnic and racial problems, human rights, and the problems of senior citizens are some of the salient and enduring unresolved social issues that continue to evoke controversy within the United States and in other nations. Global and

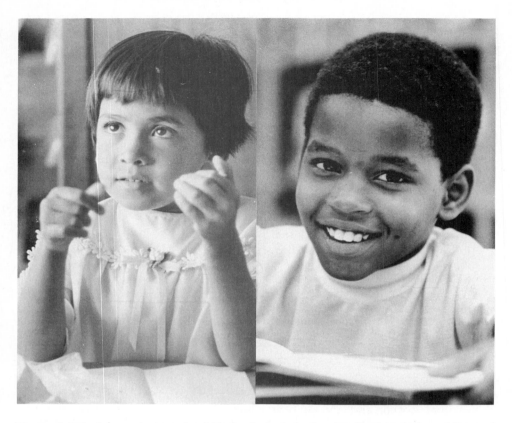

The social studies curriculum should help students to develop the knowledge, skills, and attitudes needed to participate in action to shape public policy in their communities, nation, and world. (*Source:* Washington State Office of Public instruction; Toledo Public Schools; Robb Mitchell, Lake Washington School District (Seattle); Edna Kellman, Seattle Public Schools.)

international topics, issues, and problems should also be an important part of the social studies in all grades.

A major goal of the social studies should be to help develop citizens who have the commitment and the skills needed to help close the gap between the democratic ideals of our nation and societal realities. Throughout U.S. history, the rights of various groups have continued to expand. However, there is still a wide gap between our democratic ideals and societal realities. The social studies curriculum should provide a forum where students can openly examine the conditions of various groups in society, analyze and clarify their values related to these groups and issues, decide on courses of action, and take citizen action when it is appropriate and feasible. Chapter 7 is devoted to teaching social issues.

A modern social studies curriculum is also characterized by unit teaching and the use of a wide variety of resources. Wood defines a unit as:

An organization of various activities, experiences, and types of learning around a central problem, or purpose, developed cooperatively by a group of pupils under teacher leadership; involves planning, execution of plans, and evaluation of results.[9]

Units may or may not be developed cooperatively by the teacher and the students. However, they do provide for both group and individual projects and activities and consequently allow students to play an important role in determining the direction of their own learning. A unit may be organized around a topic such as "Canada: Our Neighbor to the North," around a concept such as culture, or around a decision-problem or issue such as "What Actions Should We Take Regarding World Hunger and Poverty?"

SCOPE AND SEQUENCE IN THE SOCIAL STUDIES CURRICULUM

The social studies curriculum varies within different states, counties, and school districts. However, some characteristics are rather consistent throughout the United States. In the earliest grades the social studies curriculum is usually characterized by units and learning experiences focusing on the most familiar institutions and social systems, such as the home, the family, the school, the neighborhood, and the community. State history is usually studied in the fourth grade. United States history is usually studied in three grades: fifth, eighth, and eleventh.

Within these broad topic categories, a wide variety of approaches are used to teach the social studies in U.S. schools. At the high school level, many schools offer a variety of elective courses—such as sociology, psychology, and problems of democracy. Primary grade teachers use many different approaches to teach about the school, the family, and the community.

Teachers can implement many of the characteristics of a modern social studies curriculum within the traditional scope and sequence pattern that dominates U.S. schools. Primary grade teachers can teach about the family and the community by requiring students to memorize isolated facts. Too often this is done. However, topics such as the family and the community can also be taught by using key concepts from the social science disciplines to organize lessons and units, and to teach students how to conceptualize, to generalize, and to analyze their values. Chapter 2 illustrates how a unit on the family can be organized around key social science concepts. A unit on "Women in American History Textbooks" in Chapter 3 illustrates how topics in U.S. history can be taught while teaching students social science inquiry skills. Throughout this book, we suggest ways in which teachers can teach higher-level concepts and skills, value analysis, decision-making, and citizen action within the context of the dominant social studies curriculum pattern in U.S. schools.

THE EXPANDING COMMUNITIES OF HUMANS

The *scope* (what is taught and in what depth) and *sequence* (when it is taught) pattern that dominates the social studies curriculum in the United States was heavily influenced by Paul R. Hanna. Hanna believed students should study smaller communities first and then increasingly larger ones. Hanna called this sequence the "Expanding Communities of Men." This pattern had dominated the social studies curriculum for many years when Hanna restated it in an important article published in 1963.[10] Hanna emphasized that students should study the various human communities in the sequence described below. He noted that the specific grade placement of each of these communities was less important than the *sequence* suggested.

The child's family community
The child's school
The child's neighborhood

The child's local communities: city, county, metropolis, country
The child's state community
The child's region-of-states community
The U.S. national community
U.S. and Inter-American community
U.S. and Atlantic community
U.S. and Pacific community
U.S. and world community

Hanna's expanding communities of humans concept was severely criticized by some social studies educators during the 1960s and 1970s. They criticized it for a variety of reasons. They questioned the assumption that students should only study those communities in which they functioned most intimately and argued that television often brings distant communities within reach of today's youth. They also argued that the expanding communities concept often leads to an overemphasis on the Western world and to the neglect of non-Western nations, women's history and culture, and the experiences of ethnic groups in the United States. However, despite the strong criticisms it received during the 1960s and 1970s, the expanding communities of humans pattern is the most common social studies scope and sequence plan in the United States. However, counties, states, and school districts often implement the plan in diverse and creative ways. California departed from it significantly in the framework it adopted in 1987 (see pages 15–16).

When Superka and his colleagues studied social studies topics in the United States, they found that the following topics were the most frequently taught at the grade levels indicated.[11] Notice how similar this sequence is to Hanna's expanding communities of humans pattern.

Grade	**Topic**
Kindergarten	Self, school, community, home
1	Families
2	Neighborhoods
3	Communities
4	State history, geographic regions
5	United States history
6	World cultures, Western hemisphere
7	World geography or history
8	American history
9	Civics or world cultures
10	World history
11	American history
12	American government

Examples of Topics and Units
for Grades Kindergarten Through Eight

Below is a list of social studies topics and units that are usually studied in the elementary and junior high school grades. What is taught in each grade varies widely according to school district. However, our intent here is to describe what might be a typical sequence of topics and units for each grade level.

KINDERGARTEN

Social studies units in kindergarten usually help children to develop a better understanding of themselves and other people. The school, the home, and holidays and celebrations are typical topics.

> How we are alike and different
> Rules at home and at school
> Holidays and celebrations
> Our wants and needs

FIRST GRADE

Units in the first grade often deal with relationships in the home and school. A range of social science concepts can be used in the first grade to help students gain new perspectives on family and school life.

> What is a family?
> Kinds of families
> How we help our families
> How families change
> How schools and families are alike and different
> What people do in schools
> Conflict and cooperation at home and at school

SECOND GRADE

Units in the second grade often focus on the neighborhood, people in groups, and groups and neighborhoods in other communities and nations.

> What is a group?
> Groups we belong to
> What is a neighborhood?
> Why do groups change?
> Why do neighborhoods change?
> Cooperation and conflict in groups and neighborhoods
> How groups and neighborhoods help us satisfy our needs and wants
> A neighborhood in Japan

THIRD GRADE

Units in the third grade often focus on local communities, the city, and communities and cities in other nations.

> What is a city?
> What is a community?
> How people meet their needs in communities
> How people meet their needs in cities
> A comparison of three cities: Washington, D.C., Tokyo, and Rome
> How cities are governed
> The economic life of cities

FOURTH GRADE

Common topics in the fourth grade are the state, the world as the home of humans, and regions of the United States and the world.

> The first peoples of our state
> The government and economy of our state
> The history of our state
> Regions of South America
> Regions of the United States
> The peoples and cultures of Africa

FIFTH GRADE

The geography, history, and culture of the United States are the most common fifth-grade topics. The early periods of United States history are usually emphasized. The rest of North America and nations in South America are also sometimes studied.

> The First Americans
> European explorations in America
> The growth of the European colonies in America
> The quest for independence
> The birth of a new nation
> The peoples and cultures of the United States
> Women in United States history
> The cultures and peoples of Latin America
> Canada: our northern neighbor

SIXTH GRADE

Units in the sixth grade often focus on the geography of the earth and the peoples who live in various parts of the world.

The geographic and cultural regions of the world
The peoples and cultures of Africa
The peoples and cultures of Australia
The peoples and cultures of Asia
The peoples and cultures of Eastern Europe
The peoples and cultures of Western Europe
The peoples and cultures of the Middle East

SEVENTH GRADE

In the seventh grade, students frequently continue the study of world cultures and regions begun in the sixth grade.

Greek and Roman civilizations
The spread of Islam
Medieval days and ways in Europe
The development of nations
Science, reason, and the Enlightenment
The nature of the non-Western world
Conflict and challenge in the Middle East

EIGHTH GRADE

The history and development of the United States is studied in the fifth, eighth, and eleventh grades. The intent in the eighth grade is to give students a more in-depth understanding of the nature of United States history and culture than was gained in fifth grade.

The cultures of North America before the coming of the Europeans
The Europeans explore the Americas
The European colonies in America
The American Revolution
A new nation
The westward movement
Ethnic groups in American history
Women who left their marks on history
Slaves and the slave community
A divided nation
The long, sad war
The United States as a world power

THE SCOPE AND SEQUENCE DEBATE

The "Expanding Communities of Humans" scope and sequence plan is the dominant one in U.S. schools. It has, however, stimulated much controversy and debate within the last decade. Few social studies educators are completely satisfied with it. However, it has remained prevalent in part because there is little agreement about what should replace it. The National Council for the Social Studies (NCSS) has been active in efforts to develop a new scope and sequence plan. It has sponsored a number of debates and hearings at its national meetings about what should be an appropriate social studies scope and sequence for the twenty-first century. In 1982, the Council appointed a Task Force on Scope and Sequence to develop a plan for the profession to consider, debate, and possibly endorse.

The plan developed by the Task Force, which was issued as a preliminary position statement by the Council, stimulated much discussion and debate.[12] However, it brought social studies educators no closer to consensus about what should be an appropriate scope and sequence plan for students in the twenty-first century. Many social studies educators observed that obtaining national consensus about an appropriate social studies scope and sequence plan for the United States was neither possible nor desirable. However, other educators and many publishers believe that a nationally accepted scope and sequence plan is both possible and essential. Publishers would like such a plan to help them to develop and publish marketable textbooks. Some social studies educators believe that all U.S. students should experience a common social studies curriculum that will enable them to acquire essential knowledge, insights, and values about their nation and the world.

The NCSS Task Force on Scope and Sequence did not embrace a particular scope and sequence plan. However, it did develop an illustrative scope and sequence plan (see Table 1.1) that can be used to develop the knowledge, values and beliefs, and skills the Task Force identified. The NCSS continues its effort to identify the knowledge and skills in the social studies needed for effective citizenship in the nation and world. It has appointed a National Commission on the Social Studies to identify the components of an effective social studies curriculum for U.S. citizens. The Commission consists of distinguished scholars and social studies educators as well as prominent citizens.

A HISTORY-BASED SOCIAL STUDIES CURRICULUM

In 1987, the California State Board of Education adopted a social studies curriculum framework that differs in several significant ways from the expanding communities of humans framework described earlier in this chapter.[13] It is centered in the chronological study of history, emphasizes history as a story or narrative, incorporates the study of literature to deepen historical understanding, and introduces a new curricular approach for grades kindergarten through three (see Table 1.2). Biographies, myths, fairy tales, and historical tales are used extensively in these grades to evoke interest in history and to enhance historical understanding. The California framework also emphasizes studying selected historical events in depth rather than covering many events superficially, incorporates a multicultural perspective throughout, and requires the study of world history in three different

TABLE 1.1. Illustrative Scope and Sequence (Developed by the National Council for the Social Studies Task Force)

Kindergarten	Awareness of Self in a Social Setting
Grade 1	The Individual in Primary Social Groups: Understanding School and Family Life
Grade 2	Meeting Basic Needs in Nearby Social Groups: The Neighborhood
Grade 3	Sharing Earth-Space with Others: The Community
Grade 4	Human Life in Varied Environments: The Region
Grade 5	People of the Americas: The United States and Its Neighbors
Grade 6	People and Cultures: The Eastern Hemisphere
Grade 7	A Changing World of Many Nations: A Global View
Grade 8	Building a Strong and Free Nation: The United States
Grade 9	Systems That Make a Democratic Society Work: Law, Justice, and Economics
Grade 10	Origins of Major Cultures: A World History
Grade 11	The Maturing of America: United States History
Grade 12	One-year course or courses required—selection(s) to be made from the following: Issues and Problems of Modern Society Introduction to the Social Sciences The Arts in Human Societies International Area Studies Social Science Elective Courses: Anthropology, Economics, Government, Psychology, Sociology

SOURCE: Reprinted with permission of the National Council for the Social Studies from "In Search of a Scope and Sequence for Social Studies," *Social Education*, Vol. 48 (April 1984), pp. 254–255.

grades: six, seven, and ten. The framework also provides for students to participate in school and community service programs and activities. The California framework is also unique because the study of U.S. history and geography is limited to the twentieth century in the eleventh grade.

THE PUSH FOR FACTS AND HISTORY

The debate about what should constitute the social studies curriculum was not confined to social studies educators during the 1980s. Some of the harshest criticisms of the social studies and the schools in general were penned by specialists in the academic disciplines who argued that students were graduating from high school who were culturally illiterate. These students, argued the critics, do not know basic facts about U.S. history, such as when the Constitution was ratified or when the Civil War occurred. E. D. Hirsch, Jr., made this argument in his highly successful and widely reviewed book, *Cultural Literacy: What Every American Needs to Know.*[14] This book was on *The New York Times* best-seller list for almost six months. Its popularity indicated that it articulated important concerns among U.S. citizens about what students were

TABLE 1.2. The History–Social Science Framework for California Public Schools

Kindergarten	Learning and Working Now and Long Ago
Grade 1	A Child's Place in Time and Space
Grade 2	People Who Make a Difference
Grade 3	Continuity and Change
Grade 4	California: A Changing State
Grade 5	United States History and Geography: Making a New Nation
Grade 6	World History and Geography: Ancient Civilizations
Grade 7	World History and Geography: Medieval and Early Modern Times
Grade 8	United States History and Geography: Growth and Conflict
Grade 9	Elective Courses in History–Social Science
Grade 10	World History and Geography: The Modern World
Grade 11	United States History and Geography: Continuity and Change in the Twentieth Century
Grade 12	Principles of American Democracy (One Semester) and Economics (One Semester)

SOURCE: Reprinted with permission from *History–Social Science Framework for California Public Schools Kindergarten Through Grade Twelve* (Sacramento: California State Department of Education, 1988), p. 29.

learning in school. An argument similar to Hirsch's was presented by Lynne V. Cheney, Chair of the National Endowment for the Humanities, in *The American Memory: A Report on the Humanities in the Nation's Public Schools*.[15] Cheney argued that students were not literate in U.S. history and literature because the schools emphasized process rather than content.

Ravitch and Finn extended the argument developed by Hirsch and Cheney. They attempted to document how little U.S. students know about history and literature in their book, *What Do Our 17-Year-Olds Know?*[16] The authors described how students gave many incorrect answers to multiple-choice test items that assessed their recall of factual knowledge in history and literature. Ravitch has argued that the replacement of "history" teaching with the teaching of the "social studies" is the primary cause of what she considers the cultural and historical illiteracy of the nation's elementary and high school students.[17] She believes that the problem can be solved by teaching students larger doses of history throughout the elementary and high school grades. She has called the teaching of the other social sciences in the schools "tot sociology."[18]

The push for more history in the schools was supported by a number of organizations and institutions during the late 1980s, including the National Endowment for the Humanities. In 1988, it funded a Center on History at the University of California at Los Angeles.[19] The Center examined how history is taught in elementary and secondary schools. The Bradley Commission on History in Schools developed recommendations to improve the teaching of history in the nation's schools. The Commission, foundation-funded, was made up of teachers and prominent historians. In its report, the Commission recommends the study of substantially more history in the schools.[20]

The tense debate between those who argue that history should be the focus of the social studies and those who maintain that the social studies should be interdisciplinary, with an important component of history, has existed for decades. This debate intensifies from time to time, particularly when the schools are being attacked by reformers, especially by those outside the formal educational establishment. The Ravitch and Finn book is similar to the report published by *The New York Times* in 1943, which was based on the results of a U.S. history test given to college freshmen. It concluded that these students had a "deplorable lack of knowledge about the United States' past."[21] Social studies educators, such as Erling M. Hunt, argued that the test was "of questionable validity, amateurishly graded, poorly administered, and concerned exclusively with the ability to remember information."[22]

We will present our interpretation of the new movement for more history and factual information in the social studies curriculum in Chapter 9, which focuses on the nature and teaching of history. *History is viewed in this book as an important but not dominant part of the social studies curriculum.* An *interdisciplinary* social studies curriculum, which draws heavily upon history and geography, as well as upon the behavioral sciences—and which focuses upon higher levels of knowledge and thinking skills—is essential to helping students develop the skills and values needed to make decisions on complex social, political, and economic issues in our global world society.

DECISION-MAKING: THE HEART OF THE SOCIAL STUDIES

In an important and influential article published in 1960, Shirley Engle stated that decision-making should be a major goal of social studies instruction. More recently, Engle and Ochoa have developed a curriculum framework for a decision-making focused social studies curriculum.[23] The curriculum proposed by Engle and Ochoa has these strands:

> Environmental Studies
> Institutional Studies
> Cultural Studies
> Social Problems
> Problems in Decision-Making
> Internship in Citizenship
> Electives
> A Democratic School Environment

We also believe that the social studies should help students attain the skills needed to recognize and solve human problems, analyze and clarify values, and make sound, reflective decisions that will contribute to the perpetuation and improvement of their communities, nation, and world. Our perception of the proper goal for the social studies resulted largely from a realization that citizens—students, homemakers, factory workers, businesspersons, labor leaders, politicans, welfare recipients, and all others—must each day make personal and public decisions that will affect their lives and their community, nation, and world. These are the kinds of nagging decision-problems with which citizens must often deal:

> Should I take the job at Tony's or at Bell's?
> Should we buy a house, a condominium, or continue to rent?
> Should we stop fertilizing our lawn so that more fertilizer will be available for crops?
> Would Taylor be a better member of Congress than Kitano?
> Should I vote for or against the school bond issue?
> Should I become active in the Anti-Nuclear Weapons League?

Yuppie?

Individuals are not born with the capacity to make reflective decisions. Decision-making is a skill that must be developed and practiced. When individuals develop the ability to make reflective decisions, they can act intelligently. We believe that the most important goal of the social studies should be to develop reflective *citizen actors*. We are using *citizen* to mean a member of a democratic state or nation. *Citizen actor* refers to an individual who makes a deliberate effort to influence his or her political environment, including its laws, public policies, values, and the distribution of wealth. The activities in which he or she participates are *citizen action*. Citizen action may, of course, be effective or ineffective.

We are assuming that decision-making skills can be developed, that humans can be trained to reflect before acting on problems, and that individuals can learn to act on their freely made decisions. We cannot expect individuals to act on decisions they have been forced to make. In the decision-making model introduced later in this chapter, the individual must be able to choose freely from many alternative courses of action, *consistent with human dignity*, before we can characterize his or her behavior as decision-making. This model is discussed in detail in Chapter 15.

Essential Components of the Decision-Making Process

KNOWLEDGE

Reflective decisions cannot be made in a vacuum. Social knowledge is one necessary component for sound decision-making. If two people (a couple) try to decide whether to join and be active in the Anti-Nuclear Weapons League, they can make a better decision if they know the extent of the nuclear buildup in each nation, how successful past negotiations among the leading powers have been in reducing nuclear proliferation, and what steps other

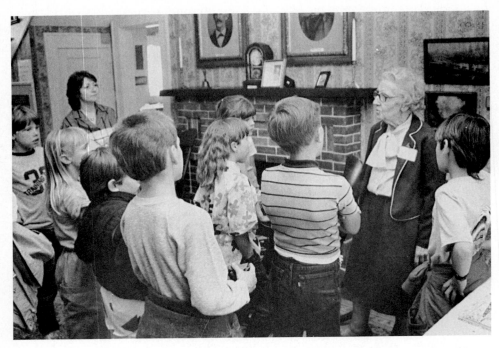

Social science inquiry produces the knowledge that students need to make reflective decisions. This photograph shows a class visiting a community museum to gather information about the history of their community. (*Source:* Terri Malinowski, Northshore School District, Seattle.)

than a nuclear buildup might be successful in preventing conflict and war. By studying historical and political information on the nuclear arms race, the couple would be able to make some informed predictions about the possible consequences of an escalating nuclear race among nations. They could consequently make a more reflective decision about whether to join and become active in the Anti-Nuclear Weapons League.

Methods and Ways of Attaining Knowledge   Knowledge is needed to make reflective decisions. There are many ways of knowing or attaining knowledge. Kerlinger has summarized four methods of knowing described by Charles Peirce, a philosopher.[24] When people use the *method of tenacity,* they hold firmly to what they know to be true—it is true because they hold firmly to it and have always believed it. Individuals seek out established belief when they use the *method of authority.* When individuals argue that they know something to be true because it is "agreeable to reason" and self-evident they are using the *a priori method.* Peirce argues that we need a method to attain knowledge "by which our beliefs may be determined by nothing human. . . . The method must be such that the ultimate conclusion of every man shall be the same. Such is the *method of science.*"[25]

A further discussion of the hypothetical couple mentioned above will clarify the four methods of knowing. When trying to decide whether they should join the Anti-Nuclear Weapons League, the couple may derive knowledge related to their decision-problem by the *method of tenacity*. The couple may conclude that an escalating nuclear race will help to prevent war and maintain peace among nations. The couple reaches this conclusion because they have always believed that nations tend to be aggressive and that only the threat of force can maintain peace.

The couple may have no firm beliefs about the nuclear buildup and little information. They may seek out an *authority* to get information about nuclear weapons and the nuclear buildup. The couple may hear a professor of sociology talk about nuclear weapons on a television talk show. The professor, who is a strong advocate of a nuclear buildup by his own nation, argues that this is the only way to maintain peace. He also argues that the Western nations have experienced their longest period of peace since nuclear weapons were invented and produced.

The couple may use still a different method for obtaining knowledge about nuclear weapons and the nuclear buildup. They may, without seeking

"As if worrying about a nuclear disaster isn't bad enough, now they tell us our school is a fall-out shelter!" (*Source:* Ford Button. Reprinted with permission).

an authority, or sources of information about nuclear weapons, discuss them and conclude that it is self-evident that nuclear weapons are needed to keep peace in the world.

Limitations of Ways of Knowing   It is not difficult to state the limitations of the ways of knowing just discussed and illustrated. Some of the methods have more serious limitations than others. The method of tenacity is not an effective way of gaining knowledge because humans are capable of believing and holding firmly to almost anything imaginable. A brief study of history and anthropology will reveal that humans, throughout history, have held beliefs that they later considered outdated and bizarre. Beliefs in ancestor gods, shamans, witch doctors, and water witching indicate the tremendous range of human beliefs that have existed in many times and places. People's capacity to create beliefs today is as great as in any previous time in history. Some people refuse to live on the thirteenth floor of an apartment building. Others carry charms, such as a rabbit's foot, for good luck. Humankind's ability to create and imagine is one of the most important characteristics which distinguish humans from other primates.

The method of authority is perhaps the most valuable of the three methods discussed above. We could not live organized and productive lives without relying a great deal on authorities because we live in a highly specialized world. When a doctor prescribes medicine, we assume that it will help heal our illness. We depend on authority when we plan trips using a road map, look up words in a dictionary, have our income tax completed by an expert, or act on the advice of a counselor.

While authorities are necessary in our highly specialized world society, a reliance on authority is unwise under certain conditions and in some situations. A sociology professor may state publicly that nuclear arms are needed to keep peace in the world when he does not know the key facts about nuclear weapons. The professor may be a specialist in small organizations, and may base his opinions about nuclear war primarily on his personal values. Individuals are often perceived as authorities when they lack specific training in a given area, or they may be assumed to have conclusive information about problems when the knowledge in the field is scant and sparse. Citizens tend to put too much faith in and to expect too much from "experts." Persons with complicated medical or learning problems often expect doctors or educational experts to give them rapid cures or quick solutions. They are often disappointed and angry when they discover that experts frequently disagree about cures and solutions. In our discussion of the nature and teaching of history in Chapter 9, we note how historians often present conflicting interpretations of the same past events.

As Kerlinger points out, the *a priori method* of knowing is very limited in deriving knowledge, because what is self-evident to one person may not be self-evident to another. People can hold opposite beliefs about the same things. Each will argue that his or her knowledge is self-evident. One person may argue that it is self-evident that rapid nuclear buildups by the major nations are needed to keep them at peace. Another may argue just as strongly that it is obvious that the rapid growth of nuclear buildup will lead to a nuclear holocaust.

The Scientific Method: a Way of Attaining Knowledge   The limitations of the tenacity, authority, and *a priori* methods suggest that we need a more reliable way of attaining valid knowledge. We should not be bound either by traditional belief systems or the opinions of authorities. A person should be able to repeat the procedures of the method and derive similar conclusions. Different people who use the method should derive similar, if not identical, conclusions. In other words, the method should be public rather than private. It should be largely independent of the values and biases of the individual using the method. The method that comes closest to meeting these requirements is the scientific method. This is the method used by social scientists to derive knowledge—facts, concepts, generalizations, and theories. We will refer to this method as *social science inquiry* or *social inquiry*. The steps in social science inquiry are discussed in detail in Chapter 3.

   If our hypothetical couple (trying to decide whether or not to join the Anti-Nuclear Weapons League) were to use the scientific method to gain the knowledge needed to make a reflective decision, they would do several specific things. First, they would state clear and researchable questions related to the decision-problem, such as:

   How many nuclear weapons are held by the major powers?
   How successful have nuclear weapons been in deterring wars?
   How successful have treaties designed to limit nuclear weapons been?
   What ways can be used to maintain peace among nations other than a
      nuclear buildup?
   What are the possibilities of a nuclear war starting accidentally?
   What are the possibilities for the survival of humans after a nuclear war
      and a nuclear winter?

   After stating the major questions related to their decision-problem, the couple would then try to define the major concepts in their questions, such as *nuclear weapons, nuclear war, treaties,* and *peace.*
   Our hypothetical couple would then state some of their own hunches about nuclear weapons and their consequences. They would gather data to answer questions and to test hypotheses from a wide variety of sources, including books, magazines, and primary documents. The couple would then evaluate, compare, and analyze the data they had gathered. Even though the couple would use the knowledge in making their decision, they would realize that the knowledge is tentative and must be constantly compared with new findings and discoveries.
   Our preference for the scientific method is by now clear. While it is not a perfect method, we believe that it is the most effective and efficient means of obtaining knowledge. Peirce overstates the value of the scientific method

when he suggests that "our beliefs are determined by nothing human. . . ." As we will point out in our discussion of values, the scientific method is based on human values and assumptions. Bernice Goldmark has insightfully pointed out some of the assumptions on which this method is based:

> The scientific method is based on the assumption that truth is neither absolute nor unchanging. Rather, truth is a judgment that, by the agreement of an informed community, produces desirable results. . . .
>
> It is on this assumption that we argue that all judgments should be held as hypotheses to be tested, evaluated, and reconstructed. . . .[26]

The scientific method also assumes that people can obtain consensus regarding generalizations and statements by using a method that is public, systematic, and repeatable. Persons who accept this method and reject the others value public over private and idiosyncratic knowledge. The *a priori* method, unlike the scientific method, is a private or "internal" method of knowing. An individual using this method derives conclusions on the basis of what is self-evident to him or her. What's self-evident to one person may not be self-evident to another. The scientific method attempts to derive knowledge that can be independently obtained by persons using the method at different times and places. However, personal values and assumptions do affect the products of this method. The problems we select and the questions we formulate are determined by our values, purposes, and social environment. These factors influence the outcome of scientific inquiry. However, these factors are less important in social inquiry than they are in other methods of attaining knowledge.

As we indicated above, knowledge is one essential component of the decision-making process. *We prefer the scientific method for attaining knowledge because it is systematic, self-correcting, open-ended, and public.* Knowledge used to make reflective decisions must be derived by an inquiry process. Decisions made on the basis of knowledge derived by intuition or tradition will not satisfy our *reflective* criteria. Before students can make reflective decisions, they must learn to use methods of social science inquiry to derive knowledge in the form of facts, concepts, generalizations, and theories.

Reflective citizen actors need not independently derive every bit of knowledge they use in making decisions and solving problems. This would be impractical. Not much human progress would be made; few reflective decisions would be possible. However, citizen actors cannot intelligently apply or judge knowledge unless they are aware of the processes used to derive it and are able to use the methods of the social scientists to derive knowledge when it is necessary and appropriate (for example, when authorities conflict). In a democratic nation, the scientific method should not be the exclusive property of a scientific elite. It should be shared by all members of the society who make decisions that affect the governing of the community, nation, and world.

INQUIRY AND DECISION-MAKING

Social knowledge, derived by a scientific process, is only one of the essential components of the decision-making process. Before we discuss other elements of the process, it is appropriate (1) to indicate how *social science inquiry* differs from *decision-making* and (2) to point out why social science inquiry is necessary but not sufficient for making reflective decisions. In this discussion we will also suggest how the ends of social science inquiry and decision-making differ.

The basic aim of social science inquiry is to derive knowledge in the form of facts, concepts, generalizations, and theories. The goal is to accumulate as much knowledge as possible. While the social scientist is primarily interested in producing knowledge, the decision-maker or citizen actor is mainly interested in how the knowledge derived by the social scientist can be used to help him or her solve problems and make decisions.

> *Social science inquiry produces knowledge; in decision-making, knowledge is selected, synthesized, and applied.*

However, as we have previously stated, the reflective consumer of knowledge must be familiar with the methods used by the professional social scientist to derive knowledge and must be able to use the method.

Knowledge in social science inquiry tends to be specialized. Each group of social scientists studies only those aspects of reality they feel are the appropriate concerns of their disciplines. They may ignore many important social problems and issues or study them from a limited perspective. The social scientist fragments reality in order to study it from a unique perspective. Reflective decision-makers and citizen actors must use the knowledge from all the various social science disciplines to solve personal and public problems. *In decision making we select, synthesize, and apply knowledge from diverse sources.* No one discipline can adequately help citizen actors to make decisions about the complex problems that confront humankind.

> *Knowledge alone is insufficient for reflective decision-making.*

Reflective citizen actors must learn how to synthesize the information they obtain from many sources and apply it to complex social problems. Figure 1.1 and Tables 1.3 and 1.4 indicate how a citizen actor may attempt to decide what actions he or she should take regarding global hunger and poverty. Figure 1.1 illustrates how various social scientists may view the problem. Note how each of the social scientists views the problem from a very restricted perspective, while the citizen actor attempts to synthesize knowledge from various disciplines and sources (including his or her own inquiries) and use it in making a decision that can guide his or her action regarding the problem of global hunger and poverty. Table 1.3 shows how the decision-maker tries to clarify his or her conflicting values about global hunger and

HISTORIAN
Analyzes events that culminated in global hunger and poverty; illuminates similarities between hunger and poverty today and in previous historical periods.

ECONOMIST
Studies the economic factors that contributed to the development of global hunger and poverty. Suggests that the standards of living in the world's affluent nations will have to be reduced if the problems of global hunger and poverty are to be solved.

POLITICAL SCIENTIST
Studies the political consequences of a world community that is made up of *"have"* and *"have not"* nations. Suggests that power struggles and war might result if the world's scarce resources are not more equally distributed among the rich and poor nations.

SOCIOLOGIST
Analyzes the effects of hunger and poverty on the norms, values and socialization practices among the victims of hunger and poverty. Suggests that severe hunger and poverty has a cogent impact on socialization practices.

PSYCHOLOGIST
Analyzes the nature and extent of aggression and frustration that develop among people who are victims of severe hunger and poverty.

ANTHROPOLOGIST
Studies how the responses to severe poverty and hunger are alike and different in various cultures. Concludes that responses to hunger and poverty are influenced by both cultural and biological factors.

GEOGRAPHER
Studies how hunger and poverty influence people's perceptions of their physical environment and their interactions with it.

CITIZEN ACTOR

INDEPENDENT INQUIRY INTO GLOBAL HUNGER AND POVERTY

VALUE CLARIFICATION
(See Table 1.1 for detailed illustration)

KNOWLEDGE
Selected—evaluated

REFLECTIVE DECISION-MAKING
Involves using knowledge acquired to identify alternative courses of action and to predict their possible consequences. An attempt is made by the citizen actor to choose a course of action that is most consistent with his or her values. (See Table 1.2 for a detailed illustration of this process.)

REFLECTIVE CITIZEN ACTION
Acting in a way to promote or realize the ends valued.

Reflective citizen actors synthesize and apply knowledge from many disciplines to help them make decisions about the action they will take regarding global hunger and poverty. They may also apply knowledge that they have derived from their own inquiries. The synthesis of *knowledge* (in the form of facts, concepts, generalizations, and theories) and *values* results in a *decision* which involves selecting a course of action from many possible alternatives, including inaction.

FIGURE 1.1 Citizen actor's decision-problem: What actions should I take regarding global hunger and poverty?

TABLE 1.3. Value Clarification (Poverty and Hunger)*

Order of Priority →

Struggle for self-preservation ⟷ Resignation

Willingness to pilfer and steal ⟶ Refusal to "rip off"

Compassion for those in need ⟷ Contempt for the "shiftless"

Work through established social agencies (organized) ⟷ Give help directly to needy individuals (personalized)

Civic programs that give priority to human needs and social improvement (food stamps, aid to dependent children, surplus food distribution, welfare to the old, handicapped, and unemployed) ⟷ Civic programs that give high priority to economic and other goals (highway construction, public buildings, environmental or pollution control)

*In this example, values are conceptualized as existing on a continuum. An individual's value preferences may vary in intensity periodically, but are generally committed toward one end of a continuum. To act intelligently, the individual must arrange his or her values into a hierarchy of preference. The level of commitment to a particular value will greatly determine its place in the the hierarchy. In Chapter 15 we present a model for teaching value inquiry. The basic steps of this model are outlined in Figure 1.3.

TABLE 1.4. The Decision-Making Process (Global Hunger and Poverty)

A. If I donate money to a world relief organization,

THEN I. . .

1. will be helping an organization that is already set up to help solve the problem of global hunger and poverty.
2. may help save a starving child's life.
3. will feel I am doing something to help eliminate world hunger and poverty.

BUT I. . .

4. will make only a small effort in behalf of my concern.
5. will have to do without some goods I wanted to buy with the money.
6. may be doing little to help starving people because some relief organizations use most of the money they collect to pay overhead costs.

C. If I form an organization to help solve the problem of global hunger and poverty,

B. If I give up eating meat,

THEN I. . .

1. will be making a strong statement about my concern for global hunger and poverty.
2. will be increasing the amount of meat available on the world's market.
3. will be disassociating myself from "overconsuming" Americans.
4. will be able to eat more cheaply.

BUT I. . .

5. will be doing nothing to assure that the meat that I do not eat will get to the world's starving people.
6. will have to give up a group of foods that I enjoy eating very much.
7. will have to find other foods to substitute for meat.
8. will experience difficulties when I am eating out or eating with others.

D. If I run for election to a local political office,

TABLE 1.4. *(continued)*

THEN I...

1. will be organizing my efforts in a concerted public way.
2. may involve a substantial number of people who feel much as I do.
3. may be able to get food to many starving children and adults.

BUT I...

4. will have to make a heavy investment of time and energy in the organization.
5. may find it difficult to interest enough people to work for and contribute to the organization.
6. may be criticized by existing relief organizations for "duplicating efforts."
7. may not succeed in raising needed funds.

E. If I choose to do nothing (inaction),
THEN I...

1. do not really have a strong concern about global hunger and poverty.
2. may not have the courage of my own conviction.
3. will not risk taking actions that may not succeed.

THEN I...

1. may be able to help reduce hunger and poverty within my own community.
2. could express my views publicly at city council meetings to be reported in the media.
3. could influence or advocate the effective distribution of more food to the poor through changes in local and national laws.
4. could see that such laws were enforced if my views were sustained and the laws were enacted.

BUT I...

5. may not succeed in getting elected to the city council.
6. might find myself a lone voice without support on the city council.
7. could lose my political effectiveness if I could not engage in trade-offs on other issues.
8. may risk compromising my views or watering them down to achieve any action related to poverty.

BUT I...

4. will not be justified in criticizing others for their inaction on problems related to global hunger and poverty.
5. will have to live with the fact that thousands of people are starving to death each year while I am living in relative affluence.

poverty. We have yet to discuss the value dimension, which is an important component of the decision-making process. Table 1.4 illustrates how the citizen actor determines a course of action.

Figure 1.2 illustrates how a reflective citizen actor and a social scientist might show concern about poverty in a hypothetical community. Note that their purposes—and therefore the main problems they formulate—are essentially different. The social scientist is interested primarily in building theory. As Redfield points out, the social scientist's "main objective is accurate description. Social scientists are scientific in that they are concerned with. . . what is, not what ought to be."[27] However, citizen actors are interested in both what is and what ought to be.

PROFILE

James P. Shaver

Helping Students to Understand Public Issues

James P. Shaver, Professor of Education and Associate Dean for Research at Utah State University, is a major and important voice in the movement to incorporate a study of public issues into the social studies. In an influential article published in *Social Education* in 1967, Shaver argued that the social studies is too often considered the social sciences simplified for teaching purposes. He stated that the examination of public issues faced by citizens in a democratic society should be the heart of the social studies and that the socal studies curriculum "must draw on sources other than the social sciences if the intellectual skills taught are to be adequate to the demands of political-ethical controversy."

In *Teaching Public Issues in the High School*, a book he coauthored with Donald W. Oliver, a Harvard education professor, Shaver and Oliver present a theory of teaching public issues to high school students as well as data on the results of their experimental public issues curriculum. Shaver also coauthored, with A. Guy Larkins, a public issues program for students, *Decision-Making in a Democracy*, published by Houghton Mifflin. A past president of the National Council for the Social Studies, Shaver is the editor of a book sponsored by that organization, *Handbook of Research on Social Studies Teaching and Learning*.

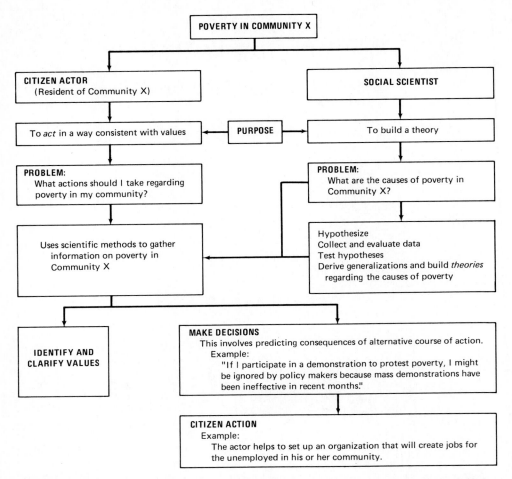

FIGURE 1.2 How a reflective citizen actor and a social scientist might approach the problem of poverty in community X.

THE VALUE COMPONENT OF DECISION-MAKING

After they have derived higher-level knowledge from their own and others' inquiries, reflective citizen actors must try to relate the facts, concepts, generalizations, and theories to their own values before deciding to act. What people do with their knowledge depends largely on the values they hold in regard to the decision-problem components.

Thus *value inquiry* is a very important part of the decision-making process. Value inquiry should help decision-makers identify the sources of their values, determine how they conflict, identify value alternatives, and choose freely from them. *However, students should be required to justify their moral choices within the context of societal values such as human dignity, justice, and equality.*[28] As Ochoa points out, the student must be explicitly encouraged to "establish a linkage between his or her goals and higher values. . . ."[29] If students are not required to justify their moral choices in terms of higher societal values, value teaching will run the risk of becoming relativistic and ethically neutral.

Students must be given the opportunity to freely make value choices. However, individual choice must be defended and made within a framework of societal values.[30] The student should be encouraged to predict and to consider the possible consequences of alternative values, and be helped to clarify conflicting and confused values. Not only are conflicting values widespread in the larger society, but within individuals there are many divergent beliefs, attitudes, and values. Many individuals who are active in religions that preach brotherhood are intolerant of other cultural and religious groups.

Before individuals can make sound decisions and act reflectively, they must be helped to clarify their conflicting and confused values. *We believe that value inquiry and clarification is one of the most important phases of the decision-making process.* Value issues are perhaps the most baffling problems that face both individuals and society. While we probably have the sophistication and means to *solve* many of our pressing human problems, we have neither clarified our value positions on them nor developed a commitment to solve them.

Let us return to the couple that was trying to decide whether they should join the Anti-Nuclear Weapons League. We will illustrate how values played an important role in their final decision. The couple gathered data about many different aspects of the nuclear buildup and of previous treaties by the leading nations to control the arms race. They read books, magazine articles, and listened to authorities who had conflicting opinions about nuclear proliferation. The couple concluded that both those authorities who argue for the need to maintain nuclear strength and those who warn about the possibility of a nuclear holocaust make compelling points. They believe that the information is far too complex and contradictory to accurately predict the effects of the escalating nuclear buildup. The couple values maintaining world peace as well as protecting human life from a nuclear holocaust. However, they decide to base their decision primarily on their value commitments. The couple decides that they value preventing a nuclear war far more than preventing other kinds of conflicts among nations. They will join and become active in the Anti-Nuclear Weapons League.

The couple's attitudes and values, more than the knowledge they acquired, determined their decision and consequent action. However, knowledge enabled them to clarify their values and to know what values they considered most important. While knowledge is necessary for sound decision-making, it is not sufficient. *The attitudes, beliefs, and values of citizen actors are often the most important determinants of their behavior.*

DECISION-MAKING AND THE SOCIAL STUDIES CURRICULUM

The main goal of the social studies should be to help students develop the ability to make reflective decisions and to take successful action to solve personal and public problems. Knowledge, derived by an inquiry process, and values, analyzed and clarified by value inquiry, are essential components of the decision-making process. The relationship between these components is illustrated in Figure 1.3. Decision-makers must select, synthesize, and apply knowledge from various social science disciplines and clarify their values before they can act reflectively on the perplexing problems in our global world society.

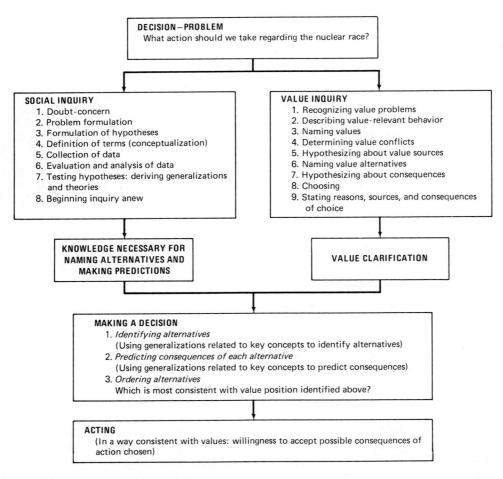

FIGURE 1.3 The decision-making process.

The social studies curriculum should help students gain proficiency in *inquiry, valuing,* and *decision-making* skills. Inquiry, valuing, and decision-making each consist of a cluster of interrelated skills, as will become evident in later chapters. Each cluster of skills contains highly interrelated elements. We separate them in this text to facilitate discussion and to emphasize the need for systematic instruction in each. Lessons should also be planned to give the student practice in relating each set of skills to the others, since the ultimate goal of social studies education is to help students make sound decisions and act reflectively. Historical content illustrating great decisions that people in the past had to make can be used to teach students decision-making skills. In the Inquiry Strategy for this chapter, students are asked to decide what decision Thomas Jefferson should make regarding the Louisiana Territory. This case can be used when the class is studying the period after the War for Independence. Similar strategy activities are found throughout this book.

Examples of Decision-Problem Units

Decision-making skills can be taught within the context of the dominant curricular framework found in most school districts and discussed earlier. Below are examples of *decision-problems* that students can study at the various grade levels. These problems can be studied as part of regular topical social studies units or they can be unit topics themselves. The specific ways in which decision-problems can be taught within the context of existing curricula will become clearer as you progress through this book.

KINDERGARTEN AND FIRST GRADE: THE HOME, SCHOOL, AND COMMUNITY

What should we do as a family to make our community safe?

What should we do as a class and a school to better solve conflicts and problems that occur on the playground and during recess?

What actions should we take in school to help poor families in our community?

SECOND AND THIRD GRADES: NEIGHBORHOODS AND COMMUNITIES

What should we do to help reduce pollution in our community?

What should we do to help improve safety in our neighborhood?

What should we do to get to know better the many different kinds of peoples and cultures in our community?

What should we do to get more people in our community to vote for the school levy?

FOURTH GRADE: STATE HISTORY

What should we do to get the state legislature to provide more money for the schools?

What action should we take regarding the nuclear waste sites in our state?

What action should we take regarding the controversy over Indian fishing rights in our state?

What action should we take to help solve the problems caused by the fact that we do not have a state income tax?

FIFTH GRADE: UNITED STATES HISTORY

What action should we take regarding the nuclear buildup in our nation?

What action should we take to help women attain more opportunities in our communities and nation?

Since we cannot vote, what actions should we take regarding the current presidential election?

SIXTH AND SEVENTH GRADES: WORLD CULTURES, GEOGRAPHY, AND WORLD HISTORY

What action should we take regarding the Israeli-Arab dispute in the Middle East?

What action should we take regarding the world's refugee problem?

What action should we take regarding world hunger and poverty?

What action should we take regarding the rapid buildup of nuclear weapons in the world?

EIGHTH GRADE: AMERICAN HISTORY

What action should we take regarding pollution in our nation?

What action should we take regarding the new federal policy toward federal land and parks?

What action should we take regarding the high rate of unemployment in our nation?

What action should we take regarding discrimination against different groups in our nation?

SUMMARY

We described some of the salient characteristics of a post-industrial society and the kind of social studies curriculum needed to help students become effective citizens in a rapidly changing world. The major goal of the social studies should be to help students attain the knowledge, skills, attitudes, and values needed to become reflective decision-makers and citizen actors. The social studies program should have goals in four major categories: (1) *knowledge,* (2) *skills,* (3) *attitudes and values,* and (4) *citizen action.* A modern social studies program should also help students deal reflectively with the major social issues and problems that face their communities, nation, and world. Teachers who wish to implement innovations in the social studies must do so within the context of the expanding communities of humans scheme which predominates in most U.S. schools. We have described ways in which this can be done. More examples are given in later chapters.

Developing decision-making skills should be a major goal of the social studies. One of the essential components of decision-making is knowledge. Reflective decisions can be made only when knowledge is *scientific, higher-level,* and *interdisciplinary.* Reflective decision-makers must not only be able to use and to recognize scientific knowledge, but to derive it themselves when necessary and appropriate. The knowledge on which reflective decisions are based must also be powerful and widely applicable so that it will enable the decision-maker to make the most accurate predictions possible. Higher-level concepts and their related generalizations are necessary for making accurate predictions. Thus the decision-maker must be able to derive these forms of knowledge. Knowledge that serves as a foundation for reflective decisions must also be interdisciplinary. Knowledge from any one discipline is insufficient to help us make reflective decisions on complex social issues such as war, pollution, and gender inequality.

While scientific, higher-level interdisciplinary knowledge is necessary for sound decision-making, it is not sufficient. Reflective decision-makers must also be able to identify and clarify their values, justify their value choices within the context of societal values (such as human dignity), and relate the concepts and generalizations they formulate to their values. The synthesis of knowledge and values constitutes the process of decision-making. During this process, citizen actors use social science concepts, generalizations, and theories to identify alternative courses of action and to predict their possible consequences. They order their values into a hierarchy, and choose a course of action most consistent with their value position and with human dignity. Finally, they take action based on their decisions to resolve personal problems or to influence public policy.

INQUIRY STRATEGY: WHAT SHALL THOMAS JEFFERSON DECIDE?

When the class is studying the period after the War for Independence in U.S. history, ask them to read the following case study. Then divide the class into three groups about the same size. One group will develop arguments and evidence to support the purchase of the Louisiana Territory; another group will develop arguments and evidence that Jefferson had insufficient evidence on which to make a defensible decision. The third group will develop arguments and evidence against the purchase of the Louisiana Territory.

The Dilemma

Should President Jefferson buy the Louisiana Territory? He has no legal authority to do so. Moreover, such a step might bring on a war with Spain. But *not* to buy Louisiana might mean losing the chance to add vast new territories to the new nation.

In 1801, Thomas Jefferson came into office as president of the United States. On July 4, 1803, President Jefferson received a letter from Paris. For long, anxious months he had been waiting for this message. But now, before opening it, he hesitated. Was it good news or bad? Had he got what he so badly wanted for the nation? Or was this letter a refusal that would create problems threatening the future of the United States?

The letter was from Robert Livingston, American minister to France. Jefferson had sent him there to make a treaty with Napoleon, the French ruler.

Jefferson opened the letter. As he started reading, he caught a sharp breath of surprise. He continued reading, with growing astonishment and delight. But as he finished the message, his first relief gave way to dismaying second thoughts.

This letter was not the answer he had expected. It went far beyond his greatest hopes. But if he let stand the arrangement that Livingston had made, the consequences might be alarming. Sadly he wondered—if he let this treaty stand, would he ever again know peace of mind?

By Livingston's treaty, Jefferson had bought what would be half a nation.

He had bought more land than any human being, before or since, had ever bought. He had bought one million square miles of North America. That had not been Jefferson's intention. He had asked Livingston to try to buy the port of New Orleans from Napoleon. Instead, as Jefferson's agent, Livingston had bought the entire French territory of Louisiana.

But I have no right to buy Louisiana, Jefferson realized. Even though he was president, under the Constitution of the United States he had no authority to buy foreign territory.

His political enemies would pounce on this action. They would accuse him of being a man who violated his most sacred principles. They would charge that Thomas Jefferson, who insisted so firmly that the Constitution must be upheld with extreme care to obey all its clauses exactly as they were written, now had shamelessly violated it!

Jefferson had maintained that the rights of the states must never be lessened by a strong central government. Now he had plotted to reduce the states' authority and to enormously strengthen the federal power.

Jefferson, who had preached stern economy with treasury funds, now was pouring out many millions of dollars to buy—what? A million square miles of harsh, barren land. And that was not the worst.

In buying Louisiana, it might be that the United States had bought an enormous amount of trouble. With gloomy foreboding, Jefferson realized that perhaps he had started a quarrel with Spain that would lead to war. Moreover, it was likely that this purchase would arouse political problems that would cause strife and disunity in the nation for generations to come.

Sadly Jefferson tried to reassure himself. He was buying territory from France only to make sure that the growth and prosperity of the United States would be helped, not hindered.

Had he made a ghastly mistake?

There still was time. He could still cancel the purchase.

But should he?*

What do you think Jefferson should do? Why?

Follow-up Activity

Create a scenario in which Jefferson is meeting with his cabinet to consider the treaty. Have different students role-play the parts of the Secretaries of State, Treasury, and War. What advice might each give Jefferson? What values might each hold? Jefferson was a strong advocate of Republican party principles, yet if he accepted the treaty and all its implications, he would certainly be acting like his despised opponents, the Federalists. How might Jefferson justify his seemingly conflicting value positions? What risks and consequences are involved? The president and the secretaries engage in a lively debate. At the end, Jefferson announces his decision and defends his position.

DISCUSSION QUESTIONS AND EXERCISES

1. Examine several books by futurist authors such as Daniel Bell's *The Coming of Post-Industrial Society,* Alvin Toffler's *The Third Wave,* and John Naisbitt's *Megatrends.* Also look for more recent books that deal with the future. What are the implications of these books for planning the social studies curriculum?

2. Examine several school districts' curriculum guides in the Curriculum Materials Center in your university library or in local school districts. How are the scope and sequence plans in these guides similar to and different from the expanding communities of humans plan described in this chapter? How can a teacher implement a curriculum which focuses on decision-making and citizen action within the context of the expanding communities of humans scope and sequence idea? Develop a sample lesson for a designated grade to indicate how this can be done.

3. What difficulties might teachers encounter when trying to structure a social studies unit or lesson around social issues? What steps might they take to minimize such difficulties?

4. Identify a personal or social problem on which you are required to make a decision such as "Should I prepare for a career rather than or in addition to teaching?" or "What actions should I take regarding pollution in my community?" If you do not currently face such a problem, select one on which you might be required to make a decision.

*Story written by George Shaftel. Reprinted with permission of the author.

    a. Make a list of the knowledge you would need (or the questions you would have to ask) to make a decision.

    b. What values do you hold strongly regarding this problem? Try to list them in a hierarchy of preference. See Table 1.3.

    c. What are some decisions you might have to make? What consequences might they have? Write down your thoughts in the style of Table 1.4.

5. Recall your own experiences in social studies classes from kindergarten through high school. What were your classes like? What kinds of things did your best social studies teachers do? What activity in social studies do you remember as the one from which you learned the most (or was the most fun or the most exciting)? Compare your experiences with the goals, curriculum, and types of learning activities advocated by the author of this chapter. Are there discrepancies between what you have experienced and what the author recommends as sound theory and practice? If so, how do you explain these differences?

6. Assume that during a primary-grade valuing lesson you are reading an open-ended story in which two small boys who desperately needed some money find a wallet containing ten dollars in cash. At this point the story ends. If, after asking the students what they would do in a similar situation, a student says he would keep the money and destroy the wallet, what would be your response? What should be your role as a teacher in value education? Why? Do you feel there are certain values teachers have a responsibility to inculcate in children? If so, what are these values? Make a list of such values and compare it with those of other members of your class.

7. In this chapter the author described four social studies curriculum frameworks: (1) Hanna's Expanding Communities of Humans (1963); (2) The NCSS Task Force Scope and Sequence (1984), Table 1.1; (3) the California History–Social Science Framework (1988), Table 1.2; and (4) decision-problem units, pp. 33–34. Given the goals of social studies described in this chapter, select the curriculum framework that you think best meets these goals. Explain and defend your choice.

8. Arrange to visit a school where you can observe a social studies lesson being taught. By careful observation, try to identify the key ideas and other major objectives that the teacher is trying to teach. After the lesson, talk with the teacher to determine whether your ideas are consistent with his or hers.

9. Demonstrate your understanding of the following key concepts presented in this chapter by writing or stating brief definitions of them.

    a. citizen
    b. citizen actor
    c. citizen action
    d. decision-making
    e. knowledge
    f. interdisciplinary knowledge
    g. higher-level knowledge
    h. the method of tenacity
    i. the *a priori* method
    j. the method of authority
    k. social science inquiry or inductive method

l. structure

m. value inquiry

NOTES

1. Alvin Toffler, *The Third Wave* (New York: William Morrow, 1980); John Naisbitt, *Megatrends: Ten New Directions Transforming Our Lives* (New York: Warner Books, 1982); Daniel Bell, *The Coming of Post-Industrial Society* (New York: Basic Books, 1976).

2. Alvin Toffler, "Civil Rights in the Third Wave," *Perspectives: The Civil Rights Quarterly* (Summer 1982), p. 35.

3. Naisbitt, *Megatrends*; Rosabeth Moss Kanter, *Men and Women of the Corporation* (New York: Basic Books, 1977).

4. James A. Banks, "Cultural Democracy, Citizenship Education, and the American Dream," *Social Education*, Vol. 47 (March 1983), pp. 178–179, 222ff.

5. Jean Fair, "Skills in Thinking." In Dana G. Kurfman, Ed., *Developing Decision-Making Skills*, 47th Yearbook (Washington, D.C.: National Council for the Social Studies, 1977), pp. 29–68.

6. Helen McCracken Carpenter, Ed., *Skill Development in the Social Studies*, 33rd Yearbook (Washington, D.C.: National Council for the Social Studies, 1963), pp. 310–327; Hilda Taba et al., *A Teacher's Handbook to Elementary Social Studies*, 2nd ed. (Reading, Mass.: Addison-Wesley, 1971), pp. 128–131.

7. David W. Johnson and Frank P. Johnson, *Joining Together: Group Theory and Group Skills* (Englewood Cliffs, NJ: Prentice-Hall, 1975).

8. Revision of the NCSS Social Studies Curriculum Guidelines. *Social Education*, Vol. 43 (April 1979), p. 266. See also Fred M. Newmann, *Education for Citizen Action: Challenge for Secondary Curriculum* (Berkeley, CA: McCutchan, 1975).

9. Carter V. Good, Ed., *Dictionary of Education* (New York: McGraw-Hill, 1959), p. 587. See also Wilhelmina Hill, *Unit Planning and Teaching in Elementary Social Studies* (Washington, D.C.: U.S. Government Printing Office, 1965).

10. Paul R. Hanna, "Revising the Social Studies: What Is Needed?" *Social Education*, Vol. 27 (April 1963), pp. 190–196.

11. Douglas P. Superka, Sharryl Hawke, and Irving Morrissett, "The Current and Future Status of Social Studies," *Social Education*, Vol. 44 (May 1980), pp. 362–369.

12. Report of the National Council for the Social Studies Task Force on Scope and Sequence, "In Search of a Scope and Sequence for Social Studies," *Social Education*, Vol. 48 (April 1984), pp. 249–262.

13. *History–Social Science Framework for California Public Schools, Kindergarten Through Grade Twelve,* (Sacramento: California State Department of Education, 1988).

14. E. D. Hirsch, Jr., *Cultural Literacy: What Every American Needs to Know* (Boston: Houghton Mifflin, 1987).

15. Lynne V. Cheney, *The American Memory: A Report on the Humanities in the Nation's Public Schools* (Washington, D.C.: National Endowment for the Humanities, 1987).

16. Diane Ravitch and Chester E. Finn, Jr., *What Do Our 17-Year-Olds Know? A Report on the First National Assessment of History and Literature* (New York: Harper & Row, 1987).

17. Diane Ravitch, *The Schools We Deserve: Reflections on the Educational Crises of Our Times* (New York: Basic Books, 1985), pp. 112–132.

18. Diane Ravitch, "Tot Sociology: On What Happened to History in the Grade Schools," *The American Scholar*, Vol. 56 (Summer 1987), pp. 343–354.

19. Robert Rothman, "1.5 Million Awarded for Center on History," *Education Week*, Vol. 7, No. 27 (March 30, 1988), p. 4.

20. Bradley Commission on History in Schools, *Building a History Curriculum: Guidelines for Teaching History in Schools* (Washington, D.C.: Educational Excellence Network, 1988).

21. Daniel Roselle, Ed., *Voices of Social Education 1937–1987* (New York: Macmillan, 1987), p. 50.

22. Roselle, p. 50.

23. Shirley H. Engle, "Decision-Making: The Heart of Social Studies Instruction," *Social Education*, Vol. 44 (May 1980), pp. 302–304, 306ff. This article is reprinted in Daniel Roselle, Ed., *Voices of Social Education 1937–1987* (New York: Macmillan, 1987), pp. 74–81; Shirley H. Engle and Anna S. Ochoa, *Education for Democratic Citizenship: Decision Making in the Social Studies* (New York: Teachers College Press, 1988).

24. Fred N. Kerlinger, *Foundations of Behavioral Research*, 3rd ed. (New York: Holt, Rinehart and Winston, 1984).

25. Kerlinger, p. 6.

26. Bernice Goldmark, *Social Studies: A Method of Inquiry* (Belmont, CA: Wadsworth, 1968), p. 215.

27. Robert Redfield, "The Social Uses of Social Science," No. 8013, pp. 1–2 (Columbus, OH: Charles E. Merrill). Reprinted from *University of Colorado Bulletin*, Vol. 47 (May 24, 1947).

28. Donald W. Oliver and James P. Shaver, *Teaching Public Issues in the High School* (Boston: Houghton Mifflin, 1966).

29. Anna S. Ochoa, "Now, More than Ever . . . Decision-Making and Related Skills." In Jack Allen, Ed., *Education in the 80s: Social Studies* (Washington, D.C.: National Education Association, 1981), pp. 100–112.

30. Oliver and Shaver, *Teaching Public Issues in the High School*.

FOR FURTHER READING

Bellah, Robert N., Richard Madsen, William M. Sullivan, Ann Swidler, and Steven M. Tipton. *Habits of the Heart: Individualism and Commitment in American Life.* New York: Harper & Row, 1985.

Boulding, Kenneth E. *Human Betterment.* Beverly Hills: Sage Publications, 1985.

Brown, Lester, et al., *State of the World: A Worldwatch Institute Report on Progress Toward a Sustainable Society.* New York: Norton, 1989.

Engle, Shirley H., and Anna S. Ochoa. *Education for Democratic Citizenship: Decision Making in the Social Studies.* New York: Teachers College Press, 1988.

Fuller, R. Buckminster. *Critical Path.* New York: St. Martin's Press, 1981.

Kurfman, Dana G., Ed. *Developing Decision-Making Skills,* 47th Yearbook. Washington, D.C.: National Council for the Social Studies, 1977.

La Raus, Roger, and Richard C. Remy. *Citizenship Decision-Making.* Menlo Park, CA: Addison-Wesley, 1978.

Shaver, James P., and William Strong. *Facing Value Decisions: Rationale Building for Teachers,* 2nd ed. New York: Teachers College Press, 1982.

The Global 2000 Report to the President: Entering the Twenty-First Century. New York: Penguin Books, 1982.

2

Unit and Curriculum Planning

THE NEED FOR AN
INTERDISCIPLINARY PERSPECTIVE

The main goal of the social studies should be to help students develop the ability to make reflective decisions so that they can solve personal problems and, through citizen action, influence public policy. Sound decisions cannot be made in a vacuum; they must be based on knowledge. Reflective decisions must be based on scientific knowledge.

Reflective decisions must also be based on *interdisciplinary* knowledge. The reflective decision-maker should be able to see human events from the perspectives of several different disciplines. Knowledge from any one discipline is insufficient for making personal and public decisions and for understanding the complex nature of human behavior. To understand complex problems such as global hunger, poverty, inflation, and unemployment the citizen actor not only needs to use economic concepts, but concepts from disciplines such as political science, sociology, and history.

To successfully influence public policy, the citizen actor must select, synthesize, and apply knowledge from all the social sciences, as well as from philosophy and the humanities. The social scientist fragments the universe to study it more easily. The social studies help students view human behavior in a broad context. The behavior of the family is neither economic nor anthropological, but it can be profitably viewed through the special lens of each of these disciplines. When planning interdisciplinary units, it is important for you to realize that the social science disciplines are not specific content, *but represent specialized ways to view the same human behavior.* Human behavior is not fragmented. Scientists fragment it in order to study it from unique points of view.

The social science disciplines are discussed extensively in Part III. The separation of the discipline chapters in this book was done to emphasize the contributions that each discipline can make to an understanding of complex social issues, and not to suggest that any one discipline in and of itself is sufficient to explain human behavior or to solve human problems.

TEACHING INQUIRY, VALUING, AND DECISION-MAKING SKILLS

Inquiry, valuing, and decision-making each consists of a cluster of highly interrelated skills. Students should have practice in developing each of these sets of skills, as well as practice relating them. You can plan separate units and lessons that teach inquiry, valuing, and decision-making skills, or you can build units to teach all three sets of skills. The long-range goal should be to help students become adept in the processes of decision-making and citizen action. Thus, you should plan units and lessons that will give students practice in relating these sets of skills as often as possible. However, for purposes of emphasis, this chapter discusses and illustrates strategies for social inquiry. Chapter 15 treats value inquiry and illustrates how these skills can be combined to help students become reflective decision-makers and citizen actors.

THE INTERDISCIPLINARY UNIT

A unit is a series of interrelated activities designed to attain specific changes in student behavior. Most units contain these components:

1. The topic or problem.
2. The objectives.
3. Initiation activities.
4. Developmental activities.
5. Evaluation activities.
6. Culmination activities.

Social science units should ideally be structured around a number of organizing or key concepts, such as those discussed in Part III. In this chapter, we will illustrate how a conceptual unit can be built within the framework of a traditional social studies curriculum. You will most likely teach in a school that has a traditional social studies curriculum. The final part of this chapter discusses building a conceptual curriculum within schools or districts that wish to change their social studies curricula in substantial ways. Table 2.1 shows the parts of a conceptual unit with examples from a unit on the family discussed later in this chapter.

TABLE 2.1. The Parts of a Conceptual Unit

 1. **Unit Topic**
    The family

 2. **Key Concepts** *(only two are shown here)*
    Scarcity, role

 3. **Key Generalizations** *(only two are shown here)*
    Every individual and society faces a conflict between unlimited wants and limited resources. This creates the need for decision-making. *(Scarcity)*
    Every member of a society must function in many different roles. *(Role)*

 4. **Subideas**
    Mother and Father often want to buy two or more things when they have only enough money for one of them. *(Scarcity)*
    Father does different things when he goes shopping or to work. *(Role)*

 5. **Objectives**
    The students will be able to list examples and nonexamples of *scarcity.*
    The students will be able to list the different *roles* in which they function.

 6. **Initiation Activities** *(these activities are designed to start the unit in an interesting and exciting way)*
    The students will be asked what a family is and to state their ideas.
    The students will be shown pictures of different types of families and asked to state how they are alike and different.

 7. **Developmental Activities** *(these activities are the heart of the unit)*
    The teacher reads *A Hundred Penny Box* by Sharon Bell Mathis.
    This powerful story is about a family that includes a great-great aunt. A conflict develops between mother and the aunt.
    Each student brings a story about a family to class that is shared.

 8. **Evaluation Activities** *(these activities, which are ongoing throughout the unit, are designed to determine the extent to which the students are mastering the concepts and generalizations being taught)*
    The students are asked to list three examples of *scarcity* in their family.
    The students are asked to list several roles performed by themselves and by their parent or parents.

 9. **Culmination Activities** *(during this phase of the unit, the major ideas that were studied are highlighted, reviewed, and interrelated)*
    Groups of students are asked to write and present skits that show *scarcity.*
    The students are asked to list as many different kinds of families as they can.

10. **A Resource Bibliography** *(includes sources for both students and the teacher)*

SELECTING AND ORGANIZING KEY CONCEPTS FOR INTERDISCIPLINARY UNITS

How you select the key concepts that will constitute your units will depend to a great extent on the degree of freedom you have. Most school districts have curriculum guides that provide a basic framework for the local social studies program; their main purpose is to ensure that the instructional program is sequential and developmental. Guides are therefore usually intended to function only as guides, not as blueprints that you are expected to follow slavishly. Curriculum guides may also contain suggested teaching strategies and instructional resources, which you may use in a way that will best enhance student growth and achievement. These comments are not intended to suggest that you should ignore the guidelines provided by your school district; rather, you should implement a program, within your district's guidelines, consistent with modern social studies theory and practice. Theory and research suggest that units should be organized around key concepts and generalizations. Such units will enhance students' understanding, retention, and transfer.[1]

The social studies guides of most school districts specify a number of topics that the teachers of each grade are expected to cover. Those topics usually reflect the "expanding communities of humans" or the "expanding environment" approach; in the primary grades, the students study institutions with which they are most familiar and thus can understand most easily (see Figure 2.1). Most often, the home, school, holidays, community helpers, and the local community are studied in the primary grades. In the middle grades the state, exploration, pioneer days, and the histories of the United States and the Western Hemisphere are studied. European and U.S. history usually constitute the program for the junior high school grades. Increasingly, students are studying non-Western cultures and nations throughout the elementary and junior high school grades.

As the students move through the grades, they study behavior and institutions increasingly more remote from their direct experiences. We will not present a critique of the expanding environment approach, but rather emphasize the fact that *you can structure a conceptually oriented curriculum within the framework of a traditional social studies program.*

This approach was taken in the Taba Social Studies Project. The directors of this project identified eleven key concepts from the various social science disciplines plus a number of related generalizations, and used content samples of the traditional program to develop the key ideas identified. The eleven organizing concepts are *causality, conflict, cooperation, cultural change, differences, interdependence, modification, power, societal control, tradition,* and *values.*[2] In the first grade, content samples are selected from the family, a traditional topic for the primary grades. Content samples are selected from the state, another traditional topic, for the fourth-grade program. While the structure of the Taba Social Studies Program is drastically different from

Teachers must plan jointly to develop a conceptual social studies curriculum that helps students to develop an increased understanding of concepts as they progress through the grades. (*Source:* Terri Malinowski, Northshore School District, Seattle.)

traditional social studies programs, the topics are quite traditional. Approaching curriculum reform using this approach will allow you to maintain a degree of stability in the curriculum. You will also be able to use many of your available instructional materials and resources. There is also a legal reason for approaching curriculum reform within a traditional framework. The study of the history of the state and the United States is mandated by most state governments. A final advantage of initiating a new program within a traditional framework is that you will feel more secure and will be more likely to implement it.

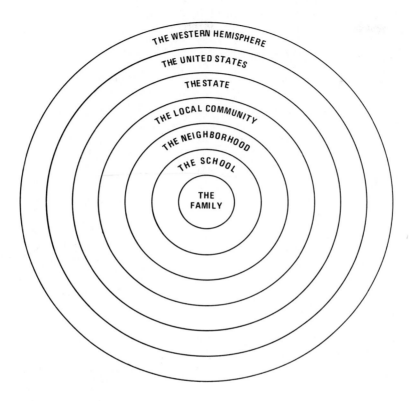

FIGURE 2.1 The expanding environment approach to curriculum construction. The traditional social studies curriculum is based on the concept of the expanding environment. Children study the human community that is closest to their actual experiences. As they move through the grades, they study increasingly larger communities. Teachers who are required to plan units within this structure can use organizing ideas from the disciplines to help children better understand the communities in which they live.

NEW WINE IN OLD BOTTLES: TEACHING NEW CONCEPTS WITH TRADITIONAL CONTENT

If you have a social studies curriculum guide, you should begin planning your units for the year by carefully studying the topics you are required to teach, such as the home, the school, community helpers, and United States history. You should then study a list of key concepts from the social science disciplines so that you can decide which ones can be most effectively and meaningfully taught with the content you are required to teach. Key concepts from the social sciences are found in Part III. They are listed in Table 2.2.

Criteria for Selection of Concepts

What *criteria* can you use to select appropriate ideas for development? You should first consider the prior experiences of the students. If they have been introduced to specific concepts in a previous grade, you should further develop and expand these concepts, perhaps introducing new related concepts that will enhance their understanding of their social environment and help them become better decision-makers. You should also select concepts around which a great deal of data and content can be organized. While all key concepts within the social sciences can be used to organize and categorize a great deal of information, some concepts are more powerful than others— that is, they are more encompassing. The concepts selected should have the "power to organize and synthesize large numbers of relationships, specific facts, and ideas."[3] This does not mean that low-order concepts should never be selected, but the goal should be to select the most powerful ones when all factors are considered. Both *scarcity* and *exchange* are key economic concepts, but *scarcity* is a much more powerful idea. Taba offers the following criteria for selecting *organizing* or *key* concepts for a conceptual curriculum:

1. *Validity:* Do they adequately represent ideas of the discipline from which they are drawn?
2. *Significance:* Can they explain important segments of the world to-day?

TABLE 2.2. Key Social Science Concepts

History	Sociology	Anthropology
Change	Socialization	Culture
Leadership	Roles	Diffusion
Conflict	Norms and sanctions	Tradition
Cooperation	Values	Acculturation
Nationalism	Social movement	Ethnocentrism
Exploration	Society	Cultural relativism
Historical bias		Rite of passage

Political Science	Economics	Geography
Power	Scarcity	Location
Social control	Production	Spatial interaction
State	Interdependence	Urban spatial patterns
Interest group	Specialization and division	Internal structure of a city
Political socialization	of labor	Cultural diffusion
Political participation	Voluntary exchange	Environmental perception

3. *Appropriateness:* Are they suited to the needs, interests, and maturational level of the students?
4. *Durability:* Are they of lasting importance?
5. *Balance:* Do they permit development of both scope and depth?[4]

Some consideration should also be given to the content that must be studied when key concepts are selected for study. Some content can be more profitably viewed from certain disciplinary perspectives than from others. For example, it is easier for students to grasp the concept of *culture* when they study U.S. families as well as families in other societies. Students cannot fully appreciate how much we are creatures of our own culture until they have viewed other ways of living and behaving. The concept of *power* can be understood more readily if students study an Indian nation than if they study community helpers, even though certain ideas about the political system can be learned when workers in the community are studied.

You should also select concepts from as many disciplines as is practical and appropriate. In other words, all social studies units should be *interdisciplinary.* The only way to assure that units are interdisciplinary is to select concepts from several disciplines during the initial stages of unit planning. Good judgment and sound selection criteria are important because it will not be possible for you to select concepts from each of the social sciences for every unit. Even though concepts from a particular discipline may not be identified initially, during class discussions you can occasionally help students view the content from other social science perspectives. However, only careful planning will ensure that specific concepts and ideas will be learned by your students.

Identifying Specific Concepts for a Unit

Helping students to view human behavior from the perspectives of the various social sciences will provide them with a sophisticated understanding of their social environment so that they can become reflective decision-makers and citizen actors. They have many daily experiences that can be profitably viewed through the lenses of various disciplines. Without the conceptual tools of the social scientist, students may and often do study topics such as the family, the community, and the school, and memorize a list of disorganized facts that are largely meaningless and quickly forgotten. However, if they learn organizing ideas when they study these topics, they will gain an understanding that can be further developed with new content in later grades. This knowledge will contribute greatly to their understanding of the world in which they live. The following example will illustrate how a first-grade teacher, Mr. Jones, who is required to teach "The Family," might select key concepts from the disciplines in order to structure an interdisciplinary unit.

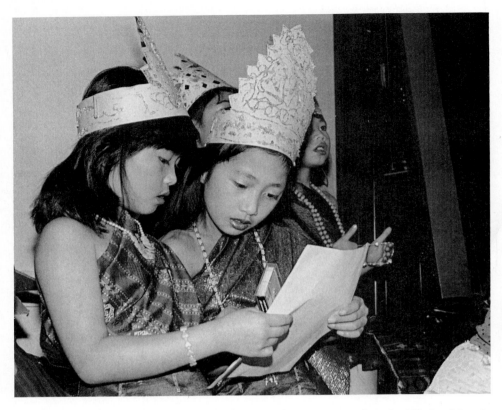

A conceptual curriculum allows the teacher to select a range of content that relates to and excites students from diverse backgrounds and cultural groups. (*Source:* Edna Kellman, Seattle Public Schools.)

AN INTERDISCIPLINARY UNIT ON THE FAMILY

Mr. Jones studies a list of concepts such as those listed in Table 2.2. As he studies the concepts of each discipline, he asks himself this question, "Which concepts from this discipline will best help my students understand the family as a social institution and become better decision-makers and reflective citizen actors?" He first looks over the key concepts of anthropology. Initially, he thinks that *culture* is a concept with which the children should be familiar, but he decides that they can better understand this concept if they also study families in other cultures. At this time, he does not have the materials necessary to introduce the children to another culture. He therefore decides not to introduce the concept at this time, but will introduce *culture* when the class studies communities later in the year. By that time, his materials on the Hopi Indians will have arrived. He feels that the other anthropological concepts cannot be fruitfully introduced until the children are familiar with the concept of *culture,* since that is the most important concept in the discipline. Mr. Jones is quite familiar with the structure of anthropology and the other disciplines.

Next he studies the key economic concepts in Table 2.2, reviews their meanings, and decides that *scarcity, interdependence, production,* and *voluntary exchange* are not only concepts that the children should know, but are ideas that can be very effectively developed with content samples drawn from the life of an American family. He feels that he already has selected enough concepts for a unit, but remembers that social studies units should be *interdisciplinary* and not just about economics. He reviews the key concepts in geography and political science. He decides that the only appropriate concept within these two disciplines for his family unit is the political science concept of *social control.* Certainly all children have rules at home that they must obey, and they should gain a better understanding of *social control.*

In studying the sociological concepts on our list, he immediately sees how closely *role* is related to one of the economic concepts he has selected, *interdependence.* He thus decides to select *role.* He also selects *socialization, norm,* and *sanction* because these concepts are related to the political science concept he chose, *social control.* If children study laws, they should know how laws relate to norms and sanctions. He is tempted to add other concepts to his list, but realizes that it is best for children to gain a working knowledge of a few concepts rather than to learn a large number of them superficially. Let's review the concepts Mr. Jones identified and the disciplines from which they were selected:

Discipline	**Concepts Selected**
Economics	*scarcity*
	interdependence
	production
	voluntary exchange
Political science	*social control*
Sociology	*socialization*
	norm
	sanction
	role

Mr. Jones is certain that his unit will be an interdisciplinary one because he has selected key concepts from economics, political science, and sociology, even though he did not select concepts from *all* the social science disciplines. He believes that it is neither practical nor possible for him to try to teach concepts from all the disciplines in one unit. He will teach other units during the year, and at that time will introduce ideas from the other disciplines. He feels that students should be exposed to the ideas and ways of thinking used by all social scientists. As he looks over his list of concepts, he realizes a point that had been made by his professor in social studies methods: although the social sciences have unique ways of looking at human behavior, the concepts and key ideas they use are far from being mutually exclusive. Political scientists often use key sociological concepts in their research. He notes how the political science concept of *social control* is related to the sociological concepts of *norms* and *sanctions*. *The interrelatedness of the social sciences is far from being a disadvantage to the social studies teacher; rather, it is a great advantage because their interrelatedness makes it easier to plan units that cut across discipline lines.*

IDENTIFYING RELATED GENERALIZATIONS

We have explained how Mr. Jones, who is required to teach about the family in the first grade, might go about selecting organizing concepts from the disciplines in order to structure an interdisciplinary unit. Once you have identified key concepts for a unit, you must then identify key *generalizations*. *Organizing* or *key generalizations* guide the selection of low-order generalizations or subideas, specific content samples, and teaching strategies. Generalizations that are related to organizing concepts are found in Part III of this book. Like key concepts, key generalizations should be powerful. They should summarize in general terms many facts and a great deal of specific information. They should also be empirical statements that can be scientifically tested. They should not be value or normative judgments. Some lists of generalizations are value judgments that cannot be scientifically tested (see Chapter 3). Mr. Jones selects the organizing generalizations shown in Table 2.3 that are related to the key concepts already identified.

Identifying Subideas

After you have identified the organizing generalizations related to the key concepts you wish to develop, you should identify the *subideas* related to the organizing generalizations. Subideas are low-order statements that relate to the specific content you are required to teach. Examples of subideas that Mr. Jones might select for his unit are found in Table 2.3.

DETERMINING UNIT OBJECTIVES

When you identify the key concepts and generalizations for a social science inquiry unit, most of the objectives of the unit will have been determined, although they have not been articulated. A major objective of a social science inquiry unit is to have the students *state or write*, in their own words, the organizing generalizations you have identified. The students should also be able to demonstrate an understanding of the key concepts in the unit. When the concepts are named, students can demonstrate their understanding by *identifying* examples and nonexamples of them. Often you will not choose to teach primary-grade children the labels for concepts used by social scientists, even though you expect them to understand such concepts. In such cases, the

TABLE 2.3. Key Generalizations, Subideas, and Related Concepts

Generalizations and Subideas	Related Concepts
1. *Generalization:* Every individual and society faces a conflict between unlimited wants and limited resources. This creates the need for decision-making. (Economics) *Subidea:* Mother and father often want to buy two or more things when they have only enough money for one of them.	Scarcity
2. *Generalization:* All members of a society are interdependent: individual producers of goods and services exchange with others to get the goods and services they need to satisfy their basic needs. (Economics) *Subidea:* Mother and Father work to make money to buy the goods and services the family wants and needs.	Goods Services Interdependence Production Consumption Voluntary exchange
3. *Generalization:* In every society and institution, regulations and laws emerge to govern the behavior of individuals; individuals usually experience some form of punishment when authorities catch them breaking laws. (Political science) *Subidea:* Father and Mother make rules for children about going to bed, eating, watching television, crossing the street, and playing.	Social control
4. *Generalization:* All human behavior is learned from other human beings through group interaction. (Sociology) *Subidea:* Our parents teach us how to walk and talk.	Socialization
5. *Generalization:* Every member of society must function in many different roles. (Sociology) *Subidea:* Father does different things when he goes shopping or to work.	Role
6. *Generalization:* Norms and sanctions shape the behavior of group members. (Sociology) *Subidea:* We get angry when members of our family do not treat us in the expected ways, and let them know it.	Norms Sanctions

objective is for the children to recognize the concept when it is stated in familiar terms. For example, if the concept is *norm*, you might ask the children to list things around the house that "you are expected to do." The children will then be able to respond with examples of the concept.

Another major objective of a social science inquiry unit is for the students to be able to use the *method* of social science inquiry to derive generalizations. Social science consists of *knowledge* (concepts and generalizations) as well as a *method* of inquiry. Because social knowledge is tentative and subject to constant revision, it is extremely important for students to be able to use the method of the social scientist to derive knowledge. While students need knowledge on social issues, knowing the *method by which scientific knowledge is derived is vastly more important*. Thus, throughout the unit, you should emphasize the *process* of knowing. (The method of science is discussed in considerable detail in Chapter 3.) Basically, it involves (a) formulation of the problem, (b) formulation of hypotheses, (c) conceptualization, (d) collection of data, (e) evaluation and analysis of data, (f) derivation of generalizations, and (g) inquiry into the methods used to solve the problem. You will not be able to provide practice for the students in each of these skills during each unit. However, the goal should be to help them attain maximum proficiency in each skill. These steps in the process and the practice of them should be kept constantly in mind when units and teaching strategies are planned. You might plan specific strategies to develop some of these skills during each unit. For example, during the family unit, you might want to stress how we formulate hypotheses and test them.

The major goals of social science inquiry units that we have identified can be summarized as follows: (1) The students will be able to state or write, in their own words, the organizing generalizations of the unit; (2) they will be able to identify examples and nonexamples of the key concepts of the unit; and (3) they will be able to use the process of social inquiry to solve a scientific problem. These objectives are stated in very general terms. However, depending on their purposes, you can state them as specifically as necessary. For example, in his statement of objectives for our sample family unit, Mr. Jones might want to write out each of the generalizations the children will be expected to state in their own words, and to list the concepts that they will be expected to understand. Also, the inquiry skills can be stated much more specifically. For example, regarding the skill of hypothesizing, you might state, "When given a problem and sources of data, the student will be able to state a testable hypothesis." This kind of specific statement could be made for each skill that the inquiry process comprises.

Organizing the Unit

When the organizing concepts and generalizations have been identified and the subideas stated, you can organize the unit in a logical and meaningful fashion. In looking over the concepts Mr. Jones identified in our example, we note that he identified the following concepts in the order indicated:

1. *Scarcity*
2. *Interdependence, production, voluntary exchange*
3. *Social control*
4. *Socialization*
5. *Role*
6. *Norms, sanctions*

Mr. Jones feels that his unit will be more effective if he teaches first some of the concepts that he identified later, and then teaches those he selected earlier. For example, the children can better understand the concept of *scarcity* if they are acquainted with the idea of *role*. He decides that role is a basic concept that should be introduced before any of the other ideas. Since people learn their roles through a process of *socialization,* he decides to teach *socialization* next. Then *norms* and *sanctions* will be taught; they shape a person's behavior during socialization. *Social control* is also a part of the socialization process. The concept of *interdependence* will help students see the relationships between different roles. *Scarcity* is chosen as the last main concept to develop because Mr. Jones feels that it can be more easily grasped once the other concepts are understood. The prior experiences of the students and the relationships between the key concepts should be the main determiners of the organization of the conceptual-inquiry unit.

Formulating and Outlining Activities:
The Developmental Phase of the Unit

The activities and teaching strategies are the heart of any unit. If the organizing concepts and generalizations have been carefully selected and stated, they should serve as an effective guide to the formulation of appropriate teaching strategies and learning activities. The activities and strategies should relate directly to the central ideas of the unit. *No activity should be included within a unit unless you clearly see how it contributes to the development of the ideas and skills you have identified.* The subideas related to the key concepts and generalizations are stated primarily to ensure that activities are related to the key ideas and to guide in their formulation. Traditional units often contain a long list of activities and teaching strategies whose relationship to the central ideas of the unit is not clear. This practice can best be avoided by writing the key concepts and generalizations to be developed on one side of a sheet of paper and the activities or teaching strategies on the other side, as illustrated in Table 2.4. The statement of the activities or teaching strategies can be as general or specific as necessary. In our example, we have stated the activities in fairly general terms, largely to conserve space. The major strategies and activities used to develop the key ideas of a unit are referred to as the *developmental phase* of the unit.

Initiating the Unit

You should plan beginning activities that will stimulate student interest and curiosity. An exciting beginning is one of the best assurances of a successful and meaningful unit. If students are bored at the beginning of a unit, you must seriously doubt whether it will have the intended outcome. The introductory phase of a unit deserves careful thought and planning. To stimulate student interest and questioning, you can arrange materials related to the unit topic around the room. These materials might include captivating pictures, interesting books, and objects the students can handle. You can also read to the students an intriguing story related to the unit topic and encour-

TABLE 2.4. Concepts, Generalizations, and Activities

Concepts and Generalizations	Activities
Socialization All human behavior is learned from other human beings through group interaction.	1. Viewing pictures of parents showing children how to do such things as tie their shoes, swim, ski, and eat properly. 2. Naming specific things our parents taught us. 3. Naming the different kinds of clothes we wear to school, to worship, and to play, and who taught us to dress in these ways. 4. Discussing how we treat other people and who taught us how to treat them. 5. Summarizing and generalizing about the things that we learn from other members of our family.
Norms, sanctions Norms and sanctions shape the behavior of group members.	1. Listing ways in which we are expected to speak to our parents. 2. Listing ways in which we are expected to treat our parents and grandparents. 3. Discussing other things members of the family expect us to do. 4. Listing the kinds of things our parents do to us when we do things that they do not expect us to do. 5. Listing the kinds of things members of our families do and say when we do the things they expect us to do. 6. Discussing why members of our family treat us differently when we do things that are expected and things that are not expected. 7. Listing the kinds of things we expect members of our family to do, and what we do and say when they fail do them. 8. Summarizing and generalizing about family norms and sanctions.

age them to ask questions about it. A record can be kept of these questions. To start the unit in our example, you might read a book about family life, such as Sydney Taylor's fascinating book about life in a Jewish family, *All-of-a-Kind-Family*, or John Steptoe's book about a family made up of a father and two children, *My Daddy Is a Monster . . . Sometimes*. A recording, filmstrip, or short film can also introduce units effectively. A unit can also be introduced with a role-playing situation or a dramatic incident. Creative teachers think of many different ways to capture student interest and stimulate curiosity during this important unit phase.

Evaluation Activities

You should plan evaluation activities that can be implemented throughout the unit. Evaluation should be an ongoing and not an "end-of-unit" activity. It is

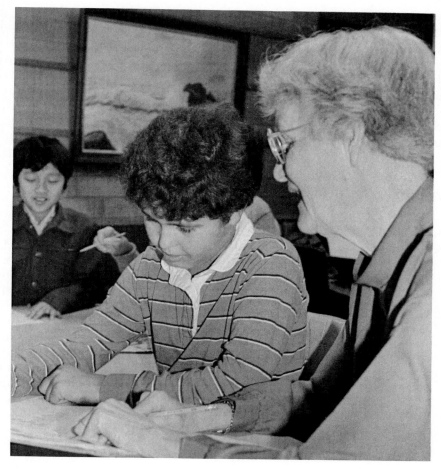

Evaluation should be an ongoing activity that occurs throughout the unit. This child is receiving important feedback from his teacher that will enable him to increase his abilities and skills. (*Source:* Edna Kellman, Seattle Public Schools.)

usually appropriate, however, to plan general kinds of evaluation activities for the end of the unit. Since effective evaluation is an ongoing process, you might find it helpful to indicate (perhaps with asterisks) which activities within the developmental phase of the unit are intended for evaluation purposes. Too often, evaluation is considered only as a paper-and-pencil test. While a test is a legitimate evaluation exercise, to think of evaluation as merely a written test is much too narrow. Evaluation should be thought of in broad terms, and the objectives of the unit should be kept clearly in mind when evaluation activities are planned. Checklists, rating scales, role-playing situations, and group discussions can all be used as effective evaluation exercises. Students may be presented with a problem, such as "What kinds of things do we learn from our parents?" and asked to act out the correct answer in a role-playing situation.

When inquiry skills are assessed, it will often be necessary to give students new data to determine whether they are able to state hypotheses, evaluate data, and test generalizations. To test students' ability to identify *roles* and to form generalizations about them, Mr. Jones may read a story about family life among the Hopi Indians and ask the students to describe the roles of the different family members and to state a generalization about these roles. A similar exercise could assess the students' understanding of *socialization*. If they understand this concept, they will be able to state ways in which the behavior of Hopi children is shaped by the norms and sanctions within their families.

Culminating Activities

You should plan activities that will summarize the various parts of the unit. During this phase of the unit, the major ideas studied are highlighted, reviewed, and interrelated. Culmination activities may consist of reviewing *data retrieval charts* (see Table 4.2) made during the unit, giving oral reports, conducting discussions, participating in role-playing situations, or presenting short skits that highlight the key ideas studied. In the past, culminating activities often consisted of highly rehearsed pageants that were attended by parents and other members of the school community. However, while sharing may be desirable under certain circumstances, the emphasis of culminating activities should be on *summarizing the major ideas learned,* and not on entertaining parents or other students. During the culminating activities, you may also gain helpful ideas about concepts to teach in future units. You may realize that certain concepts and key ideas need further study and clarification. Thus, culminating and evaluating activities are not by any means mutually exclusive. The various parts of a unit are discussed separately for purpose of emphasis. In reality, the parts often blend together.

Resource Bibliography

During the early stages of planning, you should start compiling lists of resources you will need to develop the key concepts and ideas of the unit. Some teachers have found it advantageous to collect source material even before actual plans are made. They keep folders in which they place all pictures, clippings, and other materials that relate to specific topics. This greatly facilitates the planning and initiation of a unit. When planning a bibliography, you should consider more than written, factual material. Literature, art, and music are rich sources that can and should be used to help students grasp key ideas in the social sciences. The resources should also include the filmstrips, pictures, films, and computer courseware you plan to use. All resources should be gathered or requested well in advance. Anyone who has taught can tell a disappointing story about how a lesson was ruined because the book or filmstrip that was needed at a particular moment was not available. Often these incidents result from poor teacher planning. A film may have been ordered too late or the specific location of a book was not rechecked. It is often helpful to have a written list of resources for both the students and you. You will often find it necessary to study a number of books on a topic before you can teach it successfully. Some teachers have found it helpful to duplicate the list of resources available to the students so that they may locate extra copies of resource material when they want to study the subject in greater detail than is done in class.

The Daily Lesson Plan

Once your unit is constructed, you have clearly in mind the major components of your social studies lessons for several weeks. However, the components of each day's lesson should be planned to assure effective instruction and meaningful learning experiences. The lesson plan should relate directly to the major unit plan. The main components of the daily lesson plan are described in Table 2.5. Like the unit, the daily lesson plan can be as general

TABLE 2.5. Example of a Daily Lesson Plan

1. Key Concept
Role

2. Organizing Generalization
We function in many different roles.

Subideas:
a) Family members function in different roles at home.
b) Family members function in many different roles away from home.

3. Objective
The students will be able to state, in their own words, the organizing generalization above.

4. Developmental Activities
a) Listing things parents do at home.
b) Listing things parents do away from home.
c) Listing things children do at home and away from home.
d) Discussing how roles may conflict.
e) Viewing pictures of parents functioning in many different roles.
f) Viewing pictures of children functioning in many different roles.

5. Summary and Evaluation Activities
a) Summarizing and generalizing about how we function in many different roles.
b) Viewing pictures of a Hopi Indian family and naming the roles of family members.
c) Contrasting Hopi family roles with those in Anglo-American families.

6. Materials and Resources
a) Children's experiences.
b) Pictures of parents and children engaged in many different activities.
c) Pictures of a Hopi Indian family engaged in a variety of activities.

or as specific as is necessary. In general, the inexperienced teacher will find it advantageous to make more detailed lesson plans than the veteran teacher. The concepts, generalizations, and objectives of the daily lesson plan should be taken from those listed for the major unit plan. As a general rule, you should try to develop no more than one concept and generalization during a daily lesson. Some lessons may only develop concepts; others can be planned to help students develop general statements about concepts. Table 2.5 illustrates how you may develop the concept of *role* and a related generalization in a daily lesson.

DEVELOPING A SPIRAL CONCEPTUAL CURRICULUM

In the first part of this chapter we discussed how a teacher in a school district with a traditional social studies curriculum can build conceptual units within such a framework. We will now consider a different problem. Some schools and districts are so dissatisfied with the existing social studies curriculum that they wish to develop a totally new one. A curriculum committee made up of teachers in these districts may be asked to develop a new social studies curriculum. You may be on such a committee sometime in the future in your district.

The first step in developing a spiral conceptual curriculum is to identify a list of key concepts the students will study throughout the elementary and junior high school grades, beginning in kindergarten. These concepts will be developed sequentially and in greater depth in each higher grade (see Figure 2.2). *The concepts selected should be powerful ones that can encompass many topics and a great deal of information.* In the model curriculum discussed below, five key concepts from different social science disciplines are identified: *socialization, scarcity, cultural differences, power,* and *physical environment.* When the committee is selecting key concepts for the curriculum, it should make sure that concepts are selected from a range of disciplines so that the curriculum will be *interdisciplinary.* When the key concepts are identified, an organizing or key generalization is then selected for each key concept. Related subideas are then selected for each of the key generalizations.

When these parts of the conceptual curriculum have been identified, the committee has the option of specifying *content samples* to be used to develop the key concepts and generalizations or of concluding its work when a curriculum framework is developed. In most school districts, however, specific content samples for developing the key concepts and generalizations are identified for each grade level.

In our model curriculum, specific content for each grade level is not identified. (See Table 2.6.) However, a major concept, called a *focused concept,* is identified for each grade level. Several key related questions are also identified for each grade level. (See Table 2.7.) The focused concepts, such as *human institutions* and *human communities,* are studied from the perspectives of the key concepts and generalizations identified for the total curriculum.

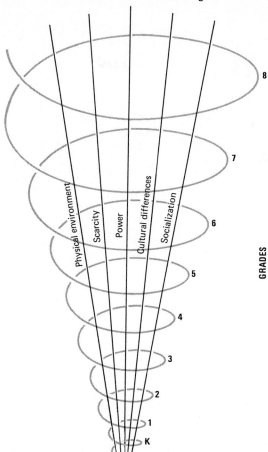

FIGURE 2.2 The spiral development of concepts within our model social studies curriculum. The curriculum is organized around five key concepts from the various social science disciplines. Two of the concepts (*socialization* and *cultural differences*) are introduced in kindergarten. Three are introduced at Level 1 (*socialization, cultural differences,* and *power*). All five of the concepts are studied in Levels 2–8. The concepts are developed at an increasing degree of complexity at each successive level.

At Levels 2 through 6, each of the focused concepts is studied from the various perspectives of five organizing concepts and related generalizations. At Level 1, only three of the organizing concepts and related generalizations are used to study the focused concept. Only two of the organizing concepts and related generalizations are used to study the focused concept at Level K. Table 2.6 summarizes the conceptual framework for our sample curriculum. The focused grade-level concepts and the key questions are shown in Table

TABLE 2.6. A Model Conceptual Curriculum

Level	Conceptual Focus in Levels	Socialization	Scarcity	Cultural Differences	Power	Physical Environment
		An individual's behavior is influenced by the social system in which he or she participates.	Individuals and groups face a conflict between unlimited wants and limited resources.	Cultural differences influence the behavior of individuals and groups.	Rules and laws govern the behavior of people in a social system.	The physical environment influences the behavior of people in a social system.
Level 6	Social problems and social movements	Individuals join movements to resolve social problems.	Scarce goods and resources cause problems within societies.	Cultural and ethnic differences cause problems in a social system.	Power struggles exist between nations and societies, thus causing international political problems.	Human utilization of natural resources creates social problems.
Level 5	Human cultures	An individual's culture strongly influences his or her behavior and values.	Cultures satisfy their needs for goods and services in many different ways.	Conflict usually results when people from different cultures and subcultures interact.	Laws and rules govern behavior in all cultures.	The physical environment influences how a culture develops.
Level 4	Human societies	Individuals within a society share behavioral characteristics.	Scarcity is a problem in all human societies.	The existence of subcultures within a society increases social conflict.	Political systems emerge in all human societies.	The physical environment influences the nature of a social system.

Level 3 Human communities	An individual's behavior is influenced by the community in which he or she is socialized.	Members of a community depend on each other to satisfy their needs for goods and services.	Cultural and ethnic minorities within a community usually function in more than one cultural environment.	Individuals frequently form groups to influence political policy.	Different human groups use the same physical environment differently.
Level 2 Human institutions	Institutions help people to meet their needs.	Economic institutions help people to exchange goods and services.	Institutions exist in all cultures.	Political institutions help societies to maintain stability.	The physical environment influences the structure of institutions.
Level 1 Human groups	An individual's behavior is influenced by the groups to which he or she belongs.		Cultures influence the nature of human groups.	Groups are governed by rules and sanctions.	
Level K Identity	An individual's identity is highly influenced by the people in his or her social environment. An individual's identity strongly influences his or her behavior.		An individual's culture and ethnic group influence his or her identity.		

2.7. Our model curriculum is interdisciplinary in two ways. The focused concepts, which are chosen from different disciplines, are viewed from the perspective of concepts from various disciplines. The interrelationship of the focused concepts is illustrated in Figure 2.3.

TABLE 2.7. Focused Concepts for the Levels and Related Questions

Level	Focused Concept for Level and Related Key Questions
Level K	*Identity* Who am I? How did I become the person I am? How does my view of myself affect me? How do other people become who they are? What will I be like in the future? What can I do to feel better about who I am? (Decision-making)
Level 1	*Human groups* How do people function in groups?* How do groups affect people? What human needs do groups satisfy? What problems do groups experience? What problems are groups likely to experience in the future? How do, and might, people try to solve them? (Decision-making)
Level 2	*Human institutions* How do people function in institutions?* How do institutions affect people? What human needs do institutions satisfy? What problems do institutions experience? What problems are institutions likely to experience in the future? How do, and might, people try to solve them? (Decision-making)
Level 3	*Human communities* How do people function in communities?* How do communities affect people? What human needs do communities satisfy? What problems do communities experience? What problems are communities likely to experience in the future? How do, and might, people try to solve them? (Decision-making)
Level 4	*Human societies* How do people function in societies?* How do societies affect people? What human needs do societies satisfy? What problems do societies experience? What problems are societies likely to experience in the future? How do, and might, people try to solve them? (Decision-making)
Level 5	*Human cultures* How do cultures influence people's behavior?* What human needs do cultures satisfy? What problems do cultures experience? What problems are cultures likely to experience in the future? How do, and might, people try to solve them? (Decision-making)
Level 6	*Social problems and social movements* What persistent social problems have people experienced throughout history?*

TABLE 2.7. *(continued)*

Level	Focused Concept for Level and Related Key Questions
Level 6	*Social problems and social movements* (Cont.) How have people tried to solve these problems? How do social problems affect people? How can we solve our social problems today? (Decision-making) What major social problems might people face in the future? How might these problems be solved?

*These questions will focus on people in both the *past* and the *present*. Thus history will be an integral part of the program. Future studies will also be an integral part of the program because of the parallel questions dealing with the future.

Helpful references for teachers that deal with future studies are Alvin Toffler, *Future Shock.* New York: Bantam, 1970; Charles Neitz and Michael Washburn, *Creating the Future.* New York: Bantam, 1974; Lester R. Brown, *World Without Borders.* New York: Vintage, 1972; Alvin Toffler, Ed., *Learning for Tomorrow: The Role of the Future in Education.* New York: Vintage, 1974: and Draper L. Kauffman, Jr., *Teaching the Future: A Guide to Future-Oriented Education.* Palm Springs, Calif.: ETC Publications, 1976. The Kauffman book includes rnany specific teaching strategies and student activities.

The Valuing and Decision-Making Component of the Curriculum

We stated earlier that knowledge is one of the important components of the decision-making process. This chapter focuses on the knowledge component of decision-making. Students need to master facts, concepts, and generalizations in order to make reflective decisions and to take thoughtful citizen action. *Values are another important component of decision-making.* The Inquiry Strategy on page 67 is an example of a valuing strategy Mr. Jones can use in the unit on the family described earlier in this chapter. Each social studies unit should contain valuing and decision-making exercises.

Values and value inquiry are discussed in Chapter 15. When a curriculum committee designs a conceptual curriculum, it should indicate the kinds of value problems and issues that can be discussed. These problems and issues should be related to the content samples and concepts being studied. The curriculum committee should also indicate what possible decision-problems can be studied when the concepts and content are studied. The valuing and decision-problems identified by the committee should be enduring and persistent problems that it will take many generations of citizens to solve. Problems such as global hunger and poverty, inflation, the nuclear race, and the discrimination against various racial and ethnic groups are enduring problems that warrant inclusion in the curriculum.

The Skills Component of the Curriculum

Knowledge is the product of social inquiry. Clarified and democratic values are the product of value inquiry. While it is very important for students to

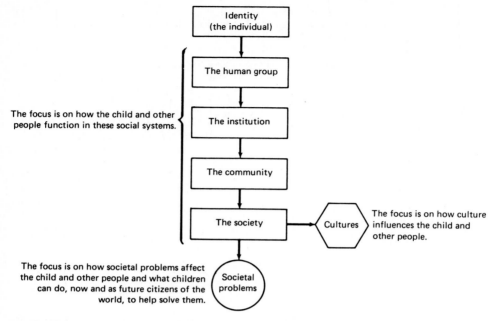

FIGURE 2.3 The interrelationship of the focused concepts.

master facts, concepts, and generalizations and to develop democratic values, *it is just as important, if not more important, for them to gain proficiency in the processes involved in gathering and evaluating knowledge and in deriving democratic values.* An important goal of the social studies curriculum should be to help students develop proficiency in social science inquiry and value inquiry skills. Sanders lists the following characteristics of a skill:[5]

1. A skill is a physical, emotional, and/or intellectual process.
2. A skill requires knowledge, but knowledge alone does not insure proficiency.
3. A skill can be used in a variety of situations.
4. A skill can be improved through practice.
5. A skill is often made up of a number of subskills that can be identified and practiced separately.

A social studies curriculum committee should identify the skills that should be introduced and extended in each grade when it formulates a conceptual curriculum. It should identify *social science inquiry, value inquiry, decision-making,* and *citizen-action* skills. A model of social inquiry is illustrated in Figure 1.3 and discussed in detail in Chapter 3. Value inquiry, decision-making, and citizen-action skills are discussed in Chapter 15. Chapter 5 discusses a range of skills, including communication skills, map reading skills, time-space skills, and group participation skills. The skills discussed in Chap-

INQUIRY STRATEGY: WHAT SHOULD THE CANGEMI FAMILY DO?

Mr. and Mrs. Cangemi live in Detroit, a very big city in Michigan. They have four children, Kate (14), Bob (12), Randy (9), and Kristin, the baby, who is just 2 years old. Mr. Cangemi has a good job working in a large factory helping to make new cars. Mrs. Cangemi works too. She is a teacher in the high school in their town. Kate, Bob, and Randy help their parents with many of the chores around the house and especially with Kristin, the baby. During the daytime Kristin goes to a nursery school when Mr. and Mrs. Cangemi are at work. Usually Mrs. Cangemi picks Kristin up at the nursery about 5 P.M. after school.

One day the Cangemis got a telephone call. Mr. Cangemi's mother, who lived far away in Phoenix, Arizona, was 75 years old and had fallen and broken her hip. She lived alone and there was no one to help her. She could not walk or take care of herself, or go to the store or do any of the usual things she did for herself. The doctor said she would need someone to take care of her for six months or more until she fully recovered and could walk again.

The children and the parents were very concerned. "What will happen to Grandma? What should we do to help her?" That night at supper the whole family, including little Kristin, sat around the table and talked about what they could do about this sudden turn of events in their family. They knew that Grandma liked her home in Phoenix where it was warm and sunny almost every day. She did not like to come back to Detroit to visit her family because it was often very cold and snowy in the winter, and in the summer it got much too hot. Besides, none of her friends lived there anymore. What should the Cangemi family do?

Questions

1. Can you retell this story in your own words?
2. What do you think the Cangemi family should do? Can you explain why?
3. Do they have any choices about what they could do? What would be the best choice? The poorest choice? Could you explain why?
4. What choice would Grandma like best? Like least? Why?
5. Is there anything Grandma's friends or neighbors in Phoenix could do to help out? Should they be the ones to help, or should her family in Detroit provide all the help?

The value issues and conflicts in this case study include:

1. Providing care for aging parents who no longer live close by.
2. Readjustment of family life if either parent goes to Phoenix for any longer than a few days.
3. Unplanned financial strain—both parents are already working.
4. The loss of independence for Grandma leading to loneliness, anxiety, frustration, and helplessness (common among the elderly).
5. Bringing Grandma home to Detroit may be the only option to ensure needed care, but (given her attitudes) it may be very disruptive to the existing family life.

ter 5 are *subskills* of social science inquiry, value inquiry, decision-making, and citizen-action skills. An example will make this point clear. The fifth step of the model of social inquiry presented in Chapter 3 is "Data Collection." The students need a range of other skills in order to "collect data," including skills in locating books, using reference books, reading maps and globes, observing, and note taking. While we will defer a detailed discussion of the subskills that constitute social science inquiry, value inquiry, decision-making, and citizen action to other chapters, below are examples of the kinds of subskills that students need to carry out these processes:

Social Science Inquiry Skills

> Reading
> Speaking
> Listening
> Concept formation
> Observation
> Gathering and organizing information
> Interpreting maps and globes
> Time-space orientation
> Interpreting graphs and charts
> Summarizing and generalizing

Value Inquiry Skills

> Observing
> Analyzing points of view
> Distinguishing facts from opinions
> Detecting biases
> Critical reading
> Justifying and defending a position

Decision-Making Skills

> Identifying generalizations
> Evaluating the accuracy of generalizations
> Identifying alternative courses of action
> Using generalizations to predict alternative courses of action
> Relating values to specific courses of action
> Defending a particular course of action

Citizen Action Skills

> Working with others in groups
> Oral and written communication
> Persuasion, compromise, and bargaining
> Forming coalitions with other individuals and groups
> Communicating a social concern to a large public

SUMMARY

This chapter highlights a basic point underlying the theory of social studies education in this book: students must become reflective decision-makers and citizen actors in order to solve personal problems and influence public policy. Decisions must be based on knowledge; reflective decisions must be based on scientific knowledge. The scientific knowledge the citizen actor uses to make reflective decisions must reflect the perspectives of a number of disciplines; social problems are too complex for a single discipline to provide enough knowledge to help us solve them.

This chapter illustrates how the teacher can build units that teach students to view topics and social problems from an interdisciplinary perspective. Methods for building conceptual units within school districts that have traditional social studies curriculum frameworks were discussed. Ways to structure a conceptual curriculum within districts that are substantially revising their curricula were also discussed and illustrated. The need to include valuing and decision-making skills as components in a curriculum plan was highlighted. The next chapter discusses social science inquiry and its products: *facts, concepts, generalizations,* and *theories.*

DISCUSSION QUESTIONS AND EXERCISES

1. Why is it necessary for students to view social problems from the perspectives of several disciplines in order to make sound decisions?
2. Select a current social problem and develop a teaching plan that will help students to view the problem from the perspectives of history, sociology, anthropology, geography, political science, economics, and psychology. From each of these disciplines, list at least one key concept and related generalization that can help students to better understand the social problem.
3. Structure an interdisciplinary unit on a topic traditionally studied in the elementary and junior high school grades—such as the family, the school, the neighborhood, or the community—including the following components: (1) unit topic, (2) key concepts and generalizations from at least four different social science disciplines, (3) subideas that are related to each of the key generalizations and to the specific institution selected for study, (4) objectives stated in behavioral terms, (5) initiation activities, (6) developmental activities, (7) evaluation activities, (8) culminating activities, and (9) a list of resources for both the students and you.
4. Work with a group of students to structure an *outline* of a K–8 interdisciplinary social studies curriculum for a hypothetical school district. The outline should indicate the key concepts and generalizations that will be developed, recommended content samples for developing the key ideas, and a list of the units for each grade or level. The rationale and criteria the group will use to identify the key concepts, generalizations, and content samples should also be stated.
5. Examine a school district social studies guide in the curriculum library of your college. Evaluate the guide using the following criteria questions: (1)

Does the guide include key concepts and generalizations from all the social science disciplines? (2) Are the concepts and generalizations accurate? (3) Are the key ideas within the curriculum developed with appropriate content samples? (4) Are the key ideas within the curriculum developed at an increasing degree of complexity in successive grades? (5) Are the objectives related to the key ideas stated? (6) Are the objectives stated in behavioral terms? (7) Are the units within the curriculum divided in a way that will facilitate the learning of the key ideas stated? (8) Will the activities develop the major ideas stated in the curriculum? (9) Are sound evaluation strategies a part of the curriculum? (10) Does the curriculum contain a sufficient number of resources for both the teacher and the pupils?

6. Demonstrate your understanding of the following concepts and terms by writing or stating brief definitions for each of them. Also tell why each is important:

   a. interdisciplinary
   b. unit
   c. initiation activities
   d. developmental activities
   e. evaluation activities
   f. culminating activities
   g. interdisciplinary curriculum

   h. conceptual curriculum
   i. spiral curriculum
   j. key or organizing concept
   k. key or organizing generalization
   l. scope and sequence chart
   m. interdisciplinary perspective
   n. skills

NOTES

1. Jerome S. Bruner, Jacqueline J. Goodnow, and George A. Austin, *A Study of Thinking* (New Brunswick: Transaction Books, 1986).

2. Mary C. Durkin and Kim Ellis, *The Taba Social Studies Curriculum: Four Communities Around the World* (Menlo Park, CA: Addison-Wesley, 1969), Grade Three, pp. v–vii.

3. Durkin and Ellis, *The Taba Social Studies Curriculum,* p. v.

4. Hilda Taba, *Teachers' Handbook for Elementary Social Studies* (Reading, MA: Addison-Wesley, 1967), p. 18; also see second edition of this book, Hilda Taba, Mary C. Durkin, Jack R. Fraenkel, and Anthony H. McNaughton, *A Teacher's Handbook to Elementary Social Studies: An Inductive Approach*, 2nd ed. (Reading, MA: Addison-Wesley, 1971).

5. Norris M. Sanders, *Classroom Questions: What Kinds* (New York: Harper & Row, 1966), p. 27. See also June R. Chapin and Richard E. Gross, *Teaching Social Studies Skills* (Boston: Little Brown, 1973).

FOR FURTHER READING

Atwood, Virginia A. *Elementary Social Studies: Research As a Guide to Practice.* Washington, D.C.: National Council for the Social Studies, 1986.

Baron, Joan Boykoff, and Robert J. Sternberg, Eds. *Teaching Thinking Skills: Theory and Practice.* New York: W. H. Freedman, 1986.

Chapin, June R., and Richard E. Gross. *Teaching Social Studies Skills.* Boston: Little Brown, 1973.

Clarke, Wenworth, and Frederick E. Green, Eds. *Contemporary Initiatives in Social Studies Education.* Boca Raton, FL: Social Issues Resources Series, Inc., 1985.

Fraenkel, Jack R. *Helping Students Think and Value: Strategies for Teaching the Social Studies,* 2nd ed. Englewood Cliffs, NJ: Prentice-Hall, 1980.

Martorella, Peter H. *Elementary Social Studies: Developing Reflective, Competent, and Concerned Citizens.* Boston: Little Brown, 1985.

Rogers, Vincent, Arthur D. Roberts, and Thomas P. Weinland, Eds. *Teaching Social Studies: Portraits from the Classroom.* Bulletin 82. Washington, D.C.: National Council for the Social Studies, 1988.

3

Teaching Social Inquiry and Its Products: Facts, Concepts, Generalizations, and Theories

THE METHOD OF SOCIAL INQUIRY

The Nature, Goals, and Assumptions of Social Inquiry

To make reflective decisions, students need to master facts, concepts, and generalizations. However, because knowledge changes and often becomes obsolete, they also need to master the skills needed to produce knowledge. Teachers should emphasize the process used to attain knowledge more than the knowledge itself. The process for *attaining* knowledge can always be used by students to attain the facts, concepts, and generalizations needed to make reflective decisions and to act to influence public policy. We call the process used to attain facts, concepts, generalizations, and theories *social inquiry, social science inquiry* or *the scientific method*.

The major goal of social science inquiry is to build theories. However, social scientists must formulate facts, concepts, and generalizations in order to build theories. Social scientists believe that they can best help society by building theories. Theories can be used to understand, explain, predict, and control behavior. Social scientists do not consider theories absolute. The scientific method allows them to constantly expand, change, and reconstruct theories.

Social inquiry is based on a number of assumptions about the natural world and about human beings. We discussed them briefly in Chapter 1. It is important for teachers and students to know these assumptions so that they are keenly aware of both the strengths and limitations of science. Science assumes that human behavior, like that of all other beings, has causes that can be determined by systematic study. This assumption rejects the notion that human behavior is determined by magical or supernatural forces. Science also assumes that there is enough order, permanence, and uniformity in nature to permit study and generalizations. If things in our environment changed drastically from day to day, we would be unable to make any generalizations about the world and about human behavior.[1] Science also makes these assumptions:

All objective phenomena are eventually knowable. . . .

Nothing is self-evident; truth must be demonstrated objectively. . . .

Truth is relative (to the existing state of knowledge); absolute or final truth may never be achieved. . . .

All perceptions are achieved through the senses; all knowledge is derived from sensory impressions. . . .

Humans can trust their perceptions, memory, and reasoning as reliable agencies for acquiring facts. . . .[2]

In addition to having a number of basic assumptions, the scientific method also has a number of requirements that the scientist must fulfill. Berelson and Steiner have summarized the basic requirements of science:

The procedures are public.

The definitions are precise.

The data collecting is objective.

The findings must be able to be reproduced.

The approach is systematic and cumulative.

The purposes are explanation, understanding, and prediction.[3]

INQUIRY IN THE SOCIAL SCIENCE DISCIPLINES

Sociologists, anthropologists, economists, and political scientists use similar but not necessarily identical methods to test and to derive knowledge. However, the kinds of questions studied by different social scientists and their respective key concepts, generalizations, and theories distinguish them more than their methodologies. Participant observation, interviews, sample surveys, and the case study are methods used to collect data in several disciplines. The sociologist's concern for *socialization* and the political scientist's interest in *power* distinguish these two disciplines more than their methodologies. Also, social scientists in one discipline often use the concepts, generalizations, and theories from other disciplines. Thus, the social science disciplines are themselves *interdisciplinary*.[4]

Although the methods used by social scientists in the various disciplines have many common characteristics, some of the disciplines use special methods of data collection or use certain research strategies more often than others. The social psychologist uses laboratory experiments perhaps more often than any other social scientist. The sample survey is used frequently in sociology and political science but less often in anthropology. Participant observation and field work are the primary research methods used by anthropologists. Although each group of social scientists sometimes uses unique research methods, an attempt is made below to present a basic model of inquiry that is shared by all social scientists. It is one that students should use, often in a modified fashion, when they try to answer the questions asked at the beginning of social studies lessons and units.

A MODEL OF SOCIAL INQUIRY

Problem Formulation

Before scientists can begin research on any problem or issue, they must clearly state the questions to be answered. Scientists must also have an inter-

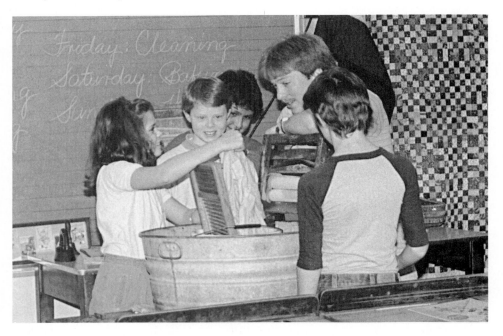

Activities that help students to understand how people lived in earlier times can help them to formulate questions that are complete, precise, and testable. The children in this photograph are washing clothes using a tub and washboard. Many farm families washed clothes in this way before electricity came to their communities in the 1940s and 1950s. (*Source:* Edna Kellman, Seattle Public Schools.)

est in answering the questions. Scientific questions must be *complete, precise,* and *testable.* "What were the children' s attitudes?" does not satisfy our criteria because we do not know which children or what kinds of attitudes to study. "What were the attitudes of colonial American children toward school?" meets our criteria of a scientific question because it is complete, precise, and testable.

Some complete and precise questions are not testable because they are not scientific. "Should the school year in the United States be extended to 11 months?" is not a scientific question and therefore cannot be answered with social inquiry methods. This is a decision-problem question, and the answer must reflect a synthesis of knowledge and personal values. Scientific inquiry can help us to make decisions and attain goals we value. Value inquiry can contribute to value clarification. However, social inquiry cannot determine our values. Social inquiry can help us answer this question: "What effects will a longer school year have on the academic achievement of elementary school students in the United States?" However, regardless of the answers that social inquiry might provide to this question, different individuals, because of their values, will decide differently about whether the school year in the United States should be extended to 11 months.

Helping students to identify and formulate precise, explicit, and testable questions is one of the most challenging tasks you will face in the inquiry-oriented classroom. The ability to ask good questions is a developmental skill that should be systematically taught beginning in kindergarten. Questioning strategies are discussed in detail in Chapter 4. The inquiries that students make can be no better than the questions they pose.

Example   A junior high school teacher begins a unit with a content analysis of several U.S. history textbooks. The teacher divides the class into several small groups and asks each group to read quickly through one chapter or unit in one of their history textbooks. Each group is asked to list "all the people who are mentioned by name" in their book. Following the completion of the task by the small groups, the teacher makes a list on the blackboard consisting of all the people mentioned by name in the history textbooks. After listing these names, the teacher asks the students to describe different ways of grouping the persons listed (e.g., by occupation, by historical period). One possible grouping will be by sex of the persons listed. After listing all the people mentioned by name and by sex, the students will observe that the list of men is much longer than the list of women.

The teacher asks the class:

Why do you think more men are included in our history textbooks than women?

What kinds of things do people do who are "remembered" in history? What makes a person historically important?

Can you think of any historically important women who might have been included but were not?

Who do you think writes most of the history books we use in school, men or women?

The teacher introduces a new concept:

Written history is what is recorded and passed down about the past. It is not necessarily what actually happened. The teacher further explains the concept of written history. The teacher asks the students to state questions stimulated by the lesson. The students state these questions, and the teacher writes them on the board:

How are textbooks written?
Who determines what gets included in a textbook?
Who chooses textbook authors?
How do historians determine which women to include in textbooks?
Why are more men than women included in our history books?
Why is written history not always the same as what actually happened in the past?

The teacher tells the class that all of the questions are excellent. He tells the students that while they will find some answers to each of these questions during this unit, the main question that they will study is *Why are more men than women included in our history textbooks?*

Formulation of Hypotheses

After scientists have stated precise and researchable questions, they then make tentative statements to guide their inquiry. We do not actually test questions, but statements related to them. The tentative statements that scientists use to guide inquiries are called *hypotheses.* Hypotheses are informed guesses that scientists make when answering their questions. They are very important in social research. They help to guide and focus it.

Hypotheses must have certain characteristics. They must be related to the questions formulated and be testable. The most effective hypotheses are based on prior knowledge and existing theories. Good hypotheses are not formulated in a vacuum. They are intelligent and not ignorant guesses. If a class were trying to formulate hypotheses about the attitudes toward school of colonial American children, the students would state much more informed and useful hypotheses if they had some knowledge about colonial children. The teacher must provide students with background information before they can formulate useful and intelligent hypotheses. Often a story, a filmstrip, or a short reading at the beginning of a unit can give the students the information needed to formulate useful hypotheses. A primary resource can also be used to help students to develop and state hypotheses, as is done in the Inquiry Strategy on page 78.

Example The junior high school teacher continues the unit on women in U.S. history textbooks by setting the stage for the development of hypotheses. First, he shows the students some photographs of men and women in various roles during the colonial and Revolutionary periods of U.S. history. He also reads selections from several books about women's roles in the development of the United States. The teacher then solicits hypotheses from the students. He says:

"We found that there were 14 times as many men mentioned in our history books as there were women mentioned. Why do you think this is the case? Think of as many different possible ideas as you can and be prepared to support your reasons."

The students state *hypotheses* and the teacher writes them on the board:

1. Only a few women did anything important back then. If a woman had done something important, she would be in the book the same as a man.
2. Women were busy at home and with children and so they couldn't be explorers and pioneers and politicians. What women did was important, but they didn't do the kinds of things that get written in history books.
3. Men have always written the history books, and they chose to write about what men do. There were just as many important women explorers, pioneers, inventors, and politicians. They were left out of the books on purpose by the men historians.

The students copy the hypotheses the class has formulated, the main question the class will study during the unit, and the other questions the class asked during the problem formulation stage.

Definition of Terms: Conceptualization

At some stage early in the inquiry process, students must try to explicitly define their major terms and concepts. Defining terms so that they have research implications is a major problem for social scientists. There is little consensus about the meaning of many important concepts and terms in social science. *Culture, social class, aggression,* and *stress* are important social science concepts that are defined differently by various social scientists.

Sometime early in the social studies unit, the teacher and the students must try to operationally define the major concepts that will be studied in the unit. Although we are listing *definition of terms* as a specific step in the inquiry process, in reality it, like the other steps of our inquiry model, may occur at different times during the unit. Each step, while often occurring in the order identified in Figure 3.1, may occur at different times and more than once during the inquiry process. The steps of the inquiry process are not linear, as Figure 3.1 suggests, but complex and multidimensional. In our unit on women in U.S. history textbooks, for example, the teacher felt that the concept *written history* was so important to the unit that he defined it during the problem formulation stage rather than waiting until the other major concepts were defined. There may be disagreement among social scientists about con-

INQUIRY STRATEGY: DEVELOPING HYPOTHESES USING A PRIMARY RESOURCE

Sojourner Truth, a former slave, became active in both the antislavery and the women's rights movements. Ask the students to read this excerpt from a speech she gave at the Ohio Women's Rights Convention in 1851. Then ask them to state some hypotheses about what rights women had and did not have in 1851. Ask them to do research on the life and times of Sojourner Truth to test their hypotheses. They should note how the rights of Black and white women were alike and different.

> That man over there says that women need to be helped into carriages, and lifted over ditches, and to have the best place everywhere. Nobody ever helps me into carriages, or over mud-puddles, or gives me any best place! And ain't I a woman? Look at me! Look at my arm! I have ploughed, and planted, and gathered into barns, and no man could head [do better than] me! And ain't I a woman? I could work as much and eat as much as a man—when I could get it—and bear the lash as well! And ain't I a woman? I have borne five children, and seen them most all sold off to slavery, and when I cried out with my mother's grief, none but Jesus heard me! And ain't I a woman?
>
> Then they talk about this thing in the head; what's this they call it? That's it, honey [intellect]. What's that got to do with woman's rights? . . . If my cup won't hold but a pint and yours holds a quart, wouldn't you be mean not to let me have my little half measure full? . . .
>
> If the first woman God ever made was strong enough to turn the world upside down all alone, these women together ought to be able to turn it back, and get it right side up again! And now they are asking to do it, the men better let them.
>
> Obliged to you for hearing on me; and now old Sojourner Truth ain't got nothing more to say.*

*Adapted from *Narrative of Sojourner Truth, a Northern Slave* (New York: 1853).

cepts used in social studies units, but the teacher and the students need to reach agreement about how the concepts will be defined for the purpose of their inquiry.

Example　The teacher asks the students questions about the terms and concepts they will be dealing with so that some agreement on definitions can be reached. The class agrees on the following definitions of the key concepts:

> *Past events* are actual events that occurred only once, never to occur again.
> *Historical statements* (or "facts") are the statements that historians write about past events. They are quite different from the actual event. An infinite number of facts can be stated about any past event.
> *Historians* are people who study the past and write historical statements.

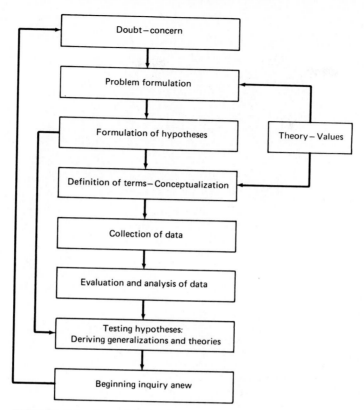

FIGURE 3.1 A model of social inquiry. Note that in the inquiry model, doubt and concern cause the inquirer to formulate a problem. The problem that he or she formulates does not emanate from a vacuum, but is shaped by his or her theoretical and value orientation. Like the social scientist, the elementary-school child will need to draw on *knowledge* to be able to ask intelligent and fruitful questions. In social science inquiry, *theory* is the main source of fruitful questions. While these are the basic steps of social inquiry, they do not necessarily occur in the order illustrated above. This figure indicates that generalizations in social science are continually tested and are never regarded as absolute. Thus, social inquiry is cyclic rather than linear and fixed.

To be *biased* is usually to tell only part of what happened or to tell something only from the point of view of one particular group, race, sex, or nation. Historians may be biased in their choice of subjects to write about, selection of resource materials, organization and presentation of historical statements, and interpretation of material.[5]

Historically important people are those who have made significant personal contributions to the course of human events, whether or not they are generally included in history textbooks.

You can use photographs like this one, which shows a Texas cotton-picking family looking for cotton to pick in September 1931, to help students formulate questions and hypotheses about the Great Depression. (*Source:* The National Archives, Washington, D.C.)

Collection of Data

Questions are answered and hypotheses are tested by the data and information the inquirer gathers. Social scientists use many methods to collect data, to test hypotheses, and to derive generalizations and theories. The *experiment*, the *sample survey*, and the *case study* are the three major methods used by social scientists. The historical study and content analysis, as well as other techniques, are also used by social scientists to gather data.

The *experiment* is a laboratory situation structured by an investigator to determine how concepts (or variables) are related. To determine how one concept influences another, the researcher attempts to control all concepts in an experimental situation.

Using an experiment with students in elementary and junior high school poses many problems: moral and ethical concerns about voluntary participation, concerns about the immaturity of young children and protecting them from undue invasions of personal privacy. However, role playing and simulation activities can be effectively used to help students discover how certain situations and concepts affect human behavior. One creative teacher used role playing to help her students discover how discrimination affects its victims. This simulation is dramatized in the educational film *Eye of the Storm*.[6] During one class period, the teacher discriminated against students with brown eyes; in another, those with blue eyes. Simulation games such as *Sunshine, Star Power,* and *Democracy* can also be used to teach students how different situations influence human behavior.

The *sample survey* is widely used in social science to gather data. A sample survey consists of a *sample* and a *survey*. A *sample* is a part of a population, usually randomly selected. A *survey* measures some characteristic of a population, such as its opinions and attitudes toward defense spending.

The *sample survey* is much easier to use with students than the experiment. Students can develop instruments to sample opinions and attitudes among their own classmates, other students in the school, faculty, and adults in the community. An unlimited number of important questions face every community. Students can learn the techniques for conducting sample surveys stratified on the basis of age, section of town, occupation, ethnic origin, and other variables.

Students can learn to sample community attitudes on a proposed highway relocation, a new bond issue, or candidates in an election. They can gather important demographic data by sample surveys concerning occupations, types of homes, businesses, religious preferences, traffic counts on major arterials, air pollution, and the use of public parks, libraries, and museums.

Scientists use the *case study* method when they study the characteristics of one element in a population in depth. Sociologists have used this method widely to analyze the characteristics of cities and various political and social institutions with special characteristics. The Lynds studied "Middletown" (Muncie, Indiana) over an extended period of time. Voting habits, social class structure, and educational and religious institutions in this midwestern town were studied in great detail. Similar case studies were Brasstown (Hollingshead); Yankee City (Warner); and Elmtown's Youth (Hollingshead).

Sociologists often study juvenile delinquents, criminals, mental patients, and other persons with special problems. The case study method is more valuable for deriving fruitful hypotheses than for testing them. This method is limited because the findings derived from it cannot usually be generalized, with a high degree of confidence, to other individuals and institutions.

A number of possibilities exist for students to engage in the participant-observer type of case study. Students can work for a time in the school cafeteria, the stockroom, the library, or the principal's office to observe work functions and social interactions. They might also serve as street-crossing guards or members of a student council. In the larger sphere, it is not at all unrealistic to think of older students participating in the work of various municipal groups such as the fire or police departments, courts, or social agencies. These activities do suggest, however, that students must plan to spend larger parts of the day outside the school itself, actively engaged in social inquiry in the real community, and less time studying the artificial world of the textbook.

Example   During the unit on women in U.S. history textbooks, the teacher asked:

Where can we find some information about our problem of why there are relatively few women mentioned in our history textbooks?

The students responded:

We could invite a historian from the university to come and tell us how historians get their information to write history books.

We could look for diaries or journals written a long time ago that tell what the lives of women and children were like.

We could go to the school and public libraries and look for biographies of famous American women.

We could check the media center for films or filmstrips or picture sets on famous women.

Some of us could watch the same TV program or movie and each write down our own historical statements. Then we could read our statements to the class and see how each person was biased and recorded the event differently.

The teacher replied:

These are all very good suggestions, and you will no doubt think of even more as you begin to work. Remember that we have three hypotheses we want to test:

1. Only a few women are mentioned in our history textbooks because only a few women did anything important.
2. Women did historically important things, but they were not the kinds of things that are generally recorded in history textbooks.
3. There were just as many women who did important things such as invent or explore, but the men historians don't write about them because they are biased in favor of other men and their activities.

How can we divide the work to be done and share the information once we have gathered it?

After much class discussion, the class decided to divide into three committees to gather and present information to the class. Two weeks later each committee made a presentation.

The committee on hypothesis 1 made a large bulletin board that included pictures and capsule biographies of a large number of historically important women who had been "forgotten" in their history books.

The committee on hypothesis 2 divided into subcommittees and prepared written reports and simulated TV shows to dramatize the roles of women and children during each of the main periods of U.S. history (e.g., colonial, Revolutionary, pioneer, WWII). The students decided to emphasize the contributions of women to the development of the new nation in all possible areas of human endeavor, including the arts, sciences, and other frequently neglected areas of history.

The committee on hypothesis 3 searched (in vain) for women explorers in the fifteenth through seventeenth centuries, for as many women as men who held important positions in the Revolutionary government, for as many female as male inventors, and for as many female as male military leaders. After some period of indecision and discussion, the committee decided to focus on why history books concentrated on political, economic, and diplomatic history and not on social history and why women had, in fact, when compared with men, done little in these areas. One subcommittee decided to present a report to the class on the current status of women in the United States and how women's roles are in the process of rapid change.[7] This group presented reports on contemporary women in politics, economics, and the military, as well as women (and men) in the arts and sciences.

Evaluation and Analysis of Data

Social inquirers must try to determine the credibility and meaning of their data. The tools they use to gather information have a significant effect on the information's meaning and use. If researchers use instruments that have been tested and validated by other scientists, they can usually put more faith in their data than researchers who construct their own instruments and assume, without adequate evidence, that they actually measure the concepts being studied.

When inquirers are evaluating information, they must carefully examine its source and the methods used to gather it, and try to identify its shortcomings and limitations. Researchers may encounter documents, artifacts, art works, and other types of evidence whose origin and nature are unknown. They must try to formulate fruitful hypotheses about their origin, relate them to known data, and determine whether they are important for the testing of their hypotheses. Much information that researchers will encounter will be useless for their purposes. The questions and hypotheses that researchers formulate help greatly in identifying pertinent and significant information.

Historical documents may pose special problems for inquirers. Students may not only be required to determine their source and nature, but also whether the authors' statements are accurate or untrue. Letters, reports, and other documents must be rigorously examined by the careful inquirer.

Example   In the unit on women in U.S. history textbooks, the students tried to determine the validity and reliability of their information. Following the presentation of each committee report and the class discussion that followed, the students asked such questions as:

Did the committee consult several sources?

Were authorities consulted and if so, what were their qualifications?

Did the committee members distinguish between sources that based their arguments on *opinion* as opposed to *facts?*

Did the committee try to present findings that supported the hypothesis as well as findings that did not support the hypothesis?

Did the committee often use emotionally charged words? If so, why?

Testing Hypotheses: Deriving Generalizations and Theories

Social scientists begin the research cycle with questions, which are usually related to an existing theory or some other body of knowledge. However, questions per se cannot be directly tested. Hypotheses related to the questions are formulated. When the data are gathered and analyzed, researchers try to determine whether their hypotheses can be verified with the information that has been gathered.

If hypotheses are verified during the process of inquiry, they become generalizations. *We can consequently think of generalizations as verified or tested hypotheses.* As different scientists develop generalizations related to the same major concepts, theories are developed and verified. A *scientific theory* consists of a system of interrelated high-level generalizations (laws or principles) that have been tested and found to be valid.

Example Throughout the inquiry on women in U.S. history textbooks, the students looked at their hypotheses and tried to see how they compared with the information they were gathering. They concluded that the questions raised at the beginning of the unit were complex; there were no simple answers. They rejected hypothesis 1 because it was not supported by their research findings. They found partial support for hypotheses 2 and 3 but felt neither was entirely true. Also, neither was sufficient to answer the major question raised in their unit. The students formulated these generalizations:

In the past, most historians have been men because women were primarily occupied in the home with child rearing and because women received less opportunity for formal education.

The writing of some male historians has reflected their personal biases, the times in which they lived and wrote, and the lack of availability of information written by or about women.

In the past not as many women as men were active in political, diplomatic, and economic affairs because such public activities were not considered proper vocations for women.

Women's roles in the United States are changing rapidly because women now have smaller families, longer life spans, and higher levels of education. Technological developments and the increasing expansion of human rights in the United States are also changing the roles of women.

Beginning Inquiry Anew

When researchers have found data to support their hypotheses and theories, they still must continue research to further test them. (See Figure 3.1.) While theories can be supported with new data and information, they can never be conclusively established. *Scientific knowledge is neither absolute nor unchanging. It must be viewed as tentative and must continually be tested, evaluated, and reconstructed.* Social inquiry is cyclic rather than linear and fixed. Social knowledge may change when new data are discovered, when new assumptions and ways of viewing behavior emerge, when new ideologies within a society arise, or when a scientific revolution occurs. Kuhn states that a scientific revolution occurs when a paradigm (or theoretical system) replaces another in a discipline.[8] When behavioral psychology emerged in 1913, it did not replace Freudian or gestalt psychology. However, it seriously challenged these theories and had a revolutionary impact on modern psychology.

Students should learn that generalizations formulated during a unit should be regarded as tentative and not as absolute. They should be encouraged to continue challenging their findings, their assumptions, and to continue examining the questions studied during the unit. When they encounter new information about a topic studied in class, they should be encouraged to bring it to class to share and to display on a bulletin board. This bulletin board might be called "New Findings and Insights." It could be used to post new findings related to topics the class has studied in science and the language arts as well as the social studies.

Example   After the students formulated their generalizations during the unit on women in U.S. history testbooks, the teacher asked them:

1. Can we be certain that our generalizations are accurate?
2. What other sources can we use that may give us new information related to our generalizations?
3. Can social scientists ever be certain that their generalizations are completely accurate? Why or why not?
4. Sometime social scientists change generalizations that they have already published. What kinds of developments do you think cause them to do this?

The teacher gives an optional assignment: During the rest of the school year, I would like you to share any news items, magazine articles, or other resources that report new information related to this unit with the class. We will discuss these items briefly near the end of our social studies period and post them on the bulletin board. You can earn five extra points for every news item you bring that meets our criteria.

When giving the assignment, the teacher shared with the class an item he clipped from his newspaper over the weekend that met the critera he had stated. It read in part:

Western Women: Some U.S. History Books Need Revision

Whenever scholars gather in the future to ponder the history of the American West, they will have to reckon with the deliberations of an unusual gathering of modern-day women in Sun Valley a few weeks ago.

. . . Citing recent research, much of it based on diaries and interviews with people who had known women pioneers, conference delegates painted a picture of frontier life either ignored or distorted in earlier accounts.

The "real" story of Western women of those days was often one of unremitting home-building and homemaking toil mixed with political activism on such issues as suffrage and mining-town labor contracts. Other women went cowboying or homesteading by themselves.

. . . Sooner or later, a lot of history books will have to be rewritten.[9]

THE PRODUCTS OF SOCIAL INQUIRY: FACTS, CONCEPTS, GENERALIZATIONS, AND THEORIES

The method used by the social scientist to derive knowledge was discussed in the first part of this chapter. The importance of the inquiry process is emphasized throughout this book. The results or products of inquiry are also important because *facts, concepts, generalizations*, and *theories* help individuals to understand human relationships and to make sound personal and public decisions. Even though the products of social inquiry are subject to constant reconstruction or revision (and thus process is important), citizens must at any given time use the most helpful facts, concepts, generalizations and theories they can find. This part of Chapter 3 focuses on the nature of knowledge, and suggests teaching strategies to help elementary and junior high school students learn facts, concepts, and generalizations.

Facts

Factual knowledge consists of specific data about events, objects, people, or other things that can be or has been verified by the senses. Facts are the particular instances of events or things that in turn become the raw data or the observations of the social scientist. Facts are usually stated in the form of simple, positive statements.

Albany is the capital of New York State.
There are 1000 meters in a kilometer.
The earth revolves around the sun.

Factual data are often presented in the form of tables and charts, and in almanacs, gazetteers, or similar reference books. These include quantities of diverse data—population of cities, tide tables, the number of votes cast in recent presidential elections in various states, counties, cities, and so forth. It should be made clear, however, that *facts* are the actual data themselves. When readers inspect the data and begin to discover trends, or to compare population data for 1970 and 1980, they are then beginning to *interpret* the data and to make inferences about the facts. This is a higher-order intellectual skill, part of the process of generalizing that will be discussed later.

Some statements that appear to be factual assertions are colored by perceptual biases or value judgments that may not be entirely obvious to the reader. Let us take the statement "Sir Francis Drake was an English hero." Most students studying early colonial history would probably be willing to accept that as a verifiable fact since it is repeated so often in their texts. There are also many popular pictures of Drake being knighted by Queen Elizabeth I for his exploits. But what about those exploits? Surely from a Spanish point of view the statement might have been written "Sir Francis Drake was an English pirate." The gold he brought home to his Queen was taken (stolen?) from captured Spanish treasure ships returning from Mexico. In short, one queen's *hero* was another king's *pirate*. Similar statements could be made about such relative words as *poverty* and *wealth*, or perhaps *starvation* and *adequate diet*.

The Fact/Concept Debate

Considerable debate took place during the 1980s about the extent to which facts should be emphasized, as opposed to concepts and higher-level understandings. The social studies reform movement that emerged during the 1960s was heavily influenced by the work of learning theorists such as Bruner and Schwab.[10] These theorists provided empirical and theoretical evidence suggesting that teachers should emphasize the *structure* of the disciplines, which consists of a discipline's key concepts, generalizations, theories, and methods of gathering data. When students learn the structure of a discipline, comprehension, transfer of learning, and motivation are increased.

During the 1980s, public concern that students might not be learning enough facts in school was heightened by newspaper headlines about declining scores on national standardized tests and by several books that were widely discussed and reviewed, including *American Memory* by Cheney, *Cultural Literacy* by Hirsch, and *What Do Our 17-Year-Olds Know?* by Ravitch and Finn.[11] The authors of these books argue that U.S. students are not learning enough facts in school—that the problem developed because U.S. educators emphasize process and concepts rather than facts in the social studies and other school subjects.

While the school critics contend that process rather than knowledge of specifics (facts) is emphasized in school, careful studies of school practices indicate that the opposite is the case: Teaching in the schools, especially in the social studies, is dominated by textbook learning, the memorization of isolated and often meaningless facts, and "teacher talk."[12] It is significant that the critics of educators and the schools have largely ignored this extensive and impressive body of research.

The way to improve the cultural literacy of our nation's citizens and their knowledge about U.S. society is clearly more complicated than teaching them more facts. We can best improve the historical and cultural literacy of students by teaching them powerful concepts and generalizations of the social sciences, but making sure that these key ideas of the disciplines are buttressed by sufficient factual knowledge. When teaching about the *acculturation* that has taken place in the United States, for example, teachers should make sure that students can list specific ways in which African-American music influenced and became a part of the U.S. mainstream culture, as well as specific ways in which African-Americans have assimilated aspects of the mainstream culture. Many of the values that African-Americans have about family life and work were taken from the U.S. mainstream culture.[13]

When you teach students factual knowledge, you should have clear goals in mind. In the preceding example, you would have students learn facts about African-American culture and U.S. mainstream culture in order to teach them about acculturation. Some facts, such as the names of the 50 states, you might ask students to memorize simply because this is information they will frequently use if they are literate citizens of the nation. However, you should stress the *process* of constructing knowledge and its nature even when you ask students to memorize such lists. For example, you can divide the class into four groups, and ask each group to research the origins of the names for 12 or 13 states and why each state has its name. This exercise will help students learn about the process of knowledge construction as well as make the names of the states more meaningful and consequently easier to remember.

Concept Learning

A concept is an abstract word or phrase that is useful for classifying or categorizing a group of things, ideas, or events.[14] To illustrate this definition, examine the following list of words:

boy   cat   dog   man   rat

What single word or short phrase can you think of that appropriately names or labels the group? At first glance you might be inclined to say *animal*, since all the words describe a kind of animal. If you have recently studied biology, you might add *carnivore*, *mammal*, or *vertebrate*, since these are also common characteristics of the group. You might be tempted to include *domestic* though that word would not really apply to *rat* unless we were referring to white rats that might be kept as pets. Teachers who have taught in the primary grades where reading skills are emphasized are quick to use such labels as: *three-letter words*, *middle-vowel words*, or *consonant-vowel-consonant* (CVC) pattern. You would undoubtedly discover many other possibilities. The point is that each of these words is a possible label or name for the group since it categorizes each item in the class according to some special characteristic that all share in common. Words that label or name a group of common objects are called *concepts.*

Several important features of concepts should be noted. For example, among the possible concept terms suggested above, *animal* and *three-letter words* are more inclusive than some of the others. Indeed, it might be possible to subordinate some of the terms into a hierarchy such as the following:

> I. Animal
> > A. Vertebrate
> > > 1. Mammal
> > > > a. Carnivore

In some cases, the concept term applies only partly or in a qualified way to all members of the group, such as the term *domestic* in the example above. The concept term is also abstract. It is not specific or concrete since it refers to an entire class or group of objects.

Learning to use concepts is a vital part of our thinking processes. They enable us to sort out the great variety of objects, events, ideas, and stimuli with which we come into contact each day. Thus, they help reduce the complexity of the environment by separating the great amount of data to be processed by the brain to more manageable portions. Reflecting this, our English language is filled with many abstract words often expressing very complex ideas.[15] The social studies curriculum provides a number of examples of concepts:

family	government	cooperation	power
community	republic	cultural change	interdependence
society	federal system	conflict	tradition
nation	democracy	law	social control

In addition, concepts have varying degrees of *abstractness* and can be thought of as existing on a continuum. For example:

Concrete		*Abstract*
family	←————————→	nation
fight	←————————→	revolution
local ordinance	←————————→	international law
village	←————————→	megalopolis

One type of abstract concept that requires special attention is the *relational* concept. Relational concepts define a particular association between attributes or distinguishing characteristics. Concepts involving distance and time are perhaps the most common relational ones in social studies: year, century, mile, light year, outer space, latitude, longitude, great circle route. Other relational concepts are much more abstract: uncle, great-grandfather, mother-in-law, foster parent, fellow countryperson. It is particularly difficult for young children to understand concepts like these because they have not had sufficient experience with the basic facts themselves, or with abstracting the common attributes to establish the particular relation or association involved. For example, it takes considerable practice with a calendar for a six- or seven-year-old child to count up 30 days, learn that that period is called a month, and then recognize that there are approximately four weeks in a month. Most adults are satisfied to think of a century as a "very long time" or have only a foggy notion of the concepts *great-uncle* and *grandniece*.[16]

INTERDISCIPLINARY CONCEPTS

Having a knowledge of the basic concepts from the various social science disciplines allows one to consider a problem that spans several disciplines, or is interdisciplinary in its scope. Broad ranging topics such as the city, international peace, and poverty can be considered from a variety of perspectives, each avoiding the parochialness of a single point of view. An example of a set of high-order, interdisciplinary concepts used in a social studies curriculum is found in Table 2.6 (pp. 62–63).

HOW CONCEPTS ARE LEARNED

Concept formation is a complex intellectual task. According to the classical approach, it consists of the ability to sort out a group of observations on the basis of one or more common characteristics, to abstract and generalize these discriminating features, and to apply a word or phrase to the observation that appropriately names or labels it on the basis of its discriminating characteristics. *In short, conceptualization is the process of categorizing, classifying, and naming a group of objects.*[17]

Children begin to form concepts very early in life. This becomes evident as soon as they can identify correctly a variety of common objects such as chair, light, table, or dog. By the time most children begin the primary grades, they already have a speaking vocabulary that includes many concept terms. These include concepts for most of the objects in their environment, such as the persons in their immediate family, the things in their homes, and the foods, clothes, and utensils they use each day. Furthermore, television has brought children into frequent contact with many things quite distant from their own environment. They may know more about these than about things that are more immediate and close to them. Children have probably developed a number of relational concepts such as *inside, outside, from, to, up*, and *down*, but often have confused and incomplete ideas about the meaning of other important relational concepts such as *smaller than, less than, larger, more than, the next one, the one before, double, like, unlike*, and the *number names* for quantities. Nor do children understand just how their close family relatives such as grandparents, uncles, or aunts are related to their own parents and themselves.

Nature of the Learning Experience   As indicated above, many concepts are learned informally before children enter school. Experiences and the many events and things in their environment provide direct and immediate learning situations. The objects encountered are concrete and specific, often with vivid sensory stimuli. Learning in the school classroom, however, tends to be proximate rather than direct, and more symbolic and abstract than concrete. Because the school setting is more formal and structured, you must provide many opportunities for students to gain experience with the events represented by the concept. Young children in the primary grades (to follow Piaget's developmental stages) need frequent experience with concrete realities that can be seen, heard, or manipulated. Older students in the middle and upper grades also need experience with the events or things involved, but the materials may be more abstract or symbolic. For example, primary grade students might use pictures, drawings, or dolls to develop simple aspects of the concept *family*, whereas students in the fifth or sixth grade might use a diagram with a variety of symbols to chart the familial ties in an extended family. The older students would spend considerably less time on this topic since the more basic elements of the concept *family* will have already been developed.

Examples and Nonexamples of Concepts   Research indicates that concepts are learned most effectively when a number of *positive* examples of the concept are presented.[18] Students are able to discern the relevant characteristics and to make appropriate discriminations when the examples of a *city*, such as Boston, Paris, or Tokyo, are not confused with special cases such as Vatican City or East Berlin. *Negative* examples illustrate characteristics that are opposite from those positively associated with the discriminating features. For example, *liberty* may be illustrated by the excesses of license; the need for *laws* and *regulations* by the possibility of anarchy; *honesty* and *integrity* by the evidence of wrongdoing and corruption. Although it is true that some learning does occur with negative examples, learners are forced to spend an inordinate amount of time inefficiently searching for the appropriate clues leading them to the discriminating characteristic. In addition, they must try to remember all the characteristics that do not apply, which usually far exceed those that are included in the concept. Yet, ironically, most classroom discussions that we have observed on the concepts of *liberty*, *law* or *integrity* have dealt almost entirely with negative examples. This is not to say that exceptions should not be discussed, only that they should not be introduced until the positive aspects of the concept have been carefully developed so that students can easily make the correct discriminations.

Complexity of Examples   Because the social studies curriculum contains so many complex concepts, it is important that we consider three aspects related to complexity: focusing on the essential characteristics, choosing between realistic versus simulated experiences, and progressing from simple to complex concepts.

Suppose, for example, a class is studying the concept *assembly line production.* If we were to start by taking the class to a factory without any prior class development of the concept, the students would be overwhelmed by the complexity of factors. Which are the *essential characteristics:* the large stores of materials, the protective clothing worn by the workers, or perhaps the great amount of machinery present? Obviously, the teacher would have had to introduce the idea of a moving table on which the product was placed, and as the table was moved rapidly through various parts of the factory different groups of workers added something or made some change in the product until it reached its finished form. This could be done through a short 8-mm film loop or a set of animated transparencies, each illustrating several different examples—for example, auto production, or a meat-packing plant, with a nonexample of a local jeweler repairing a watch, or a shoemaker resoling a pair of shoes.

Once the students have understood the essential characteristics, a field trip to see an assembly line in actual operation would be more profitable.

"The first thing you must learn is they say one thing and mean another." (*Source:* Herbert Goldberg. Used with permission.)

Students could then attend to the essential characteristics and not be diverted by the fascinating but irrelevant cues.

Using the same example, let us examine the problem of choosing between *realistic versus simulated experience* when a concept is being presented for the first time. Abundant research evidence from the areas of industrial and military training has indicated that simplified line drawings, models, animated films, or simulated mock-ups are usually far more effective in teaching a concept than direct observation or involvement. These devices eliminate most of the irrelevant cues and emphasize strongly, often by vivid colors, the essential characteristics. As we indicated above, the field trip to the factory to see an assembly line is a complex learning activity. Undoubtedly, students will see many new and exciting things for the first time, many having little or nothing to do with the concept *assembly line*. As Travers has pointed out, humans have a limited capacity to handle the onrush of new information, and the brain tends to eliminate those stimuli which it cannot sort out and relate to other existing impressions and ideas.[19] It is very likely that some students will miss entirely the concept *assembly line*, and little will have been gained from the field trip. Thus, a teacher must weigh carefully the value of heightened motivation and interest that will result from a field trip, versus the value of simplicity and accuracy that is to be gained from the use of a simulated experience when a concept is first introduced.

VERBALIZING A CONCEPT

One of the factors related to concept attainment is the ability of the student to verbalize the concept. Verbalizing is distinguishing orally or in writing the discriminating characteristics and giving the concept an appropriate name. Such a skill is important in social studies if students are to use concepts freely and readily in sorting out large amounts of data and if they are to have a repertoire of powerful analytical terms for making comparisons and contrasts in the process of developing generalizations from several samples of data.

Many students at first have some kind of intuitive grasp of the concept and are able to recognize those items that belong to a group and those that do not. They find it difficult, however, to state the basis for their discrimination and can often give no reason for why an item belongs in a particular group other than "Well, because it just does." In short, they may be able to identify (and possibly use) a concept, but not be able to define it adequately in words.

This problem is due not only to the lack of adequate abstract terms in the young child's vocabulary, but also to the fact that the process of conceptualizing involves three separate tasks: *observing, classifying,* and *defining,* all of which involve separate response modes. Studies have demonstrated that the quality of concept definition improves when students are given even limited amounts of practice in making definitions at the same time that they make the discriminations, even when they are not told how good the definition is.[20] Teaching strategies should ensure, then, that students are given adequate practice in naming or defining a concept, at the same time that they identify the discriminating features used in classifying the items in the group. Teachers should recognize, too, that students will grope for adequate words to express the concept and will often use awkward phrases because they have not learned the precise abstract word. One class of third-grade youngsters studying manufacturing agreed on the phrase "things-that-you-make-all-in-a-line" as their name for the concept *assembly line*. It was not until a day or two later when the teacher was certain that most of the students had attained the concept that she suggested that they substitute the more technical word "assembly line." For students with low verbal fluency or poor language development it is doubly important that the teacher concentrate on the skill of defining as well as the skill of discriminating.

A strategy for teaching concepts based on curriculum and psychological principles is presented in Table 3.1. It consists principally of having the teacher ask a series of questions designed to elicit from the students the essential task of *listing*, *grouping*, and *labeling*.

CURRENT ISSUES IN CONCEPT LEARNING

Recent studies in concept learning have raised a number of new issues that challenge the "classical" approach described above.[21] They present new models of the structure of concepts and a new theory on the process of how concepts are learned. They also suggest that you as a teacher must be more keenly aware of the cultural context that different groups of students bring with them as they learn to interpret and establish meanings for complex social science concepts.

The Structure of Concepts

The classical model of a concept assumes that all the essential characteristics or attributes must always be present. While this may be satisfactory for relatively simple conjunctive concepts (where the elements are additive), it presents serious learning problems for complex, abstract concepts that are often disjunctive in form (that is, some of the elements may or may not be present).

To meet these difficulties, two alternative models have been proposed: the *exemplar model* and the *social context model*. Proponents of the *exemplar* model have suggested that concepts be identified on the basis of attributes that are most typically present, rather than insisting that all attributes must always be present—somewhat like Wittgenstein's "family resemblance" notion.[22] In this model you would present to students a number of best examples (most typical) of the concept with little or no attention to poor examples (least typical). In a recent study, this method of presenting only the best examples proved to be the most effective strategy when compared to three other strategies of concept learning.[23] Thus, many complex concepts in social

TABLE 3.1. Developing Concepts: Listing, Grouping, Labeling, and Defining a Concept

This task requires students to group a number of items on some kind of basis. The teaching strategy consist of asking students the following questions, usually in this order.

Teacher Asks	Student	Teacher Follow-Through
What do you see (notice, find) here?	Gives items.	Makes sure items are accessible to each student. Lists the items on chalkboard, transparency, individual list, pictures, or item card.
Do any of these items seem to belong together?	Finds some similarity as a basis.	Communicates grouping. For example, underlines in colored chalk, marks with symbols, or arranges pictures or cards.
Why would you group them together?*	Identifies and verbalizes the common characteristics of items in a group.	Seeks clarification of responses when necessary.
What would you call these groups you have formed?	Verbalizes a label (perhaps more than one word) that appropriately encompasses all items.	Records.
Could some of these belong in more than one group?	States different relationships.	Records.
Can we put these same items in different groups?†	States additional different relationships.	Communicates grouping.
Can you explain (define) the name or label of this group?	States a definition.	Records the definition.

*Sometimes you ask the same child "why" when he or she offers the grouping, and other times you may wish to get many groups before considering "why" things are grouped together.
†Although this step is important because it encourages flexibility, it will not be appropriate on all occasions.
SOURCE: *The Taba Social Studies Curriculum* (Menlo Park, Calif.: Addison-Wesley, 1970), vol. 6, p. xxii. Reprinted with permission.

studies such as ethnicity, social class, alienation, justice, or poverty might well be taught using this best example (most typical) model.

The *social context* model suggests that the brain forms a unitary representation of a concept, a nonanalytic, perhaps intuitive learning, that merges specific instances of a concept within a context of actions, expectations and relationships to other concepts.[24] Consider the concept of a *birthday party*. For many young children this is an eagerly awaited day, an enjoyable time with family and friends, games, ice cream and cake, gifts, and a vague awareness that they have grown another year older. In this model, while the party itself may be the essential attribute, it is the context of the special day, the expectation of how people, actions, and events are likely to interact, and the relationship of this day to the larger concepts of age or maturity that give meaning to the concept of birthday party. Similarly, the concept of *basketball game* or *play-off tournament* has a much larger social context than *ball* or *players*, which make up only a part of the concept. Thus, you may find this model much more useful for teaching some complex concepts in social studies such as *civil rights demonstration, lobbying, the presidential primary system,* or *terrorism.*

Schemata and the Process of Learning Concepts

Drawing upon recent research in cognition, linguistics, and artificial intelligence, psychologists have proposed the theory that the mind makes use of underlying *schemata* or frameworks as it organizes and processes information.[25] According to the schemata theory, the mind tends to build frameworks which contain slots or placeholders into which we put new data or experiences. They are dynamic structures constantly undergoing change. The mind integrates new information by establishing relationships between the new data and what is already known and stored in the long-term memory of the brain. Schemata are the building blocks of cognition or thinking processes.[26]

Schemata, or frameworks, are developed out of the cultural background of the student, and prior experiences provide the context for interpreting or deriving meaning from written text or social situations. Thus, children who understand how a neighborhood convenience store functions would have appropriate schemata for understanding the concept of supermarket or department store, but they may have no schemata for understanding the concept of bargaining at a bazaar in the Middle East or bidding at an art auction.

Similes and metaphors seem to enhance the process of relating new information to previously learned data. You might begin a discussion about the concept of *election* by saying, "Winning a presidential primary election is like winning a state championship in a basketball tournament." The schemata theory has been derived from research studies in socio-linguistics and has had a major influence on the teaching of reading in schools.[27] Scholars cite similar trends beginning to emerge in teaching social studies and urge further investigation into ways that teachers can add new and often conflicting information about culturally different people and societies into students' existing schemata.[28]

Generalizations

Generalizations are statements of the relationship of two or more concepts. These statements may range from very simple to very complex. Sometimes they are referred to as principles or laws. The following statements are generalizations.

As people interact with their physical and social environment, both they and the environment are changed.

All persons and groups of persons depend on the other persons and groups for satisfaction of needs.

Conflicts and inequities often result from assigning value to particular categories of differences, such as white skin or high intelligence.

Cultural change is accelerated by such factors as increased knowledge, mobility, and communication, operating both within and between cultures.

Generalizations such as those above provide us with a useful means of expressing the relationship between accumulated facts and information in a highly organized and systematic way. They eliminate the need for us to go back to original statements again and again. In a sense generalizations become a kind of shorthand for the knowledge that we accumulate during our life experience. They are also useful as a means of helping us explore new situations.

Traditionally, schools have passed on these accumulated generalizations in an expository manner. Teachers have lectured or talked about them. The authors of textbooks have incorporated them as statements of truth. In most cases they have been presented as statements to be learned and accepted with little or no discussion about their derivation or validity. Typically, generalizations have been used in a deductive manner; that is, students have accepted the truth of the statements and then sought examples that illustrate them in particular detail or in local application.[29]

The point of view taken in this text is that students in elementary and junior high schools should have the maximum opportunities to derive generalizations for themselves. While there certainly is a place for deductive learning, it is our position that this mode of learning has occupied far too large a part of students' learning experiences. In contrast, students have had little opportunity to learn the skills and processes involved in deriving generalizations for themselves.

ANATOMY OF GENERALIZATIONS

A generalization expresses a relationship between two or more concepts. For example, let us take two very simple concepts: rain and temperature. What can we say about their relationship? We might be able to make a very *simple* statement such as "When it is cold, rain changes to snow." While most young children will already have had enough experience in their lifetime to validate this statement, a more complex generalization might make a statement about the relationship of rainfall and temperature and their effect on vegetation. In such cases, it may be possible to generalize that the combination of warm weather, large amounts of rainfall, and fertile soil produces great amounts of vegetation.

Relationships between two or more concepts are often expressed by verb phrases such as *grows larger, declines, is influenced by, is associated with, causes changes in,* or *varies with.* Earlier we spoke of generalizations as "verified hypotheses." It is a good test of a generalization, therefore, to try to recast the statement into the "if . . . then" form. Not only does this force the relationship into clearer perspective, it also requires that the concepts be stated in sequence so that their logical cause and effect or other association is plainly evident. Thus, the two examples given above could be rewritten as:

If it is cold, *then* the rain will change to snow.
If there is a combination of warm weather, large amounts of rainfall, and fertile soil, *then* large amounts of vegetation will be produced.

We propose this rule of thumb: *If* a generalization cannot be recast into an "if . . . then" form, *then* it is probably only a statement that summarizes factual knowledge.

Some generalizations, of course, are very limited in scope. The data they are derived from may be limited to the experience of a single individual or they may refer to a single town or region in the United States. For example, we may have "the growth of the lumber industry in the Pacific Northwest depends in large measure on the annual rainfall." This statement is obviously limited because of the restrictions on the data from which the relationships were derived. The source of evidence is the annual rainfall and the economic growth of the lumber industry in the Northwest. A very different series of generalizations might be developed if we were to analyze the amount of rainfall in Thailand and its effects on the rice crop. These two examples require widely contrasting sources of data. If we extend this by adding the sample data on rainfall and production of rice in Louisiana, and another sample that provides data on the amount of rainfall and the yield of wheat in the Soviet Union, we may begin to get some broad inferences from a series of widely divergent samples about the influence of rainfall and temperature on vegetation.

Other generalizations, however, have universal application throughout people's cultural experience. Empirical data from all times and all cultures can be used to support the relationship stated between the concepts. For example:

In every society rules emerge to govern the affairs of people.
Culture tends to standardize human behavior and to stabilize societies by developing many interrelated and elaborate institutions.

HIGH- AND LOW-ORDER GENERALIZATIONS

As you can see from the discussion above, generalizations can be classified on the basis of the range of their application. Some are universal in their scope; others are very limited in their applications. For convenience we have called these high-order, intermediate-level, and low-order generalizations. In the following paragraphs we have sketched out a progression of generalizations from high to low. As the arrow indicates, these can be read in any direction, from high to low (deductive), or from low to high (inductive).

High-Order Generalizations

These generalizations have *universal* application. They apply to all people at all times. Generalizations of the highest order are often called laws or principles.
Example: Interaction between a people and their environment influences the way in which they meet their needs.

Intermediate-Level Generalizations

These generalizations apply to particular regions of the world, cultures, or historical eras.
Example: Americans who moved westward from the eastern seaboard during the eighteenth and nineteenth centuries modified their life-style to meet the demands of frontier living.

Low-Order Generalizations

These generalizations are based on data from only two or three small samples such as a group of cities in a particular region.
Example: An abundance of moisture together with a long, warm growing season provide good conditions for growing grapes in the San Francisco Bay area and along the southern shore of Lake Erie.

Summarizing statements. In contrast to the various levels of generalizations outlined above, summarizing statements tend to sum up a series of facts or observations derived from a *single* sample, such as manufacturing in Boston, temperature variations in a single town, or even as broad a topic as the American Revolution. No matter how much data may be accumulated on any of these topics, this kind of activity still remains a *summarizing* and not a generalizing statement if the data are drawn from a *single* sample.

You should not regard long factual summaries as generalizations. *It is not until comparisons and contrast are made with two or more samples and relationships established between important concepts* (or *variables*) *that one can be said to be engaged in the process of generalizing.* In one study, this method was found superior to two other methods of teaching economic concepts to fifth-grade students.[30] Table 3.2 illustrates a strategy for teaching students to generalize.

GENERALIZATIONS IN CURRICULUM DESIGN

In planning a unit of study, a teacher usually starts by specifying the end product of the students' learning. This serves as the target or focus for all

TABLE 3.2. Inferring and Generalizing

This cognitive task requires the students to interpret, infer, and generalize about data. The teaching strategy consists of asking the students the following questions, usually in this order.

Teacher Asks	Student	Teacher Follow-Through
What did you notice? See? Find? What differences did you notice (with reference to a particular question)?	Gives items.	Makes sure items are accessible—for example, chalkboard, transparency, individual list, pictures, or item card. Chooses the items to pursue.
Why do you think this happened? Or, how do you account for these differences?	Gives explanation that may be based on factual information and/or inferences.	Accepts explanation. Seeks clarification if necessary.
What does this tell you about . . . ?	Gives generalization.	Encourages variety of generalizations and seeks clarification when necessary.

This pattern of inviting reasons to account for observed phenomena and generalizing beyond the data is repeated and expanded to include more and more aspects of the data and to reach more abstract generalizations.

SOURCE: Hilda Taba, Mary C. Durkin, Jack R. Fraenkel, and Anthony H. McNaughton, *A Teacher's Handbook to Elementary Social Studies: An Inductive Approach* (Reading, MA: Addison-Wesley, 1971), p. 75.

other planning. Stated in behavioral terms, for example, the learning outcome might be

> Having completed a unit of study on world cultures, students will write statements that approximate the generalization: *Cultures vary from society to society. Any given culture changes in the course of time. Some behaviors and institutions within a culture are universal while others vary widely, even during the same period.*

Using this as the final goal toward which all activities should point, the teacher can then begin to plan in reverse the content, materials, and learning experiences that would be appropriate to help the student ultimately arrive at this generalization. Figure 3.2 shows a schematic outline of the process. It should be emphasized again that this diagram represents the teacher's planning activity, which is to a large measure a deductive process. The students' learning activities, however, start from the bottom of the diagram, and proceed inductively toward the high-level generalization.

In each of the chapters on the disciplines (Chapters 9 through 14), there are examples of concepts and generalizations from the various social sciences.

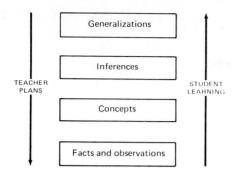

TEACHER
PLANS

STUDENT
LEARNING

FIGURE 3.2 Relationship of generalizations, concepts, and facts.

Sample generalizations from these chapters are presented in Table 3.3. Chapter 2 describes interdisciplinary approaches and illustrates how generalizations from the various social science disciplines can be used to study topics and problems.

You should realize, however, that lists of generalizations are in themselves only

TABLE 3.3. Key Social Science Generalizations

Discipline	Generalizations
History	Wherever human beings have lived, conflicts between individuals, groups, and nations have arisen.
	A historian's view of the past is influenced by the availability of evidence, his or her personal biases and purposes for writing, and the society and times in which he or she lives and writes.
Sociology	All characteristically human behavior is learned from other human beings through group interaction.
	The group exerts social control over its individual members through the use of sanctions.
Anthropology	Cultures use a diversity of means to attain similar ends and to satisfy common human needs.
	Cultural exchange takes place when groups with diverse cultures come into prolonged contact. Cultural change may disrupt a society.
Geography	The physical environment influences how a culture develops and how it solves the problems of survival.
	An individual's perception of his or her physical environment is influenced by his or her culture and experiences within that environment.
Political science	In every society and institution, regulations and laws emerge to govern the behavior of individuals and groups.
	Rules and laws reflect the basic values within a society or institution.
Economics	Every individual and society faces a conflict between unlimited wants and limited resources.
	All members of society are interdependent. Individual producers of goods and services exchange with others to get the goods and services they need to satisfy their basic wants.

lists. When provided in state or local curriculum guides, they are intended to serve as *guides.* In most cases, it remains for you to work out the practical problem of relating concepts and generalizations to appropriate content, instructional materials, and teaching strategies geared to your students.

Theories: Nature and Examples

Theory is the highest form of knowledge and is the main goal of science. Theories help us to explain and to predict human behavior. Although total agreement on the definition of the term does not exist, most social scientists would agree that a scientific *theory* consists of a set of testable interrelated lawlike statements or high-level generalizations. The high-level generalizations that make up a scientific theory must

1. show the relationship between clearly defined variables or concepts,
2. constitute a deductive system and be logically consistent (unknown principles must be derivable from known ones), and
3. be a source of testable hypotheses.

Unlike physical scientists, social scientists have developed relatively few theories consistent with the definition above. Partly, this is because the social sciences are much newer fields than the physical sciences. Also, data on human behavior are much more difficult to collect and verify than data about our physical environment. However, social scientists have been successful in formulating a number of *partial* theories. The theories illustrated below are partial because they attempt to explain and predict only limited aspects of human behavior. They try to explain why suicide rates vary among different groups. *Grand* or *inclusive* theories try to explain, with a few statements or generalizations, all group behavior or a total class of things. Darwin's theory of evolution, Newton's corpuscular theory of light, and Einstein's theory of relativity are examples of grand theories in the biological and physical sciences. Social scientists have not been able to develop grand or all-encompassing theories universally accepted by the scientific community. However, the Freudian and Marxist theories are grand in scope and attempt to explain most human behavior in a few principles.

EXAMPLES OF THEORIES

Durkheim's Theory of Suicide   One of the first empirical social science theories, Durkheim's theory explained the low suicide rate in Spain.[31] Durkheim's system satisfies all the characteristics of a theory described above.

1. In any social grouping, the suicide rate varies directly with the degree of individualism.
2. The degree of individualism varies with the incidence of Protestantism.

3. Therefore, the suicide rate varies with the incidence of Protestantism.
4. The incidence of Protestantism in Spain is low.
5. Therefore, the suicide rate in Spain is low.

Merton's Theory of Suicide Merton has formulated and tested a theory to explain the lower incidence of suicide among Catholics than among Protestants:[32]

1. Social cohesion provides psychic support to group members subjected to acute stresses and anxieties.
2. Suicide rates are functions of *unrelieved* anxieties and stresses to which persons are subjected.
3. Catholic (and specified additional groups) have greater social cohesion than Protestants.
4. Therefore, lower suicide rates should be anticipated among Catholics than among Protestants.

THEORIES IN THE SOCIAL STUDIES CURRICULUM

Social studies educators have done relatively little work related to the teaching of theories to students. A few writers have suggested that curriculum builders should identify those social science theories that will best help students to make decisions and teach the concepts and generalizations that comprise them. There are many partial theories in the social sciences that you can use in teaching. These include such theories as Rogers's theory of personality and behavior, Schlesinger's theory of political ambition, and Lenski's theory of social stratification. Arthur M. Schlesinger, Jr.'s interesting theory about cycles in U.S. history—the thirty-year alternation of liberal and conservative forces—can provide students in the middle and upper grades with a unique lens through which to view history and contemporary events.[33]

A theory approach to curriculum construction is a promising one. However, we have no models or examples of social studies curricula structured around theories. More work related to the teaching of theory must be done before specific curriculum recommendations can be made. Nonetheless, during a study of some concepts (such as suicide, prejudice, political ambition, and social stratification), especially in the middle and upper grades, you might draw on theories such as those presented above to guide your selection of generalizations to teach and to help your students to better understand and predict behavior.[34] Like all forms of knowledge, social theory has limitations. It is tentative and does not always specify conditions or exceptions. Despite these limitations, theory is the most powerful form of knowledge that has yet been devised. Table 3.4 illustrates the relationship between the various categories of knowledge discussed in this chapter.

TABLE 3.4. The Relationship of the Categories of Knowledge

This figure illustrates the relationship between *facts, concepts, generalizations,* and *theories.* Note that each category of knowledge is dependent for its development on the element below it.

Theory: Durkheim's theory of suicide

Generalization: In any social grouping, the suicide rate varies directly with the degree of individualism.

Concepts: Suicide rate; Individualism

Fact: Only 7.6 persons per 100,000 committed suicide in Spain in 1965, compared to 16.3 per 100,000 in the United States.*

*Based on data reported in the *Statistical Abstract of the United States* (Washington, D.C: U.S. Government Printing Office, 1969), p. 81.

SUMMARY

The main goal of the social studies should be to help students develop the ability to make reflective decisions. They can then influence public policy by participating in effective citizen action. Knowledge is one essential component of the decision-making process. The first part of this chapter discusses the goal and nature of social inquiry and describes a model students can use to test hypotheses and to derive knowledge. Students must be given systematic practice in each of the skills that constitute this model in order to become adept decision makers. This chapter also highlights the assumptions, limitations, and basic requirements of science. *Scientific knowledge is neither absolute nor unchanging. It should be regarded as tentative and must be continually tested, evaluated, and reconstructed.*

The second part of this chapter describes the nature of social knowledge. Emphasis in elementary and junior high school social studies should be on the process of inquiry and not on its products. However, the products of inquiry—facts, concepts, generalizations, and theories—are essential for structuring experiences whereby students can learn inquiry modes, and thus help to solve important personal and public problems. Without higher-level predictive knowledge, or the products of inquiry, the decision-maker is not competent to act. The reflective citizen actor must make use of the best available knowledge.

Factual knowledge consists of specific data about events, objects, people, or other things that can be verified by the senses. *Concepts* are abstract words useful for classifying groups of facts, events, or ideas on the basis of common characteristics. *Generalizations* are statements showing a relationship between two or more concepts. A *scientific theory* is a set of interrelated high-level generalizations capable of explaining and predicting behavior. Partly because of the emerging status of theory in the social sciences, the teaching of social science theory in the schools has not been systematically explored by social studies educators.

DISCUSSION QUESTIONS AND EXERCISES

1. What are the essential factors that distinguish one social science discipline from another? Give examples to support your answer. What implications does your answer have for planning social studies experiences for elementary and junior high school students?

2. What are the *assumptions* of science? Why is social science unable to answer many of the questions people are most vitally interested in? List several questions that social science cannot answer. List several questions that social science cannot answer, but whose resolution can be aided by the wise use of the scientific method.

3. The model of social inquiry presented in this chapter consists of a series of skills. Plan lessons designed to help students gain proficiency in:
   a. formulating problems   d. collecting data
   b. hypothesizing   e. evaluating and analyzing data
   c. conceptualizing   f. deriving generalizations.
   You may use one or several questions to develop your plans.

4. Explain and give examples of how a teacher may help students to implement each of the following types of studies:
   a. the experiment   c. the case study
   b. the sample survey

   What difficulties might a teacher encounter in trying to help students implement each type of study? How might these difficulties be overcome?

5. Make a list of 10 facts that can be or have been verified about some important recent event or problem (e.g., the presidential election campaign, consumer protection programs, a racial conflict, a prolonged strike, or a campus controversy). Are any of these "facts" distorted by biased or prejudiced perceptions of the data?

6. Using the list of 10 facts pertinent to any *one* of the events or problems suggested in Question 5, categorize them into groups and label them with an appropriate concept word or phrase. Can some of the items be interchanged between groups? Does this affect the concept term applied to the groups?

7. The terms *concept* and *generalization* are often confused and substituted for each other. How would you distinguish one from the other?

8. Using some of the concepts you formulated in Question 6, write four generalizations that might be developed from them (assuming the data are available to support them). Test each generalization by recasting it into the conditional "if . . . then" form to check for the logical relationship among concepts. (The purpose of this exercise is to develop practice in formulating the statement of a generalization, not necessarily in finding the data to verify it.)

9. Think back over the social science courses you have had. With what major theories from one or more of the disciplines are you familiar? To what extent do they meet the criteria for theory identified in this chapter? If students were familiar with this theory, how might it contribute to their understanding of concepts and generalizations? How might it contribute to more effective decision-making?

10. Demonstrate your understanding of the following key concepts by writing or stating brief definitions for each:

a. social inquiry (process)
b. knowledge (product)
c. hypothesis
d. conceptualization
e. experiment
f. sample survey
g. participant observation
h. the requirements of science
i. the assumptions of science
j. fact
k. concept
l. generalization

m. hierarchical order of concepts
n. abstract concept
o. concrete concept
p. relational concept
q. interdisciplinary concepts
r. positive examples of concepts
s. negative examples of concepts
t. generalizations
u. high-order/low-order generalizations
v. summarizing statements
w. theories

NOTES

1. Carlo L. Lastrucci, *The Scientific Approach: Basic Principles of the Scientific Method* (Cambridge, MA: Schenkman, 1963), pp. 37–47.

2. Lastrucci, pp. 42–46.

3. Bernard Berelson and Gary A. Steiner, *Human Behavior: An Inventory of Scientific Findings* (New York: Harcourt Brace & World, 1964), pp. 6–7.

4. Gerald N. Grob and George Athan Billias, Eds., *Interpretations of American History*, Vol. II: Since 1877, 5th ed. (New York: The Free Press, 1987).

5. Henry Steele Commager and Raymond H. Muessig, *The Study and Teaching of History* (Columbus, OH: Merrill, 1980).

6. See the book describing this film [William Peters, *A Class Divided: Then and Now*, expanded ed. (New Haven, CT: Yale University Press, 1987)] and the 1985 follow-up of it (the 1985 follow-up of the film is called *A Class Divided*). *Eye of the Storm* is distributed by the Anti-Defamation League of B'nai B'rith (823 United Nations Plaza, New York, NY 10017). *A Class Divided* is distributed by PBS Video (1320 Braddock Place, Alexandria, VA 22314–1698).

7. Edward T. James, Janet Wilson James, and Paul S. Boyer, *Notable American Women: A Biographical Dictionary*, Vols. 1, 2, and 3 (Cambridge: Harvard University Press, 1971).

8. Thomas S. Kuhn, *The Structure of Scientific Revolutions*, 2nd ed., enlarged (Chicago: University of Chicago Press, 1970).

9. *The Seattle Times*, August 28, 1983, p. A18.

10. Jerome S. Bruner, *The Process of Education* (New York: Vintage Books, 1960); Joseph J. Schwab, "The Concept of the Structure of a Discipline," *The Educational Record*, Vol. 43 (July 1962), pp. 197–205.

11. Lynne V. Cheney, *The American Memory: A Report on the Humanities in the Nation's Public Schools* (Washington, D.C.: National Endowment for the Humanities, 1987); E. D. Hirsch, Jr., *Cultural Literacy: What Every American Needs to Know* (Boston:

Houghton Mifflin, 1987); Diane Ravitch and Chester E. Finn, Jr., *What Do Our 17-Year-Olds Know? A Report on the First National Assessment of History and Literature* (New York: Harper & Row, 1987).

12. James P. Shaver, O. L. Davis, and Susan W. Helburn, "The Status of Social Studies Education: Impressions from Three NSF Studies," *Social Education*, Vol. 43, pp. 150–153; John I. Goodlad, *A Place Called School: Prospects for the Future* (New York: McGraw-Hill, 1984).

13. James E. Blackwell, *The Black Community: Diversity and Unity*, 2nd ed. (New York: Harper & Row, 1985).

14. Jerome Bruner, Jacqueline Goodnow, and Gerald Austin, *A Study of Thinking* (New York: Wiley, 1977); E. E. Smith and D. L. Medin, *Categories and Concepts* (Cambridge: Harvard University Press, 1981); William B. Stanley and Robert C. Mathews, "Recent Research on Concept Learning: Implications for Social Education," *Theory and Research in Social Education*, Vol. 12 (Winter 1985), pp. 57–74.

15. Giovanni Sartori, Ed., *Social Science Concepts: A Systematic Analysis* (Beverly Hills: Sage, 1984).

16. Stephan J. Thornton and Ronald Vukelich, "Effects of Children's Understanding Time Concepts on Historical Understanding," *Theory and Research in Social Education*, Vol. 16 (Winter 1988), pp. 69–82.

17. Smith and Medin, op. cit.

18. Roger F. Yoho, "Effectiveness of Four Concept Teaching Strategies on Social Concept Acquisition and Retention," *Theory and Research in Social Education*, Vol. 14 (Summer 1986), pp. 211–223.

19. Robert M. W. Travers, "Transmission of Information to Human Receivers," *Educational Psychologist*, Vol. 2 (1964), pp. 1–5.

20. Hilda Taba, *Teaching Strategies and Cognitive Functioning in Elementary School Children* (Cooperative Research Bureau Project #2404. U.S. Office of Health, Education, and Welfare, San Francisco State College, 1966).

21. Stanley and Mathews, pp. 57–74.

22. E. H. Rosch and C. B. Mervis, Eds., *Cognition and Categorization* (Hillsdale, NJ: Erlbaum, 1978); L. Wittgenstein, *Philosophical Investigations*, 2nd ed. (New York: Macmillan, 1958).

23. Yoho, pp. 211–223.

24. K. Nelson, "Cognitive Development and the Acquisition of Concepts," *Psychological Review*, Vol. 81 (1974), pp. 267–285.

25. R. B. Millwar, "Models of Concept Formation," in R. E. Snow, P. Federico, and W. E. Montague, Eds., *Aptitude, Learning and Instruction*, Vol. 2 (Hillsdale, NJ: Erlbaum, 1980), pp. 245–275.

26. D. E. Rumelhart, "Schemata: The Building Blocks of Cognition," in R. J. Spiro, B. C. Bruce, and W. F. Brewer, Eds., *Theoretical Issues in Reading Comprehension* (Hillsdale, NJ: Erlbaum, 1980).

27. R. C. Anderson and P. D. Pearson, "A Schema Theoretic View of Basic Processes in Reading Comprehension," in P. D. Pearson, R. Barr, M. Kamil, and P. Mosenthel (Eds.), *Handbook of Reading Research* (White Plains, NY: Longman, 1985). Robert Calfee and Priscilla Drum, "Research on Teaching Reading," in M. C. Wittrock

(Ed.), *Handbook of Research on Teaching*, 3rd ed. (New York: Macmillan, 1986), pp. 808–809, 837–843.

28.   Beverly J. Armento, "Research on Teaching Social Studies," in M. C. Wittrock (Ed.), *Handbook of Research on Teaching*, 3rd ed. (New York: Macmillan, 1986), pp. 946–947. William B. Stanley and Robert C. Mathews, "Recent Research on Concept Learning: Implications for Social Education," *Theory and Research in Social Education*, Vol. 12 (Winter 1985), pp. 57–74.

29.   Shirley H. Engle and Anna S. Ochoa, *Education for Democratic Citizenship: Decision Making in Social Studies* (New York: Teachers College Press, 1988).

30.   James Betres, Michael Zajani, and Patricia Gumieniak, "Cognitive Style, Teacher Methods and Concept Attainment in Social Studies," *Theory and Research in Social Education*, Vol. 12 (Summer 1984), pp. 1–18.

31.   George C. Homans, "Contemporary Theory in Sociology," in Robert E. L. Faris, Ed., *Handbook of Modern Sociology* (Chicago: Rand McNally, 1964), p. 957.

32.   Reported in Alex Inkeles, *What Is Sociology? An Introduction to the Discipline and Profession* (Englewood Cliffs, NJ: Prentice-Hall, 1965), p. 101.

33.   Arthur M. Schlesinger, Jr., *The Cycles of American History* (Boston: Houghton Mifflin, 1986).

34.   Leon H. Warshay, *The Current State of Sociological Theory: A Critical Interpretation* (New York: David McKay, 1975).

FOR FURTHER READING

Beyer, Barry K. *Developing a Thinking Skills Program*. Boston: Allyn & Bacon, 1988.

Bruner, Jerome S., Jacqueline Goodnow, and George A. Austin. *A Study of Thinking*. New Brunswick, NJ: Transaction Books, 1986.

Hunkins, Francis P. *Teaching Thinking Through Effective Questioning*. Needham Heights, MA: Christopher-Gordon Publishers, 1989.

Roselle, Daniel, Ed. *Voices of Social Education 1937–1987*. New York: Macmillan, 1987.

4

Teaching Higher-Level Thinking with Questions

Social inquiry about important issues and problems requires people to use higher-level thinking processes, such as conceptualizing factual data, hypothesizing about possible solutions, and generalizing to larger settings. You can help students learn these thought processes by skillfully asking appropriate questions that lead students from simple to complex thinking tasks. Research conducted during the past twenty years has amply demonstrated that student learning improves when teachers use appropriate questioning practices, particularly those that involve higher-order thinking processes.[1]

This chapter will examine classroom questions, both oral and written, from a number of considerations: (1) the purpose and function of questions, (2) their use as elements in the teaching strategies related to social inquiry, valuing, and decision-making, (3) various ways of classifying classroom questions, and (4) several simple instruments for observing and analyzing the levels of questioning and for providing feedback to you about your own questioning performance.

THE PURPOSE AND FUNCTION OF CLASSROOM QUESTIONS

Although questions may be used to serve a number of purposes, their most frequent use has been as a means of testing students' knowledge, often at the end of a chapter in a book or a unit. The rapid, oral questioning by the teacher has traditionally served as a useful means of review or summary for a lesson, or as a preliminary introduction to new material. To a lesser extent the same function is served by short written tests, or end-of-chapter questions in a textbook. In contrast, the much broader, open-ended questions such as "How do you suppose the Indians got to America in the first place?" serve as motivating devices to arouse curiosity and to focus students' thoughts in a particular direction at the start of a lesson or a larger unit of study. Other types of questions focus on both the learning process and the content being studied. For example:

> What can you infer from this data?
>
> What comparisons or contrasts can you make about the economic aspects of nineteenth-century life in a New England town from their tax records and household inventories?
>
> What can you generalize about the economic life of that period?
>
> Are those generalizations still valid today?
>
> Can you predict (or hypothesize) what changes might occur in the economic aspects of New England towns (or cities) in the next three decades?
>
> How could you validate this prediction (or hypothesis)?

Although such questions represent an ideal frequently discussed and encouraged in the professional journals and methods textbooks, what actually occurs in the classroom seems to fall far short of these goals. A number of

Dramatic and role-playing stituations motivate students to learn and are sources of thoughtful student questions. This photograph shows students participating in a simulated television program. (*Source:* Edna Kellman, Seattle Public Schools.)

studies have pointed out that although teachers' objectives are often stated or intended to be at high intellectual levels, the types of questions teachers ask, whether in oral discussion or as written test items, most often require only the recall of a previously learned answer.[2] Your questions should require more than appropriate content responses. They should also require students to use various learning processes such as forming concepts, proposing hypotheses, and developing generalizations. Especially important is the challenge from students and teachers alike:

How do you know?
Where are the data to support that conclusion?
Why do you feel that way?
On what basis do you consider that solution good (or bad)?

In the following pages we shall show how questions such as these can be built directly into the model of social inquiry discussed in Chapter 3.

A STRATEGY OF QUESTIONING
FOR SOCIAL INQUIRY

The model of social inquiry shown in Figure 3.1 (p. 79) is composed of a series of elements: (1) expressing doubt or concern, (2) formulating a problem and recognizing the theoretical position or the values implicit in it, (3) formulating working hypotheses, (4) defining or clarifying the key terms in the hypotheses, (5) collecting data, (6) analyzing and evaluating the data, and (7) testing the hypotheses and deriving generalizations.

> *Expressing Doubt:* To begin a unit of study that involves social inquiry, first plan for a situation that introduces some form of incongruity, contradiction, or dissatisfaction so that the students will perceive a problem and see some need to solve it. The nature and scope of the problems will vary, of course, with the age and maturity of the students and their previous experiences, but the essential task remains the same: to arouse the students' curiosity and to motivate them to inquire.
>
> *Starting with a Value Question:* One approach is to begin with a value question and then shift to a scientific question. Because the value question tends to include a strong element of controversy and emotional tone, it quickly arouses interest and motivation. Several examples follow which show how this shift can be made.

Problem 1: Playground Rules

> *Value Questions:* After a fight on the playground over the use of the basketball court you might ask the class, "Do you really think the rules are unfair in this school? Do some students seem to get special favors?"

After some minutes of open discussion, during which students would express their opinions and perhaps vent some pent-up anger or frustration, you might attempt to shift the focus by asking scientific questions related to the problem.

Scientific Questions: What are the rules regarding the use of the basketball courts? How is time scheduled? Is there a plan for rotating the courts to prevent one group of students from using it all the time? What provision is there for settling disagreements once they arise?

Although all the questions posed above are contemporary ones, the same technique can be used to arouse interest in studying problems that have their roots in the past.

Problem 2: Constructing a New Freeway

Value Questions: Should we construct a six-lane freeway through the heart of the central residential district? This will displace 900 or more families. Can they find other places to live that they can afford?

Following some discussion by the class, it might help to shift the focus of the discussion to scientific questions.

Scientific Questions: How many lanes will be needed on the new freeway to handle the expected volume of traffic to and from the city? By 1995? By 2000?

What will be the impact on the community of efforts to link up a major east-west interstate highway with the principal north-south one? How many homes or businesses will have to be relocated? Will the highway effectively cut one part of the community off from another? Are new shopping centers or playground areas being planned? Are there homes currently available for those people whose homes will be demolished?

Problem 3: Minorities in the Suburbs

Value Question: Should African-Americans move into white suburbs? After students have given their opinions and have discussed the question for a while, you might shift the focus toward scientific questions related to the original value question.

Scientific Questions: How does the presence of minority groups in a previously all-white community affect the availability of jobs, the quality of education in the schools, etc.? What types of discrimination do African-Americans face in predominantly white communities?

Problem 4: Dropping the Atomic Bomb

Value Question: Should the United States have dropped the atomic bombs on Hiroshima and Nagasaki and caused the loss of thousands of lives and the complete destruction of the two cities?

Students who are sensitive to the implications of mass destruction of humanity will have many opinions, views, and feelings on this important topic. To prevent the class discussion from becoming a mere exchange of opinions, you must help to shift the focus by asking scientific questions related to the strategic decision made by President Truman and his advisors.

Scientific Questions: What were the strategic considerations involved in the decision? What responses had Japan made to the various peace overtures made? How did President Roosevelt's "unconditional surrender" doctrine affect the strategic thinking of World War II?

Many of the typical social studies topics can be approached in the same way: topics such as voting rights, "taxation without representation," the westward movement, and the Monroe Doctrine. The point is that value questions tend to arouse student interest and motivation and, wherever possible, you should capitalize on them to begin a problem of social inquiry. In Chapter 15, we discuss other strategies for teaching value-laden issues.

Starting with a Scientific Question

Not all problems, however, lend themselves easily to starting with a value question. You should vary your procedures so that a class will not become bored by the same approach to every problem. You can skillfully pose what Festinger[3] has called "cognitive dissonance" by introducing a "discrepant event" as an intellectual teaser to arouse curiosity and motivation. Some examples that might be used are

1. How can the Eskimos live in the extremes of the Arctic climate when people who have recently moved north from temperate zones have great difficulty adjusting to the new climate?
2. Why does the city of Seattle have so little snow when other cities at the same latitude or even lower, such as Minneapolis, Chicago, Cleveland, Rochester, and Boston, all have so much more?
3. Why can a nation with such a high standard of living as the United States have more than 30 million people living in poverty? (About 250 million people lived in the United States in 1989.)

These examples illustrate ways of using questions to arouse motivation and interest in a problem. Either of the two approaches shown above may be used. Starting with the value question first has the advantage of introducing a strong emotional element that helps to elicit student interest. You must then take steps to shift the focus of the discussion so that it will center on the scientific questions. If a value question is inappropriate as a starter or the topic does not lend itself, then a scientific question framed in such a way as to create "cognitive dissonance" by posing a discrepant event may be used to arouse interest and motivation.

Finally, we repeat a cautionary note raised in Chapters 1 and 3. While we reassert strongly that values are an essential consideration in social science inquiry and decision-making, we note that some value issues are heavily laden with emotional overtones. Thus, you must judge the merit of the value questions by such criteria as the age and maturity of the students, their ability to understand the issue, and its relevance to the school curriculum. This is not to suggest that difficult or controversial value questions should be avoided, or that unsolved problems of the future should not be raised, but only that you should choose them with care, thoughtfulness, and appropriateness to the curriculum. Questions that have only shock effect for young students or that invade personal privacy should be avoided.

Problem Formulation

The next stage of the inquiry process is to take the aroused interest and begin to identify the components of a problem. The problem must be one that is researchable, for which there is some possible answer, about which some hypotheses or test questions can be formulated, data collected, and generalizations drawn.

1. Is marijuana harmful? How is it different from alcoholic beverages? What are the social consequences of using drugs?
2. The American shipbuilding industry has been declining steadily since the 1920s. What has the government done to protect its maritime interests and to prevent almost all its import-export trade from being carried in "foreign flag" vessels?
3. What was our town like in the "olden days"? How did it get that way? How did it change as different groups of people came to live in it?
4. How have democratic societies in the past maintained a balance between the need to achieve a consensus on certain common values and the right of people to dissent?

In the framework described in Chapter 3, these problems are identified as *scientific questions.* Working hypotheses can be formulated for each, concepts clarified, data gathered and analyzed, and generalizations derived. Each can be verified by repeated inquiries. Each makes use of data from one or more of the social sciences.

Another approach to formulating an inquiry problem is to pose the same questions as *value questions,* rather than scientific ones. Value questions emphasize the "should" or "ought" of a possible course of action and often imply that some course of action is prized over some other. Here are the same four questions rewritten as value questions:

1. Should we legalize the use of marijuana as we did with liquor?
2. Should the government continue to support the shipping industry but not the trucking industry?

3. Should our town pass a new zoning ordinance to prevent the building of a new low-income housing project?
4. The early Puritans banished Roger Williams into the wilderness of Rhode Island for his "obnoxious heresies." Should we take similar action against some of the very outspoken critics of today?

CONTROVERSIAL ISSUES

Questions such as those listed above readily engage student interest and enthusiasm in the topic. At the same time, however, they are also controversial and come quickly to the heart of conflicting value patterns in the community. Although few school officials would deny their rightful place in the school curriculum, they are often relegated to the corner as sensitive topics requiring "special attention." As a result, they are seldom asked in any serious way. Too often, little scientific inquiry has preceded them and no reliable data have been gathered. The teacher is often left with the bland assertion "each person is entitled to his or her own opinion." True, perhaps. But we strongly take issue with the corollary assertion that "one opinion is as good as another." An unsubstantiated or uncritical judgment is certainly not as good as one that has been carefully made by weighing the alternatives, analyzing relevant data, and selecting the choice consistent with one's value system. To help you avoid this uncritical approach, we will deal with strategies for exploring value questions in Chapter 15. For our purpose here, let us simply say that the value question can be used to formulate a worthwhile problem for investigation.

THEORIES AND VALUES

One further issue should also be raised: that of formulating a problem within the context of a particular theory or value structure. If the problem were geographic, that is, concerning the development of a city at a particular place, you might help students phrase questions in terms of the city's central location and spatial distance from other cities: "How far is this city from other settlement areas? Is it centrally located and conveniently accessible from all points?" Such questions borrow from the theories of urban geography that attempt to explain the location of cities in terms of space and distance.

In quite the same way, one's value position can also shape the formulation of a problem. The question can be worded so that a normative word or phrase spells out the framework of the question and the dimensions of the problem. Note how the italicized word gives a particular thrust or direction to the following questions:

What is the most *efficient* route for the construction of this new interstate highway?

How can school desegregation be accomplished within the concept of *neighborhood school* pattern?

> What role did English *pirates* such as Sir Francis Drake play in the decline of Spain as a world power?

Note that in the first two examples given above *efficiency*, rather than aesthetic quality or relocation of people, dictates the solution of the highway route. Desegregation must be accomplished in such a way as to preserve the traditional values of the local school—implying not only the limited use of transportation, but also the retention of residential patterns and local control of school policies. Finally, the word *pirates* assumes that the English were villainous for having seized the Spanish treasure at sea, but makes no similar implication about the Conquistadores, who plundered the Incas and the Aztecs to obtain the gold in the first place. From another point of view, the noble title "Sir" suggests the way in which England's Queen Elizabeth I chose to view the same exploits as heroic deeds furthering England's national interests.

Photographs are rich sources for generating hypotheses. This photograph, which shows women trimming currency in 1907, can be used to help students formulate hypotheses about women's work roles today and yesterday. (*Source:* The National Archives, Washington, D.C.)

DEVELOPING THE HYPOTHESES

Each of the problems illustrated above is still insufficiently focused to be well researched or to guide the inquirer's research. Before a question can be fruitfully researched, it must be clearly defined, and related hypotheses must be formulated. In Chapter 3, we discussed the key functions of hypotheses and ways of distinguishing them from other kinds of statements. Here we shall introduce several formats for stating hypotheses.

The simplest way of stating a hypothesis is to make a simple statement that states the expected relationship between concepts in a statement to be tested. For example, a class that is studying industrialization might hypothesize: "The development of new technology results in the growth of new industries and increased productivity." A primary class that is studying local communities might hypothesize, "The larger a community is, the more services it provides for its residents." To be sure, statements such as these look much like generalizations, yet it should be made clear that they are merely statements *whose truth is yet to be tested.* For complex problems, it·may be that a class will develop several hypotheses, each one related to the problem.

Another way of stating the hypothesis is to use an "if . . . then" format. This makes unmistakably clear the conditional and tentative nature of the statement. The examples cited above might be rephrased to read: "*If* there is a new development in technology, *then* there will be a growth in the number of new industries and in the amount of productivity." The second hypothesis might be phrased: "*If* the number of people in a community increases, *then* the community will provide more services for the people." The chief value of the "if. . . then" format is that it requires the student to set the concepts in their correct relationship and makes much more readily apparent any fallacies in the logic of the hypothesis. In addition, the conditional format of the "if" statement allows the students to give fuller reign to their hunches and best guesses. It allows them to send up trial balloons, whereas the statement format tends to suggest a more polished and finished result.

Perhaps a word should be added about the problem of the logic of the conditional "if . . . then" hypothesis. You must be alert to the problems faced by students when language becomes confusing. If a statement is worded negatively or double negatives are used when a positive assertion is intended, students will be confused. As a simple rule, it is perhaps best to state the conditional hypotheses in a positive form and avoid the use of negatives wherever possible. If opposite or inverse relationships exist, positively phrased relational concepts should be introduced. Using the example of the community study again, the alternate hypotheses might be: "If the population of a community declines, then the community can provide fewer services to the residents." This is a much simpler form to deal with than a negatively phrased hypothesis such as: "If the population does not increase, then the community will not increase the services it provides." Not only might the logic be fallacious, but the evidence might not support it either, for many other possibilities may exist under which a community might increase the services it offers.

Logical fallacies are another problem. For most students, the rules of formal logic are much too abstract and complex to tackle in a straightforward way. These might be better left to upper-grade classes in the junior or senior high schools. Young students can learn to deal, however, with the problem of the sufficiency of evidence and whether the conclusion is warranted from the data presented. Operating in a simple, inductive framework, you can help students question the size of the sample, its representativeness, and the extent to which the evidence presented validly represents the conditions and the conclusions expressed in the hypothesis.

One further problem to be mentioned in connection with hypothesis formation is the definition of terms. Some words—such as *culture, standard of living, productivity,* and the like—must be carefully defined so that data can be found about the hypothesis. When complex or abstract concepts are used, it is important to clarify and sharpen the hypotheses by carefully defining terms. This will help to guide and direct the collection of data so that valid conclusions can be drawn.

Collection of Data

Central to the task of social inquiry is the collection of data that bear on the problem. As we indicated above, the carefully formulated hypothesis sets the stage to guide and direct the collection of the data. It sweeps away the irrelevant and focuses sharply on the specific questions at issue. If students have defined the terms in their hypothesis carefully, they can then begin searching for appropriate data. It is important, however, that you see that sources for data are available for the questions that students are most apt to ask, for nothing is more frustrating to the students than to have developed fine hypotheses, and then have no resources for gathering pertinent data.

Many methods for gathering data are available to the social studies teacher. In Chapter 3, we discussed how the experiment, the case study, and the sample survey can be used in the social studies. Basically, each of these methods asks: *Who? What? When? Where?* and *How?*

What tools did the Iroquois Indians have before they came into contact with the white settlers? Afterward? Where and how were they used? What evidence is available? Is the evidence direct or must we make inferences from other data?

What beliefs did the Iroquois hold about their origin? Life in an afterworld? Or the forces of nature such as the sun, wind, rains, etc.? What evidence do we have? Or must we infer it from some secondary source?

Similar questions can be raised about the problem of technology and industrialization, as well as about the size of the community and the number of services it offers.

As we gather these data, it becomes important to ask questions about the source of and evidence for the data. Is the source primary or secondary? Do we have direct evidence or is it based only on inference? If the class is interviewing a parent or town official, is the interviewee reporting his or her own observations or direct knowledge, or is it perhaps only hearsay (i. e., passing along what someone else has said)?

Despite the use of a single textbook in many classrooms, the teacher still has many other options. Publishers have produced supplementary materials or kits that contain original documentary source materials (some in edited form), maps, charts, statistical data, transparencies, filmstrips, 8-mm closed loop cartridges, and audio tape cassettes. Software has been developed for classroom microcomputers that will provide large arrays of data for simulating decision-making on such topics as westward expansion, national elections, and agricultural and economic development in developing nations. Moreover, much of this data has been programmed so students can predict and plot out on a graph the trend of the data over time, or the effect if certain variables are altered. Thus microcomputers now make it possible for students to ask "What would happen if. . .?" and to obtain valid data to evaluate a proposed course of action. These newer resource materials are discussed more fully in Chapter 8.

Collecting and Recording the Data

One of the problems associated with data gathering in any investigation is the problem of collecting and recording it in some simple and convenient form. A simple device developed by Hilda Taba and her associates is the data retrieval chart. This is no more than a chart that allows students to log in the data they have found in answer to a series of questions related to the basic concepts involved in the hypothesis. Its chief value is that it can easily be expanded to include more than one data sample; it allows students to ask the same questions across two or more samples. Thus comparisons and contrasts can be easily made. A data retrieval chart related to the Iroquois Indians is shown in Table 4.1. Each of the questions is related to one of the concepts, and the chart forms an easy method of collecting and recording a relatively large amount of data in an abbreviated form. The exact questions to be asked can be agreed on in a class discussion, and the potential is present for adding additional questions or more concepts as the research progresses. A key point to stress here is the open-endedness of this approach. Students are limited only by the kinds of questions they ask and the data sources available to them.

Deriving Generalizations

A strategy for formulating generalizations was outlined in Chapter 3. In this chapter, we call attention to the types of questions asked and their sequence in relation to the hypotheses that have been formulated and the data that have been gathered. Let us use the problem, "How did the colonists in North

TABLE 4.1. Data Retrieval Chart: Iroquois Indians

Analytical Concepts and Related Questions	Before Contact with Colonists	After Contact with Colonists
Tools What kind of tools did the Iroquois use: For hunting? For food? For farming? Other uses? What were they made of? Where did they get the material? How plentiful?		
Beliefs What did the Iroquois believe about: Origin of their tribes? Life after death? The forces of nature? Did they have a folklore or mythology? Taboos?		
Religious Practices How did they express their beliefs? Dances, ceremonies? Did they perform special ceremonies in honor of the gods? Was there a special person in charge of ceremonies? Were there special rites at birth, death, marriage, adolescence? Did they wear charms, amulets, or dress that had special meaning?		

America influence the cultures of the Iroquois Indians?" When the data retrieval chart (Table 4.1) is filled in, it is then possible to ask a series of questions about the data that helps to establish *relationships, explanations, inferences,* and *meaning.*

> *Discrimination of Data:* What do you notice about the data on the Iroquois' use of tools during these two time periods? About their beliefs and religious practices?
> *Comparison and Contrast:* What similarities do you see? What differences?

Relationships: What things seem to be connected to one another?
Explanation: How do you account for this? What may have caused what?
Inference: What do these data mean? Suggest? Or infer?
Generalization: What can you conclude from all this? What can you say
    that is generally true, based on these two data samples?

It is important to stress here that the series of questions listed above is designed to result in the formation of inferences and generalizations, which by their very nature tend to be more abstract than any of the single instances of data, or any summation of them. We stress this because the past practices of teaching have been so heavily loaded in favor of the collection and memorization of vast collections of isolated data. Little or no effort has been made to establish relationships in any meaningful way. What counted most was that the facts were true and verifiable; they could be pointed to with certainty and without equivocation.

In contrast, the process of developing inferences and generalizations takes considerable time and requires much give and take among students and between students and you. Most important, the process must be free of any dogmatic conclusions since the results depend so heavily on the varied ways in which the students conceptualize the relationship among data, develop explanations, and seek inferences beyond the literal meaning of the data. Thus, the strategy has much flexibility and a high degree of open-endedness, provided you are willing to accept student ideas and help the student expand on them.

A caution should be added about the level of abstraction of the generalization. As indicated in Chapter 3, generalizations may be of high or low order depending on the scope of the sample from which the data have been drawn and the universality of the application. In the example of the Iroquois, the generalization is limited both to that group and to the time period of the early contact with white settlers. For the generalization to have a higher level of meaning, data from similar samples of cultural contact must be gathered from other groups and times. If this were to be the major emphasis of study, students might plan to examine, in addition to the Iroquois, the contact and cultural exchange between the Romans and the Goths, the Aztecs and the Spanish conquerors, and the New England Yankees and the European immigrants. Table 4.2 shows how a data retrieval chart might look when additional samples of data are used to study one's own local community and its past.

While much has been said about the use of high-order generalizations for organizing a curriculum and about the development of theory based on a well-integrated set of high-order generalizations, you must be aware that this is a long and slow process. Most of the work studied at particular grade levels will yield relatively low- or intermediate-order generalizations. What is important, however, is that schools must place greater stress on the coordination between grade levels to maximize the potential cumulative effect. Only when students learn to build consecutively on previously developed work will they

TABLE 4.2. Data Retrieval Chart: The Changing Nature of Our Town

Analytical Concepts	During Indian Days	Period of Early Settlers 1660–1740	Our Town a Century Ago	Our Town Today
Geographical Site Boundaries? Physical features? Climate? Natural resources? How used?				
Technological Development What tools used? New machines invented? Other discoveries?				
Utilization of Place and Space Location of homes? Farms? Businesses? Mills? Factories? Percent of town for each?				
Population Distribution Indians? Farmers? Merchants? Mill hands? Ethnic groups? Religious groups? Density? Rate of growth?				
Connecting Links Main roads? Where to where? New routes? Old or abandoned routes?				

be able to develop high-order generalizations or gain experience in synthesizing these into larger packages called theories.

Summary of the Discussion on Generalizations

We have shown how a deliberate strategy of questioning can be built into the model of social inquiry presented in Chapter 3. Distinctions were made between the need to arouse interest on the part of the student and the identification of the problem itself and its components. Problems can be formulated as either scientific or value questions. Techniques were suggested for focusing on the hypothesis as a framework to guide and direct the search for data. Two possible formats were suggested for the hypothesis: the statement form and the conditional "if. . . then" form. A number of ways were suggested for gathering data related to the hypothesis. Emphasis was placed on the use of analytical questions that flowed from the basic concepts used in the problem. The data retrieval chart was presented as a convenient method of recording and collecting data for the questions asked in the data-gathering process. Finally, a series of questions was presented that can be used to teach students to make inferences and generalizations. These questions stressed the processes of discrimination, comparison and contrast, relationships, explanation, inference, and generalization. Distinctions were made about the level of generalizations that could be developed in classrooms and the problems related to formulating high-order generalizations and relating these to a comprehensive theory.

HIGHER LEVELS OF QUESTIONING

In the preceding section we discussed a strategy of questioning based on a model of social inquiry. In this section, we shall describe another strategy of questioning, based on a somewhat different model of thinking processes: Bloom's *Taxonomy of Educational Objectives: Handbook I—Cognitive Domain*.[4]

Bloom and his associates originally developed the taxonomy as a tool for classifying educational objectives. They identified six levels of instructional goals. The first deals with the recall of specified knowledge; the remaining five deal with various cognitive or intellectual skills: comprehension, application, analysis, synthesis, and evaluation. A chart showing the operational definitions of each of these categories is presented in Table 4.3.

Built into the taxonomy is an assumption that the categories are cumulative and hierarchical. One must have knowledge in order to comprehend. Application requires both knowledge and comprehension. Each of the higher-level categories progresses similarly by including all the categories below it, as shown in Table 4.3. The hierarchical notion is based on the increasing degree of complexity and sophistication of the cognitive processes as well as their cumulative character. Let us see how the operational definition of each category of the Bloom taxonomy can be used to describe different levels of questioning.

Knowledge Questions

A knowledge-level question requires the student to *recall* specific facts, names, places, trends, previously learned concepts, generalizations, or theories. The key factor is that the student is expected to produce from memory some previously learned knowledge.

**TABLE 4.3. The Taxonomy of Educational Objectives—Cognitive Domain:
A Hierarchical Classification of Intellectual Abilities and Skills**

Knowledge (memory)

Ability to recall, to bring to mind the appropriate material which may include

terminology
classification
trends
criteria
methodology
generalizations
structure

Comprehension

Ability to know what is being communicated and to be able to make some use of the materials or ideas contained in it.
Such behavior involves:
translation into other terms or forms;
interpretation, a reordering of ideas and understanding of their interrelationships;
extrapolation, the making of estimates or predictions based on understanding, tendencies, trends, or conditions described in the communication.

Requires:
Knowledge

Application

Ability to use ideas, principles, and generalizations in new situations.
Involves being able to remember and bring to bear on given new material the appropriate generalizations and principles.

Requires:
Knowledge and comprehension

SOURCE: Adapted from Benjamin S. Bloom, Ed., *Taxonomy of Educational Objectives: Handbook I—The Cognitive Domain* (New York: McKay, 1956). Reprinted with the publisher's permission.

CLASSROOM SITUATIONS

Knowledge questions are most often used when students have read material in a text or reference book, watched a film or videotape, or completed a unit of study. The question refers specifically to what has been studied previously. The expected or correct answer is usually a verbatim repetition from the text, a class discussion, or some similar source. Given such settings, typical knowledge-level questions include:

Analysis

Ability to identify the component parts of an idea and to establish the logical relationships of the parts to the whole. The activity involved must emphasize the use of inductive or deductive reasoning processes in some form.

Requires:

Knowledge, comprehension, and application

Synthesis

Ability to draw on elements from many sources and put these together into a structure or unified organization or whole not clearly there before.

Requires:

Knowledge, comprehension, application, and analysis

Evaluation

Ability to make judgment about the value, for some purpose, of ideas or procedures, solutions, methods, materials. Uses criteria (determined by student or given to him) for appraising the extent to which particulars are accurate, effective, economical, or satisfying.

Requires:

Knowledge, comprehension, application, analysis, and synthesis

1. List the major cities in the northeast region of the country.
2. Give some of the main reasons for the growth of manufacturing.
3. What were Jefferson's views on liberty?
4. Identify the main causes of the Civil War.

KEY WORDS

A number of key words can be identified in your questions. These give students clues to the cognitive level expected in the reply. There is reason to believe that the use of this kind of "grammar of the interrogative" can be very fruitful in helping students learn to use higher-level cognitive processes.

Some examples of key words usually indicating a knowledge-level question are

define	identify	name	show	tell
describe	list	recall	state	write

Comprehension Questions

A comprehension-level question requires the student to understand the meaning of an oral or written communication and to make some use of it. Three important subcategories are included within the large category of comprehension: *translation, interpretation,* and *extrapolation.*

In a *translation* question, students are expected to express an idea in similar or equivalent terms. They are not expected to explain or reason with the idea, but only to restate it in a way that approximates its literal meaning. "Tell in your own words. . ." is one of the simplest forms of a translation question.

Interpretation requires the ability to relate things to one another, to reorder, to put into some arrangement or sequence, to establish relationships by comparing or contrasting, or to separate essentials from nonessentials.

Extrapolation requires a student to predict or estimate an event from a known pattern or trend. This frequently includes the ability to project trends on the basis of statistical data or occasionally to interpolate when data are missing.

The key factor is the ability to make appropriate inferences as to the probable trend or continued direction of the event, phenomenon, or pattern of ideas that can still be regarded as legitimate extensions of the original data.

CLASSROOM SITUATIONS

From the explanation given above, one can readily see that comprehensive questions have the potential for being a vital part of many classroom activities. The data retrieval charts introduced earlier in this chapter (Tables 4.1 and 4.2) offer many possibilities for teaching students to compare and contrast data, to establish relationships between items, to seek explanations, to state implications, and to make inferences. In primary grades, children might simply point to different items in a picture and orally explain the relationships involved. In a much more sophisticated way, students in an upper grade might use a graph to predict the probable trend of population increase or decline in large urban centers. In contrast to the knowledge-level questions which involve the recall from memory of a previously learned response, all these activities are new experiences for the student. Thus a test question must use materials or situations different from those used previously in class study. To repeat the same question without change reduces it to the knowledge-recall level. Given such conditions, typical comprehension-level questions might include:

1. Explain how "division of labor" takes place in a factory.
2. Contrast the systems of education found in the United States, France, and the Soviet Union. What aspects do they have in common?
3. Explain in your own words the statement attributed to Clemenceau, "Wars are too important to be left to generals."
4. Given census data for 1960, 1970, 1980, and 1990 for the 10 largest cities in the United States, what trend do you see emerging? What would you predict the population of these cities to be in 2000? 2010?

KEY WORDS

Some key words that usually indicate a comprehension-level question are

compare	estimate	illustrate	relate
conclude	explain	infer	reorder
contrast	extend	interpolate	rephrase
demonstrate	extrapolate	interpret	tell in your own words
differentiate	give an example of	predict	
distinguish	hypothesize	rearrange	

Application Questions

In an application question, students are required to demonstrate that they can make use of some previously learned relationship or idea. An application question differs from comprehension-level questions in that the student is not told specifically how to apply a particular idea, but must be able to select the appropriate idea, concept, or principle and apply it correctly to the given situation. In short, application requires students to transfer their learning to a new situation with little or no direction.

CLASSROOM SITUATIONS

Application questions most often require students to solve some problem, to construct something such as a model farm or town, to put some skill into practice, or to take some appropriate form of action within the social context of the real world outside the classroom. Primary grade students who have studied transportation routes and the exchange of goods and services might apply these concepts and related generalizations by constructing a model town and play acting with toy trains or trucks. Older students can apply ideas and concepts by role playing a session of the United Nations or a state legislature as it attempts to decide some important issue. Simulation games, such as *Democracy* or *Napoli,* although designed with a set of quite specific rules, require students to apply the principles of the political process to a fast moving and exciting game that comes very close to approximating the real-life situation. Finally, the social studies classroom meets the real world when students actually apply what they are learning by engaging in social action situations. This may take the form of participation in a student council (provided it has a truly meaningful role in a school and is not simple window dressing), writing letters to the editor, collecting signatures on a petition for some local issue, or ringing doorbells in support of a political candidate. Given such settings, typical application questions might include:

1. Using the sand table, develop a plan for and build a model layout of a medieval manor or estate.
2. Locate as many different kinds of material as possible on the Pilgrims' first Thanksgiving using the card catalog and various kinds of reference materials in the school library.
3. Write a play (or role playing a scene) that illustrates the controversy about whether or not the United States should have joined the League of Nations after World War I.
4. Develop a plan for calling the community's attention to the seriousness of the environmental pollution problem. Gather the necessary data and be prepared to present it at a public hearing on the topic. (The class has recently completed a study of pollution of the environment. The community seems unaware of the problem.)

KEY WORDS

Some key words that usually indicate an application-level question are

apply	demonstrate
build	develop
construct	solve

Analysis Questions

The analysis-level question requires a student to break down an idea into its component parts and distinguish these parts with a conscious knowledge of their relationship to one another. This involves three different abilities.

First, the student must be able to distinguish assumptions from conclusions, to determine whether a conclusion is warranted from the evidence presented, or to detect the presence of an unstated but implied assumption that may invalidate the initial premises. Second, the student must be able to recognize the relationship of part to whole, to recognize which facts are essential to support the main thesis, or to distinguish relevant from irrelevant data. The third is the ability to recognize the form or organizational structure of a statement or set of ideas, and to relate this to the overall intent or meaning. Thus, a student can recognize various parts, such as the major theme and local variations in a political candidate's speech, the techniques of persuasion in advertising or propaganda, or the viewpoint or bias of a writer in a historical account.

The difference between *interpretation* and *analysis* questions depends on the extent to which the student is *aware of and makes use of the formal processes of reasoning.* At the interpretation level, a student may make inferences and generalizations, or formulate hypotheses, without reference to the formal processes involved. For the same processes to be at the analysis level, the student must be consciously aware of these intellectual processes and the organizational structure.

CLASSROOM SITUATIONS

The strategies of teaching for social inquiry, valuing, and decision-making discussed in this book offer many possibilities for analytical thinking. It should be noted, however, that thinking at the analysis level involves a considerable degree of abstract reasoning. The processes identified above dealing with the logical quality of thought, and the form of expression they take, are rather high level and complex. All too often students simply have no experience with this type of thinking process. It is important that students have sufficient practice and experience with thinking at the analysis level. The inductive strategies described in the preceding pages for making inferences and generalizations should provide the kind of experience necessary to help develop abstract thinking.

Given sufficient experience with this mode of thinking, then, it is possible for students to distinguish a fact from an opinion, a hypothesis from a generalization, or to determine whether the evidence gathered is sufficient to warrant the conclusion that is drawn. Students at upper-grade levels can learn to detect unstated assumptions in arguments, or identify elements of form and style in primary source materials that indicate personal points of view, biases, or prejudices, as distinguished from objective evidence. They can also learn to identify specific techniques of persuasion borrowed from mass media advertising, now being used so frequently in political campaigns. Commonly available material, such as bumper stickers, lapel buttons, billboards, newspaper ads, and TV spot commercials for political candidates all can be used to illustrate such techniques as the half-truth, the catchy slogan, the appeal to selected values, stacking the deck in favor of one side, the deliberate distortion, and the big lie. For students to be able to recognize the *intentional* use of these techniques when they come upon them in campaign literature or in public statements gives evidence of analytical thinking. Given such settings, typical questions at the analysis level might be

1. Analyze the following slogans. What techniques of persuasion are used in them?
    > The United States: Love it or leave it.
    > Keep your local police force independent.
    > Law and order.
    > Save the whales.
    > No Nukes.
2. Having studied the problem of cultural change following contact between the Iroquois Indians and the white settlers, a class might

formulate the generalization "A technologically less advanced society will quickly adopt aspects of the technology and belief systems of a more technologically advanced society when such societies come into extended contact." You might challenge this generalization by asking: "What data support the notion that the change will occur quickly? Or that the belief system will necessarily change because the technology is adopted? Isn't there an assumption that *all* technologically less advanced societies will react this way? Are the data from one case study sufficient to warrant this broad generalization?"

3. Analyze the views of white slaveholders as described by Frederick Douglass, an ex-slave, in his autobiography, *Narrative of the Life and Times of Frederick Douglass,* and by former slaves in Botkin's *Lay My Burden Down: A Folk History of Slavery.* Make a similar analysis of the accounts written by historians such as Ulrich B. Phillips, John Hope Franklin, Kenneth P. Stampp, and Eugene D. Genovese. What evidence is there in the choice of words, style, or form to indicate the writers' viewpoints about the white slaveholder?

KEY WORDS

Some key words that usually indicate analysis-level questions are

analyze	compare	discriminate
categorize	contrast	distinguish
classify	detect	recognize

Synthesis Questions

In a synthesis question, students are expected to be able to respond by combining or integrating a number of facts into some arrangement *that is new for them.* This often takes the form of a plan, a proposal, or some product such as a story. Synthesis differs from application in that the form of the final product is not specified, nor are the ways in which the elements may be combined. It is this feature that makes the synthesis a unique and creative activity.

In contrast to the types of questions discussed above, where each implies a particular form of thinking process, the synthesis question usually gives no cues to the student and is intended to be broad and open-ended. It does not imply any right answer, but instead assumes a variety of possible solutions, any or all of which could be acceptable. In short, it seeks divergent, rather than convergent, thinking.

CLASSROOM SITUATIONS

There are many possibilities for using creative synthesis questions in the social studies class. In the elementary school, the variety of reasons for early exploration can be synthesized into a fictional story or a carefully written paragraph. Other common forms of synthesis include writing a short play, role playing, preparing a mural, a bulletin board, or a showcase display. Most frequently overlooked, especially in the primary grades, is the short oral statement synthesizing (but not merely restating) a group of explanations for some event into a broader proposition. Here, too, is the chance for students to speculate freely and imaginatively on possible courses of events or actions, using factual data, interpretations, or new relationships to support their conjectures. "What would happen if . . . ?" "What are the possible courses of action. . .?"

Given the settings described above, typical synthesis questions might include:

1. What solutions might be proposed for the problems of air pollution?
2. What possible solutions might have been open to President Truman immediately prior to the beginning of the Korean War?
3. In how many different ways can prisoners in jails engage in rehabilitation programs?

KEY WORDS

Some key words that usually indicate a synthesis-level question are

create	formulate a solution	propose a plan
develop	make up	put together

Evaluation Questions

The evaluation question asks the student to make a judgment about the worth, merit, or value of something. Is it good or bad, beautiful or ugly, trivial or worthwhile? Students must appraise, assess, or criticize some idea, statement, or plan on the basis of specific standards or criteria that they have developed or that may be provided by you or some other source. Thus, students must indicate the criteria on which they have made their judgment and supply appropriate data to justify their positions. In short, the evaluation level requires much more than an unsubstantiated opinion based purely on personal whim or opinion.

CLASSROOM SITUATION

There are many situations in which a student can make an evaluative judgment, especially in the decision-making mode of inquiry discussed in Chapter 1. If several alternatives are given, a student must select one, using some appropriate criteria. Under these conditions, the evaluation level is heavily cognitive, even though a judgment about worth or value is being made.

Typical evaluation questions might be:

1. Which policy will result in the greatest good for the greatest number?

2. For what reasons would you favor. . . ?
3. Which books would you consider of greatest value? Upon what criteria?
4. Evaluate that idea in terms of cost and community acceptance.

It is important to note that the student must make an informed judgment on the worth, merit, goodness, or evil of something based on a set of criteria and supporting data. Helping the students learn to identify appropriate criteria is just as important as is the making of the value judgment. The evaluation must be supported by data. It is important to recognize, however, that different students can arrive at different evaluations depending on the criteria established and the data presented to them. Thus, a student is not necessarily right or wrong in the evaluation that he or she makes. Rather, it is the appropriateness of the criteria and how well he or she has supported the judgment with data or a rationale.

Although much social studies software teaches low-level knowledge and skills, some of the computer simulation programs can help students to formulate and respond to creative and divergent questions. (*Source:* Terry Malinowski, Northshore Public Schools, Seattle.)

KEY WORDS

Key words that would indicate an evaluation-level question are

choose	evaluate	select
decide	judge	which do you consider

Creative and Divergent Questions

Finally, we wish to stress the importance of creative and divergent thinking in social studies and the need to ask questions that stimulate these intellectual processes. Creative thinking involves the formation of new ideas, novel or unconventional approaches to old problems, or some different arrangement of existing parts or ideas in order to create something entirely new. It is the opposite of rote memory, copying, imitating, or making minor variations in a familiar pattern. Closely related is the term "divergent thinking," which refers to open-ended, unconventional or nontraditional thinking. It is in sharp contrast to convergent thinking, which emphasizes the single, limited, or traditionally approved "right answer." We do not underestimate the importance of accuracy in basic factual knowledge, or the knowledge of established traditions; nevertheless, problem solving and decision-making in the twenty-first century will surely require new insights, unique approaches, and radical departures from many of our customary or traditional ways of thinking.

There is only a thin line between the creative and imaginative response and fantasy. Indeed, the fantasy or science fiction written by Jules Verne in the 1890s about travel to the moon and other planets has become the scientific reality of our day! Thus, you should not label a student's novel or unusual solution to a problem as "silly" or "impossible," but should rather encourage the student to explain the chain of reasoning or new insights that led to the solution. Schools should do everything possible to encourage creative abilities in students. You should also be slow to criticize or dismiss highly unusual ideas, nonconformist approaches, or challenges to conventional mores or wisdom.

It is a sad commentary upon the history of science that the insights and theories of some of our most brilliant scientists—Galileo, Newton, Darwin, Freud and Einstein—were for many years rejected and dismissed by teachers, scientists, and intellectuals as impossible or bizarre. Yet, ultimately, each revolutionized our thinking and changed the course of developments in their fields.

For these reasons we encourage you to ask and prod students with such questions:

1. How many different ways could that be done?
2. What new approaches could you suggest to remedy the weakness of this plan?

3. Could we rearrange the parts of this mural on exploration and discovery to create a new effect?

4. Are there some approaches that have not been tried yet? What would it take to make them feasible or workable?

SUMMARY

Two questioning strategies were presented in this chapter. The first was based on the model of social inquiry developed in Chapter 3. It suggested a variety of questions that could be used for each step of the inquiry model. The other strategy was based on the six levels of cognitive processes identified in Bloom's *Taxonomy*. We discussed the cognitive activity required at each level and identified a series of key words that could be used to form questions at each cognitive level. Lastly, we discussed the importance of creative and divergent questions in helping students to develop new, unique, or unconventional approaches to problem solving and decision-making.

DISCUSSION QUESTIONS AND EXERCISES

1. Children in the primary grades often study some aspect of their local community. Write some questions that might be used to express doubt or concern to begin the process of social inquiry: (1) a value question followed by (2) scientific questions.

2. Take several conventional topics such as the westward movement, the American Revolution, the writing of the U.S. Constitution, or the Age of Exploration and prepare an opening value question for each. Then show how the discussion could be shifted by asking appropriate scientific questions.

3. A social inquiry problem can often be begun by introducing a "discrepant event" as an intellectual teaser to arouse curiosity and motivation. Select three such situations and write questions involving a discrepant event that could be used to start an inquiry study.

4. Using the questions you prepared in Questions 1 through 3, write suitable hypotheses for each that could be used in a social inquiry study. Write each first in the statement form, and then in the "if . . . then" format.

5. The use of the conditional "if . . . then" form for stating hypotheses has been described in this chapter. What are some of the advantages and limitations of this approach? What difficulties related to the rules of logic and semantic confusion should be expected? How can they be minimized?

6. Using any of the hypotheses you wrote for Question 4, prepare a data retrieval chart for gathering appropriate information. Be sure you identify the major concepts from the hypothesis and list a number of related questions that will help guide the search for data under each concept. Identify two or more possible samples (time periods, cultures, nations, etc.) that would provide good sources for making comparisons with the data found (see Tables 4.1 and 4.2).

7. Classroom questions can be written at a variety of cognitive levels. Take any one of the areas you identified above for social science inquiry. Write a question at the knowledge level of Bloom's *Taxonomy*. Then expand the same topic into six questions, one at each of the levels of the taxonomy.
8. Select a social science inquiry problem different from the one used in Question 7. Write several creative or divergent questions.
9. Define and illustrate each of the following terms:

a. value question
b. scientific questions
c. cognitive dissonance
d. "if. . . then" proposition
e. data retrieval chart
f. taxonomy
g. cognitive domain

h. the six categories of the Bloom *Taxonomy* (knowledge, comprehension, application, analysis, synthesis, evaluation)
i. convergent questions
j. divergent questions
k. creative questions

NOTES

1. For a comprehensive overview of questioning techniques and their use in teaching, see William W. Wilen, Ed., *Questions, Questioning Techniques, and Effective Teaching* (Washington, D.C.: National Education Association, 1987); also William W. Wilen and Ambrose A. Clegg, Jr., "Effective Questions and Questioning: A Review of Research," *Theory and Research in Social Education*, Vol. 15, No. 2 (Spring 1986), pp. 153–161.

2. Meredith D. Gall and Tom Rhody, "Review of Research on Questioning Techniques," in William W. Wilen, Ed., *Questions, Questioning Techniques, and Effective Teaching* (Washington, D.C.: National Education Association, 1987).

3. Leon Festinger, *A Theory of Cognitive Dissonance* (Stanford: Stanford University Press, 1957).

4. Benjamin S. Bloom, Ed., *Taxonomy of Educational Objectives: Handbook I: Cognitive Domain* (New York: McKay, 1956).

FOR FURTHER READING

Gall, Meredith, and Tom Rhody. "Review of Research on Questioning Techniques," in William W. Wilen, Ed., *Questions, Questioning Techniques, and Effective Teaching*. Washington, D.C.: National Education Association, 1987.

Hunkins, Francis P. *Involving Students in Questioning*. Boston: Allyn & Bacon, 1976.

Hunkins, Francis P. *Teaching Thinking Through Effective Questioning*. Needham Heights, MA: Christopher-Gordon Publishers, 1989.

Wilen, William W., Ed. *Questions, Questioning Techniques, and Effective Teaching*. Washington, D.C.: National Education Association, 1987.

Wilen, William W., and Ambrose A. Clegg, Jr. "Effective Questions and Questioning: A Review of Research," *Theory and Research in Social Education*, Vol. 15, No. 2 (Spring 1986), pp. 153–161.

PART _____ II

Skills, Issues, and Materials

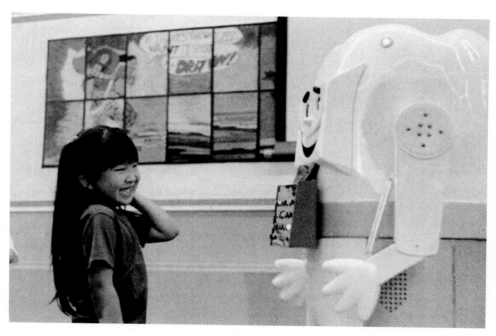

(*Source*: Edna Kellman, Seattle Public Schools.)

Part II focuses on several important components of a sound social studies curriculum: skills, social issues, and materials. While reflective citizen actors must master facts, concepts, and generalizations, it is also essential that they gain proficiency in the processes involved in gathering, evaluating, and processing knowledge. Reflective citizen actors need thinking skills, social science inquiry skills, academic or study skills, and the skills needed to function effectively in group discussion and research. Chapter 5 discusses these important skills. Most of the materials used to gain proficiency in social studies skills are reading materials. Chapter 6 describes ways that social studies teachers can help students to improve their reading skills.

Reflective citizen actors frequently use their knowledge and skills to help them make decisions on important social issues. Some of the important social issues within our nation and world are described in Chapter 7. Activities that can be used to help students gain information about these issues are also described. Social issues are society's unresolved problems. These problems deeply concern large numbers of citizens, and citizens strongly disagree about their causes and solutions. Citizens also have deep value commitments to social issues. Social issues can be used effectively to help students develop decision-making and citizen action skills.

To gain the knowledge needed to participate successfully in a democratic society, citizen actors need to use a wide variety of resources. Information from any one source will not enable citizens to acquire the range of views and perspectives needed to make reflective decisions and to take successful citizen action. Chapter 8 discusses a range of resources that you can use to help students formulate concepts and generalizations, to clarify their values, make decisions, and to participate in reflective citizen action. The materials discussed include reading materials (such as the textbook), visual, audio and audiovisual materials, the microcomputer, and the community.

5

Teaching Social Studies Skills

The social studies curriculum is designed to help students attain the knowledge, attitudes, and skills needed to participate effectively in a democratic society. Chapter 3 describes the knowledge components of the social studies curriculum, which include higher-level concepts and generalizations needed by citizens to make reflective decisions. Skills are an important component of the social studies program and are discussed in several chapters in this book. Social science inquiry skills are discussed in Chapter 3; value inquiry and decision-making skills in Chapter 15. This chapter discusses skills that should be an important part of a decision-making-focused social studies curriculum: thinking skills, map and globe skills, time and chronology skills, group skills, and writing skills.

TEACHING THINKING SKILLS

Helping students develop and increase their proficiency in thinking skills should be an important goal of the social studies. While this is an accepted goal of social studies education, it is difficult to find a clear definition and a specification of thinking skills in the educational literature. Beyer, who has done extensive work on teaching thinking skills, defines thinking as a search for meaning and as a "mental process by which individuals make sense out of experience."[1] He identifies two major components, or operations, of thinking: *cognitive* and *metacognitive*.[2] Individuals engage in the cognitive operation when they generate or attempt to find meaning. Metacognition involves thinking about thinking.[3] The major cognitive operations in thinking identified by Beyer are shown in Table 5.1.

Thinking consists of a number of processes, including describing, infer-

TABLE 5.1. Major Cognitive Operations

I. Thinking Strategies

Problem Solving	*Decision Making*	*Conceptualizing*
1. Recognize a problem	1. Define the goal	1. Identify examples
2. Represent the problem	2. Identify alternatives	2. Identify common attributes
3. Devise/choose solution plan	3. Analyze alternatives	3. Classify attributes
4. Execute the plan	4. Rank alternatives	4. Interrelate categories of attributes
5. Evaluate the solution	5. Judge highest-ranked alternatives	5. Identify additional examples/nonexamples
	6. Choose "best" alternatives	6. Modify concept attributes/structure

II. Critical Thinking Skills

1. Distinguishing between verifiable facts and value claims
2. Distinguishing relevant from irrelevant information, claims, or reasons
3. Determining the factual accuracy of a statement
4. Determining the credibility of a source
5. Identifying ambiguous claims or arguments
6. Identifying unstated assumptions
7. Detecting bias
8. Identifying logical fallacies
9. Recognizing logical inconsistencies in a line of reasoning
10. Determining the strength of an argument or claim

III. Micro-Thinking Skills

1. Recall	*Reasoning*
2. Translation	inductive
3. Interpretation	deductive
4. Extrapolation	analogical
5. Application	
6. Analysis (compare, contrast, classify, seriate, etc.)	
7. Synthesis	
8. Evaluation	

SOURCE: Reprinted with permission from Barry K. Beyer, *Practical Strategies for the Teaching of Thinking* (Boston: Allyn & Bacon, Inc., 1987).

ring, analyzing, conceptualizing, generalizing, applying, and making decisions. We will discuss how you can help students develop and increase their competence in each of these skills.

Describing

Students must learn to make careful observations in order to write accurate descriptions. Students cannot make sound inferences or formulate concepts and generalizations unless they are able to carefully observe and to accurately

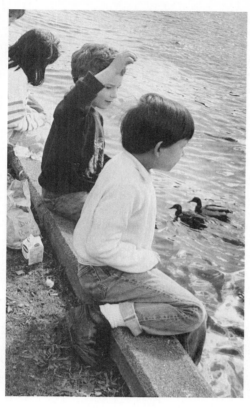

Field trips and excursions can help students to develop the ability to make careful observations needed to write accurate descriptions. (*Source*: Edna Kellman, Seattle Public Schools.)

describe their observations. To help students develop and enhance their observation and describing skills you must give them ample opportunities to observe and describe behavior in a variety of situations. Role-playing episodes, photographs, films, sound recordings, and other media can be used to enhance students' observational skills. Here are some activities that can be used to teach students to make careful observations and accurate descriptions:

One group of children in the class role plays the open-ended story "Tell-Tale" by George Shaftel.[4] After the role play, the students make a list of the major actions that occurred in the story.

A group of students makes observations in the cafeteria for a one-week period to determine the most popular foods.

A group of students conducts a small study to determine whether men or women buy more groceries at a particular store on a Saturday morning between 9:00 A.M. and 12:00 noon.

The students watch television commercials for a one-week period to determine how women are depicted.

The students view Medieval, Renaissance and French Impressionist paintings and describe the characteristics of the paintings of each period.

Making Inferences

When social scientists observe and describe, they try to tell exactly what happened without making guesses about what the observed behavior means. When they interpret and develop hypotheses about what their observations mean, social scientists are making inferences. Social scientists make inferences in order to try to understand and explain behavior. Students should be given practice in both making observations and making inferences about what they observe. However, they should be keenly aware of the differences between *observation* and *inference* and know when they are practicing each skill.

After students have made observations and descriptions while participating in the kinds of activities described above, they can then make inferences about the behavior they observed. If they find during the observation of food preferences in the cafeteria that hot dogs are more popular than beef stew, they can make some inferences about why this is the case. However, the students should realize that, while many of their inferences may be correct, the inferences are actually hypotheses which must be tested before they can be accepted as valid knowledge. While students may assume that hot dogs are preferred to beef stew because hot dogs taste better than beef stew, their inference will become less certain if they do a survey and find that the most important factor that influences choice of a dish at lunch time is the dish chosen by close friends.

Analyzing Information

The ability to make careful observations and to formulate inferences will help students analyze information. When students analyze information, they identify its parts and establish a logical relationship of the parts to each other and to the whole. You can use reading, visual, and audiovisual materials to help students increase their skills in analyzing information. The following questions and activities can help students to develop and increase their ability to analyze materials:

Listen to this audiotape by Helen Caldicott, an antinuclear war advocate. Read "Three Controversies," in Edward Teller's book, *Better a Shield Than a Sword: Perspectives on Defense and Technology* (New York: The Free Press, 1987). List the major assumptions that Caldicott and Teller make about nuclear weapons. How are they alike? How are they different?

This list contains both facts and inferences about nuclear weapons. Which are facts and which are inferences?

In this selection on the removal of the Cherokee from their Georgia homeland to Oklahoma in 1838–1839 the author makes a number of conclusions and generalizations. Do the facts he presents support his conclusions and generalizations? Explain.

What are the major points made in this passage? What other points are made? How are the major points and subpoints related?

Which of the following statements best describes the film on the feminist movement we viewed?

Conceptualizing

The ability to conceptualize is important because concepts are needed to formulate important generalizations and principles. Hilda Taba and her colleagues developed some useful strategies for helping students attain and develop concepts.[5] Some of these strategies are discussed in Chapter 3.

In the Taba strategy for *developing a concept*, begin by having the students generate a list of items by asking them a question and writing their responses on the board or butcher paper. After the class has studied a unit on urbanization, you can ask a question such as "Why do families move from the city to the suburbs?" Each of the reasons the students state is listed on the board or butcher paper. When the students have listed as many reasons as they can, then ask them to group the items in as many different ways as they can. Each student can be asked to form a group. Tell the students that the items can be

What concepts about immigration can this photograph help students to develop? It shows federal immigration officials inspecting European immigrants arriving at Ellis Island in 1923. (*Source*: The National Archives, Washington, D.C.)

grouped in many different ways and that items placed in one group by one student can also be placed in another group by a different student. They should be encouraged to group items in many different ways.

Once the students have grouped the items, ask them to name or label the groups. They will find that labeling a group is the most difficult part of the process of conceptualizing, which in this strategy consists of *listing, grouping,* and *labeling.* When the students have made a list of items, grouped them, and labeled the groups, they can be asked to think of ways the groups may be changed and extended to include other items on the list. They should also be encouraged to think of other ways the items on the list may be grouped.

Another Taba strategy is called *attaining a concept.* This is a deductive strategy in which you first introduce the concept label, such as *rite of passage,* then ask students to repeat the label, and finally present them with an example of the concept, such as a description of a puberty ceremony in a preliterate culture. You can then present the students with other examples. You might have them read a description of a traditional Jewish wedding, view a film on a birth ceremony in a preliterate society, and read a description of a funeral in an American novel. You can then offer students *nonexamples* of the concept and ask them to define the concept. You can determine the students' level of mastery by asking them to identify examples from a list of examples and nonexamples. (See Table 5.2.)

Generalizing

When students form generalizations, they formulate *statements* which show how concepts are related. It is therefore important for students to be able to develop and to attain concepts before they are asked to formulate generalizations. It is also important for students to be able to make accurate descriptions, to infer, to analyze data, to differentiate, and to compare and contrast before they can formulate generalizations. The ability to formulate accurate and valid generalizations is one of the most important and sophisticated skills in the social studies.

To formulate valid higher-order generalizations, students must study several different content samples, determine how the data from different cultures and societies are alike and different, and formulate valid statements for the different sets of data. If students are studying the political system in three different nations—the United States, the United Kingdom, and the Soviet Union—the class can be divided into three research groups. Each group could study the political system of each nation in depth. When the students come together as a whole class to share and to pool their information, they can enter their data on a data retrieval chart such as the one in Table 5.3. Data retrieval charts can help students to formulate generalizations because they enable them to clearly see relationships. After studying the

TABLE 5.2. The Taba Strategy for Attaining Concepts

Teacher	Student	Teacher Follow-Through
1. Say this word after me . . .	Repeats word.	Makes sure the word is pronounced correctly.
2. This is an . . .	Looks at object, listens to description given,	Checks for any who may not be able to see or hear.
3. This is also an . . .	or reads statements which are illustrative examples of the concept.	
4. This is *not* an . . .	Looks at new object, or listens to new description, or reads statements which are not samples of the concept (but which may be similar, in similar form, etc.)	Checks again.
5. Show me an . . . or Tell me what you think an . . . is or Which of these describes an . . . or Is this an . . .	Points to object. Defines the concept. Selects from one or more descriptions.	Shows additional objects or gives fresh descriptions to test. Has students write down their definitions.
6. Asks: How then would you define an . . .	Gives summary generalization (definition) of concept.	Checks for accuracy.

SOURCE: Hilda Taba, Mary C. Durkin, Jack R. Fraenkel, and Anthony H. McNaughton, *A Teacher's Handbook to Elementary Social Studies* (Reading, MA: Addison-Wesley, 1971), p. 71.

three political systems, the students may develop generalizations such as these:

> In each of the three nations, some individuals and groups are authorized to make decisions that all citizens must obey.
> The ways in which the three nations determine which groups will make binding political decisions differ.

TABLE 5.3. The Political System in Three Nations

	The United States	The United Kingdom	The Soviet Union
What major individuals make binding political decisions?			
What major groups or bodies make binding political decisions?			
How are these individuals and groups chosen?			
In what ways can individual citizens participate in the political system?			
What is the level of citizen participation in the political process?			
To what extent can political views be freely expressed?			
What are the major political parties?			
To what extent are the rights of minority political parties protected?			

Decision-Making and Citizen Action

Decision-making problems and situations give students opportunities to apply the concepts and generalizations they formulate. Using concepts and generalizations to identify alternative courses of action and to predict their possible consequences is an important part of the decision-making process. When students study a social issue—such as the growth of nuclear weapons—and try to determine what course of action they should take regarding it, generalizations help both to identify alternative courses of action and to predict possible consequences. Courses of action that a class may identify when studying this issue include (1) taking no action; (2) joining and supporting a national antinuclear organization; and (3) writing letters to members of Congress.

Generalizations about the growth of nuclear weapons and the competition between the most powerful nations will enable the students to predict that alternative 1 will most likely result in the continued escalation of nuclear weapons. Generalizations about influencing public policy will enable the students to predict that if they choose alternative 2 they will have only a small— if any—influence on national and international policy. However, they will have more influence joining and working with a national group than working alone as a small class. They are also more likely to develop a sense of personal and political efficacy if they choose alternative 2 rather than alternative 1; they will realize that they took some action to help solve the problem, even though their chances of making an impact on national or international policy is minimal. They may also conclude that alternative 2 is more consistent with their values than alternative 1.

Generalizations about ways to influence national policy will enable the students to predict that writing letters to senators and congressional representatives is one of the least effective ways to affect public policy. Letters have little influence on legislators unless they are received in massive numbers. What the students will most likely conclude, after considering these and other alternatives, is that as a class they can have little influence on national and international policy regarding nuclear weapons. However, they can take some small actions. They have a commitment to make the world a safer place. Thus, a reflective course of action for them is to join and contribute to a national organization working to curb the nuclear weapons race.

Some students in the class, however, may choose to take no action. While they are committed to making the world a safer place in which to live, they believe nuclear weapons help keep the world at peace. These students believe nuclear weapons pose no serious threat to human survival. They have examined the same data during the unit as the members of the class that decide to join an antinuclear organization. However, they interpreted the data differently and decided on a different course of action. *In a decision-making unit or lesson, students must be able to freely choose alternatives consistent with their values within a democratic classroom atmosphere.* They should, however, be encouraged to examine and to reflect upon their values and to consider value alternatives and different ways to interpret data.

Students need to think about issues in social studies classes. Thinking does not occur in a vacuum. Thinking is also more fruitful if the issue is important to students. Important social issues, to which students have strong attachments and commitments, should be used frequently in social studies classes to give students opportunities to practice and reinforce their thinking skills. Thinking serves its most important purpose when it enables students to make better decisions and to take action that helps solve problems and improve the human condition.

TEACHING MAP AND GLOBE SKILLS

Social studies teachers should help students develop space and time concepts. Social studies content often deals with people, problems, and issues that are distant in both time and space. When students study medieval Europe, you should help them understand how very long ago that period was in Western history and how far removed Europe is from their homes and communities. Time lines and work with dates can help students to better understand time concepts. Map and globe concepts and skills can increase understanding of spatial relationships.

Introducing Maps

A map is a drawing of a part or all of the earth's surface. You can introduce the concept of a *map* to young children by working with them to make a map of their classroom. When preparing the map of their classroom, you should make sure that the children understand that when a map is made the view is looking down from above. You can reinforce the concept of a map by asking the children to draw a map of one of the rooms in their homes, which they can share and discuss in class. The children can also build maps with blocks and mold them in clay.

You can prepare the class for doing a map of a section of their neighborhood by taking them on a walking tour of the section and asking them to observe and note various buildings and landmarks. If possible, you should take the students to a tall building from which they can observe the section of

FIGURE 5.1 A neighborhood map.

the neighborhood they will be showing on their map. This will help them to see the neighborhood from a map-like perspective.

To keep the map simple, only several important buildings can be included on the map, as illustrated in Figure 5.1. This map can be used to introduce the students to several important concepts related to maps, including *legend* (or key) and *grid*. You can work with the class to make a new copy of the map, using symbols rather than written descriptions to show the locations of the school, the church, the hospital, the drug store, the barber shop, and the department store. The class might decide that it will use the symbols shown in Figure 5.2 to represent the buildings.

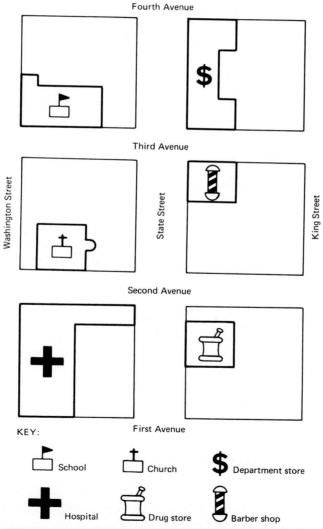

FIGURE 5.2 A neighborhood map with a pictorial legend.

Teachers whose students are in the middle and upper grades can draw vertical and horizontal lines on the map to make a grid system. Numerals and letters can be used to label the grids. The students can be taught to use the grid system by locating buildings such as the school, the church, the hospital, and the department store on the map.

Introducing the Globe

Students should be introduced to the globe in the primary grades. It is important for students to be introduced to a globe early because maps greatly distort the land and water forms on the earth and their relationships. Students who memorize the relationship of the continents shown on a Mercator projection have a very distorted concept of the size of Greenland and the relative distance of Asia from North America. Students must also be introduced to the globe in order to understand the cardinal directions.

You can introduce the globe to students by showing them an illustration of the nine planets that revolve around the sun and explaining that the earth is one of these nine planets. You can explain that the globe is a small model of the earth.

THE CARDINAL DIRECTIONS

When the globe is introduced, you can introduce some of its important features and help students to learn the cardinal, or most important, directions. You should point out the imaginary line around the center of the globe called the *equator*. The North and South Poles should also be introduced. You can then tell the students that north is toward the direction of the North Pole and that south is toward the direction of the South Pole. The students should also learn that when they face north, their back is toward the south, their left hand is toward the west, and their right hand is toward the east. Asking the students to observe the direction in which the sun rises and sets will help them to better understand the cardinal directions. The sun rises in the east and sets in the west. The students can also observe the sun on a sunny day to help them locate the cardinal directions. Shadows point toward the north at noon because the sun is south.

Students often learn the misconception that north is up and south is down on a map because this is the case on most of the maps they see. Unfortunately, some teachers also reinforce this misconception. This common misconception should not be taught or reinforced for several reasons. Up is away from the center of the earth and down is toward the center of the earth. Where north appears on a map depends on the kind of map projection being viewed. On a map projection showing only the Northern Hemisphere (see Figure 5.3), for example, north and south are seen from a perspective that belies the notion that north is at the top of the map.

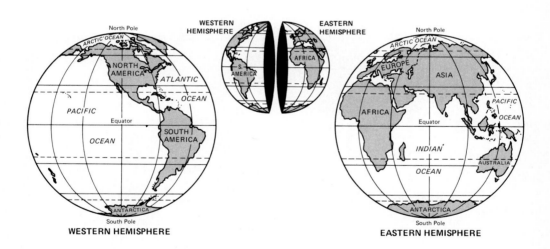

FIGURE 5.3 The hemispheres. (*Source:* Reprinted from Herbert H. Gross, Compiler, *Follett Student Atlas*. Chicago: Follett Publishing Company, 1983, p. 9.)

HEMISPHERES AND PROJECTIONS

The students should be helped to see how the earth as a sphere can be conceptualized as consisting of two hemispheres. A hemisphere is half of a sphere. The equator, the imaginary line equidistant from the North and

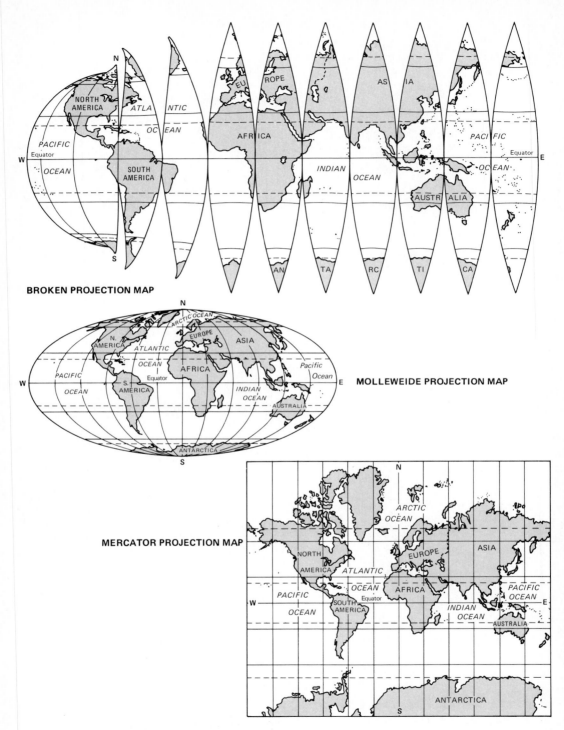

FIGURE 5.4 Map projections. (*Source*: Reprinted from Herbert H. Gross, Compiler, *Follett Student Atlas*. Chicago: Follett Publishing Company, 1983, p. 8.)

South Poles, divides the earth into the Northern and Southern Hemispheres. The earth can also be conceptualized as Eastern and Western Hemispheres when it is divided into two equal parts along an imaginary line that runs north and south. The Northern, Southern, Eastern and Western Hemispheres are illustrated in Figure 5.3.

After the students have been introduced to the concept of hemispheres, they can then be introduced to various kinds of projections of the earth's surface. It is not possible to show a sphere like the earth on a flat surface like a map without distortions. However, maps were created and are frequently used because they are much more convenient to carry than a globe, enable us to view the whole earth at once, and can show much more detail than globes. Map makers have created more than 200 kinds of projections, which are ways to draw a flat map of the earth's surface.

The purpose of a map largely determines the kind of projection a map maker uses. All flat maps distort the earth's surface. However, some types of projections are more accurate than others. Figure 5.4 illustrates three common types of projections: the Mercator, the Mollweide, and the Broken projection. These projections can be used to help students discover the different ways in which maps depict and distort the land and water forms of the earth. They can notice, for example, the extent to which Greenland is oversized on the Mercator map and the accuracy of the size, but distortion in shape, of the land forms on the Mollweide projection.

This teacher is helping his students to develop important map skills. (*Source*: Seattle Public Schools.)

LATITUDE AND LONGITUDE

A knowledge of the parallels of latitude and the meridians of longitude will deepen students' understanding of the globe and help them use these concepts to locate land and water forms on the globe. Students should understand that parallels of latitude and meridians of longitude are imaginary lines drawn on maps and globes to help locate places on the earth.

You can introduce the parallels of latitude by locating the equator on a globe and explaining to the students that the equator is at 0 degrees latitude and that the latitudes north of it are north and those south of it are south. The lines north and south of the equator are numbered from 1 degree to 90 degrees of latitude at the North and South Poles. One degree of latitude is about 69 miles. Parallels of latitude run in an east-west direction and are used to pinpoint locations north or south of the equator.

Meridians of longitude are imaginary lines that run in a north-south direction. They are used to pinpoint locations in an east-west direction. Meridians of longitude are measured by degrees in an east or west direction from the Prime Meridian. The Prime Meridian runs through the original site of the Royal Observatory located in Greenwich, England, which is a suburb of London. The east and west meridians of longitude run from 0 degrees at the Prime Meridian to 180 degrees where they meet at the International Date Line. The days change at the International Date Line. It is Sunday east of the line and Monday west of the line at the same time. Students learn about the importance of the International Date Line in the Inquiry Strategy. Figure 5.5 shows parallels of latitude and meridians of longitude on a globe. You can ask students to use parallels and meridians to locate land and water forms on the earth. However, map and globe skills practice should take place within the context of ongoing social studies units and lessons as often as possible. They should not be isolated exercises that relate to little else in the social studies curriculum.

READING AND INTERPRETING MAPS AND GLOBES

Middle and upper grade students can be introduced to more complicated maps and globes and taught more complex map and globe concepts. They can be taught the concept of *scale* and can make a correctly scaled map of a small area. Locations on maps and globes must be drawn on a scale that is many times smaller than the actual area of the earth shown. The makers of maps indicate the extent to which the water and land forms on a map have been reduced in the map's key or legend. The scale is often made in a statement such as "one inch equals 1000 miles," or expressed as a ratio: 1:1000. The scale may also be shown with a line divided into segments showing how many miles each segment of the line represents. When introducing the concept of scale, you should point out to the students that every place on the map has been reduced to the scale stated in the map's legend. If the students decide to develop a map to scale of a small area, such as a room or the school grounds, they will be required to use precise measurements and

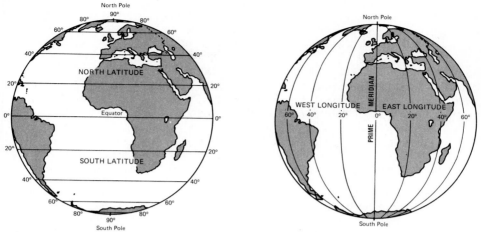

The parallels on globes or maps show the degrees of latitude north or south of the equator. The equator is 0°, the poles are 90°.

The meridians show the degrees of longitude east and west of the Prime Meridian. Both east and west longitude run from 0° to 180°, where they meet.

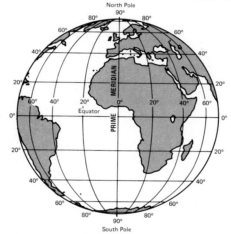

On a globe, notice that 180%east or west longitude is on the opposite side of the world from the Prime Meridian. This is where the International Date Line is located. Here the days change. When it is Sunday east of the line, it is Monday west of the line.

FIGURE 5.5 Parallels of latitude and meridians of longitude. (*Source*: Reprinted from Herbert H. Gross, Compiler, *Follett Student Atlas.* Chicago: Follett Publishing Company, 1983, p. 10.)

quantification techniques. Making a map to scale of a small area is a fruitful activity that students can undertake as a mathematics–social studies project.

Students in the middle and upper grades should be introduced to the various kinds of special purpose maps and to the way in which color is used to delineate political boundaries, distinguish bodies of land from bodies of water, and to show various levels of elevation. Maps that show political boundaries between cities, states, and nations are frequently used in the social studies. Other special purpose maps, showing climate, population, and the

INQUIRY STRATEGY: AN IMAGINARY WINTER HOLIDAY TRIP TO ANOTHER LAND

This activity is designed to teach the students about times zones and the International Date Line, how the seasons differ above and below the equator, foreign currency, and how the celebration of Christmas or Chanukah is influenced by the type of climate and cultural setting.

1. The students will break up into groups and plan a winter holiday vacation to another land. Students in North America or Europe should plan a trip to Sydney (in Australia). Students in Australia or New Zealand should plan a trip to New York City (in the United States). Teachers in other parts of the world should adapt this lesson accordingly. We describe the trip as if it were being planned in North America or Europe.
2. One group of students should plan the trip itinerary. Working with a travel agent, they should obtain information about flights to Sydney, the time and day they would leave their city, and the time and day they would arrive in Sydney. They should choose the most convenient flight from their home city to Sydney. Given this information, they should determine how many hours the flight takes and why the day changes when they fly from their city in North America to Sydney.
3. A second group should obtain information about vacationing in Australia from the library, from travel agents, and by writing to the Australian Consulate-General (360 Post Street, San Francisco, CA 94108).
4. A third group should determine the rate of exchange between Australian and U.S. dollars, and find out the cost of hotels and other goods and services in Sydney. This group will also tell the students how and where they can convert U.S. dollars to Australian dollars and what the current exchange rate is. They can find the current exchange rates in the daily financial sections of *The Wall Street Journal* and *The New York Times*. You can create more interest in this activity by exchanging several U.S. dollars for Australian currency at a local commercial bank and showing it to the class. (Make the request in advance, because some commercial banks require several days to acquire foreign currency). Children are quite interested in currency of other nations.
5. A fourth group should complete a report on how Christmas or Chanukah is celebrated in Sydney, as well as how these celebrations in Sydney differ from those in their home city in North America. They can read various sources, in addition to interviewing people who have lived in Australia or who have traveled there at Christmas time. They will discover, for example, that the celebration of Christmas in Sydney is influenced by the fact that it takes place in the summer (as compared to the winter in New York City) and that Christmas in the United States tends to be celebrated much longer and with many more commercial aspects than Christmas in many other parts of the world.
6. Each of the groups will share its report when the class takes an imaginary trip to Sydney during the Christmas or Chanukah season.

distribution of resources and occupations, are also used in social studies lessons and units. Combination maps, showing political boundaries, vegetation, and national boundaries, can be used successfully with upper grade students but are often not appropriate for students in the primary and intermediate grades. Road, city, and state maps can frequently be used to help students better understand the location of places within their community.

INTRODUCING LAND AND WATER FORMS

When they study the globe, students in the middle and upper grades should learn to identify the major land and water forms that make up the earth. They should also learn how to locate some of the major nations they will be studying. While studying the globe, the students will quickly discover that most of the earth's surface is made up of water rather than land. There is over two times more water than land on the earth's surface.

You should ask the students to locate the continents on the globe (the major land forms): Asia, Africa, North America, South America, Antarctica, Europe, and Australia. The students can explore a number of interesting questions when studying the continents, such as:

In which continents do most of the world's population live?
In which continents are the world's most technologically developed nations located?
In which continents do we find the poorest nations of the world? Why?

After the students have located the major continents, they can then identify the major water forms, the oceans. The major ones are the Pacific, the Atlantic, the Indian, and the Arctic. When studying about the oceans, students can investigate their importance in the history of the development of Western nations and their economic and political importance in today's world.

IMPORTANT MAP AND GLOBE SKILLS

Table 5.4 on pp. 158–159 is a list of map and globe skills that students should develop competency in during the elementary and junior high school grades.[6]

TEACHING TIME AND CHRONOLOGY

Social studies materials often contain references to time. Many of these refer to definite time concepts, such as month and year; others refer to indefinite time concepts, such as a long time ago, a generation, a period, or an era. Time concepts are relational concepts. Relational concepts define a particular association between attributes or distinguishing characteristics. Relational concepts are difficult for young children to understand. They have not had sufficient experience with the basic facts, or with abstracting the common attributes, to establish the particular relation or association involved. For example, it takes considerable practice with a calendar for a six- or seven-year-old child to count up 30 days, learn that that period is called a month,

TABLE 5.4. Map and Globe Skills

I. Interpreting maps and globes.
    A. Orient the map and note directions.

    1. Use cardinal directions in classroom and neighborhood.
    2. Use intermediate directions, such as southeast and northwest.
    3. Use cardinal directions and intermediate directions in working with maps.
    4. Use relative terms of location and direction, such as near, far, above, below, up, and down.
    5. Understand that north is toward the North Pole and south toward the South Pole on any map projection.
    6. Understand the use of the compass for direction.
    7. Use the north arrow on the map.
    8. Orient desk outline, textbook, and atlas maps correctly to the north.
    9. Use parallels and meridians in determining direction.
    10. Use different map projections to learn how the pattern of meridians and that of parallels differ.
    11. Construct simple maps which are properly oriented as to direction.

    B. Locate places on maps and globes.

    1. Recognize the home city and state on a map of the United States and on a globe.
    2. Recognize land and water masses on a globe and on a variety of maps.
    3. Identify on a globe and on a map of the world the equator, tropics, circles, continents, oceans, and large islands.
    4. Use a highway map for locating places by the number-and-key system; plan a trip using distance, direction, and locations.
    5. Relate low latitudes to the equator and high latitudes to the polar areas.
    6. Interpret abbreviations commonly found on maps.
    7. Use map vocabulary and key accurately.
    8. Use longitude and latitude in locating places on wall maps.
    9. Use an atlas to locate places.
    10. Identify the time zones of the United States and relate them to longitude.
    11. Understand the reason for the International Date Line, and compute time problems of international travel.
    12. Consult two or more maps to gather information about the same area.
    13. Recognize the location of major cities of the world with respect to their physical setting.
    14. Trace routes of travel by different means of transportation.
    15. Develop a visual image of major countries, land forms and other map patterns studied.
    16. Read maps of various types which show elevation.
    17. Understand the significance of relative location as it has affected national policies.
    18. Learn to make simple sketch maps to show location.

    C. Use scale and compute distances.

    1. Use small objects to represent large ones, such as a photograph compared to actual size.
    2. Make simple large-scale maps of a familiar area, such as a classroom, neighborhood.

TABLE 5.4. *(continued)*

3. Compare actual length of a block or a mile with that shown on a large-scale map.
4. Determine distance on a map by using a scale of miles.
5. Compare maps of different sizes of the same area.
6. Compare maps of different areas to note that a smaller scale must be used to map larger areas.
7. Compute distance between two points on maps of different scale.
8. Estimate distances on a globe, using latitude; estimate air distances by using a tape or string to measure great circle routes.
9. Understand and use map scale expressed as representative fraction, statement of scale, or bar scale.

D. Interpret map symbols and visualize what they represent.
1. Understand that real objects can be represented by pictures or symbols on a map.
2. Learn to use legends on different kinds of maps.
3. Identify the symbols used for water features to learn the source, mouth, direction of flow, depths, and ocean currents.
4. Study color contour and visual relief maps and visualize the nature of the areas shown.
5. Interpret the elevation of the land from the flow of rivers.
6. Interpret dots, lines, colors, and other symbols used in addition to pictorial symbols.
7. Use all parts of a world atlas.

E. Compare maps and draw inferences.

1. Read into a map the relationships suggested by the data shown, as the factors which determine the location of cities.
2. Compare two maps of the same area, combine the data shown on them, and draw conclusions based on the data.
3. Recognize that there are many kinds of maps for many uses, and learn to choose the best map for the purpose at hand.
4. Understand the differences in different map projections and recognize the distortions involved in any representation of the earth other than the globe.
5. Use maps and the globe to explain the geographic setting of historical and current events.
6. Read a variety of special purpose maps and draw inferences on the basis of the data obtained from them and from other sources.

and then recognize that there are approximately four weeks in a month. Most adults are satisfied to think of a century as a "very long time" or have only a foggy notion of a millennium.

The development of a mature sense of time and chronology is a slow, complex, sequential, and cumulative task.[7] Consequently, it is not realistic for elementary and junior-high school teachers to expect their students to completely master time and chronology concepts. Your goal should be much more modest: to help students increase their ability to understand and interpret time concepts and to understand how past and present events are inter-related.

The teaching of time concepts should be done primarily within the context of social studies content and units. If time concepts are taught in isolation, they will be less meaningful to students and will not help them to understand how past, present, and future historical and social events are interrelated.

You should identify the major time concepts and historical periods in the content and materials you plan to teach during the year. Once these concepts and periods are identified, you can formulate activities and teaching strategies that will help students master them within the context of particular units. You can best help students to master time and chronology concepts by personalizing them and making them as concrete as possible. Definite time concepts that you will want your students to develop include second, minute, hour, day, week, month, year, decade, and century. Indefinite time concepts—such as long ago, a short time, and an era—are more difficult for students to understand than definite time concepts. You will also need to help students understand concepts such as B.C. and A.D. when they are studying the development of civilization. You can use activities such as the following to help students increase their skill in using time concepts:

1. To teach the idea that time is relative, ask the students to be silent for five minutes and then to clock five minutes when they are playing one of their favorite games.
2. Ask the students to make a family tree. Have them write birthdates for their parents and grandparents and relate those dates to famous historical events.
3. The students can make a personal time line, including such events as their birthdates, when they started school, when they moved into their new home, and when their parents were born.
4. The students can bring and share photographs of themselves at various points in their lives.
5. The students can keep a multiple time line for the school year on which they pictorially note events that were happening at the same time in the various locations and cultures studied.
6. The students can construct a time line of the history of their school. They can also include other important historical events on the time line.

DEVELOPING GROUP SKILLS

The Nature and Importance of Groups

Human beings are socialized within groups and learn their basic values, beliefs, and behaviors from other individuals within group situations. People become human by interacting with other human beings in groups. Thus groups are important both for the survival of humankind and for teaching people how to become human. A mere collection of individuals does not constitute a group. Rather, a group is a collection of individuals sharing certain purposes, goals, a sense of identity, and a relatively long-term relationship. Johnson and Johnson define a group as a "collection of persons in face-to-face interaction, each person aware of his own relationship, each aware of the membership of others, and each getting some satisfaction from participating in the activities taking place."[8]

Individuals belong to many different kind of voluntary and involuntary groups which help them to satisfy a wide range of needs. Babies and young children depend upon the family for survival. Religious groups help individuals to satisfy their spiritual needs and to answer complex questions about life, death, and morality. Other groups help individuals to satisfy their need to belong, for companionship, and for status. Groups are especially important in a highly modernized society characterized by widespread alienation and an erosion of traditional community beliefs, norms, and moral authority.

Many traditional groups and group attachments have fallen victim to modernization and urbanization. As a result, many individuals in modernized Western societies have experienced an acute sense of alienation and often search to satisfy group needs in unorthodox and socially unacceptable ways. The rise of cults and other nontraditional groups and organizations to some extent reflects the search by individuals in modernized societies for important group attachments and affiliations.[9] Humans have a need for both individuality and group membership.

The Need to Develop Group Skills

Individuals need to develop competency in group skills because of the importance of the group in a democratic society. Individuals who have highly developed thinking skills and are very knowledgeable are not likely to become effective citizens if they cannot function competently in groups. They must know how to exert influence within a group. Effective citizens in a democratic society must be able to exert influence in public affairs by convincing groups of the importance of the goals to which they are committed and to mobilize group support for their goals. Individuals also need proficient group and human relations skills in order to perform successfully on their jobs. Most people who have problems on their jobs have the technical skills to perform successfully but lack essential human relations skills.

Students should be helped to gain increased proficiency in group skills in each of the subject areas in elementary and junior high school. However, the social studies has a special responsibility to help students develop proficiency in group skills. One of the major goals of the social studies is to help students become effective citizens in a democratic society. Effective group skills are essential for this role.

The Nature of Group Skills

You must be aware of the nature of group skills in order to help students increase their proficiency. Students must have opportunities to practice group skills in order to become more competent in group situations. Just as students must practice baseball to increase their ability to play, they must have repeated opportunities to function in group situations to become more skilled group participants. However, for students to increase their group skills, certain conditions must exist in the practice situation. Some of these conditions are discussed and illustrated below.

The task given to the group of students must be within their ability range. Students must experience success in group situations to increase their proficiency in group skills. If a group of students is given a task beyond their skill level, they will be frustrated and the group situation is likely to contribute little to their skill development. As a matter of fact, when a group of students is given a task beyond their skill level, they are likely to develop negative attitudes toward group work and to view it as a waste of their time.

You should carefully tune group task assignments to the skill level of the students within the group. If a group of students who are poor readers are given a group assignment to prepare a report that requires extensive reading, the group experience will be frustrating and unrewarding. However, if they are given a group task that requires them to make a construction, a map, or to present a role play of an incident from a story the class has read, they will be more likely to have a successful experience and to further develop their group skills.

Group tasks should be motivational and meaningful to each group participant. Each member of the group must feel that he or she can both contribute something to and gain something from it. Unless students feel that they both contribute to and gain something from a group experience they will view the experience negatively. If the group task is such that some of the students feel that they can accomplish it more successfully working alone than working in a group, the group experience is likely to be viewed negatively. Consequently, when group assignments are made, you should make sure that they can be done better by a group than by individual students working alone. You should provide opportunities for students to complete tasks and assignments both individually and in group situations. Some tasks are completed more successfully by individuals; others are completed more successfully by groups. A book report and reports on the lives of individuals are usually best done by one student; a dramatization, a construction, and a research report on an entire nation can usually best be done by students working in groups.

The task and goals for the group should be clearly understood both by the leader and by all group members. When you give group assignments, make sure that students clearly understand the task. When group tasks are given to students who have had little experience in group situations, you will need to monitor the group as it works to make sure that it is carrying out the assigned task. When you begin group work in class, it is a good idea to start with one group, gradually creating more groups as the year progresses. As more students gain proficiency in group skills, you can eventually have all the students working on group projects at the same time.

Both participation and leadership should be distributed among all group members. All students have a need to participate and to make meaningful contributions, but they also need to exercise some leadership functions. Both teachers and chairs of committees and study groups should be sensitive to this principle of group life. If care is not exercised with a group, one or two individuals are likely to dominate the group and do most of the work. While most groups in social studies classes need a chair, the chair should be sensitive to individuals' needs to exercise leadership. Many opportunities arise for individuals other than the chair to exercise leadership functions. The chair can help by asking different individuals within the group to assume responsibilities for various tasks. As the teacher, you can make sure that all individuals within a group have the opportunity both to participate and to exercise leadership by carefully monitoring the groups as they work and encouraging reluctant students to participate and contribute. Ask those who like to dominate to share the participatory and leadership functions with others in the group.

Groups function best when power and influence are distributed equally, based on expertise, ability, and access to information rather than on authority.[10] If this principle is applied, each member of the group will have an opportunity to exercise influence and power sometime during the life of the group.

Every group will experience problems when disagreements and conflicts arise and minority opinions are expressed. In an effective group, conflicts among members with different views and opinions are encouraged and dealt with openly in a negotiated way.[11] You will need to help students develop conflict-resolution skills to learn how to resolve conflicts within groups successfully.

Table 5.5 summarizes some of the important characteristics of effective and ineffective groups. You should keep these characteristics in mind when you plan group experiences.

The Improvement of Group Skills

Students need to develop a range of group skills to become effective citizens in a democratic society. They need to learn how to become successful leaders, effective followers, and how to make productive contributions to groups. The ability to be a good listener, to express a strong opinion as well as to compromise, and to identify with others in situations different from one's own are also important group skills. Effective group members are able to see things

TABLE 5.5. Comparison Between Effective and Ineffective Groups

Effective Groups	Ineffective Groups
Goals are clarified and changed to give the best possible match between individual goals and the group's goals; goals are cooperatively structured.	Members accept imposed goals; goals are competitively structured.
Communication is two-way and the open and accurate expression of both ideas and feelings is emphasized.	Communication is one-way and only ideas are expressed; feelings are suppressed or ignored.
Participation and leadership are distributed among all group members; goal accomplishment, interval maintenance, and developmental change are underscored.	Leadership is delegated and based upon authority; membership participation is unequal with high-authority members dominating; only goal accomplishment is emphasized.
Ability and information determine influence and power; contracts are built to make sure the individual goals and needs are fulfilled; power is equalized and shared.	Position determines influence and power; power is concentrated in the authority positions; obedience to authority is the rule.
Decision-making procedures are matched with the situation; different methods are used at different times; consensus is sought for important decisions; involvement and group discussions are encouraged.	Decisions are always made by the highest authority with little group discussion; members' involvement is minimal.
Controversy and conflict are seen as positive keys to members' involvement, the quality and originality of decisions, and the continuance of the group in good working condition.	Controversy and conflict are ignored, denied, avoided, or suppressed.
Interpersonal group and intergroup behavior are stressed; cohesion is advanced through high levels of inclusion, affection, acceptance, support, and trust. Individuality is endorsed.	The functions performed by members are emphasized; cohesion is ignored and members are controlled by force. Rigid conformity is promoted.
Problem-solving adequacy is high.	Problem-solving adequacy is low.
Members evaluate the effectiveness of the group and decide how to improve its functioning; goal accomplishment, internal maintenance, and development are all considered important.	The highest authority evaluates the group's effectiveness and decides how goal accomplishment may be improved; internal maintenance and development are ignored as much as possible; stability is affirmed.
Interpersonal effectiveness, self-actualization, and innovation are encouraged.	"Organizational persons" who desire order, stability, and structure are encouraged.

SOURCE: David W. Johnson and Frank P. Johnson, *Joining Together: Group Theory and Group Skills* (Englewood Cliffs, NJ: Prentice-Hall, 1975), p. 5. Reprinted with permission of the publisher.

from a different frame of reference and to empathize with others in diverse situations. Effective group members are also able to communicate successfully and to negotiate and compromise. They have a strong sense of identity with group goals and respect the rights and opinions of other group members.

Students will differ greatly in the level of their group skills. Individual students will be strong in some group skills and weak in others. Some students will be highly capable of taking leadership functions within the group, but will lack the ability to be good followers and participants when they are not functioning in leadership roles. Other students will be good followers but will lack the ability to function adequately in leadership roles. Students need to develop the skills to be good followers as well as good leaders. One of the teacher's major responsibilities is to carefully observe students in group situations and to give them feedback about their skill development. Feedback is essential to help students improve their group skills. You can use a checklist

TABLE 5.6. Group Observation Checklist

Name of Student: Group Situation Observed:	Grade: Date:		
	Rarely	*Sometimes*	*Always*
1. Carefully listens to others.			
2. Contributes useful ideas to the group.			
3. Functions well as a group leader.			
4. Takes every opportunity to lead.			
5. Functions well as a follower.			
6. Helps the group stick to the task.			
7. Has a strong interest in the group.			
8. Shows interest in opinions different from his or her own.			
9. Demonstrates his or her ability to compromise and to help resolve conflict.			
10. Is able to express his or her opinions clearly.			
11. Is able to exercise influence within the group.			
OTHER COMMENTS:			

similar to the one in Table 5.6 to observe and record student behavior in group situations.

Group Activities and Projects

Students must have practice in group situations to improve their group skills. You should begin to give students experience in group situations in the primary grades. Groups in the primary grades should be kept small and their tasks should be simple. Two students might be given group assignments, such as erasing the board for a day, watering the plants, or making a house with blocks.

In the middle and upper grades, groups can be assigned more academically oriented tasks. During a unit on Latin America, sixth-grade students might be divided into research groups to study the four nations covered in the unit: Colombia, Brazil, Argentina, and Chile. This kind of assignment can be made only after the students have developed sufficient research and group skills. When establishing research groups to study a topic, you should make sure that the scope of the group task is clear and limited. In our example, the class could develop an outline that would be used by each study group. The outline might include the following as major topics: the political system, education, industry, agriculture, and religion.

A range of instructional goals can be achieved in group situations in the middle and upper grades. Writing a script based on a story the class has read, producing and presenting the story in a school assembly, making charts and graphs, collecting pictures and artifacts, making videotapes, interviewing, and various kinds of reports and discussions are tasks that can be successfully achieved in groups.

Reports and discussions are frequently used in social studies classes. You can help students increase their skills in discussion groups. You can help students formulate guidelines for participating in discussions, provide students feedback on their own behavior in discussion groups, and give them opportunities to observe other students in discussion groups.

TEACHING WRITING SKILLS IN THE SOCIAL STUDIES

The rich content in the social studies provides many opportunities for you to extend and enrich students' speaking, listening, and writing skills. While the major goal of the social studies should be to help students to develop the knowledge and skills needed to become competent citizens, the reinforcement of language arts skills is an important component of the social studies curriculum. Effective citizens must be able to write, speak, and listen competently. Competence in these skills will also enable students to better attain goals more germane to the social studies.

Writing as a Form of Thinking

When teaching and extending writing skills in the social studies, you should realize and help students to understand that writing is primarily a form of thinking. Clear and effective writing results when the writer has carefully thought about the subject or topic, clearly organized his or her ideas, and formulated them in lucid English. Thus the first and most important step in effective writing is to determine the purpose of the essay, its intended audience, and the form and content that will best enhance the purpose. Purpose and audience should be the main determiners of the nature and structure of the writing project. A successful persuasive essay on nuclear proliferation will differ significantly from an essay designed mainly to inform the reader about nuclear weapons. Both essays might be factually accurate. However, the writer who wants to persuade and convince successfully will select a different set of facts from the writer who merely wants to inform. The tone of the essays is likely to be different. The persuasive writer will, for example, use more emotion-evoking adjectives than the writer who wants to inform.

Summary Writing

You should provide practice in writing for different purposes during social studies lessons and units. In the primary grades, students can be given ample practice in summary writing. The major purpose of summaries is to accurately summarize the works of other authors in the students' own words. Summary writing can be taught successfully to primary grade students, to students who have had little previous writing experience, and to students who have poor writing skills. Summary writing does not require students to formulate new ideas, but merely to express the ideas of other writers in their own words. However, students must have a sufficient level of understanding of a written work to summarize it successfully.

When teaching summary writing in the primary grades, you can ask the children to summarize topics, paragraphs, or excerpts that they have read, viewed, or listened to during social studies lessons. You can list the students' summary statements on the board or butcher paper in simple but clear and complete sentences. During a unit on the community, you can ask students to state three major points made about communities in a textbook selection or a filmstrip. When you write these statements on the board, make sure they are accurate summaries of the text or filmstrip. They should also be in complete sentences (not sentence fragments) and grammatically correct.

After the students have had ample practice in dictating summaries of materials as a class, you can ask them to work in small groups and then individually to prepare summaries (in lists). Eventually, they should be required to formulate their lists of sentences into paragraphs and to complete their writing assignments independently. When teaching students to formulate their lists of sentences into paragraphs, you should introduce or review the concept of a paragraph and the topic sentence. The topic sentence states the main idea of the paragraph as briefly as possible. In the middle and upper grades, you can require students to prepare summaries of materials in short compositions that consist of a number of interrelated paragraphs.

Synthesis Writing

In the middle and upper grades, students can be introduced to synthesis writing. In this form of writing, students are required to research a topic, such as "Women in the West," and to synthesize the ideas from at least two different authors. Synthesis writing requires higher-level thinking skills than summary writing. The writer is required to summarize the ideas of two or more writers and to integrate them into a single composition. Outlining skills will help students to successfully synthesize and interrelate ideas, interpretations, and facts from two or more authors on a single topic.

When students do research and read to prepare a composition on "Women in the West," they should jot down main ideas and subideas related to major topics and subtopics in outline form. Main topics for the outline might include:

    I.   Work
   II.   Recreation
  III.   Health
  IV.   Raising children
   V.   Religion

Often a writer will need to do exploratory reading before knowing what the appropriate main topics and subtopics should be for a particular composition.

When teaching composition and outlining skills, you should not convey the idea that research and writing is a rigid process, such as first developing a detailed outline, reading, and then writing. In reality, these processes might go on at the same time. Writers often do exploratory reading on a topic, develop a skeleton outline, begin a rough draft of the composition, and outline the composition in more detail mentally as they write without developing a highly detailed outline like those often found in English composition textbooks. The microcomputer, with word processing software, has greatly influenced the writing process for many writers. Since editing and changes are very easy to make when writing on a word processor, writers tend to be more tentative in their planning of compositions, more exploratory, and more prone to make significant changes during the writing process.

When you first assign synthesis compositions, an example of the assignment should be done with the class as a whole (see Chapter 8, pp. 243–244). The scope of the assignment should be limited and explicit. A first synthesis writing assignment might be to ask the students to use two references (an encyclopedia and a trade book) to describe the Jamestown settlement in 1607.

When students prepare synthesis writing assignments, they should be taught how to summarize the authors' ideas in their own words, to interrelate the ideas of several authors, to identify a direct quotation, and to cite references in a simple way. Students should learn as early as possible that an author's words belong to him or her just as other kinds of property and that an author's works should always be respected and credited.

Analytical and Critical Writing

In both summary and synthesis writing, the writer is concerned primarily with accurately summarizing the ideas of other authors. Students in social studies classes also need to develop and refine higher-level thinking and writing skills, such as thinking about and extending ideas they read, hear, or view, critically analyzing them, determining perspectives and points of view, evaluating the validity of arguments, and distinguishing facts from opinions. Students practice these skills when they do analytical and critical writing.

You can provide practice in analytical and critical writing by asking students to write responses to newspaper editorials, to analyze the treatment of women in television commercials, and to compare the treatment of the Civil War in two different textbooks. To successfully write analytical and critical compositions, students will need many in-class opportunities to identify the biases, points of view, and frames of reference of different authors. One effective way to help students develop skills in analytical and critical writing is to work with them as a class in identifying and naming the perspectives and points of view of writers and contrasting them with their own views and the views of other writers.

*Exercises for Teaching Analytical
and Critical Writing Skills*

1. Read the account of the American Revolution in our textbook. List the major assumptions the author makes about (1) the British and (2) the American colonists.
2. Read this editorial (provided by the teacher) on the new immigrants that have come to the United States since 1970. Write one or two paragraphs that present another point of view.
3. In a short essay, compare and contrast the ideas of Booker T. Washington and W.E.B. DuBois about the education of African-Americans in the nineteenth century.
4. Read several accounts of nuclear weapons and the possibilities of nuclear war. Summarize the major assumptions and points of view of each author in a brief composition. In the last part of the composition, state your own views about nuclear weapons.
5. Read one of the books on this list (provided by the teacher) and write a critical review of it in 500 words. Do not summarize the book. Assume that the reader is familiar with its contents. Use all of your 500 words to critically discuss the book.

6. After viewing the film *How the West Was Won and Honor Lost*, write a short paragraph which states the major message communicated about Indians. State another way that Indian history can be viewed.

Creative Writing

Content in the social studies can serve as an excellent springboard for creative writing. In creative writing in the social studies, the student is asked to assume various roles and positions in different historical periods and to write diaries, speeches, letters, editorials, and other compositions from particular points of view and perspectives.

To write successful creative essays in the social studies, the student must have in-depth knowledge of the historical period, the culture, the people, and the particular role of the person he or she assumes. Creative writing assignments provide an excellent opportunity for students to synthesize and apply the knowledge gained in social studies lessons and units. During the culminating phase of a unit on medieval life, the students can be asked to write a composition on "My Life as a Knight." While the specific events in the essay will be fictitious, the composition should accurately reflect the culture and times of the medieval period. The students can also be asked to assume roles from the past and to complete writing assignments such as those listed below.

Creative Writing Assignments
in the Social Studies

1. You are Harry S. Truman in 1945. Write a speech explaining why you decided to authorize the dropping of the atomic bomb on Japan at Hiroshima (August 6) and Nagasaki (August 9).
2. You are a mother and a black slave living in South Carolina in 1850. Two of your three children have just been sold to the owner of another plantation in another state. They will be taken from you and sent to the new owner in a few days. Write an entry in your diary about this event and describe your feelings.
3. You are a newspaper writer living in San Francisco in 1942. You work for William Randolph Hearst. The Japanese-Americans are being sent to internment camps. Write an editorial about the internment for your newspaper.
4. The year is 1885. You are an immigrant from Italy who has settled in New York City. You have found a job in a factory. Write a letter home to Italy telling about your new country, your job, problems, hopes, and dreams.

Making Writing Assignments
in the Social Studies

Students in the middle and upper grades are frequently asked to write book reports, short research papers, biographies of important people, and answers to examination questions in social studies classes. When making these kinds

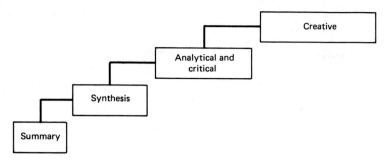

FIGURE 5.6 A typology of writing skills in the social studies. Writing in the social studies should reinforce skills that students learn in the language arts and help them to develop increasingly higher-level thinking and writing skills using social studies content.

of assignments, you should make sure that they require students to use higher-level thinking skills. As often as possible, these assignments should require students to do analytical, critical, and creative writing. Writing assignments in the middle and upper grades that only require students to summarize or to regurgitate information they have read, heard, or viewed are rarely justified. However, some assignments may justifiably require students to accurately summarize information and then to interpret, evaluate, and analyze it. Book report assignments may require students to briefly summarize a book, and then to spend most of the report evaluating and analyzing it. We cannot overemphasize the importance of teaching students the difference between summary and analysis; this difference frequently eludes college students when they prepare book reports and research papers.

You should carefully review writing assignments to make sure that they require students to use higher-level thinking skills (see Figure 5.6). Social studies seat work assignments and essay examinations frequently require students to regurgitate information they have memorized. Frequent use of higher-level questions, discussed and illustrated in Chapter 4, will enable you to make sure that social studies writing assignments are meaningful, challenging, and rewarding for your students.

SUMMARY

The social studies curriculum is designed to help students develop the knowledge, attitudes, and skills needed to become successful participants in a democratic society. This chapter discusses skills that should constitute an important component of a decision-making-focused social studies curriculum: thinking skills, map and globe skills, time and chronology skills, group skills, and writing skills. To help students develop proficiency in these skills, you need to give them sufficient practice and feedback and teach skills within the context of ongoing social studies units and lessons.

DISCUSSION QUESTIONS AND EXERCISES

1. Plan a series of activities to provide students with practice in (1) describing; (2) making inferences; and (3) analyzing information. If you are teaching or student teaching, try these activities with a class or group of students to evaluate their effectiveness.

2. Develop several lesson plans using the Taba strategies described in this chapter to teach students to conceptualize and to generalize. If possible, try these strategies with a group of students.

3. Develop a lesson plan for introducing globes and maps to students in the primary and intermediate grades.

4. What problems might you experience in teaching the cardinal directions to students? How might these problems best be overcome?

5. Develop a plan for teaching students the concept of map projections.

6. How can young children best be taught time and chronology concepts?

7. What are some of the major principles of group participation discussed in this chapter?

8. Develop activities for involving students at the following grade levels in group projects: primary grades, intermediate grades, and upper grades.

9. Develop a creative writing social studies assignment for students in the intermediate grades.

10. Demonstrate your understanding of the following concepts and terms by writing or stating brief definitions for each of them. Also tell why each is important:

    a. describing
    b. inferring
    c. analyzing
    d. map
    e. projections
    f. globe
    g. parallels of latitude
    h. meridians of longitude
    i. group skills
    j. summary writing
    k. synthesis writing
    l. analytical and critical writing
    m. creative writing

NOTES

1. Barry K. Beyer, *Practical Strategies for the Teaching of Thinking* (Boston: Allyn & Bacon, 1987), p. 16.

2. Beyer, p. 17.

3. Beyer, p. 17.

4. Fannie R. Shaftel and George Shaftel, *Role Playing in the Curriculum*, 2nd ed. (Englewood Cliffs, NJ: Prentice-Hall, 1982).

5. Hilda Taba et al., *A Teacher's Handbook to Elementary Social Studies* (Reading, MA: Addison-Wesley, 1971).

6. Helen M. Carpenter, Ed. *Skill Development in the Social Studies*, 33rd Yearbook (Washington, D.C.: National Council for the Social Studies, 1963), pp. 322–327. Reprinted with permission.

7. Alice W. Spieseke, "Developing a Sense of Time and Chronology," in *Skill Development in the Social Studies*, p. 200.

8. David W. Johnson and Frank P. Johnson, *Joining Together: Group Theory and Group Skills* (Englewood Cliffs, NJ: Prentice-Hall, 1975), p. 2.

9. Fergus M. Bordewich, "Colorado's Thriving Cults," *The New York Times Magazine* (May 1, 1988), pp. 36–44.

10. Johnson and Johnson, p. 4.

11. Johnson and Johnson, p. 4.

FOR FURTHER READING

Beyer, Barry K. *Developing a Thinking Skills Program.* Boston: Allyn & Bacon, 1988.

Beyer, Barry K. *Practical Strategies for the Teaching of Thinking.* Boston: Allyn & Bacon, 1987.

Cohen, Elizabeth. *Designing Groupwork: Strategies for the Heterogeneous Classroom.* New York: Teachers College Press, 1986.

Guidelines for Geographic Education: Elementary and Secondary Schools. Macomb, IL: The National Council for Geographic Education, 1984.

Hyde, Arthur, and Marilyn Bizar. *Thinking in Context: Teaching Cognitive Processes across the Elementary School Curriculum.* White Plains, NY: Longman, 1989.

Presseisen, Barbara. *Thinking Throughout the Curriculum: A Conceptual Approach.* Philadelphia: Research for Better Schools, 1985.

Martorella, Peter. *Concept Learning: Designs for Instruction.* Scranton, PA: Intext Educational Publishers, 1982.

Slavin, Robert E. *Cooperative Learning.* New York: Longman, 1983.

Strunk, William, Jr., and E. B. White. *The Elements of Style*, 3rd ed. New York: Macmillan, 1979.

Wales, Charles E., and Anne Nardi. *Successful Decision-Making.* Morgantown: West Virginia University Center for Guided Design, 1984.

6

Teaching Reading
in the Social Studies

Most social studies materials are reading materials; therefore, helping students become better readers of these materials is important and requires careful planning. Social studies materials contain difficult concepts that make them hard to understand. This chapter is designed to help you become more aware of the reading process, the problems students encounter when they read social studies materials, and techniques you can use to help students become more successful readers. An integrated approach to improving reading is stressed, one that combines teaching of the social studies with a concern for the techniques necessary for reading social studies materials successfully. Such an approach is supported by research, but it requires positive teacher attitudes for success.[1]

KNOWING WHEN WE KNOW

An important part of any learning activity is developing an awareness of how the learning is taking place and the learner's role in making it happen. Students must get into the habit of evaluating how much they know about a subject and how much they learn when they read. They should ask themselves "What is my purpose for reading?" "What will I do with the information?" and "How should I read to fulfill my purpose?" They should also frequently ask themselves "Do I understand what I've just read?" "Does it

This chapter is contributed by Christine Caverhill Schaefer, Ph.D., President, Applied Graphics Systems, Inc., Seattle.

make sense?" "How is it related to what I know already?" "Does all the information go together?"

This self-analysis is called *metacognition,* or *metacognitive awareness.* Metacognition has been described as "knowing about knowing" and "knowing how to know."[2] Metacognition is an awareness of what must be done in order to learn. Such an awareness allows readers to determine if and when they have understood. Paired with conscious, manipulative reading strategies to increase understanding, it develops flexible readers who can alter their activities in recognition of the purpose for reading, their own backgrounds and preparation for the task, and an awareness of the text characteristics that will help or interfere with successfully fulfilling the learning task.

Research has shown that the ability to control comprehension strategies is a developmental process. That is, as children get older, this ability increases. In one study, fifth graders who were above-average readers adjusted how much time they spent on reading tasks, increasing the time when the tasks became more difficult. The below-average readers, however, failed to make this adjustment. In fact, they spent less time as the tasks became harder.[3] This shows that either the poorer readers did not know when they did not understand, or that they thought they could not understand.

Poor readers do not see themselves as in control of what they do when they read.[4] They do not understand that they must rely on background information to comprehend as well as on the textual material. They tend to see reading as decoding rather than as understanding.[5] However, your students can be taught to develop metacognitive awareness. In several studies,[6] younger and less able readers began to learn through training what proficient readers already seem to know:

> Part of being a good student is learning to be aware of one's own mind and the degree of one's own understanding. . . . [T]he problem is not to get students to ask us what they don't know; the problem is to make them aware of the difference between what they know and what they don't.[7]

Four steps for monitoring comprehension have been identified:[8]

1. Students must know *when* they do and do not know something.
2. Students must know *what* they know.
3. Students must know what they *need* to know.
4. Students must know the *usefulness* of techniques that help them learn.

These are essential for active participation, which is essential for learning. Metacognitive awareness requires active participation in self-monitoring and self-evaluation. These activities must be a reader's constant companions. For students to develop metacognitive awareness, however, teachers must train and encourage them to monitor their own learning activities. All of the other topics covered in this chapter depend on metacognitive awareness, the aspect of learning that gives the learner control over the material and options for learning from it.

CHARACTERISTICS OF SOCIAL STUDIES READING MATERIALS

When young children first learn to read, they read fiction. Most of the skills you teach in reading classes can and should be applied to the reading your students do for the social studies. However, the skills they develop for fiction cannot be applied directly to social studies materials for several reasons. First, most social studies materials are nonfiction, and the structure of most nonfiction materials is different from those of fiction. Fiction is usually written as linear text: It has an identifiable beginning, middle, and end. It is meant to be read from beginning to end so readers can see plot and character development. Social studies materials, however, are not written as linear texts. They are more like outlines that have been filled in. Each major idea is explained in detail and followed by the next major idea. If students read these materials from beginning to end, the major ideas can be lost among the details.

Second, specialized vocabulary is used in social studies materials. These words are the labels for complicated concepts that can be very abstract, and therefore more difficult to understand. An example is the abstract term *agricultural assets*. In some contexts, however, it means the same as *pigs*, a more concrete—and more easily understandable—term. Without some planning and teaching on your part, your students may have difficulty making the connection between the two terms. Frequently, the abstract concepts will be new to your students, and large numbers of new, complex concepts in-

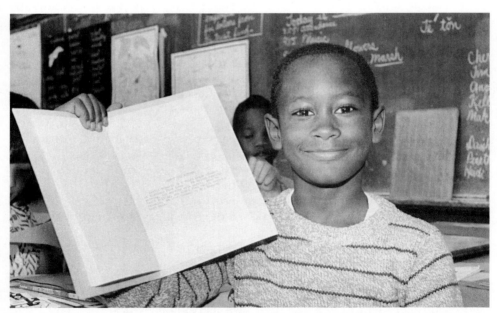

You should help students to develop an interest in reading materials because they are an important source of data in the social studies. (*Source*: Edna Kellman, The Seattle Public Schools.)

crease the difficulty of the materials. You must be concerned about how many new concepts are introduced, how they are explained, and how much prior knowledge the author assumes readers have.[9]

Third, the students' purposes for reading social studies materials are different from those for reading fiction. Gathering and remembering information are emphasized for a number of reasons—taking tests, writing reports, discussing. Applying the information to new situations is also important. "Reading to learn" replaces "learning to read" as the primary reading activity.

Finally, the authors' purposes for writing the materials are different from those in fiction. The primary purposes are no longer to entertain or to give practice in the process of learning to read, but to give information, to persuade, to present and defend points of view. Your students need to learn to read critically so they can recognize what an author is trying to do when writing these materials.

Unfortunately, many students read social studies materials as if they were fiction. Without help, they do not understand that the differences in the materials themselves and in their reasons for reading them require different reading techniques.

Before you teach your students how to read social studies materials, show them how the information is organized. A great deal of research supports the notion that a reader who understands the structure of text will have a better chance of understanding the text itself.[10] This type of reader attends to the ways in which the author develops ideas and uses the structure metacognitively. At the first level, for example, teach your students to find and use the different parts of textbooks (see Chapter 8). This need not be dull or tedious. Make it a game by using a scavenger hunt. Ask them to tell you where they can find the meaning of *abolition,* on which page they can find the date of the Monroe Doctrine, in which section they can find a map of Mexico. Make sure they must use every part of the book to finish the game so that they have some experience with each section and with the kind of information it contains.

Help your students get a preview of what is contained in the materials. Rather than making connections among units or chapters, students often think of their assignments as being separate. Show them how to use a table of contents to discover the material's scope. If they realize how the authors have organized the material, they can understand better how the various sections fit together.

Smaller sections of the materials, such as textbook chapters, also have identifiable structures that can help your students read them successfully. Teach them how to preview the material and encourage them to preview each reading assignment. Let's use a textbook chapter as a convenient example to show how this should be done, because authors and editors include features that will help students understand chapters. Most chapters have an introduction, subheadings, and a summary or conclusion. Teach your students to read these first and in that order. That will give an overview of the most important points in the chapter. If they know what the most important points are, their attention can be directed to see how they fit together. They should also look at graphical information and scan the questions at the end of the chapter. All of these things tell readers what the author thinks are the most important aspects of the text. Only after reading this "skeleton" of the chapter should students go back to read for detail.

This simple and quick strategy may well be the most important thing you can teach your students about reading nonfiction; it will save them time and help them read and understand the material better. When they don't read this way, they often cannot tell what is important and what is not, especially if their background for the subject is limited. Getting an overview first is a critical step in their learning to sift out the less important information from the most important.

Encourage your students to read their social studies materials in this way by showing them how much they can learn and remember from just previewing. First, teach them the strategy and give them practice using it. Then give them a quiz on that information. If you quiz their knowledge after several previewing sessions, you will probably notice that they use the strategy more carefully, first for the purpose of doing well on the quiz, but later for the amount of information they realize they can gain.

THE IMPORTANCE OF BACKGROUND EXPERIENCE

Background experience is necessary for understanding new concepts and events. It provides a point of reference and a structure for the world. In order to learn, we must link new information to information we already know.[11] Try explaining what *quiche* is, for example, to someone who has never heard of it or seen it before. You would probably say something like "It is like a pie but with cheese inside rather than fruit or custard." This kind of explanation is very common. We have a natural tendency to compare new ideas and new things to those we already understand because making these connections leads us to an understanding of the new idea. Some psychologists refer to "working memory" as the place where these connections are recognized and made.[12] This term indicates that the process of learning through these connections is active and dynamic, a crucial link in the learning chain.

When we read, we must constantly call on background information in order to interpret the text. This is so important to understanding that one theorist has called reading "only incidentally visual,"[13] indicating that what the reader brings to the page is more important than the text itself.

Schema theory is an attempt to show how background information is acquired, stored, retrieved, and altered, and how it helps us use that information to learn.[14] First, let's see what is meant by *schema*. If you were asked if you knew what it was like to go to a restaurant, you would probably say yes, but you probably would not think about any particular experience in a restaurant. Your schema for restaurants is a composite of all your experiences

In this photograph, the teacher is helping the student to identify key points in a selection he is reading. (*Source*: Edna Kellman, Seattle Public Schools.)

with them. From these experiences, you can probably identify the critical aspects that characterize restaurants: a customer, a waiter or waitress, and the exchange of money for food.

Every time you go into a restaurant, you compare the new experience against your schema. You are probably aware of this process only when something unexpected—something new—happens. Suppose you have gone only to fast food restaurants. Your schema for restaurants would have to include lines for placing your order, low prices, and the ubiquitous hamburger. The first time you went to an expensive French restaurant, two things would probably happen. First, you would recognize this as being "like a restaurant but with linen tablecloths, candles, and waiters in evening clothes." In other words, you would compare this new experience with your established schema. Second, you would store this information away as a kind of subset, or subschema, in case you ever needed that information again. The more experiences like this new one you encounter, the more useful the subschema would seem, and the more complete your restaurant schema would become.

Suppose for a moment you could remember your first experience in a restaurant. With nothing in your set of experiences to match this experience, you would miss several of the details and you would not understand the entire experience. This happens to students when they read about topics with which they have no experience. They miss details; they do not understand as much as they would if they had a schema to which they could compare it. In fact, they might not know enough to even ask questions about the material. If no one has questions, teachers can be led to the faulty assumption that the text has been understood.

The concept of schemata can perhaps best be understood through an analogy. A schema is analogous to a house: If you already own a house, then you have a place to put the furniture. In fact, you can organize the furniture within the house into logical groupings so that the sofa is in the living room with the chairs, and the refrigerator is in the kitchen with the stove: it all makes sense. However, if you do not have the house, then you have no place to put the furniture except in a heap on the parking strip. Just so, information assembled without structure to organize it is an incomprehensible jumble of details that is unusable until the schema is developed to keep it in order.[15]

When we read something for which we have some background, however, details suggest an appropriate schema, against which the incoming information is compared. As we read, we match the new information with the schema we have already developed. Consistencies between our background information and the new material help us understand what we read. The schema directs our attention and helps us make sense of the material. If the text becomes inconsistent with the schema, one of two things will likely happen: We will misinterpret the text to make it consistent or we will abandon that schema and look for one that is more appropriate.[16] Students who read without comparing schema to text will understand little or nothing of the information, and may be unable to select a more appropriate schema when inconsistencies appear because the inconsistencies go undetected.

Schemata (the plural of schema) are interactive. The new information must be tested and accepted or tested and rejected as it is compared to the schema. The process requires an active and thoughtful reader.

Because the concepts your students must read about in social studies materials are difficult and often new to them, you must help them develop the appropriate *schemata* to understand their reading assignments. Making sure that the materials they read are clear enough so that the appropriate schema is suggested while they read is equally important. If the text is unclear, students might not recognize that they have the background to read it successfully. You can help them by showing films, taking field trips, and providing introductions that directly link the new concepts to the students' existing experiences.

Sometimes students will collectively have a great deal of experience with a particular topic. Discovering how much they know as a group before starting a unit can help you know how much more background information is necessary for them to understand their reading assignments. At the same time, the students in your class can learn from each other, as they put their information together.

For example, suppose you are about to start a unit about the space race of the 1950s and 1960s. First ask your students what they know about the early space programs (but expect information about more current space topics as well). They might give you the following list:

astronauts	John Glenn	*Columbia*
orbit	*The Right Stuff*	*Challenger*
moon	cosmonauts	disaster
blast-off	John F. Kennedy	O-ring
capsule	Sputnik	leak
shuttle	competition	explosion
rockets	Russia	
NASA	USA	

Organize this information into a semantic map on an overhead, on the board, or on a large chart by breaking it into categories (see Figure 6.1). Use this as an introduction to the unit for comparison with the information your students will gain from what they read, from your lessons, from films, and any other material on the subject. By doing this, you will take advantage of what they know already to help them learn more,[17] by letting them see the structure of their existing schema and how that schema grows with new information.

Your students can also help organize the information, especially as they become accustomed to the technique. You can lead the whole class, helping the students find and fill in the categories. You can also have small groups of

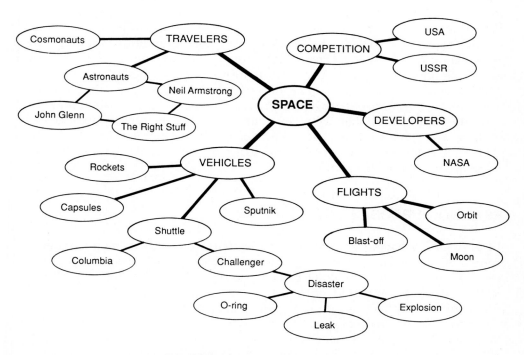

FIGURE 6.1 A semantic map.

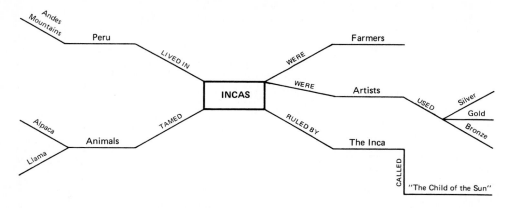

FIGURE 6.2   Structured overview.

students organize the information, putting each entry on 3 × 5 cards so that they can arrange and rearrange the information in different ways. These activities will help the students recognize their own schemata and expand the schemata before they read the assignments.

Another way to build schemata is to make *structured overviews* for your students based on their upcoming reading assignments. A structured overview looks similar to a semantic map, but the latter details what is already inside the students' heads, while the former is an outline made from information in a text. In fact, the same information can be organized in traditional outline form, but structured overviews are more graphic in showing how information is related (see Figure 6.2). Suppose you ask your students to read an article about the Incas. You can identify the main vocabulary, concepts, and information from the chapter and organize it into a structured overview. You will quickly find out if the material is consistent or confusing, and you can add information that will give your students a better background for understanding the reading assignment. Seeing the structured overview before they read helps your students see the assignment's organization and understand what is most important.

SETTING PURPOSES FOR READING

In addition to having an adequate background for understanding reading, your students need to know *why* they are reading each assignment. Set a purpose for them so they don't have to guess why the assignment was given. If they know the expected purposes for reading, their attention will be directed to what you think are the most important things to learn.

Suppose you had assigned the passage about gold mining towns below. You should give your students prereading directions such as these: (1) Read to find out how Central City became a ghost town; (2) Read to find out how Central City as a boom town was different from Central City as a ghost town.

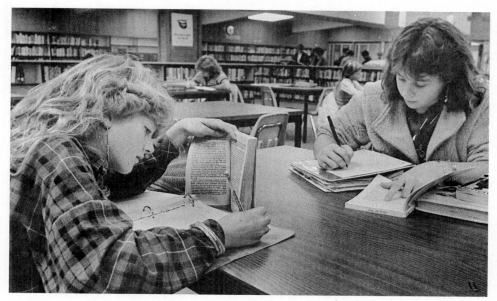

Students need to be provided an appropriate setting in which they can read social studies materials. (*Source*: Terri Malinowski, Northshore School District, Seattle, Washington.)

To answer these questions, students must read the *entire* passage. Answers found too early can discourage careful reading; the purpose is fulfilled too soon.

Notice also that prereading directions or questions are not *literal:* They do not ask for specific facts from the article. If your students look for information that is too specific, they are less likely to pick up other information from the passage.[18] On the other hand, these directions are not too general, either. Directions like "Read to find out what happened" do not give enough information for effective reading. Nor, in fact, do they do anything to suggest the appropriate schema.

TEXTBOOK PASSAGE WITH PREREADING DIRECTIONS

Guiding Directions

1. Read the following passage to find out how Central City became a ghost town.
2. Read to find out how Central City as a boom town was different from Central City as a ghost town.

Boom Towns, Ghost Towns[19]

The discovery of gold and silver brought people to the western Great Plains starting in 1858. Boom towns, as rapidly settled towns were called, grew up quickly at the sites of the mines. Most of these towns slowly became ghost towns as the gold and silver were mined out.

One such boom town was Central City, Colorado. In 1859, a miner named John Gregory discovered gold in the Colorado mountains. Miners swarmed to the spot. The month after the discovery, 3000 people were living in the mining camp they called Central City. By the third month there were more than 30,000 people.

Central City became a noisy, brawling, lawless town. It was a wealthy town, too, with plans for theaters and an opera house. Grand homes were built. Central City mines kept producing gold for about twenty years. Finally, the gold mining failed to pay enough to keep the miners interested. Most of them moved on. A few stayed in Central City, surrounded by deserted buildings and abandoned mine shafts. Central City became a ghost town.

Too many guiding questions or directions can confuse your students, so focus on the most important concepts or on details that will help students most while they read. Avoid telling them to read for the purpose of discussion or for a test, even if that will be the ultimate activity, because the purpose here is to learn new information from the text. In keeping with that purpose, give them goals that direct their attention, and then base tests and discussions on these points. Because you know more about the subject area than they do, there are certain things you know they should learn. By setting purposes for their reading, you let them in on these secrets.

You should also encourage your students to suggest purposes for their reading assignments themselves. Once they have previewed the material, they can help with this process, especially if you have developed their background information. Their active involvement in the process of setting purposes for reading is important for several reasons. It helps them become more independent readers and helps develop their judgment for discovering the important aspects of the subjects they study. Purpose setting also suggests appropriate schemata that will help them understand the reading assignments. When we read without a clear schema in mind, memory for and understanding of the information are very difficult.[20]

TEACHING VOCABULARY

Knowledge of word meanings is strongly related to reading comprehension.[21] Because of this, be sure that your students are familiar with the important vocabulary in their reading assignments *before* they are required to read them. Identifying which vocabulary words to teach is simple up to a point: The technical vocabulary is relatively easy to identify because it is often italicized or printed with definitions in the margins of textbooks. *Democracy, capitalism,* and *laissez-faire* fall into this category.

Identifying the nontechnical vocabulary words is more difficult. Some words are difficult because their secondary definitions, rather than their primary ones, are related to the social studies. *China, climate, cabinet, bill, graft, class,* and *stable* take on special meanings in social studies materials. Such words are easy to overlook when you plan teaching units because they are deceptively common in other contexts. Your students will know the primary meanings of many of these words, so they might not always know that they do not know the appropriate meaning. Research has shown that students usually know and remember only the primary definitions of words, even when secondary or tertiary meanings are supported by context.[22] So, if your students think a *cabinet* is where the president stores his *china*, there is going to be trouble.

Other kinds of nontechnical vocabulary items can also cause problems. Initials and acronyms (such as NAACP and NASA) are very common, and we might assume they are understood, but many students do not know what they mean. Figurative language (such as mother country, breaking ties, bamboo curtain, and cold war) must be explained so that students will not be confused.

Make sure, then, that your students have experience with the appropriate meanings before they read. Present the words to them *in context* so they can see how the context supports the less common meanings. Use sentences from their assignments or write your own that use the words in the same way as the text. Get your students involved in analyzing the sentences and deciding what the words mean, but also teach them how to be suspicious about word meanings by modeling analysis processes: "The space shuttle has 250,000 tiles on its surface. If they were as heavy as bathroom tiles, wouldn't the shuttle be too heavy to be launched? I'd better not assume they are the same kind of tiles. I'd better look for more information to clarify that point."[23]

Two cautions must be considered when teaching vocabulary. First, for direct vocabulary instruction, choose only the most important terms from the lesson. If you teach 25 words from each chapter, you will have considerable trouble ever getting as far as assigning the reading. Research has shown that students will remember the words we teach them and the related concepts whether the words are important to the text selection or not.[24] Do not spend time directly teaching vocabulary that is not necessary for the students' understanding of the most important parts of the text. Second, *do not* ask students to copy definitions out of a dictionary or glossary! This method is not effective for teaching vocabulary words because copying requires no thought, no comprehension, and little attention. A student who memorizes definitions does not necessarily learn the words or how to use them. Active involvement with the words *as they are used* in social studies materials will help your students understand and remember their specialized meanings. This teaches usage and appropriate contexts for the words rather than static definitions without meaning for the students.

MATCHING TEXT CHARACTERISTICS
AND READING ABILITIES

The Text—Readability

Readability is the level of difficulty of written material. High readability levels are more difficult than lower ones. Most formulas that measure readability are concerned with such things as word frequency, word length, and sentence length. These factors are used because longer words are usually less common and less likely to be part of a student's vocabulary. Longer sentences are assumed to be more difficult, more complex, and therefore harder to read and understand.

Readability is important because social studies materials are often hard to read. Difficult concepts are explained in complicated sentences. Also, materials are used in social studies classes that were not written especially for students, so there is little if any control over their level of difficulty.

Publishers usually apply readability formulas to school texts and report the results in teacher's manuals and promotional material. If you use materials that have not been measured for readability, you can figure it out very easily yourself. The Fry Readability Formula[25] is among the most commonly used. It is quick and easy to use. This formula uses the average number of sentences and syllables in randomly selected, 100-word passages. The results are plotted on a graph separated by grade level scores. The graph and rules for its use are in Figure 6.3. The results of readability formulas, however, are

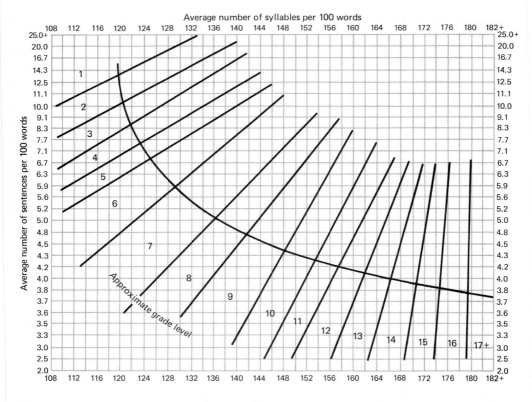

FIGURE 6.3 Graph for estimating readability—extended. *Note:* This "extended graph" does not outmode or render the earlier (1968) version inoperative or inaccurate: it is an extension. (*Source:* By Edward Fry. Reprinted from *The Journal of Reading.* December 1977. Reproduction permitted. No copyright.)

Expanded Directions for Working Readability Graph

1. Randomly select three (3) sample passages and count out exactly 100 words each, beginning with the beginning of a sentence. Do count proper nouns, initializations, and numerals.
2. Count the number of sentences in the hundred words, estimating length of the fraction of the last sentence to the nearest one-tenth.
3. Count the total number of syllables in the 100-word passage. If you don't have a hand counter available, an easy way is to simply put a mark above every syllable over one in each word; then when you get to the end of the passage, count the number of marks and add 100. Small calculators can also be used as counters by pushing numeral 1, then push the + sign for each word or syllable when counting.
4. Enter graph with *average* sentence length and *average* number of syllables; plot dot where the two lines intersect. Area where dot is plotted will give you the approximate grade level.
5. If a great deal of variability is found in syllable count or sentence count, putting more samples into the average is desirable.
6. A word is defined as a group of symbols with a space on either side; thus, *Joe, IRA, 1945,* and & are each one word.
7. A syllable is defined as a phonetic syllable. Generally, there are as many syllables as vowel sounds. For example, *stopped* is one syllable and *wanted* is two syllables. When counting syllables for numerals and initializations, count one syllable for each symbol. For example, *1945* is four syllables, *IRA* is three syllables, and & is one syllable.

neither absolute nor precise, but merely give a rough assessment of the task you are asking your students to do in reading the text.

Be suspicious if you are advised to rewrite materials to lower the readability by substituting simple, common words for difficult ones and breaking long sentences into shorter ones. This advice is impractical and undesirable for several reasons. First, few teachers have enough extra time to rewrite materials. Your time is better spent preparing students to read the materials you already use and finding other suitable materials. Second, simplifying vocabulary may yield short-term gains that are actually rather costly. The most difficult words in social studies materials are often technical terms necessary for discussing the topics. If students do not learn the precise words, they will no longer be able to discuss the topics with others who understand them, and they will not be adequately prepared for more advanced classes in which they are expected to know these terms and the concepts they represent. Sacrificing precision for the sake of "easy" readability is an extremely poor choice that can have dire results for your students.

Finally, sentence length is not always a measure of sentence complexity. Shortened, simplified sentences might not be able to support the complex ideas they must communicate. Research suggests that using short sentences to decrease the measured readability can actually make materials harder to understand.[26] Complex relationships stated explicitly in longer sentences can become implicit when the sentence is broken into shorter ones, thus requiring the reader to make inferences. This is fine if the reader is prepared to make appropriate inferences, but disastrous to comprehension if that is not the case.

For example, the following sentence contains an explicitly stated cause and effect relationship:

I stayed home from school because I was sick.

To decrease the measured readability level of this sentence, it can be broken into two sentences:

I stayed home from school. I was sick.

To the good reader, both examples are easy to understand. However, the cause and effect relationship in the pair of shorter sentences is implicit, placing the burden of inference on the reader. Because making inferences requires a higher level of comprehension than understanding literal statements, the shorter sentences—the more readable ones—are actually more difficult to understand.

Students face enormous difficulty when they read about social studies concepts and events in which they have little background. Without an adequate schema, students are unlikely to recognize the relationships and make the necessary inferences required in falsely "readable" texts.

Readability formulas can be useful, then, if you use them wisely and remember what they can and cannot do. They can do a good job of measuring *text* difficulty independent of readers and their capabilities and backgrounds. The formulas *cannot* measure students' backgrounds, experiences, or cultural identification with a topic. Similarly, readability formulas *cannot* use students' interest in or motivation for reading as a factor of readability. "Nonreaders" can surprise their teachers by fluently reading materials that interest them, while being unable to read school assignments.

The Students—Reading Levels

Students in every class vary widely in their reading abilities. Standardized test scores are not intended for placing students into instructional materials, so do not use them in this way. Standardized tests are general, and they can be ineffective or misleading; they can overestimate or underestimate a student's reading level.[27] Instead of using standardized tests, you can make and give Informal Reading Inventories (IRIs) for quick, specific information about how well your students read the social studies materials used in your class.

To construct an IRI, choose sample passages from your textbook that represent various readability levels. Use the Fry Readability Formula (Figure 6.3) to measure the readability. Choose the passages carefully. The readability may vary widely from one section to another, especially if the material was written by several authors. Do not assume that earlier sections of a book will be less difficult than later ones, even in materials that were written for use at a particular grade level.

Follow these steps to construct your own IRI (see the sample, Table 6.1):

1. Choose sample passages from your materials that are at least 100 words long. These passages must make sense when taken out of the context of the rest of the selection.

TABLE 6.1. Sample Informal Reading Inventory

This sample IRI passage is from a chapter in an eighth-grade text.[28] Its measured readability level using the Fry formula is seventh grade.

This passage will tell you about some of the women in the 1840s who believed that women and Blacks should have more rights.

Many women argued not only for their own rights but for the rights of black people. They argued for the abolition of slavery. The beginnings of the women's rights movement came from women's speeches against slavery. One woman, Lucretia Mott, began this way. She attended the World Anti-Slavery Convention in London in 1840. That convention refused to let her take part because she was a woman. It was then that Lucretia Mott realized that her own role as a woman was in some ways similar to the role of slaves: women had few freedoms; slaves had none.

When she returned to the United States, Mrs. Mott joined other concerned women. Along with Martha C. Wright, Elizabeth Cady Stanton, and Mary Ann McClintock, she called for a convention to discuss the rights of women. In 1848, the announcement of that convention appeared in a newspaper called the *Seneca County Courier.*

Literal:	1. Why was Lucretia Mott not allowed to take part in the World Anti-Slavery Convention?
	2. Who were the other women who helped her plan a convention on women's rights?
Inferential:	3. How did women's speeches against slavery help start the women's movement?
Higher-than-Inferential[29]	4. What freedoms do you think women and slaves did not have?
	5. What freedoms do you think women had that slaves did not?
Vocabulary	6. What does *abolition* mean? How do you know?

2. Write a brief introductory sentence or paragraph to give your students some background for the passage.

3. Check their comprehension by asking questions for each passage. You can ask a general question that requests a summary of the main points, or you can ask several questions that are more specific and at different levels of comprehension:

   a. Write one or two literal questions that are answered *explicitly* in the test passage.

   b. Write one or two inferential questions, requiring students to go beyond the literal information given in the passage.

   c. Write one question that asks students to go beyond the inferential level to evaluate the accuracy of the passage, to project what might happen next, to determine the author's purpose, etc.

   d. Write one or two vocabulary questions that ask the students to define a word as it is used in the passage.

Prepare several IRI passages at different readability levels. The first passage your students read should be easy so that they begin successfully. They should read progressively more difficult passages.

When you administer the IRI, ask your students to read the passages just as they would read a regular assignment. They should know *why* you are doing this: to help them become better readers of their social studies materials. Otherwise, they might regard this as just another test or assignment.[30] Either give them a time limit for reading and answering the question on paper or ask them to time their reading only. Comparing their speed with their comprehension is also important to get a better picture of their reading skills.

You might want to give two different kinds of IRIs. Sometimes you can have them answer the questions with and sometimes without looking back at the text. These tasks require different skills because not looking back depends more on memory than on recognition of important information. Be clear about what kind of information you want to get from the IRI so you can decide how to give it.

When you determine how well your students do on these passages, you are getting specific information that helps you determine the severity of the gap between text difficulty and the reading abilites of your students. This information will help you discover how much extra help they will need for reading and understanding their social studies materials. With the information you get from their scores, you can determine three levels that describe their reading.

1. If a student answers 90 percent of the questions correctly, that passage represents the level at whch he or she can read *independently.*
2. If comprehension is between 70 and 89 percent, that passage represents his or her *instructional* reading level. At this level, the material is appropriate for the student *with instruction* from the teacher.
3. If comprehension is below 70 percent, that student has reached a level of *frustration.* Students should *never* be asked to read at this level. If your students are at the frustration level with the majority of their materials, the materials are not suitable for the class.

DEVELOPING FLEXIBLE
READING SKILLS

Many people believe that good readers are fast readers, but this definition is too narrow. The mark of a good reader is not great speed but reading flexibility. Flexible readers use a variety of speeds and strategies depending on the difficulty and structure of the text, their backgrounds in the subject matter, and the purposes for reading it.[31] Inflexible readers muddle through everything at the same rate, regardless of what they know or why they are reading.

Good readers know when less information is sufficient for the task at hand and when to slow down and read more carefully. *Skimming* and *scanning* are strategies that give students reading flexibility. Teach them to skim to get an overview—the first few paragraphs, the first sentence of each paragraph, and the last few paragraphs. (They should recognize that skimming is like previewing.) Skimming is very rapid becaue much of the text is ignored. The purpose of skimming is to gain a general understanding of the material, not to find details.

Scanning is also rapid reading, but it differs rather importantly from skimming. Your students scan materials when they need to look for specific information, such as a date, a number, or a name. Teach your students to find specific information quickly by reading section headings (if they are present) to find the most probable location. They should examine that section, looking only for the kind of information they need. If they are looking for a date, for example, they should pay attention only to numbers. As each one is found, they must examine the text around it to see if it is the right set of numbers. If not, the process continues. People scan to find precise information.

Study reading is quite different from skimming and scanning, but it is the logical companion of these fast rates of reading. Once students have received prereading directions and have skimmed (or previewed) their reading assignment, they must read carefully and much more slowly. This reading requires paying attention to details as they relate to overall information, weighing accuracy of information, making connections between new and known information, and making critical judgments. It also involves rereading, taking notes, and checking definitions. Study reading also requires that students understand the purpose for reading that assignment, what they must do with the information, and if they have understood. In short, they must understand if and what they have learned.

Students are responsible for reading longer and longer assignments as they get older. They must learn to be flexible readers to complete these assignments successfully. To do that, they must learn when these strategies are appropriate and when careful reading is necessary. You should already be helping them understand *why* they read their assignments. Also help them learn to vary their rate by telling them *how* they should read each assignment. All assignments should include suggestions for how the material should be read, determined by the expected outcome.[32] After your students become accustomed to the idea of flexible reading, let them help determine how assignments should be read. They should learn to match their purpose for reading with their backgrounds and the appropriate strategy so that this process can become independent.

CRITICAL READING

The ability to read critically is essential for making decisions, for solving problems, and for effective citizen involvement. Because critical reading is a higher-level comprehension skill, it requires an understanding of literal information and the ability to make reasonable inferences. Critical readers must be able to make judgments about accuracy, to understand the author's purposes, and to evaluate text. They must also be able to decide if the material they read fulfills their purposes for reading. Becoming a critical reader is difficult because students must learn to trust their own judgment without being swayed by the power of the printed word. To do that, they must realize that politicians, advertisers, and members of special interest groups often use skills of persuasion to sway people to their points of view.

Skills that you commonly teach in your reading classes have a perfect application for helping students become critical readers of social studies materials. Sequence, for example, is an important concept in social studies materials as well as in basal readers. Understanding the sequence of events that led to the dropping of the atomic bombs on Hiroshima and Nagasaki, or the sequence of events that led to President Richard M. Nixon's resignation from office, helps students understand these events. Linking the decisions in the sequence of events with their consequences also helps students recognize cause-and-effect relationships.

Other skills traditionally found in reading textbooks—distinguishing between statements of fact and statements of opinion, drawing conclusions, and predicting outcomes—are essential for students to become critical readers. They must learn these skills, however, by examining issues systematically. You can use the inquiry method to provide a framework for your students' reading.

The inquiry method involves gathering, categorizing, and evaluating information. For example, if your students are examining the issues surrounding the nuclear arms race, they must be clear about alternatives, points of view, and potential consequences. They must be able to gather facts, so they must learn to distinguish facts from opinions, as well as understand how different interpretations of the same set of facts can lead to different conclusions, attitudes, and actions. They must learn to evaluate the source of the information—a news article, an editorial, a biased account. They must learn to examine why the material was written and for whom it was intended. They must determine who wrote the material and what the author's qualifications are. These are important aspects of critical reading.

You can encourage critical reading in prereading exercises by helping students establish criteria for comparing information. You can encourage it in post-reading exercises by asking good questions at several levels of comprehension. Good questioning can lead your students from literal understanding to inference, to evaluation, and to critical analysis. You can also use charts to summarize this information so that it can be weighed and evaluated (see Table 6.2). This evaluation leads to drawing conclusions on which decisions for action can be based, and predicting the outcome of the decisions that are

TABLE 6.2. Summary Chart on Slavery

Source	Author's Purpose	Intended Audience	Details	Conclusions
Editorial	Persuade	Contemporary readership (1864)		
News article	Inform-persuade	Contemporary readership (1864)		
Textbook	Inform	Modern (1984)		

made. When students systematically examine different points of view, they can make decisions and understand the complexities of social issues. They can also learn to understand their own values through this process. Make the issues immediate and help your students feel involved by asking them to take a stand and by helping them realize when they need more information to do so. (See the Inquiry Strategy that follows.)

Your students must become involved in the issues and understand why they are important. Even more essential, however, is that they understand why their involvement is important. They must learn that they can help shape events when they are informed and prepared to make decisions. To do this, your students must recognize the relationship between social studies concepts and the world.[33] When students learn to evaluate what they read and to make thoughtful decisions, they will have become critical readers— well prepared to accept their responsibilities as citizens of the nation and world.

Teaching Students about Questions

Students are asked myriad questions during the course of a school year, yet some never seem to understand how to go about the task of answering them. Some exciting new research has emerged that suggests that students can be taught an effective metacognitive approach to the task of anwering questions.

Much has been written about the need for teachers to ask questions at different levels of comprehension (see Chapter 4), as well as creating clusters of questions that represent a *line of questioning*.[34] A further step has been taken in teaching students what tasks the different kinds of questions represent. The readers who can identify the kinds of question asked have a better chance of actually being able to answer them because they understand where to go for the information.

In one study,[35] students were taught to identify literal, inferential, and beyond-inferential questions. The terminology that the researchers used in teaching the students was the following:

Right there questions (because they could find the answer right there in the text).
Think-and-search questions (for which they had to put together information from different places in the text and draw an inference).
On-my-own questions (which required the students to use background knowledge and the text in order to answer the question. For example, an on-my-own question for *Goldilocks and the Three Bears* is "Should Goldilocks have to pay for the property she ruined?"). This type of question requires that the students understand the text, but their answers must also be based on outside experiences.

In the study, above-average, average, and below-average readers were trained by their teachers to identify the kinds of questions being asked before answering them. While the above-average readers in the study did not make significant gains as a result of the training (probably because they already

INQUIRY STRATEGY: READING CRITICALLY

Directions

Have your students read materials from sweepstakes offers, time-share introductory offers, pyramid schemes, and the like. When they are finished, break them into groups of four to six students to answer the questions that follow. When they have completed the questions, the whole class should come together to discuss their results.

Note

This lesson is designed to accompany the many materials that most people receive in the mail stating that they "may have already won 10 million dollars or one of the fabulous prizes in Column A!"—or that they can make $250,000 merely by selling reports to other people through the mail.

The Problem

Your family has been inundated with get-rich-quick opportunities in the mail and on the telephone. Examine each situation and decide which are responsible enough to warrant participation.

Questions

1. What language (specific words and phrases) do the materials use to encourage you to participate?
2. How do they make you feel that you are only one step away from being wealthy?
3. What are your chances of winning or earning money from any of these? How can you tell? Find specific words and phrases that are clues.
4. Is it usually possible to get something for nothing? Find examples. How frequently does this happen?
5. What are the consequences of participating in each of the schemes? For example, what will it cost you in time and money, and what are the chances of reward?
6. What will you advise your friends who are tempted to participate in one of the more expensive ventures? How can you persuade them that it probably is not a good deal?

possessed the skills), the average and below-average students were greatly helped by this strategy, which gave them more control over the task. In some instances, the poorest readers who received the training did as well as the good readers in the control group, who had not received the strategy training.

This study indicates that a metacognitive approach—What is my task? What do I need to do in order to fulfill it?—is of great value to learners and can be taught effectively to the students who need it most. It reveals to the students who need the help the secrets of how fluent and able readers approach tasks.

The encouraging results of this study indicate that teaching students new strategies for monitoring their learning processes will increase ther reading skills. The 1986 National Assessment of Educational Progress report reveals that while nearly all 17-year-olds can read at a basic level, advanced-level reading skills elude more than 95 percent of them.[36] This alarming statistic clearly argues for a greater emphasis on teaching students how and when to perform higher-level reading tasks.

SUMMARY

Concern about reading is certainly not new. In the eighteenth century, Samuel Johnson stated that "People in general do not willingly read, if they can have anything else to amuse them."[37] Those students who avoid reading today choose not to read, perhaps because they have not learned to actively compare new information with existing schemata, and have not learned to monitor and evaluate their own learning processes metacognitively. Inability to fulfill reading tasks successfully can lead to an unwillingness to try.

Because social studies materials are often difficult to read, helping students develop the skills necessary to understand them must be integrated as a part of social studies instruction. Developing background information, introducing important vocabulary, teaching the structures of the materials, and encouraging flexible reading are all important for helping students read social studies materials more successfully. Students must develop an awareness of their purposes for reading and of any appropriate background information needed to read each assignment successfully. Students must also become critical readers who are able and willing to evaluate what they read so they can make good decisions and assume the rightful role of reflective citizen actors.

DISCUSSION QUESTIONS AND EXERCISES

1. For one chapter in a social studies textbook, prepare materials to help students understand the text more easily by buildng their schemata: for example, structured overviews, guiding questions or directions, films, field trips.
2. Identify the vocabulary from one textbook chapter that should be taught before your students read the material. Look for items in these categories:

   Technical Terms   Acronyms and Initials
   Figurative Language   Specialized Meanings

3. Prepare a scavenger hunt worksheet that will introduce your students to every part of their textbook.
4. Prepare a lesson plan to show your students how to read social studies

materials. It should include previewing, skimming, scanning, and study reading. It should also call attention to the structures of the materials.

5.   a.   Prepare a lesson plan that compares an editorial, a news story, and a political cartoon on the same topic. How do they differ in language, point of view, vocabulary?

    b.   Explain why critical reading is important. What can happen to students if they do not become critical readers?

6.   a.   Using the Fry Readability Formula (Figure 6.3), measure the readability of the social studies textbook you use with your students.

    b.   Discuss why the readability is higher than grade level, if it is higher. Are causal relationships clear? Are the vocabulary words important to the topics used or have they been simplified?

7.   Prepare a set of three Informal Reading Inventory (IRI) passages and questions. Use passages that are one year apart, beginning one grade level below that of your students.

8.   Demonstrate your understanding of the following terms by writing or stating brief definitions for each of them. Also tell why each is significant.

a. schema	f. purpose for reading
b. schema theory	g. guiding questions
c. metacognition	h. previewing
d. critical reading	i. flexible reading
e. Informal Reading Inventory	j. readability

NOTES

1.   Philip Berryhill, "Reading in the Content Area of Social Studies," in Mary Dupuis, Ed., *Reading in the Content Areas: Research for Teachers* (Newark, DE: International Reading Association, 1984).

2.   Ann L. Brown, "Knowing When, Where and How to Remember: A Problem of Metacognition," in R. Glaser, Ed., *Advances in Instructional Psychology* (Hillsdale, NJ: Erlbaum, 1978).

3.   John T. Guthrie, "Metacognition: Up from Flexibility," *The Reading Teacher*, Vol. 35 (1982), pp. 510–512.

4.   F. J. DiVesta, K. G. Hayward, and V. P. Orlando, "Developmental Trends in Monitoring Text for Comprehension," *Child Development*, Vol. 50 (1979), pp. 97–195.

5.   L. B. Gambrell and B. S. Heathington, "Adult Disabled Readers' Metacognitive Awareness about Reading Tasks and Strategies," *Journal of Reading Behavior*, Vol. XIII (1981), pp. 215–222.

6.   L. Baker, "Comprehension Monitoring: Identifying and Coping with Text Conclusions" (Urbana, IL: University of Illinois, Center for the Study of Reading, Technical Report No. 145, 1979); N. G. Mangano, D. Palmer, and E. T. Goetz, "Improving Reading Comprehension through Metacognitive Training," *Reading Psychology*, Vol. 3 (1982), pp. 365–374; M. E. Andre and T. H. Anderson, "The Development and Evaluation of a Self-Questioning Study Technique," *Reading Research Quarterly*, Vol. XIV (1978–1979), pp. 605–623.

7.   John Holt, *How Children Fail* (New York: Dell, 1964), pp. 28–29.

8. Jill Fitzgerald, "Helping Readers Gain Self-Control over Reading Comprehension," *The Reading Teacher,* Vol. 37 (1983), pp. 249–253.

9. Terry L. Bullock and Karl D. Hesse, *Reading in the Social Studies Classroom* (Washington, D.C.: National Education Association, 1981).

10. Bonnie J. F. Meyer, David M. Brandt, and George J. Bluth, "Use of Top-Level Structure in Text: Key for Reading Comprehension of Ninth-Grade Students," *Reading Research Quarterly,* Vol. 16 (1980), pp. 72–103; Barbara M. Taylor and Richard W. Beach, "The Effects of Text Structure on Middle-Grade Students' Comprehension and Production of Expository Text," *Reading Research Quarterly,* Vol. 19 (1984), pp. 134–146.

11. P. David Pearson and Dale D. Johnson, *Teaching Reading Comprehension* (New York: Holt, Rinehart and Winston, 1978).

12. James M. Royer, "Designing Instruction to Produce Understanding: An Approach Based on Cognitive Theory," in Gary D. Phye and Thomas Andre, Eds., *Cognitive Classroom Learning* (New York: Harcourt Brace Jovanovich, 1986).

13. P. A. Kolers, "Reading Is Only Incidentally Visual," *Psycholinguistics and the Teaching of Reading* (Newark, DE: International Reading Association, 1969), pp. 8–16.

14. P. David Pearson and Rand J. Spiro, "Toward a Theory of Reading Comprehension Instruction," *Topics in Language Disorders,* Vol. I (1980), pp. 71–88.

15. Walter C. Parker, personal communication, October 1985.

16. Pearson and Spiro, op. cit.

17. Pearson and Johnson, op. cit.

18. J. P. Rickards, "Processing Effects of Advance Organizers Interspersed in Text," *Reading Research Quarterly,* Vol. XI (1975–1976), pp. 599–622.

19. James A. Banks with Sam L. Sebesta, *We Americans: Our History and People,* Vol. II (Boston: Allyn & Bacon, 1982), p. 34.

20. J. D. Bransford and M. B. Johnson, "Conceptual Prerequisites for Understanding: Some Investigations of Comprehension and Recall," *Journal of Verbal Learning and Verbal Behavior,* Vol. 11 (1972), pp. 717–726.

21. Richard C. Anderson and F. Freebody, "Vocabulary Knowledge," in John T. Guthrie, Ed., *Comprehension and Teaching: Research Reviews* (Newark, DE: International Reading Association, 1981).

22. Jana M. Mason, E. Knisely, and J. Kendall, "Effects of Polysemous Words on Sentence Comprehension," *Reading Research Quarterly,* Vol. XV (1978–1979), pp. 10–56.

23. Christine C. Schaefer, "The Effects of Metacognitive Processing on Immediate and Delayed Memory of Extended Discourse," unpublished doctoral dissertation (Seattle: University of Washington, 1983).

24. Karen K. Wixson, "Vocabulary Instruction and Children's Comprehension of Basal Stories," *Reading Research Quarterly,* Vol. XXI (1986), pp. 317–328.

25. Edward Fry, "Fry's Readability Graph: Clarifications, Validity, and Extension to Level 17," *Journal of Reading,* Vol. 21 (December 1977), pp. 242–252.

26. Pearson and Johnson, op. cit.

27. Joseph F. Brunner and John J. Campbell, *Participating in Secondary Reading: A Practical Approach* (Englewood Cliffs, NJ: Prentice-Hall, 1978), p. 9.

28. Banks and Sebesta, op. cit., Vol. I., p. 214.

29. Timothy C. Standal, "A Simplified Taxonomy of Questions," unpublished paper (Seattle: University of Washington, 1980).

30. Ellen L. Thomas and H. Alan Robinson, *Improving Reading in Every Class,* 2nd ed. (Boston: Allyn & Bacon, 1978), p. 219.

31. Jack Holmes and Harry Singer, *Speed and Power of Reading in High School* (Washington, D.C.: U.S. Government Printing Office, Cooperative Research Monograph No. 14, Superintendent of Documents Catalog No. FS 5.230:30016, 1966).

32. Bullock and Hesse, op. cit.

33. I. W. Gaskins, "Reading for Learning: Going Beyond Basals in the Elementary Grades," *The Reading Teacher,* Vol. 35 (1981), pp. 323–328.

34. P. David Pearson. "Changing the Face of Reading Comprehension Instruction," *The Reading Teacher* (1985), pp. 724–738.

35. Taffy E. Raphael and Clydie A. Wonnacott, "Heightening Fourth-Grade Students' Sensitivity to Sources of Information for Answering Comprehension Questions," *Reading Research Quarterly,* Vol. XX (1985), pp. 282–296.

36. In William J. Bennett, *American Education: Making It Work* (Washington, D.C.: U.S. Government Printing Office, 1988).

37. G. B. Hill and L. F. Powell, *Boswell's Life of Johnson* (Oxford: The Clarendon Press, 1964), in Frank Kermode, "The Common Reader," *Daedalus* (Winter 1983), p. 3.

FOR FURTHER READING

Baumann, James. F., Ed. *Teaching Main Idea Comprehension.* Newark, DE: International Reading Association, 1986.

Bullock, Terry L., and Karl D. Hesse. *Reading in the Social Studies Classroom.* Washington, D.C.: National Education Association, 1981.

Cooper, J. David. *Improving Reading Comprehension.* Boston: Houghton Mifflin, 1986.

Johnson, Dale D., and P. David Pearson. *Teaching Reading Vocabulary.* New York: Holt, Rinehart and Winston, 1984.

Pearson, P. David, and Dale D. Johnson. *Teaching Reading Comprehension.* New York: Holt, Rinehart and Winston, 1978.

Phye, Gary D., and Thomas Andre. *Cognitive Classroom Learning: Understanding, Thinking, and Problem Solving.* Orlando: Harcourt Brace Jovanovich, 1986.

Samuels, S. Jay, and P. David Pearson. *Changing School Reading Programs.* Newark, DE: International Reading Association, 1988.

Vacca, Richard T., and JoAnne L. Vacca. *Content Area Reading,* 2nd ed. Boston: Little, Brown, 1986.

7

Teaching Social Issues and Human Rights

SOCIAL ISSUES AND CITIZEN ACTION

Social issues are society's unresolved problems that deeply concern many citizens. Citizens usually have strong value commitments related to these problems and frequently disagree about both their causes and ways to solve them. Social issues can be adequately understood only when studied from an interdisciplinary perspective. Scientific data are necessary but not sufficient for resolving social issues. Social issues have value dimensions and are deeply rooted in emotional attachments. They provide an excellent means for teaching decision-making skills and for providing opportunities for citizen action.

Social issues can be one of the most interesting and important components of the social studies curriculum. They add vitality to the curriculum and help make it significant to both students and teachers. The study of social issues gives students an opportunity to get a better understanding of the dynamic and changing nature of our society, their responsibilities as citizens in a democracy, and the importance of concepts such as equality and human dignity in maintaining a democracy.

Even though social issues are an important and necessary component of the social studies curriculum, there is evidence that many schools are bypassing their responsibility to help students learn how to examine them. There are many reasons why teachers are reluctant to teach social issues. These include fear of pressure groups, lack of knowledge about how to teach social

Cherry A. McGee Banks, President of Educational Materials and Services Center, Edmonds, Washington, coauthored this chapter.

issues, and a desire to keep society's serious problems hidden from students.

Highly organized pressure groups are active in some communities. Such groups often try to keep topics they consider inappropriate out of the classroom. Fear of controversy, however, should not prevent teachers from helping students deal reflectively with social issues. You should review your school district's policy on teaching about controversy before teaching social issues. If a school district does not have a policy on teaching controversial issues, you should inform the parents and the principal about the issues you plan to teach well in advance. This is not intended to suggest that teachers should acquiesce. However, if parents and administrators are fully informed in advance, any resulting criticism can be properly channeled toward a full and free discussion of the right to raise such issues in the classroom, rather than centered on the personality of a particular teacher.

Some teachers are reluctant to teach social issues because they feel uneasy when teaching about controversy. Their uncertainty, to some extent, reflects the value conflicts in our society. Some educators advocate indoctrination while others advocate the uncritical transmission of our cultural heritage as the best way to develop loyal and intelligent citizens. Though widely used, both of these approaches are inappropriate.

When studying social issues, students should be encouraged to examine original sources and to reach their own conclusions. Indoctrinating teachers lack a deep faith in democracy, for individuals who strongly endorse democratic ideals believe that democracy will sustain the most intense scrutiny. If students arrive at their own conclusions, their convictions will be strong and rooted in reason, not merely emotional. Emotion easily gives way to persuasion. Sound, reflective convictions will sustain the most intense challenge.

Some teachers are reluctant to teach social issues because they believe students should be shielded from society's serious problems. Whether in school or out, students eventually learn about the deep value conflicts in U.S. society. They are often star witnesses in the social conflicts of our times. Television programs, the daily newspaper, and lunchroom conversation often reflect current conflicts. Students will, perhaps more in the future than at any time in the past, be required to confront and find ways of dealing with complex social problems. You should help students to reflectively examine these problems. Unless students are aware of the problems in our society, have accurate information about them, and begin thinking about effective ways to help solve them, they cannot help close the gap between our ideals and actual behavior or become reflective citizen actors.

HUMAN RIGHTS: A FRAMEWORK
FOR THE TEACHING OF SOCIAL ISSUES

Human rights is a unifying theme that connects the social issues discussed in this chapter. Human rights, by definition, is a global issue. Human beings everywhere in the world want to live in dignity. The quest by groups such as women, ethnic minorities, and the disabled to secure equality in the United States and other parts of the world are all human rights movements. Nuclear proliferation poses a major threat to human rights because it not only makes the annihilation of the human race possible (the ultimate denial of human rights) but also causes nuclear accidents, which seriously threaten the health and lives of individuals. Nuclear accidents, such as those that occurred at Three-Mile Island, Pennsylvania, in the United States (March 31, 1979) and at Chernobyl in the Ukraine in the Soviet Union (April 30, 1986), cause citizens and leaders throughout the world to think seriously about the threats posed by nuclear energy to human survival and human rights.

Studying about the quest for human rights in the United States as well as throughout the world will help students to understand that the U.S. is neither the only nation whose documents promise its citizens basic human rights nor the only one with a wide discrepancy between its democratic ideals and its historical and current realities. The Magna Charta (1215), the British Bill of Rights (1689), and the writings of John Locke (1632–1704—the English philosopher renowned for his writings on freedom) are historical precedents to the major documents establishing equality and human rights in the United States in the late 1700s. Viewing the struggle for human rights within a global context enables students to better understand how the U.S. Declaration of Independence (1776), the Constitution (1788), and the Bill of Rights (1791) are related to earlier efforts to establish human rights in the United Kingdom and other Western European nations. Without viewing problems such as racism, sexism, handicappism, and militarism from a global perspective, students, especially those in the early and middle grades, are likely to conclude that these problems are uniquely U.S. ones.

The global approach to the study of the social issues described in this chapter will help students not only to understand that these problems are global in scope, but also to see that they are unlikely to be solved without international cooperation among nations throughout the world. For example, the nuclear accident at Chernobyl (Soviet Union) released radioactivity not only in the Soviet Union but in some neighboring European nations. As another example, the right to work is one of the basic human rights stated in The Universal Declaration of Human Rights, adopted by the United Nations General Assembly on December 10, 1948. Ethnic problems and tensions are increased in the United States when immigrants from Mexico enter the U.S. illegally because they are unable to find jobs in their native land.

The final topic discussed in this chapter, law-related issues, is a key and integral component of the quest for human rights because most of the documents and legislation establishing and guaranteeing individuals human rights have been created by national governments or by international bodies with the power to make national or international laws. However, while national governments usually have the power to enforce the laws they make, bodies that establish international laws, such as the United Nations International Court of Justice, usually have little enforcement power.

HUMAN RIGHTS IN A GLOBAL WORLD SOCIETY

Human rights are rights that every man, woman, and child has by birthright to live a dignified life that is free of poverty, illiteracy, and cultural and political repression.[1] Without protection of these basic human rights, people become dehumanized to the extent that they lose opportunities to live dignified lives. One of the most important characteristics that distinguish humans from other beings on earth is their ability to create cultures that regard human life as sacred and that promote human dignity and creativity.

Today our world is one of paradox. While we are experiencing tremendous technological growth, there are ominous threats to human rights and human welfare. Nuclear weapons—the offspring of modern science— seriously threaten human survival. Their destructive potential is beyond human imagination. Poverty, hunger, limited wars, authoritarian governments, racism, sexism, illiteracy, and international terrorism also present serious threats to human rights. The problems posed by such threats are intractable and overwhelming. Yet, as teachers and human beings, we have an inescapable responsibility to do what we can to help solve them and to improve the human condition.

It is far easier to affirm our commitment to improve human rights in the world than to take actions that will achieve this goal. It is very difficult to enforce international human rights pronouncements and laws. Some very significant documents, such as the Universal Declaration of Human Rights and the International Covenant on Civil and Political Rights, are designed to protect human rights throughout the world. Yet how do nations, committed to the protection of these rights, bring sanctions successfully against nations that violate them? Often, citizens and groups within nations focus on their unique concerns and show little interest in the rights of other citizens within their own or other nations.

A major challenge that we face in international human rights is how to create an international constituency that is not only committed to the protection of human rights throughout the world, but that also can effectively mobilize to bring decisive sanctions against nations that consistently violate those rights. Strong commitments to community and nation-state, along with a tendency to focus on their unique concerns and issues, often prevent citizens and groups from taking actions related to global issues and concerns.

It is essential for a nation's citizens to experience equity and human rights before they can realistically be expected to participate in actions to protect the human rights of other people within or outside their national borders. Citizens who are struggling to survive, who are illiterate, who feel that they have few basic rights, or who are structurally excluded from their own political system are likely to show little interest in the human rights of other groups. Consequently, the most important contribution that teachers can make to promoting international human rights is to help create conditions in social and political institutions that promote equity and human rights and that help students to see how their own human rights are inextricably bound to the human rights of other peoples throughout the world.

Violations of human rights in one nation usually have important consequences in others. When Haitian and Cuban refugees fled from their nations to the United States, they had a significant influence on the Miami area. Ethnic conflict in Miami increased. Immigrants from nations such as China, the Philippines, and Mexico also affect jobs and educational opportunities for the Chinese, Filipinos, and Mexicans already living in the United States. Yet citizens who are preoccupied with protecting and attaining their own basic rights often do not see the interrelationship between their rights and those of other world citizens.

As the difficulties involved in enforcing international human rights make clear, we can protect human rights in the international community only when a critical mass of citizens throughout the world is committed to their protection and when these citizens are able to mobilize for effective social and political action.

To help future citizens develop a commitment to international human rights, we must create situations in their communities, schools, and nations in which they are treated with dignity and equity. You can best contribute to the promotion of international human rights by creating a classroom and school environment that respects the human rights of students. The school, wrote John Dewey, should be a model democracy.[2] Human rights should be promoted, exemplified, and protected in the classroom and school. Within this kind of atmosphere, the teaching of concepts related to international human rights will make sense to students because their experiences will be consistent with what they are being taught. Attempts to teach and promote human rights in an authoritarian atmosphere will be rightfully dismissed by students as empty rhetoric and hypocrisy.

STRATEGIES FOR TEACHING SOCIAL ISSUES AND HUMAN RIGHTS

The social issues component of the social studies—taught within the framework of international human rights—should be consistent with and help to extend the goals of the social studies stated in Chapter 1: to help students develop decision-making skills and the ability to influence public policy by participating in effective citizen action. To make effective decisions related to issues such as nuclear energy, sexism, racism, and handicappism, students must master knowledge in the various social science disciplines related to these issues.

When the students have sufficient historical and sociological knowledge about an issue, such as the development and dropping of the atomic bomb on Hiroshima on August 6, 1945, they can then begin to clarify their values regarding the issue, to discuss whether they think President Truman's decision to drop the bomb was justified, and what actions they think we should take regarding the control of nuclear energy and nuclear weapons today. *It is important for students to understand the historical context in which a decision was made in order for them to discuss the decision reflectively.* When they consider

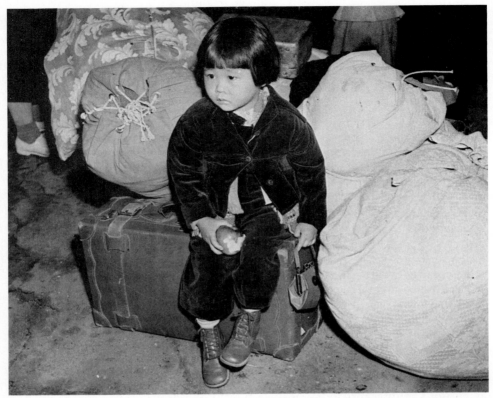

The internment of the Japanese Americans during World War II can be used to help students raise and discuss human rights issues and questions. (*Source*: The National Archives, Washington, D.C.)

President Truman's decision to authorize the dropping of the atomic bomb on Hiroshima in 1945, they should know that the United States believed that Germany was developing an atomic bomb, that many American soldiers were being killed daily in Asia, and that Japan's government was controlled by military leaders. They should also be knowledgeable about the catastrophic consequences of dropping the atomic bomb. Knowledge is an important requisite for reflective decision-making and value inquiry.

AN EXPANDING CONCEPT OF HUMAN RIGHTS IN THE SOCIAL STUDIES CURRICULUM

The study of social issues in the social studies should not be isolated but should be a continuing and integral part of daily lessons and units. While you may want to teach one or more units a year that focus on human rights issues, every unit you teach during the year has content that will enable you to deal with issues related to social issues and human rights. Social and human rights issues can be related to the content as well as to the developmental levels of the students. Students in the primary grades are concerned about fairness in their families, in the classroom, and on the playground. You can use incidents that actually happen in the classroom and on the playground, as well as case studies, to enable students in the primary grades to think about and to make decisions related to human rights issues.

The social world of young children, however, is not confined to their own families, schools, and communities. Television, books, and travel enable most primary-grade students to greatly expand their social world. You can use books, films, and photographs about families in other cultures and times (both within and outside the United States) to enable students in the primary grades to learn about human rights issues and problems that children their age experienced in the past or still experience today. *Song of the Trees* by Mildred Taylor can be used to acquaint young children with the discrimination that an African-American family experienced in Mississippi in the 1930s.[3] *Small Hands, Big Hands: Seven Profiles of Chicano Migrant Workers and Their Families* by Sandra Weiner provides a vivid and compassionate description of the problems experienced by children in a migrant family.[4] You can also use books written about children and families in other nations to acquaint primary-grade students with how human rights issues, as experienced by families in other parts of the world, are alike and different from those in the United States.[5] The global dimension of human rights and social issues teaching should be an integral component of all lessons and units.

As students progress through the grades they can deal effectively with increasingly complex content, case studies, and decision-problems related to human rights. Students often study the history of their state in the fourth grade. As they do, students can examine issues and problems related to the status of women, ethnic groups, and the disabled. They can determine the laws that exist in their state to protect the rights of these groups, the extent to which they are enforced, and the unresolved human rights issues related to these groups in their state. Indian fishing and treaty rights, as well as affirmative action for women and minorities, are examples of issues that are still controversial and unresolved in many states. Students can also do research to determine whether there are nuclear plants within their state and whether these plants are controversial or supported by most citizens because they provide important jobs.

The study of U.S. history in the fifth and eighth grades will give the class an opportunity to examine the development of the major documents (such as the Constitution and the Bill of Rights) that established human rights and equity in the United States, the limited groups to which human rights applied when these documents were first formulated, and the ways in which human rights have been expanded through the centuries to include more groups. For example, it is important to help students understand the meaning of the phrase "All men are created equal." When written in the Declaration of Independence in 1776, this phrase referred to white males with property.[6] However, the strength of documents such as the Declaration of Independence and the Constitution is that the ideas within them were able to be interpreted to include more and more groups through the years. The story of the expansion of equality and human rights in the United States, and the active role that groups such as women and minorities played in the expansion, is an important story that students should learn. They should also be helped to understand that full justice in the United States, as well as in other nations, is still an ideal and not a reality. Table 7.1 lists some landmark events in the development of human rights. These events should be incorporated into a study of human rights in the United States and in the world. The students can add events to this timeline throughout the year as they study various human rights issues.

The study of nations in various parts of the world in the upper grades gives students many opportunities to examine human rights issues and problems in a global context. You can focus on the major issues and problems related to human rights and social issues that are still unresolved, such as the nuclear race between the two superpowers (the U.S. and Russia), the conflict between Israelis and Arabs in the Middle East, apartheid in the Republic of South Africa, and political repression in various parts of the world. Important violations of human rights in the past, such as slavery in the United States and the Holocaust in Europe during World War II, should also be studied. The important documents developed by the United Nations to protect human rights throughout the world, formulated since World War II, should also be examined, such as the Universal Declaration of Human Rights (1948) and the Declaration of the Rights of the Child (1959).[7] Case studies, such as those in the following Inquiry Strategy, can be used to integrate a study of social issues and human rights into the social studies curriculum.

TABLE 7.1. Human Rights Timeline

1215	The Magna Charta
1689	The British Bill of Rights
1690	Publication of *Two Treatises on Civil Government* by John Locke
1776	The Declaration of Independence (United States)
1788	The United States Constitution
1791	The Bill of Rights (amendments to the U.S. Constitution)
1792	Publication of *Vindication of the Rights of Women* by Mary Wollstonecraft
1848	The Declaration of Women Sentiments (issued at the Seneca Falls Convention)
1851	A resolution supporting female suffrage presented in the House of Lords (Great Britain)
1859	Publication of *On Liberty* by John Stuart Mill
1865	The Thirteenth Amendment to the U.S. Constitution abolishing slavery
1866	Civil Rights Act
1868	The Fourteenth Amendment to U.S. Constitution making blacks citizens
1869	Formation of the National Women Suffrage Association (led by Susan B. Anthony and Elizabeth Cady Stanton)

conservative campus student newspaper has published several inflammatory articles that most African-American students and faculty consider insulting and demeaning.

Questions and Exercises _____

Ask the students:

1. In what ways are the case studies alike?
2. In what ways are they different?
3. What words or labels can we use to describe these case studies as a group? Try to elicit concepts such as *discrimination* and *unfair treatment*. Introduce the concept of *human rights* and explain how each of the cases is an example of how human rights are violated.
4. Divide the class into five groups. Give each of the groups one of the cases above. Ask each group to identify the problem the protagonist(s) faces in each case and what he or she should do to try to solve it. Members of each group should try to reach a consensus about what they would do if they were the protagonists. Individual students should be free to make a decision different from that of their group.

Global realities
Nuclear issues
Gender equity
Ethnic issues
Social justice for handicapped individuals

The final section of this chapter discusses law-related education because laws are often used to guarantee the rights of individuals and groups.

Global Realities

We live in an age of global realities, which affect not only our national policies, but also many aspects of our everyday life. Our economy is one of the many components of our society that reflects global realities. It is influenced both by the actions of people living within our borders and by people and nations far away.

Our economy is an example of the interdependent nature of life in the twentieth century. When Arab oil-producing nations decided to increase the price of oil in the 1970s, Americans started buying smaller, more fuel-efficient cars. Most of these cars were not manufactured in Detroit, but were available from foreign car manufacturers. Car sales for Detroit auto makers decreased in the United States and those for small, foreign-made cars sharply increased.

It is important to note, however, that while the United States was importing large numbers of foreign-made automobiles, American auto makers were exporting American-made cars to other nations. In 1977, Ford Motor Company received 42 percent of its income selling cars to countries outside North America. Exports and foreign investments account for a significant percentage of multinational American corporations' income. They also account for a significant number of jobs. In 1981, between 15 percent and 20 percent of American workers were involved in making goods for export. Exports accounted for more than $372 million for American business.[8]

In addition to manufactured goods, agricultural products, chemicals, other products, and capital are also being imported to and exported from the United States. In 1981, Americans had just over $109 million invested in assets abroad. In that same year there were nearly $78 million in foreign assets invested in the United States.[9] These facts point out the difficulty of isolating one nation's economy, culture, or politics from that of other nations. It is difficult today, and will perhaps be even more difficult in the future, to delineate significant components of our lives that are uniquely American and untouched by outside influences.

Through the years there has been a great deal of cultural exchange both within and outside the borders of the United States. Important components of U.S. culture are shared with people in other nations. We have borrowed food, clothing, music, and languages from other nations. Today it is possible to buy a McDonald's hamburger in downtown Paris or Amsterdam. You can see young people dressed in jeans in the Ginza in Tokyo as well as on Fifth Avenue in New York City. Jazz is popular in both Moscow and New Orleans.

There are many reasons for the rapid cultural exchange between nations. Sophisticated telecommunication systems make it possible for Americans to witness events in distant lands as they are occurring. It has been suggested that the daily battles that were shown on the evening news were one of the reasons that anti–Vietnam war sentiment grew in the United States. We are also coming in contact with more people from other nations. In 1981, 312,000 foreign students were enrolled in U.S. colleges and universities.

Americans continue to have a strong national identity. However, our knowledge of the people and cultures of other lands, our internationally based economy, and our growing awareness of earth as a spaceship with finite supplies is increasing our knowledge of the interrelated nature of the world we live in.

Global studies offers an excellent opportunity for interdisciplinary teaching. It also provides a way to develop social studies skills, including decision-making, valuing, and the ability to conceptualize and generalize. The world, not a nation-state, becomes the unit of analysis. Instead of learning about the culture, geography, or economy of one nation, students are taught to compare and look for relationships between the cultures, geographies, or economies of several nations. Students learn to see their actions and the actions of their government from both national and international perspectives. Most importantly, they have an opportunity to see themselves as citizens of the world and to explore the importance and responsibility of that role.

GOALS, CONCEPTS, AND ACTIVITIES FOR TEACHING ABOUT GLOBAL REALITIES

Goal 1

To help students increase their awareness and understanding of the interlocking relationships between all people and nations of the world.

Concept

Interdependence—the interaction between nations in a variety of areas, including finance, trade, communication, and travel, that transcend national boundaries.

Activities

1. Divide students into groups representing first, second, third and fourth world nations (see Table 7.2). Ask the students to research the kind of nutrition typically available in these types of nations. Then have them suggest ways that the first and second world nations can share food with third and fourth world nations.
2. Many churches, unions, and community groups such as sororities

---

TABLE 7.2. First, Second, Third, and Fourth World Nations

First World Nations

These are technologically advanced and modernized Western nations. The United States, Canada, Australia, and the nations in Western Europe are examples of first world nations. Japan is a developed nation in Asia.

Second World Nations

The term second world is used to refer to the Soviet Union and the Communist bloc nations it leads. Second world nations are characterized by a high degree of government control of the economy. First world nations usually have more mixed economies. Second world nations include the People's Republic of China, the Soviet Union, and the Eastern European nations.

Third World Nations

Third world is used to describe technologically less advanced nations; largely agrarian, poor in money and income, and with large and rapidly growing populations. Most African, Latin American, and Asian nations are third world nations. Most of the third world nations were colonized by Western nations during the period of European colonialism.

Fourth World Nations

The term fourth world nation is rarely used. However, when it is used, it refers to the poorest of the developing nations. Bangladesh is an example of a fourth world nation.

and fraternities are transnational. Invite a person from such a group
to talk to your class about why his or her organization is interested in
people in other nations.

3. Have your students write to a large bank like Chase Manhattan
    requesting an annual report. Using the annual report as a resource,
    have your students identify all of the nations that have borrowed
    money from the bank.

Goal 2

To help students develop the ability to look at the world and world
events as part of an interrelated system, not as separate, isolated nations and events.

Concept

Global perspective—a conception of the world as an integrated whole.

Activities

1. Immigrants from Europe have settled in many nations including
    Mexico, South Africa, and Australia. Have students compare the
    influence of European immigration on the native populations of
    these nations.
2. Have students find out how many languages are spoken in the
    United Nations. Then have them debate whether or not there is a
    need for an international language.
3. Select a multinational company like IBM or General Motors. Have
    students put a pin in a world map where the company has its
    headquarters. Then have them put different colored pins in the map
    to represent where the company has plants, where it gets its raw
    materials, and where its products are sold.

Nuclear Issues

We are living in a nuclear age. This requires us to be prepared to confront
and explore the facts and controversies surrounding the threat of nuclear
war, nuclear energy, and other nuclear issues. These issues are complex and
value-laden. Emotions and limited information are often an integral part of
discussions on nuclear issues.

The threat of nuclear war is an issue particularly important to young
people. They are being asked to plan for their future while living in a world
that has the means of its own destruction. The future of the world is no
longer assured. The psychological impact of this knowledge on adults, as well
as on children, is tremendous. For this reason, critics of teaching about
nuclear issues in the schools feel that discussing the threat of nuclear war
only promotes fear. It is true that fear and inaction are possible responses to

the threat of nuclear war. An American Psychiatric Association study of 1000 adolescents found that most of them felt that they had no future because they would be killed in a nuclear war before they grew up.[10] Other studies have found that students have very little concrete knowledge about nuclear issues.[11]

Immobilizing fear is more likely a consequence of too little rather than too much knowledge about nuclear issues. Students learn about the threat of nuclear war from movies, newspapers, and many other sources. Studying about the threat of nuclear war in the classroom will give students an opportunity to learn about the complexity of the issues and to explore their feelings about them. More importantly, they will have an opportunity to learn that even though nuclear war is possible, it is not inevitable.[12]

More and more schools are making efforts to include nuclear issues in their curricula. Students are learning the vocabulary, exploring their thoughts and feelings, and learning how developments like the Manhattan Project, the Cold War and the Cuban missile crisis relate to the current concern over the nuclear threat.

Students need to learn more about the complex dimensions of the nuclear threat. When the threat of nuclear war is discussed, the focus of the discussion is almost always on only two nations, the United States and the Soviet Union. Together, these two nations have 40,000 nuclear warheads. Combined, these warheads have 1 million times the destructive power of the atomic bomb dropped on Hiroshima in 1945. It is, however, a mistake to limit the discussion of nuclear arms to the United States and the Soviet Union.

The problem of nuclear arms has a very wide scope. The number of nations that have nuclear weapons or the ability to produce nuclear weapons is growing. In addition to the United States and the Soviet Union, Britain, France, China, and India have built and tested nuclear devices. Ten other nations—including Israel, Japan, South Africa, Canada, and Argentina—are capable of building a nuclear bomb. Within the next 6 to 10 years, 15 other nations including Iraq, Libya, Brazil, and Norway will probably have a nuclear bomb. The threat of nuclear war is not limited to the two superpowers. It is a world problem.

The social studies curriculum often focuses on issues that directly relate to the United States. However, the study of nuclear issues requires teachers to focus on the world community, not just on the United States. Actions taken by other nations or by people outside of our borders can have an influence on nuclear issues in the United States. Nuclear issues provide an excellent means to help students understand the interdependence of our modern world society.

While it is important for students to understand the global dimensions of the threat of nuclear war, it is equally important for them to know there is a global movement to prevent it. Groups advocating disarmament and arms control are active in Germany, Japan, the United States, and many other parts of the world. The prevention of nuclear war is an important topic that

TABLE 7.3. Nuclear Freeze, Arms Control, and Deterrence

Nuclear Freeze is a concept that relates to unilateral disarmament. Its supporters argue that we have enough nuclear weapons to defend ourselves. They feel that other nations would not feel a need to build nuclear weapons if we refused to continue building them. Critics argue that a nuclear freeze would put the United States in a position of permanent disadvantage. In addition, they feel it would prevent the development of the MX missile, B-1 bomber, and a number of other weapons they believe important to American defense. Most importantly, the critics of a nuclear freeze feel it would not prevent nuclear war and would be more likely to increase the risk of it.

Arms Control focuses on ways to reduce the threat of nuclear war. The Strategic Arms Limitation Treaty (SALT I) and the nuclear ban treaties are some of the ways the United States is working to control nuclear arms.

Deterrence focuses on a number of issues, including arms buildup. Some people believe that if the United States is able to prevent other nations from becoming more powerful, it will be able to prevent nuclear war through strength. The concept of a limited nuclear war is an outgrowth of this position.

is being widely discussed. Students should be able to discuss and critically evaluate these concepts: *unilateral disarmament, arms control,* and *deterrence* (see Table 7.3).

In discussing nuclear issues, you should be aware of the possibility of indoctrination. Diverse points of view should be presented and students should be encouraged to critically analyze them. Even when diverse points of view are presented, the study of nuclear issues in the schools is still likely to be considered inappropriate by some citizens. It is, however, one of the most important issues facing humankind. It will continue to grow in importance in future years. As such, it is an issue that cannot be ignored by social studies teachers.

GOALS, CONCEPTS, AND ACTIVITIES FOR TEACHING ABOUT NUCLEAR ISSUES

Goal 1

> To help students understand the interrelated nature of modern world society.

Concept

> Interdependence—nations mutually rely on and influence each other.

Activities

> 1. Petroleum and chromite are both important to the defense of the United States. Yet the U.S. has to import both products. Using a map, have students draw lines between five nations that are trading

partners, exchanging goods and services vital to their national defense.

2. Tell your students to pretend that the United States has been cut off from its oil supply by a Middle East nation it relies heavily on for oil imports. Ask them to describe what effects the stoppage in oil trade will have on the United States and the Middle East nation.

3. Have students in your class represent the United States, the Soviet Union, Britain, France, China, and India at a simulated conference to discuss ways to control nuclear proliferation.

Goal 2

To help students develop a high level of awareness and understanding about possible means to prevent nuclear war.

Concept

Control—the regulation of behavior by forces such as rules, laws, and treaties.

Activities

1. Ask your students to write a paper about how nations might resolve conflicts in the year 2000.

2. Have your students research SALT I and II. Then role play a meeting between the United States and the Soviet Union to discuss SALT III.

3. Many communities across the nation are taking stands on nuclear arms by popular vote or by legislative action. Find out if your community has taken such a stand. If so, invite a local official to the class to discuss how the community's stand is being implemented. If your community has not taken a stand on nuclear arms, have your students survey the community to find out what the community feels should be done to prevent nuclear war.

Have your students summarize their findings in a letter to the editor of a local newspaper.

Gender Issues

OVERVIEW

Using the work of early feminist reformers as their foundation, modern-day feminists began a movement that helped change the way women are viewed in our society. The publication of Betty Friedan's book *The Feminine Mystique* in 1963 marked a new beginning for the women's movement.[13] Friedan's position—that women had the potential and the need to work in a wide range of occupations and professions outside the home—was considered radical when the book was published. Many of the people who debated the merits of gender equity in the 1960s knew little of the nineteenth century reform movements or of the efforts of women like Sojourner Truth and Susan B. Anthony to secure basic rights for women. Studying about women gives students an opportunity to see how past events can affect those in the present and future.

Students need to examine both the past and the present experiences of women to fully understand American society. The culture, status, development, and achievement of women as a group should be explored. Women are not a monolithic group, making their study a complex and often difficult task. There are many different women, and differences in race and social class often result in diverse experiences for women. A sound curriculum must reflect both similarities and differences. A distinction should also be made between *sex* and *gender*. Sex refers to the biological characteristics that make an individual male or female. Gender describes behaviors that result from social, cultural, and psychological factors associated with masculinity and femininity within a society. Appropriate male and female roles result from the socialization of the individual within the group.

The study of women often has an emotional dimension. In some cases, emotions can make it difficult for students to examine facts related to women's issues. In other cases, you can help students use their emotions to reach an effective understanding of what it means to be a male or a female in our society. In either event, you should realize that emotions are an important factor.

Many of the questions raised by the women's movement are related to *sexism*. Sexism is prejudice and discrimination directed at individuals on the basis of their sex. Sexism in education confronts every classroom teacher, whether it is part of the formal curriculum contained in books and materials or part of the hidden curriculum communicated through behavior and attitudes, and it can have an important effect on students. For example, while the role of women in U.S. society is changing, many questions related to gender equity, such as income, are unresolved. In 1980, women in the United States with college degrees earned less than men who had completed one to three years of high school.[14] Eighty-four percent of all elementary teachers in 1977–78 were female, but only 18 percent of all elementary school principals and only 1 percent of superintendents were female.[15]

Language is one way that sexism is reflected in our society. Words and phrases such as *mankind, manpower, chairman*, and *early man* can leave students with the notion that women have not been active participants in the development of civilization. Even when words used to describe men have a female counterpart, the female word may have a very different meaning. A case in point is the word *bachelor*, whose feminine counterpart is *spinster*, a word with a very different denotation. Increased teacher awareness can play an important role in helping students understand the importance of language. You can model nonsexist language as well as point out and correct sexist language in textbooks and other materials.

When women are studied in the social studies, care should be taken to include content and examples from the experiences of women of color. This photograph shows the famous African-American singer Marian Anderson. (*Source*: The National Archives, Washington, D.C.)

When you review your class lists at the beginning of the school year, you should realize that gender is a possible factor in the academic development of your students. Many girls start out in first grade equal to or ahead of boys in reading, mathematics, and science. However, as they progress through school, girls tend to fall behind boys in science and mathematics. You should also realize that the girls in your class with high grade point averages will tend to have lower occupational goals than boys with similar grade point averages. In addition, girls will tend to have less confidence in their potential for academic and occupational success than boys.[16] This kind of knowledge can help you to successfully intervene and support your students.

While much of the literature on sexism in education focuses on women, sexism also affects men. The study of women can provide an opportunity to explore how the treatment and condition of women in our society relates to the experiences of men. Boys are much more likely to be identified as having learning or behavioral problems or to be diagnosed as hyperactive than are girls.[17] Boys are expected to be strong and not to cry even if they are hurt. After being told, year after year, not to cry and to act like a man, it is not surprising that many young men have trouble communicating their feelings and are unable to show a full range of emotions.

Sex-role stereotyping denies both men and women freedom of choice and can prevent students from developing their full potential. Students need an atmosphere that encourages them, not one that limits their hopes and dreams. Students should be helped to expand their concepts of male and female roles and to understand that gender should not determine what men and women are able to do. Teachers who use books and materials that show both men and women in nontraditional roles will help their students understand that most roles in society can be filled by both women and men.[18]

GOALS, CONCEPTS, AND ACTIVITIES
FOR TEACHING ABOUT WOMEN

Goal 1

To increase student awareness and knowledge of women in our society.

Concept

Sexism—prejudiced beliefs and behaviors that are directed against women because of their gender.

Activities

1. Have students examine their textbooks for sex biases.
2. Help your students develop a nonsexist dictionary. Give them a list of sexist words and have them suggest alternatives.
3. Read and discuss the poem "What Are Little Boys Made of?" Ask your students to rewrite the poem.
4. Ask your students to look at specified television programs for a one-week period to find out how minority women are depicted and in what kinds of roles.
5. Make a list of all the extracurricular activities at your school. Ask your students to find out if both males and females participate in each of the activities and in what proportions. Discuss their findings in class.

Goal 2

To help students examine how sex-role stereotyping influences the behavior of men and women.

Concept

Role—(sex-role stereotyping). Sex-role steroityping involves using traditional definitions of feminine and masculine to limit the behavior of males and females.

Activities

1. To open discussion on sex-role stereotyping, show your students a picture of a woman and a man and ask them to name some jobs that each of them can do. List the jobs on the board. Then ask your students if the woman can do all the jobs listed for the man and if the man can do all the jobs listed for the woman.
2. Have students examine the roles of women and men at different periods in U.S. history, such as the late 1700s, and compare those to the roles men and women function in today.
3. Ask your students to pretend they are journalists who give advice to readers. Tell them to respond to a man who wants to know if he should become a househusband and stay home with his two preschool-age children while his wife runs the family business full time.

Ethnic Groups

In recent years, school districts throughout the nation have attempted to modify their curricula to more accurately reflect the ethnic and cultural diversity within U.S. society. Much of the curriculum reform related to ethnic studies and ethnic heritage programs has taken place in the social studies because the social studies deal with human behavior and the relationships between groups.

To fully understand the cogent role that ethnicity plays in our society, ethnic studies must be broadly defined to include European-American ethnic groups as well as ethnic minority groups. When ethnic studies is broadly defined it provides an opportunity for students to learn about a wide range of ethnic groups. They are able to compare and contrast the experiences of a wide range of ethnic groups and gain valuable insights into U.S. society. Ethnic studies deals with such ethnic groups as Anglo-Americans, Italian-Americans, and Polish-Americans, as well as with ethnic minority groups such as African-Americans and Mexican-Americans. Conceptualizing ethnic studies and ethnic content broadly enables the curriculum builder to select content about different types of ethnic groups so that students, by comparing and contrasting them, can develop higher level concepts and generalizations about ethnicity within U.S. society.

Ethnic identification and affiliations are important for many groups of Americans, including African-Americans, Mexican-Americans, Irish Catholics, Jewish-Americans, and Greek-Americans. It can be a factor in selecting a marriage partner, voting in an election, and joining a social club. Because ethnicity is an important factor in American life, infusing ethnic content into the curriculum provides an excellent opportunity for teachers to examine its assumptions, purposes, and nature. Rather than viewing ethnic studies as an addition to the regular social studies curriculum, it should be viewed as a process of curriculum reform. One of the most promising aspects of ethnic studies is that it can serve as a vehicle for general curriculum reform. As such, it can result in the creation of an innovative curriculum based on new assumptions and new perspectives. Such a curriculum can help students gain novel views of the American experience and a new conception of what it means to be American.[19]

We need to teach U.S. history and culture from diverse ethnic and cultural perspectives rather than primarily or exclusively from the points of view of mainstream American historians and writers. Many social studies courses and units are taught primarily from mainstream American perspectives. These types of courses and units are based on the mainstream centric model or Model A (see Figure 7.1).[20]

Ethnic studies, as a process of curriculum reform, can and often does proceed from Model A to Model B, the ethnic additive model. In courses and units based on Model B, ethnic content is an additive to the major curriculum thrust, which is still dominated by the American mainstream perspective. Many school districts have attempted ethnic modification of the curriculum through Model B curriculum changes, black studies courses, Chicano studies courses, and special units and celebrations on ethnic groups in the elementary and middle grades are examples of Model B curricular experiences.

However, curriculum reform should proceed directly from Model A to Model C, the multiethnic model. In units and courses based on Model C, the students study historical and social events from several ethnic and cultural points of view. Mainstream American perspectives are only one group of several and are in no way superior or inferior to other ethnic perspectives. Model D (Ethno-national Model) units and courses are the ultimate goal of curriculum reform. In this curriculum model, students study historical and social events from the perspectives and points of view of ethnic groups in other nations. Since we live in a global society, students need to learn how to become effective citizens of the world community. This is unlikely to happen if they study historical and contemporary events only from the perspectives of ethnic and cultural groups within their own nation.

When studying a historical period such as the colonial period in United States history in a unit or course based on the multiethnic model (Model C), the inquiry would not end when the students viewed the period from the perspective of mainstream American historians and writers. Rather, they would ponder these kinds of questions: "How do American Indian historians view the colonial period?" "Do their views of the period differ in any substantial ways from the views of mainstream American historians?" "Why or why not?" "What was life like for Jews, African-Americans, and other ethnic groups in America during the seventeenth and eighteenth centuries?" "How do we know?" Model C units and courses allow students to view historical and contemporary events from the perspectives of different ethnic and racial groups.

A historian's experience and culture, including his or her ethnic culture, influences his or her views of the past and present. However, it would be simplistic to argue that there is one mainstream American view of history and

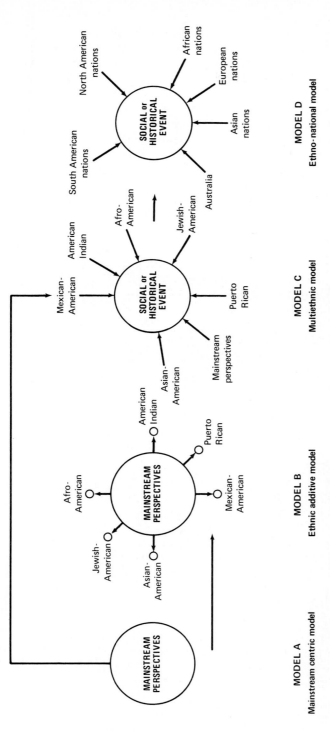

MODEL A	MODEL B	MODEL C	MODEL D
Mainstream centric model	Ethnic additive model	Multiethnic model	Ethno-national model

Ethnic studies is conceptualized as a process of curriculum reform which can lead from only mainstream perspectives on our history and culture (MODEL A), to multiethnic perspectives as additives to the major curriculum thrust (MODEL B), to a completely multiethnic curriculum in which every historical and social event is viewed from the perspectives of different cultural and ethnic groups (MODEL C). In MODEL C mainstream perspectives are among several and are in no way superior or inferior to other perspectives. In MODEL D, students study historical and social events from the perspectives of groups in several different nations. Many schools that have attempted ethnic modification of the curriculum have implemented MODEL B types of programs. It is suggested here that curriculum reform move directly from MODEL A to MODEL C and ultimately to MODEL D. However, in those districts which have MODEL B types of programs, it is suggested that they move from MODEL B to MODEL C and eventually to MODEL D types of curricular organizations.

FIGURE 7.1 Ethnic Studies as a process of curriculum reform. (*Source:* Reprinted from James A. Banks, *Teaching Strategies for Ethnic Studies,* 4th ed. Boston: Allyn & Bacon, 1987, p. 22. Used with the publisher's permission.)

contemporary events, or one American Indian view. Wide differences in experiences and perceptions exist both within and across ethnic groups. However, those who have experienced a historical event or a social phenomenon, such as racial bigotry or internment, often view the event differently from those who have watched it from a distance. There is no one mainstream American perspective on Japanese-American internment during WWII, just as there is no one Japanese-American view of it. However, accounts written by those who were interned, such as Takashima's powerful *A Child in Prison Camp*, often provide insights and perspectives that cannot be provided by people who were not interned.[21] Individuals who viewed the internment from the outside can also provide us with unique and important perspectives and points of view. Both perspectives should be studied in a sound social studies curriculum.

A study of the experiences, cultures, and crafts of U.S. ethnic groups can enrich the social studies curriculum. This photograph (1879) shows a Moki Indian weaving. (*Source:* The National Archives, Washington, D.C.)

GOALS, CONCEPTS, AND ACTIVITIES FOR TEACHING ABOUT ETHNIC GROUPS

Goal 1

To help students become more aware of how different ethnic groups have influenced American culture.

Concept

Acculturation—the exchanging of cultural traits between cultural groups.

Activities

1. Ask students to name their favorite foods. Then have them research how those foods became a part of the American diet.
2. Have students compare the values that are the basis for the environmental movement with values expressed by American Indians in the 1800s.
3. Many Americans set off fireworks on the Fourth of July. Ask your students to find out how this tradition started and what other cultures use fireworks for celebrations.

Goal 2

To help students gain a new view of who is an American and what it means to be American.

Concept

Ethnocentrism—the belief that your own ethnic group is superior to all others.

Activities

1. Show your students a photograph of a group of people representing a variety of ethnic and racial groups. Then ask them to select the person in the photograph that they feel represents an American. Have them discuss why they made that choice.
2. Make up a sample presidential ballot. Describe the people on the ballot to your students, indicating their positions on issues and their ethnic group. Then ask your students to vote. Discuss how ethnicity often plays a role in how we perceive and respond to individuals.

Handicapped Individuals

Handicapped people have been a part of United States society since its beginning. However, because they were isolated and hidden, they were generally unknown to most people in their communities. In the past, handicapped people were sometimes not even accepted by their own families. Fear, shame, and a lack of understanding caused some families to disown handicapped relatives.

Until the nineteenth century, handicapped people without families to care for them were "farmed out." The government paid people to provide room, board, and care for handicapped people. The person who put in the lowest bid was often the one who got the contract. Public concern grew as handicapped people were starved or frozen to death by their caretakers. Reforms resulted and handicapped people were sent to institutions for care.

In the 1800s most handicapped people were put into poorhouses where conditions were generally unsanitary and overcrowded.[22] Between 1870 and 1890, state institutions located outside cities were developed to provide more specialized care for handicapped people. One of their main goals was to protect handicapped people from society.

By the early 1900s, there was a marked reversal in society's attitude toward disabled people. Many people at that time believed society needed protection from handicapped people. Social Darwinism was popular and it was widely believed that most social problems were the result of unfit people having unfit children. Handicapped people were referred to as "mere animals," "subhuman creatures," and "waste products." Today these terms are completely unacceptable. Yet it is this history that both nonhandicapped and handicapped citizens must examine if they are to know and understand handicapped people in today's society.

PREJUDICE AND HOW IT AFFECTS HANDICAPPED PEOPLE

As a society, we have many reactions to handicapped people. Sometimes response to handicapped people is accepting and compassionate. However, unless this attitude is accompanied by respect, it can result in pity and be patronizing. One of the most common reactions is for people who are not handicapped to see themselves as superior to people who are. Because handicapped people are often isolated, we do not get many opportunities to learn about their abilities or disabilities. Stereotyping often results. People with Down's Syndrome are often believed to be incapable of showing emotions. Many people believe that individuals who do not have use of their arms and legs are not able to live alone.[23]

Because people sometimes feel uncomfortable or embarrassed when they interact with handicapped individuals, they tend to avoid them. Some sales clerks are slow to wait on them. Restaurants will often seat them in places where they are not likely to be seen by other customers. People on the street commonly look away, as if to pretend that they weren't there. Many of the problems experienced by handicapped people result from prejudice and discrimination. Lessons about handicapped people can profitably focus on some of the same concepts as lessons about women and ethnic groups.[24]

WHO ARE THE HANDICAPPED?

Public Law 94–142 identifies the handicapped as individuals who are mentally retarded, hard of hearing, speech-impaired, deaf, orthopedically impaired, visually disabled, learning disabled, or seriously emotionally disturbed.[25] Many people see handicapped individuals only in terms of their disability. Handicapped people are a diverse group and should be viewed as individuals who share both similarities and differences. They have the same interests and are as diverse as nonhandicapped individuals. Persons with handicaps, such as Franklin D. Roosevelt and Helen Keller, have made major contributions to our society. Consequently, many handicapped persons prefer that their disabilities be described with adjectives and not with nouns. Thus an epileptic would be referred to as a person with epilepsy and the retarded as a mentally retarded individual.

It is difficult to determine the exact number of handicapped people in the United States. The various agencies that collect data on handicapped people use different methods. This makes the data difficult to compare. The estimated number of handicapped people in the U.S. varies from 35 million to as many as 50 million. Anywhere from 8.6 percent to 12 percent of all working adults have disabilities that limit their ability to work. Special education programs are required for 5.7 percent to 9.4 percent of all school-age children.[26] Most have speech impairments, learning disabilities, or are mentally retarded.

Older people have a greater probability of being disabled than younger people. Adults between the ages of 55 and 64 are three times more likely to have a severe or occupational disability than people between the ages of 35 and 44. They are 10 times more likely to be severely disabled than people between 18 and 34. Due to the work environment and types of jobs, 13 percent of African-Americans and Hispanics—compared to 8 percent of whites and 6 percent of other ethnic and racial groups—were disabled and unable to work in 1978. Disabled people are less likely to get married and more likely to separate or divorce than the nondisabled. The divorce rate for disabled persons is about two times that of the nondisabled.[27]

WHY TEACH ABOUT HANDICAPPED PEOPLE?

Teaching about handicapped people can be an important part of citizenship education. Many of the beliefs and attitudes related to handicapped persons have tended to deny them the opportunity to participate fully in the political, economic, and social life of our nation. Many of the laws enacted to protect handicapped citizens from discrimination are often misunderstood and sometimes interpreted as giving handicapped people privileges that are not available to other citizens. Studying about handicapped citizens gives students an opportunity to examine fundamental issues such as equality, responsibility, and rights in a democracy.

GOALS, CONCEPTS, AND ACTIVITIES FOR TEACHING ABOUT HANDICAPPED PEOPLE

Goal 1

To make students aware of policy issues regarding handicapped citizens and better able to discuss and act on that knowledge.

Concept

Mainstreaming—resulted from the Education for All Handicapped Children Act of 1973, which requires that handicapped students be placed in the "least restrictive environment." This means that many handicapped students who, in the past, were educated in classes with other handicapped students are now required to be integrated into regular classrooms.

Activities

1. Have students write a letter to the school board to find out their school district's policy on mainstreaming.
2. Have students discuss how they would feel and act if they had a severely disabled person in their class. Help your students see that disabilities are on a continuum. Most people have some type of disability, such as being nearsighted or farsighted.
3. Have your students investigate where and how severely disabled people in your community are educated. Ask them to interview a person who teaches severely disabled students. Then have them discuss whether or not they believe disabled citizens are receiving all the educational benefits to which they are entitled.

Goal 2

To provide students with varying perspectives and information on the handicapped.

Concepts

Disabilities and *handicaps*—there is some disagreement over the use of these terms. Some writers use disability to refer to a medical condition and handicap to refer to a person's status as a result of the disability. Often a combination of several definitions is used by agencies.

Activities

1. Disabled in Action (DIA) and the American Coalition of Citizens with Disabilities are groups that promote civil rights for disabled people. Invite a disability rights activist from such a group to speak to your class.

2. Have students read about the disabled rights movement. Then have them role play a rally for equal employment opportunity for disabled people.
3. Have students evaluate library books on disabilities and on disabled people. Ask them to report their findings to the class.

Law-Related Issues

Since the 1960s, educators and legal professionals have developed law-related curricula and materials. In 1963, a group of concerned educators, lawyers, and other legal professionals met in Chicago under the leadership of the Chicago Bar Association. The initial plan for an educational program to promote the study of law in the schools was developed at that meeting. The Law in American Society Foundation was established to conduct teacher-training workshops and to develop curricula. The Foundation's initial work was supported by federal funds. The Foundation's program has grown and expanded since then through the development of a nationwide network of associated projects. It sponsors a number of publications, including a quarterly journal, *Law in American Society: Journal of the National Center for Law-Focused Education*. Significant contributions to the growth and development of law-related education have also been made by organizations such as Law in A Free Society and the Constitutional Rights Foundation.

Law-focused education is designed to help students obtain the knowledge and skills needed to participate more effectively in our legal institutions. A major goal of law-focused education is to help students attain the knowledge, skills, and attitudes needed to obtain their maximum rights within our legal system. Students are also taught about the responsibilities that all citizens must exercise to make our legal system work more effectively and justly.

Major attention is given to local laws, legal institutions, and law enforcement within a sound law-related curriculum. Many of the encounters that people have with the law involve county or city laws and ordinances, and not federal laws. Enforcement of these regulations varies greatly from one locality to another. The norms of the particular agency and the values and beliefs of the individuals who are enforcing or administering the law also vary greatly. When students are knowledgeable about the laws in their communities they can increase their chances for obtaining their legal rights.

The case study method and inquiry approaches are often used to teach law-focused components of the social studies program in both elementary and secondary schools. When examining case studies, especially controversial ones such as the case involving Christine Craft, students explore both the moral and legal implications of the case. They also examine their own feelings and attitudes toward the issues and people involved. Craft, a former television news anchor, sued her employer for fraud involving sex discrimination. She won a half-million-dollar verdict in her first trial. However, that verdict was overturned and a new trial was ordered. This case gives students opportunities to enhance their decision-making skills and abilities. The teacher can have students role play controversial legal cases like the Craft case, and designate different students to play the judge, the jury, defense and prosecuting attorneys, and the defendant. If the case has already been decided, the students can discuss why their verdict in the case is similar to or different from the verdict in the actual case.

Law-related education is an important component of a sound social studies curriculum. It gives students an opportunity to explore social issues from a legal perspective. Many social and human rights issues have a legal dimension. Examining the legal aspects of social issues can help students understand and appreciate the complexity as well as the promise of our democratic society. They are able to examine the wide discrepancies that often exist between our legal ideals and realities, and consider what they might be able to do to help close this gap. Law-related education also provides an opportunity to recognize and respect the legal rights and entitlements of diverse groups. Each of the social issues discussed in this chapter has important legal dimensions and has been affected by important legislation, court cases, or treaties.

GOALS, CONCEPTS, AND ACTIVITIES FOR TEACHING ABOUT LAW-RELATED ISSUES

Goal 1

To help students develop an understanding of their constitutional rights and responsibilities and to become familiar with landmark Supreme Court decisions that reflect American values.

Concept

Justice—a cardinal principle of impartial, fair action in the assignment of rewards or punishments.

Activities

1. The historic 1954 Supreme Court decision in *Brown* vs. *Board of Education of Topeka, Kansas* legally outlawed *de jure* school desegregation. Linda Brown, a young black girl, was prevented from attending her local elementary school in Topeka because she was black. Her family sued the local school board and the case went through the Kansas State court system and was eventually appealed to the Supreme Court. The Supreme Court held that school segregation was unconstitutional. Have your students review the *Brown* decision. Then ask them to pretend that they are Linda Brown in 1954 and tell how they feel about
   a. her local school
   b. her parents' suing the school board
   c. the black school she is attending
   d. the Supreme Court justices who ruled on her case

As a final activity, ask your students to write a one-page statement about how the *Brown* decision has changed our society and the problems encountered when school districts have tried to implement it. Discuss with the students why some people feel that school desegregation protects equality for nonwhites but denies both nonwhites and whites freedom of choice.

2. Contact your local Bar Association and request a speaker to come to your class and discuss the judicial power of the Supreme Court. Ask the speaker to explain how the Court, during the 1960s, expanded the protection given to people who are accused of committing a crime. Three important cases reflecting this expansion are (1) *Miranda* vs. *Arizona,* which requires the police to inform arrested persons of their rights, including the right to remain silent; (2) *Gideon* vs. *Wainwright,* which guarantees defendants subject to jail sentences the right to legal counsel; and (3) *Mapp* vs. *Ohio,* which provides protection against illegal search and seizure. At the end of this presentation, divide your class into small groups and ask each group to discuss this question: How does our society as a whole and how do you as individuals benefit from laws that protect the rights of people accused of crimes? Ask each group to summarize its discussion for the class.

3. Have your students visit a law library to gather information on the Supreme Court's position on the rights of children. Ask the librarian to explain how to use the library and to help the students locate and make copies of Supreme Court decisions in cases like *Oregon* vs. *Mitchell.* The Supreme Court upheld the right of 18-year-olds to vote in this case. When the students get back to their classroom, they can make posters highlighting some of the rights they have as children. The posters can be displayed in the classroom or throughout the school.

Goal 2

Help students to understand our society's need for rules and laws, their origin and modification, and the seriousness and potential consequences of their violation.

Concept

Responsibility—being accountable for your actions and obligations.

Activities

1. Ask your students to act out a situation in which they are stranded on an island with no adults. None of the children know where they are. They don't know what, if anything, is being done to rescue them. They only have enough food and water for two days. After

the students have acted out this situation, ask them the following questions.

   a. Was it necessary for them to decide on certain rules?

   b. If not, how did they make decisions about things like shelter and food?

   c. What are some of the benefits of having rules?

   d. Should everyone obey rules?

   e. What happens to the group when people do not obey rules?

   f. Ask students to summarize why rules/laws are necessary.

2. When our Constitution was written, women were not given the right to vote. That right was given to women by the Twenty-first Amendment to the Constitution in 1920. Ask each of your students to pretend that he or she is a famous suffragist, such as one of the Grimke sisters or Elizabeth Cady Stanton. Then ask each student to write a five-minute speech to present to the class telling why women should have the right to vote.

3. Have your students identify several rules/laws, such as the law against shoplifting, that are sometimes violated by young people. Then have your students survey all of the students at their school to find out how many students are aware of the penalties for breaking those rules/laws. Finally, ask your students to prepare and distribute to all students in the school a flyer listing several rules/laws and explaining the possible consequences for violating them.

SUMMARY

Social issues are society's unresolved problems. These problems are enduring and are not likely to be solved in the foreseeable future. They touch the lives of large numbers of citizens and therefore can add vitality to the curriculum and help make it significant to the lives of teachers and students. The controversial nature of social issues provides excellent opportunities for teaching decision-making and citizen-action skills. Social issues also provide excellent opportunities for students to analyze their values and to develop clarified commitments to important human concerns. Human rights is a unifying theme that connects the social issues discussed in this chapter.

DISCUSSION QUESTIONS AND EXERCISES

1. Define social issue. Find three news stories in a local newspaper that deal with social issues. Bring the news stories to class for a discussion of current social issues.

2. Discuss the similarities and differences among the following concepts:

   a. racism   c. handicappism

   b. sexism   d. ethnocentrism

3. Write key generalizations that are related to social issues using the following concepts:

   a. role
   b. stereotype
   c. mainstreaming

   d. interest group
   e. change
   f. freedom

4. List five citizen action strategies that can be effectively used by elementary and junior high school students to show their concern about the threat of nuclear war.
5. Interview several teachers to find out if they teach about social issues. If they do, find out what issues they teach and the methods used to teach them.
6. Demonstrate your understanding of the following concepts by writing brief definitions for each and telling why each is important.

   a. aging
   b. feminist
   c. disabled
   d. nuclear freeze

   e. global interdependence
   f. law-focused education
   g. social issue
   h. human rights

NOTES

1. A section of this chapter is adapted from James A. Banks, "Foreword," in Margaret Stimmann Branson and Judith Torney-Purta, Eds., *International Human Rights, Society, and the Schools*, Bulletin 68 (Washington, D.C.: National Council for the Social Studies, 1982), pp. v–viii. Used with permission of the National Council for the Social Studies.

2. John Dewey, *Democracy and Education* (New York: Macmillan, 1961; originally published in 1912).

3. Mildred D. Taylor, *Song of the Trees* (New York: Dial, 1975).

4. Sandra Weiner, *Small Hands, Big Hands: Seven Profiles of Chicano Migrant Workers and Their Families* (New York: Pantheon Books, 1970).

5. Ailsa and Allan Scarsbrook, *A Family in Pakistan* (Minneapolis, MN: Lerner, 1985). See this book and others in the Lerner series, "Families the World Over."

6. Thurgood Marshall, "The Real Meaning of the Constitution Bicentennial," *Ebony*, Vol. 42 (September 1987), pp. 62, 64, 66, 68.

7. These documents are reprinted in Paul D. Hines and Leslie Wood, *A Guide to Human Rights Education*, Bulletin 43 (Washington, D.C.: National Council for the Social Studies, 1969).

8. *Statistical Abstract of the United States 1982–83*, 103rd ed. (Washington, D.C.: U.S. Government Printing Office, 1982), p. 823.

9. *Statistical Abstract*, p. 823.

10. Stanley M. Elam, "Educators and the Nuclear Threat," *Phi Delta Kappan*, Vol. 64 (April 1983), p. 535.

11. Elam, p. 535.

12. "Education and the Threat of Nuclear War," *Harvard Educational Review*, Vol. 54, special issue (August 1984).

13. Betty Naomi Friedan, *The Feminine Mystique* (New York: Dell, 1963).

14. *Statistical Abstract of the United States 1982–83*, 103rd ed. (Washington, D.C.: U.S. Government Printing Office, 1982), p. 146.

15. *Interracial Books for Children Bulletin*, Vol. 10, No. 8 (1979). Special Issue on "New Elementary Curriculum Teaches Anti-Racism, Anti-Sexism," p. 7.

16. Donna M. Gollnick and Philip C. Chin, *Multicultural Education in a Pluralistic Society* (St. Louis, MO: Mosby, 1983), pp. 208–209.

17. Gollnick and Chin, pp. 208–209.

18. Kathryn P. Scott, "Effects of Sex-Fair Reading Materials on Pupils' Attitudes, Comprehension, and Interest," *American Educational Research Journal*, Vol. 23, No. 1 (Spring 1986), pp. 105–116.

19. James A. Banks, *Teaching Strategies for Ethnic Studies,* 4th ed. (Boston: Allyn & Bacon, 1987), pp. 13–23.

20. Banks, pp. 14–16.

21. Shizuye Takashima, *A Child in Prison Camp* (Montreal, Canada: Tundra Books, 1971).

22. United States Commission on Civil Rights, *Accommodating the Spectrum of Individual Abilities* (Washington, D.C.: U.S. Commission on Civil Rights, 1983), p. 19.

23. U.S. Commission on Civil Rights, p. 25.

24. James P. Shaver and Charles K. Curtis, *Handicappism and Equal Opportunity: Teaching about the Disabled in Social Studies* (Reston, VA: Foundation for Exceptional Children, 1981), p. 1.

25. Shaver and Curtis, p. 2.

26. Shaver and Curtis, p. 1.

27. United States Commission on Civil Rights, *Accommodating the Spectrum of Individual Abilities* (Washington, D.C.: U.S. Commission on Civil Rights, 1983), p. 15.

FOR FURTHER READING

Human Rights

Banks, James A., and Cherry A. McGee Banks, Eds. *Multicultural Education: Issues and Perspectives*. Boston: Allyn & Bacon, 1989.

Branson, Margaret Stimmann, and Judith Torney-Purta, Eds. *International Human Rights, Society and the Schools*, Bulletin 68. Washington, D.C.: National Council for the Social Studies, 1982.

"Human Rights," *Daedalus*, Vol. 112, No. 4 (Fall 1983), pp. i–280. This entire issue of *Daedalus* is devoted to human rights.

Multicultural Leader (quarterly newsletter). Educational Materials and Services Center, 144 Railroad Avenue, Suite 107, Edmonds, WA 98020.

Global Realities

Barney, Gerald O. (Study Director). *The Global 2000 Report to the President: Entering the Twenty-First Century*, Vol. 1. New York: Penguin, 1982.

Brown, Lester R., et al. *State of the World 1989: A Worldwatch Institute Report on Progress toward a Sustainable Society*. New York: Norton, 1989.

Hahn, Carole L. "Promise and Paradox: Challenges to Global Citizenship," *Social Education*, Vol. 48 (April 1984), pp. 240–243, 297–299.

Lamy, Steven L. (guest editor). "Global Perspectives Education," *Educational Research Quarterly*. Vol. 8, No. 1 (1983), special issue.

Nincic, Miroslav. *United States Foreign Policy: Choices and Tradeoffs*. Washington, D.C.: Congressional Quarterly, 1988.

Nuclear Issues

"Education and the Threat of Nuclear War," *Harvard Educational Review*, Vol. 54 (August 1984), special issue. See especially in this issue, Lowry Hemphill, "Curriculum Reponses to the Threat of Nuclear War," pp. 358–363. This article contains an excellent review of curricular materials for teaching about nuclear issues.

Ehrlich, Paul R., et al. "Long-Term Biological Consequences of Nuclear War," *Science*, Vol. 222, No. 4630 (December 23, 1983), pp. 1293–1300.

Hicks, David, Ed. *Education for Peace: Issues, Principles and Practice in the Classroom.* New York: Teachers College Press, 1988.

Mayers, Teena Karsa. *Understanding Nuclear Weapons and Arms Control: A Guide to the Issues*, 3rd ed., revised. Washington, D.C.: Pergamon-Brassey's International Defense Publishers, 1986.

Schell, Jonathan. "The Abolition: Defining the Great Predicament," *The New Yorker* (January 2, 1984), pp. 36–75.

Teller, Edward, *Better a Shield Than a Sword: Perspectives on Defense and Technology.* New York: The Free Press, 1987.

Turco, R. P., et al. "Nuclear Winter: Global Consequences of Multiple Nuclear Explosions," *Science*, Vol. 222, No. 4630 (December 23, 1983), pp. 1283–1292.

Weart, Spencer R. *Nuclear Fear: A History of Images*. Cambridge: Harvard University Press, 1988.

Gender Issues

Barber, James David, and Barbara Kellerman, Eds. *Women Leaders in American Politics*. Englewood Cliffs, NJ: Prentice-Hall, 1986.

Bassnett, Susan. *Feminist Experiences: The Women's Movement in Four Cultures*. Boston: Allen and Unwin, 1986.

Hymowitz, Carol, and Michaele Weissman. *A History of Women in America*. New York: Bantam Books, 1978.

Lerner, Gerda. *The Majority Finds Its Past: Placing Women in History.* New York: Oxford University Press, 1979.

Morgan, Robin, Ed. *Sisterhood Is Global: The International Women's Movement Anthology*. Garden City, NY: Doubleday, 1984.

Sadker, Myra Pollack, and David M. Sadker. *Sex Equity Handbook for Schools*. New York: Longman, 1982.

Ethnic Groups

Banks, James A. *Multiethnic Education: Theory and Practice*, 2nd ed. Boston: Allyn & Bacon, 1988.

Banks, James A. *Teaching Strategies for Ethnic Studies*, 4th ed. Boston: Allyn & Bacon, 1987.

Glazer, Nathan. *Ethnic Dilemmas 1964–1982*. Cambridge, MA: Harvard University Press, 1983.

Handicapped Individuals

Gartner, Alan, and Tom Joe, Eds. *Images of the Disabled, Disabling Images*. New York: Praeger, 1987.

Herlihy, John G., and Myra T. Herlihy, Eds. *Mainstreaming in the Social Studies*, Bulletin 62. Washington, D.C.: National Council for the Social Studies, 1980.

Shaver, James P., and Charles K. Curtis. *Handicappism and Equal Opportunity: Teaching about the Disabled in Social Studies*. Reston, VA: Foundation for Exceptional Children, 1981.

Law-Related Issues

Berry, Marry F. *Black Resistance/White Law: A History of Constitutional Racism in America*. Englewood Cliffs, NJ: Prentice-Hall, 1971.

Hepburn, Mary A., Ed. *Democratic Education in Schools and Classrooms*, Bulletin 70. Washington, D.C.: National Council for the Social Studies, 1983.

Keller, Clair W., and Denney L. Schillings, Eds. *Teaching about the Constitution*, Bulletin 80. Washington, D.C.: National Council for the Social Studies, 1987.

8

Selecting and Using Instructional Materials and Resources

To solve scientific, valuing, and decision problems, students must collect, analyze, and evaluate data from a wide variety of resources. Information and data from any one resource are insufficient to help students solve problems and answer the range of questions that will arise in the units, lessons, and problems they study. Information and data from multiple media sources present students with diverse perspectives and points of view and stimulate their different senses. Learning is enhanced when it is reinforced by different communication forms.

Students need to use data from a wide range of communication forms in order to formulate and test concepts and generalizations, analyze and clarify their values and those of others, make reflective decisions, and plan thoughtful citizen action. In this chapter we discuss a variety of data forms that can be used to introduce, extend, and enrich social studies learnings. We have classified these materials as (1) reading materials, (2) visual, audio, and audiovisual materials, (3) role playing, creative dramatics and simulation, and (4) the community as a learning resource.

SELECTING AND USING
APPROPRIATE DATA SOURCES

The textbook is the most frequently used data source in the social studies classroom. It consists primarily of verbal and visual symbols. The textbook is consequently one of the most abstract teaching tools. However, abstract materials are not always more difficult than direct experiences. Some simple explanations in textbooks (visual symbols) are much less difficult than some complex demonstrations or field trips during which students view and participate in situations and events with many complex and distracting clues.

You should determine which data source can be used to teach a concept most efficiently and accurately and which will be the most meaningful to your students. The textbook or other reading sources might best be used to introduce many concepts. Demonstrations, field trips, and dramatized experiences might best be used to extend and reinforce them. Once students have mastered the concept *assembly line* as explained in their textbooks, they might then be able to greatly benefit from a field trip to visit an assembly line at a local automobile factory. Field trips are often poor vehicles for introducing concepts. Students see many distracting and irrelevant clues on a field trip and often find it difficult to focus on the essential attributes of the concepts being studied.

Each of the data sources used in teaching the social studies, such as the textbook, the filmstrip, and the field trip, has unique characteristics making it effective for some instructional purposes and ineffective for others. The most important criteria in deciding which data source to use for a particular lesson are the lesson's objective and the nature of the learning activity. A textbook account of Puritan New England can help students acquire the facts about the witch hunts that took place during this period of U.S. history. However, a powerful work of historical fiction, such as *The Witch of Blackbird Pond* by Elizabeth George Speare, will enable students to experience the bigotry and heroism of these times when they identify with the heroine, Kit, who befriends a Quaker woman suspected of being a witch.

Our major point is that no one data source, including the textbook, the field trip, or the dramatized experience, is appropriate for each learning situation and purpose. Each data source has strengths and limitations and is appropriate for specific learning activities, purposes, and goals. No one data source should be regarded as *the* source for the social studies curriculum. Rather, you should use a wide range of data sources to help your students attain instructional goals.

READING MATERIALS

The Textbook

Most teachers in the elementary and junior high school use the textbook as their main source of information, guide to curriculum planning, and ideas about teaching activities. This is not only true for the social studies, but for other subject areas as well, such as reading, language arts, mathematics, and science. Most teachers rely heavily upon the textbook despite the fact that textbooks are often criticized by lay and professional writers.[1]

Textbooks are criticized for being boring to read, for the way in which they are developed and written (usually by teams of authors and editors), and for being shaped primarily by market rather than educational considerations. Each of these criticisms contains grains of truth as well as exaggerations. The textbook, like any human creation, has both strengths and limitations.

Many of the poor teaching practices associated with textbooks result more from the way they are used rather than from the nature of textbooks themselves. The authors, editors, and publishers of textbooks do not intend them to be the only source of information for a particular subject. Unfortunately, however, too many teachers think of the textbook as *the* curriculum and use it as the major if not the only source of information when teaching the social studies. Common statements such as "My social studies book is too big for me to cover in one year" and "I think I will be able to cover my textbook this year" indicate the extent to which many teachers regard the textbook as the curriculum.

A discussion of the nature of textbooks and some of their inherent limitations will indicate why the textbook should be considered only one important source of information in an effective social studies curriculum. Most textbooks, which are expensive to write, produce, and publish, are designed for a national audience. Consequently, it is not possible for them to reflect the unique needs of a particular region, school district, or class. Because several million dollars are usually spent producing a series of social studies books for grades kindergarten through 6, textbooks must be written and produced in such a way that they will be acceptable to many different regions and groups.

Groups concerned about promoting national patriotism, women's rights, civil rights, positive images of the handicapped, free enterprise, creationism, and global education are among the many interest groups that frequently put pressure on textbook publishers. Many of the interests these groups promote are conflicting. Consequently, textbook developers often try to avoid discussing controversial issues, so no particular group will be offended. Textbook authors frequently try to discuss important social issues, such as civil rights and the nuclear buildup, from a neutral position that no interest group will find offensive.

Textbooks in the elementary and junior high school grades are rarely the product of a single author. They are usually developed by a team consisting of authors, editors, and school district consultants. This method of developing textbooks is positive in the sense that the final book reflects the thinking and expertise of a large group of professionals. However, it makes it very difficult for an author to present unique and cogent perspectives on events, situations, and social issues.

While textbooks have inherent limitations, they also have advantages. Most social studies textbooks are well-organized, readable, attractively illustrated, and contain important if highly selective information. The social studies as presented in the textbook is the best social studies curriculum that many students ever experience. This may be because the teacher has a scant background in the social sciences, little interest in teaching the social studies, or assigns the social studies a low priority. Often most of the teacher's time in the elementary and junior high school grades is spent teaching reading, the language arts, and mathematics. Consequently, little time is spent teaching either science or the social studies. Social studies and science are taught only a few times a week in many elementary schools. When the social studies program is thin and sporadic, the textbook is a blessing because it is the only social studies curriculum that exists.

The best way to have an effective social studies curriculum in a school that devotes most of its time to teaching reading, the language arts, and mathematics is to integrate social studies concepts and content into the reading and language arts curricula. This is best done not with textbook-centered teaching, but with interdisciplinary units requiring the use of a wide variety of data sources.

Another advantage of textbooks is that the teacher is usually supplied with useful and carefully developed supplementary materials, such as a teacher's guide or edition which includes answers to questions in the textbook, tests, and teaching activities. Most textbooks also have supplementary materials for the students, such as workbooks, duplicating masters, and other aids. When used wisely and selectively, and adapted for use with their particular units, lessons, and students, these materials can be helpful. However, supplementary materials can be easily abused. This happens when teachers use a teacher's guide without adapting it to their unique situation and class. Student workbooks are often abused when teachers use them to give students busy work that is not clearly related to instructional goals.

UPDATING TEXTBOOKS

To use a textbook effectively, it must be supplemented, enriched, and updated. It is necessary to supplement and enrich textbooks because of the limited space textbooks can devote to any one topic. It is also better to relate the topics, issues, and concepts taught in the textbook to your own students and the communities and cultures in which they live. The content of textbooks also needs to be extended and enriched because they become quickly outdated. The use of old textbooks is often a serious problem in school districts that face financial problems. During financial hard times, school districts are reluctant to replace old books with new ones because of the high costs involved.

Textbooks often need to be updated when a new president is elected, an international crisis arises, or new problems grip the nation. You should use reliable local, national, and international news sources to keep abreast of current events that should be incorporated into textbook lessons. National newspapers such as the *New York Times* and the *Wall Street Journal*, national news magazines such as *Time* and *Newsweek*, and international news magazines such as the *Economist* and *World Monitor* contain valuable information that can help you keep textbooks current. Using resources such as these, you can clip important and timely news items, cartoons, and editorials, group them by categories, and file them for use at appropriate times during lessons or units. Possible categories for grouping news items and stories are

> The conflict in the Middle East
> Global hunger and poverty
> The nuclear buildup
> The presidential election
> Women's rights
> Civil rights
> Local political issues

In addition to updating the content in social studies textbooks, you need to update pictures, charts, tables, and other visual aids when these materials become dated. You may wish not only to update pictures in the textbook but to present the students with other visuals that show different aspects of a city, nation, or situation. A unit on Nigeria or Colombia may show pictures of rural villages but not of cities. Consequently, the students may acquire visual misconceptions about Nigeria and Colombia, not realizing that there are major cities such as Lagos, Nigeria, and Bogota, Colombia, in developing nations.

One of the best sources of pictures to supplement the social studies textbook is magazines such as *Life, National Geographic*, and the *Saturday Evening Post*. Ethnic magazines such as *Ebony* and *Sepia* contain pictures of ethnic groups not usually found in large numbers in magazines such as *Life* and the *Saturday Evening Post*. Parents are a good source of old copies of these magazines, since many families periodically discard old magazines. A useful PTA project is to form a clearinghouse to collect discarded magazines from parents that can be used for instructional purposes. You can also clip pictures from the magazines discarded by your own family. You should keep an ongoing file of pictures and group them by categories such as those listed above. To preserve and display them in an attractive way, pictures should be laminated.

You can use a variety of sources to update statistics, charts, tables, and other information in textbooks. One of the most useful sources for this purpose is the information and data published by the Bureau of Census. The Bureau publishes a series of useful and timely publications. One of the most helpful is the *Statistical Abstract of the United States*. Published annually, it contains census data on a wide range of topics, including population, vital statistics, immigration and naturalization, elections, energy, and foreign commerce and aid. The *Bureau of the Census Catalog*, issued periodically, contains a complete list of the Bureau's publications, grouped by topics such as agriculture, business, and foreign trade.

Almanacs, published annually by a number of commercial publishers, also contain valuable statistical information on a wide range of topics and issues. Most of the yearly almanacs are available in inexpensive paperback editions. You can buy one of these each year and, in time, have a valuable library of statistical information that can be used to compare data from different years and for inquiry exercises. The annual almanacs usually go on sale near the end of the year and are still available during the first part of the next year. The annuals that are published by encyclopedias such as *Britannica* and *World Book* also contain articles and statistics which can be used to update social studies textbooks. These are usually received each year by the school library.

You should be sensitive to the need to update the maps in textbooks. National boundaries change from time to time, especially within the developing areas of the world and in regions, such as the Middle East, where there is ongoing conflict. Many African nations changed their names when they gained independence. It is important that students learn the new rather than the old names of these nations. On older maps of Africa, Namibia and Zimbabwe are called Southwest Africa and Rhodesia respectively. Current editions of standard atlases, such as those published by Hammond and the National Geographic Society, can be used to update the maps in textbooks.

ENRICHING TEXTBOOKS

While it is necessary to update textbooks with both visual aids and information, you also need to enrich and supplement textbooks with other kinds of resources. Different points of view on issues, concepts, and events, information that relates directly to the community and cultures of your students, and art and literary resources are the kinds of materials that are needed to enrich textbooks. Art and literature, as well as other kinds of data sources, are discussed later in this chapter. We will now discuss a few other ways in which textbook lessons can be extended and enriched.

Primary grade textbooks usually include units on families, the individual, the community, the neighborhood, and the school. During a study of the textbook unit on families, you can ask the students to bring pictures of their families, discuss the kinds of families they have, and make a list of the things their families do for fun or recreation. The students can also make a list of the rules they have at home. When the community is being studied, you can survey the parents of your students to learn about their jobs. The parents' jobs can be discussed. Several of the parents can be invited to class to tell about their jobs. To culminate the unit, a field trip can be taken to places where several of the parents work.

In the fifth grade, textbooks often have units that relate to "Our Country and Other Lands." During a study of these units, the class can undertake a historical study of their community by interviewing citizens who have lived in the community for many years, visiting community museums, newspaper offices, churches and cemeteries. You can integrate this experience with the language arts and require the students to write up their community history in narrative form. It can be duplicated and shared with other classes, parents, neighbors, and other members of the community. During their study of other lands, you can survey the parents to find out which nations they have visited.

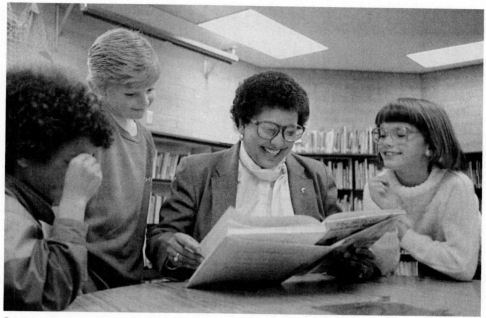

Social studies textbooks need to be supplemented with other materials and resources. This photograph shows a librarian sharing an interesting book with students. (*Source*: Robb Mitchell, Lake Washington School District, Seattle.)

Some of the parents can be invited to give their impressions of the nations they have visited and share their slides, photographs, art, and artifacts.

When using the textbook as a major data source, you should use the experiences and resources of the students, the parents, and the community to enrich and extend textbook lessons. Primary sources found in documentary histories, diaries, conflicting accounts of the same historical events, political cartoons from current newspapers, and dramatic and role-playing techniques can all be used to enrich and extend textbook learning and experiences.

INTRODUCING THE TEXTBOOK TO STUDENTS

You should not hand out the textbook to students during the first few days of the school year until you have developed a plan for introducing it. While introducing the textbook to the students, you should explain that, while the textbook is an important resource, it will be only one of many resources that will be used during the year. Some students might come to your room, because of previous experiences, with the idea that the textbook *is* the social studies curriculum.

You should introduce the textbook to the students by asking them to note the authors, the title, and the publisher. It is a good idea for the students to learn something about the authors of their textbooks. If biographical sketches of the authors are not included in the book (which is often the case in school textbooks), you might be able to obtain information about the authors of the textbook from biographical sources such as *Who's Who in America* or from one of the regional *Who's Whos*. These books are published by Macmillan.

You should explain the parts of the book to the students, including the front matter (title page, table of contents, preface, etc.) and the end matter (the appendixes, glossary, index, and other special features). You should explain the purpose of each of these sections of the book and ask the students to complete a number of activities, such as those below, that will help them to increase their skills in using the textbook:

> How many units are in the book? (Using the table of contents)
> Turn to the first page of the unit on the Civil War. (Using the table of contents)
> Find the first page on which Abraham Lincoln is mentioned. (Using the index)
> Turn to the page where the Constitution begins. (Using the appendix)
> How does the author define *Civil War*? (Using the glossary)
> Find the maps that show the states which made up the Confederacy. (Using the guide to maps)
> Locate the names of the original 13 colonies. (Using the index to locate charts)

Reference Books

You should introduce reference books to students in the primary grades and help them increase their skills in using reference books in each subsequent grade. One of the first reference books that students should learn to use is the dictionary. Picture dictionaries can be used to introduce primary grade children to the dictionary. These dictionaries define words, such as *river* and *school*, with both words and pictures. Some dictionaries for young children, such as *The Magic World of Words: A Very First Dictionary* (Macmillan), define each entry simply but show pictures of only some of the concepts. As students progress through the grades, they should be introduced to increasingly comprehensive and complex dictionaries and helped to attain the skills needed to use them.

There are a number of good dictionaries on the market designed for upper elementary and junior high school students, including *The Oxford Children's Dictionary* and the *New World Dictionary of the American Language*, Basic School Edition. You can help students to acquire skills in using a dictionary with activities such as these:

1. Asking students to rearrange a group of words into alphabetical order.
2. Asking students to write sentences illustrating the various ways in which *culture* is defined in the dictionary.

3. Asking students to tell how the words *citizen, citizenry,* and *citizenship* are alike and different.

4. Asking students to define these words and use them correctly in sentences that are related to the behavior of people: *artifact, norm, behavior, values.*

5. Asking students to find the origins of these words: *delicatessen, pretzel, tortilla, enchilada, chow mein, smorgasbord.*

Students should also be introduced to other reference books, such as encyclopedias and almanacs, in the primary grades. As students progress through the grades they should be given assignments that will help them increase their skills in using reference books. In the primary grades, you can use reference books such as those which comprise *Childcraft* to introduce children to the concept of a reference book. *Childcraft* includes several volumes that treat topics typically studied in elementary social studies, including *Places to Know, How We Get Things, Children Everywhere,* and *Holidays and Customs.* You can introduce young children to these books by reading aloud from them. When the students learn to read, you can make simple assignments requiring them to use these kinds of resources independently or in small groups.

Beginning in the middle and upper grades, social studies teachers frequently give students assignments that require use of the encyclopedia and other reference sources. Students are often asked to prepare written or oral reports, which require the use of reference books. Not infrequently, teachers will assign a written report when the students do not have the skills to select appropriate readings needed to prepare the report, to locate the needed resources, and to organize and write the report. What often happens in these circumstances is that parents do a lot of work on the reports or the students copy verbatim from encyclopedias and other reference works. In the first instance, the report is a product developed largely by parents. In the latter case, the student report is primarily a random collection of quotations from authorities.

To reduce these problems, you should make sure that the students have the skills needed to complete an oral or written report prior to assigning it. This should be done even if the skills were taught in a previous grade. Students' knowledge and skills often become rusty over the summer months. Students also attain skills at highly varying levels when they are introduced.

One way to make sure that students have the skills to complete oral and written reports is to do such a report with the class prior to making the assignment. During a unit on "Leaders and Leadership," a fourth-grade teacher asked each of the students to prepare a written report on one of the nation's presidents. However, before giving the assignment, the teacher chose one president, George Washington, and worked with the class to prepare a report on Washington. The class first did some general reading on Washington. They then made a list of major topics they wanted to cover in the report, including his childhood, education, and early career. They then made a list of resources they could use to find information about George Washington. Their list included encyclopedias, informational books in the school and public library, and U.S. history textbooks that they could borrow from the fifth grade.

The class gathered these materials and read them together. As they read the sources, they took notes and listed the main ideas from the sources under the major topics they had identified. The class then organized their notes and prepared a final outline. Finally, they wrote, edited, revised, and rewrote their report on Washington until it was polished.

Informational Books

Informational trade books intended for a general audience are another important resource you can use to enrich social studies units and lessons. These books are not intended for use as school textbooks and consequently tend to cover a wide range of topics in considerable depth. Informational trade books for children are usually written by single authors. The authors of these books can usually express points of views and positions more freely than textbook authors.

Each year hundreds of children's books are published, many of them informational books that can be used to enrich the social studies. *Children's Books in Print*, *The Elementary School Library Collection*, *Horn Book*, and *The Best in Children's Books* by Zena Sutherland can help you locate appropriate informational books for use in the social studies. Each spring, usually in April, *Social Education*, the official journal of the National Council for the Social Studies, publishes an annotated list of "Notable Children's Trade Books in the Field of Social Studies." This list includes both fiction and *informational* books that can be particularly useful.

Informational books that can be used to enrich the social studies cover a range of topics, from early colonial days to current social issues and problems. Such books can be used to initiate a unit, to test hypotheses, for dramatic and role-playing incidents, and as references when students prepare written and oral reports. Informational books can usually be found in the school and public libraries. You will need to help the students acquire the library skills needed to locate and check out informational books.

Using Fiction to Enrich the Social Studies

There is a gold mine of fiction that can be used to enrich the social studies. When used properly, fiction not only makes the social studies more interesting, it provides the students with valuable insights into historical periods that cannot be obtained easily from textbooks and informational books. Fiction used in social studies should be carefully selected and effectively used. Fiction not only enriches and adds interest to social studies units, it can help students to answer major unit questions.

Historical fiction, novels, poems, stories, and other literary forms can give students keen insights into the hopes, dreams, aspirations, and behavior of peoples who lived in the past and who live today. Students should be taught the difference between fact and fiction. However, they should also be helped to understand how literature provides unique insights into the behavior and world views of peoples.

When the fifth-grade students at one school studied the ancient Romans, they used a children's version of the *Aeneid* to help answer such questions as How did the Romans feel toward the pagan gods? What were the characteristics of an ideal Roman? and What were the favorite legends of the Romans? Each of these questions was related to the central problem of the unit: How did the ancient Romans live, think, and feel? These and other questions were identified in the early part of the unit. The students were encouraged to use a variety of sources to find the answers.

Copies of the *Aeneid* were in the room. The teacher anticipated many of the questions the students raised in the first stage of the unit and realized that the *Aeneid* would provide answers to many of them. After reading the *Aeneid* and factual sources, the students concluded that the Romans held their gods in high esteem, and that an ideal Roman, personified by Aeneas, sacrificed personal wishes for the good of his country. They also knew the legendary history of the founding of Rome.

If fictional writers thoroughly research the period they write about, their words can give the reader keen insights into past customs and practices. Elizabeth George Speare, in the *Bronze Bow*, gives a realistic portrayal of a Galilean boy's struggle to free his people from Roman oppression. This book will give students an appreciation for the Galileans' attempt to escape Roman oppression, thus giving them insight into the problems created by the expansion of the Roman empire.

Fiction can be used to make the social studies more meaningful and interesting to students. However, fictional works used in the social studies should be carefully chosen and used only when they help solve the central problems and questions raised in units and lessons. Their purpose in the unit or lesson should be clear to both students and the teacher. Students should be helped to distinguish fact from fiction. However, they should also be helped to appreciate the social and historical validity of powerful and authentic fiction.

VISUAL, AUDIO, AND AUDIOVISUAL MATERIALS

Visual materials, such as pictures, illustrations, and charts, are often used in the social studies to introduce concepts, reinforce learning, and extend understanding. We have already discussed how pictures can be used to update the content of textbooks. Audio materials such as records, tapes, and radio can also be used to enrich the social studies program. Materials combining sound and pictures, such as sound filmstrips, can also be used to enrich social studies learning. Sound films, which combine pictures, sound, and motion,

Visual materials, such as photographs, are often used in the social studies to enhance understandings and to evoke questions. This photograph shows President Lyndon B. Johnson signing the Voting Rights Act of 1965. What questions can students raise about this photograph?

can help students to experience powerful examples of concepts, value dilemmas, and decision-making opportunities.

The objectives for a lesson should be the main consideration when deciding which form of material to use and how to use it. When introducing a concept such as *culture*, photographs or artifacts might be more appropriate than a film on the Netsilik Eskimo. Most films have many distracting clues and examples, and are better used to reinforce rather than to introduce concepts.

When you use media materials with your classes, you should *prepare*, *present*, and *follow up*.[2] Brown, Lewis, and Harcleroad have identified five steps you should follow:

1. prepare yourself
2. prepare the environment
3. prepare the class

4. use the item
5. follow up

   You should prepare for using an item such as a filmstrip or film by deciding what objectives the item is designed to attain, previewing it, developing questions and activities related to it, and arranging for the delivery of the item. It is important that arrangements for the delivery of the item to your classroom be made well in advance of when you plan to use it. You should also check to make sure that the physical setting is appropriate for the item. You might need to obtain a screen to show a film or an extension cord to use a movie projector in your room.

   Prepare the class for the use of the item by giving the students an overview of it and explaining how it relates to the other unit experiences. The students should have a clear idea of what you expect them to understand from a film or filmstrip. Giving the students a list of key questions is one effective way to help them focus while viewing it.

   After viewing a film or listening to a recording, the class should discuss the major points it presented, relate these points to other learnings in the unit, and evaluate the item. The class may conclude that the film or recording was a valuable learning experience or that some other kind of experience might have been more valuable. Another possibility is that the class will conclude that, while the film or recording was excellent, they would have gained more from it had it been shown earlier in the unit.

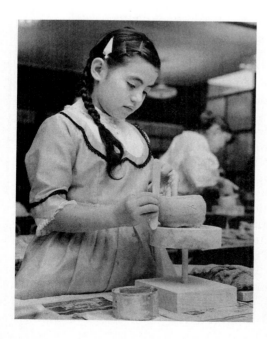

Art activities and projects can be used to enrich social studies learnings. (*Source:* Seattle Public Schools.)

Enriching the Social Studies with Art

The use of art in the social studies can add depth, meaning, and interest to social studies units and lessons. Students in the elementary and junior high school grades can be taught the visual literacy skills needed to derive social science concepts from works of art. Works of art such as paintings, drawings, sculpture, basketry, pottery, and architecture can help students to derive and test hypotheses about peoples who lived in the past and who live today.

After studying a unit on the ancient Greeks that includes a study of their architecture and a discussion of Doric, Ionic, and Corinthian orders, fifth-grade students can be helped to formulate the concept of *cultural borrowing* by looking at a picture of the Roman Pantheon. When they begin their study of the ancient Romans, the students can be asked a question such as What features of the Roman Pantheon are similar to the Greek Temple of the Olympian Zeus (the Olympium) and other Greek temples we have discussed? The students will quickly discover that both buildings use Corinthian capitals. Knowing that the Greeks developed the Corinthian order, they will correctly hypothesize that the Romans borrowed it from the Greeks.

The concept of cultural borrowing is paramount in the social sciences. You can use other examples of art to develop and extend it. Roman art is especially conducive to teaching cultural borrowing because it is highly eclectic. The Romans borrowed many art forms from the Egyptians, the Etruscans, and the Greeks. To further extend the concept of cultural borrowing, you can ask the students to name buildings in their community that use Greek and Roman architectural innovations. This may require some field research. Hardly a student will be disappointed, since nearly every community has public buildings that use classical architecture.

When studying medieval times, the students can discuss the symbolic meaning of the pointed arch and other features of medieval cathedrals. After reading several accounts of the Middle Ages and viewing pictures of medieval cathedrals, the students will be able to conclude that medieval people were preoccupied with life after death and that the medieval cathedral was the ultimate expression of this preoccupation. The pointed arch was especially effective in guiding the worshipper's eyes toward heaven. Medieval people were awed by the potent otherworldly impact of the magnificent cathedrals.

When shown a detail from a medieval stained glass window, such as those in Chartres, students can be asked to tell whether they think the figures look like real individual people or like types and symbols. The students will discover that the medieval artist was not concerned with individuals but with symbols and types. In his preoccupation with the other world, individuals *per se* were not important. Instead, Virtue, Purity, and Evil were personified.

The students can compare medieval with Renaissance paintings. They will discover that the artists of the Renaissance were more interested in this world and in individuals rather than in types and symbols. This is evident by the tendency toward portraiture during this period, by the expensive imported silks, other fabrics, and jewelry in high Renaissance paintings, as well as by the deemphasis of strictly religious subjects. In the architecture and sculpture of the period, the students can see a revival of the classical Greek and Roman traditions. Michelangelo's *David* is an excellent example of this trend.

The art and architecture of today, like that of the Middle Ages and the Renaissance, mirror central concerns. While the cathedral was the ultimate expression of the ideals of medieval Europe, the present-day preoccupation with commerce and industry is reflected in the office buildings that dominate our cities. Louis Sullivan's Guaranty Building (Buffalo), Hood and Howells' Daily News Building (New York), and many other modern office buildings of architectural merit can be viewed. The students can be taken on a field trip to study important modern office buildings in their community and their architects. Several of the architects could be invited to class to share their views of what they were trying to achieve and express in their buildings.

The students can examine works of contemporary American artists and the works of artists in their local communities. Several local artists can be invited to class to share and discuss their works. When the students study contemporary Western art, they can be helped to discover ways in which the freedom and individualism in contemporary art reflect some of the salient characteristics of modern society.

In a number of important ways, art forms can be used to enrich social studies lessons and units. The use of art to reinforce social studies learning heightens students' interests and historical insights. It also gives them a deeper appreciation for the cultural heritage of humankind.

Records, Radio, and Audiotapes

Sounds from both the past and the present can enrich social studies lessons and units. Using recordings and audiotapes is often more convenient than arranging for the showing of a film or videotape. Record players and tape recorders are easily assessible in most schools. Many elementary and junior high school students own their own tape recorders.

A number of commercial records and tapes are available for use in social studies lessons. John F. Kennedy's inspiring inauguration address, Martin Luther King's hopeful "I Have a Dream" speech, and Adlai E. Stevenson's poignant words when he conceded defeat to Eisenhower in November 1952 are examples of excellent commercial recordings. Alex Haley tells the story of the search for his roots on a commercial recording.

You and your students can make recordings. Recordings can be made of important presidential speeches and news conferences to be played and discussed in class. Your students can also make audiotapes for use in their class reports. There are some excellent programs on the radio that can be used to enrich the social studies. In our highly visually oriented age, we tend to forget that the radio is a valuable and effective tool for information as well as entertainment.

Filmstrips, Films, and Videotapes

Sound filmstrips combine pictures and sound. They are an effective teaching tool. Filmstrips can also be stopped at any point to answer student questions and to clarify and extend points made in the presentation. Commercial sound filmstrips are available on an infinite variety of topics studied in social studies classes, such as Colonial America, the Civil War, and the post-World War II era.

Many educational films on social studies topics are produced each year. Some films designed for other purposes, such as television documentaries, are also available for rental or purchase by educational institutions. If used properly, films can add vitality and interest to social studies lessons and units.

However, films should be carefully chosen, clearly related to the major objectives of the unit, be of a high technical quality, and be appropriate for students. The use of films in schools is often abused. Sometimes they are shown as fillers, to kill time or merely to entertain. At other times films are shown when their relationship to what's being studied is unclear to the students. Almost nothing is done in these instances to relate the film to instructional goals.

The discussion and activities that take place before and after a film is shown are in some ways more important than the film itself. These activities extend and clarify the understanding presented in the film and relate them to the other learnings in the unit. Without pre- and post-discussion and activities, the screening of a film might result in little learning.

Videorecorders will become increasingly available in schools as their price continues to go down. Videorecorders and videotapes can be used creatively in the social studies. Students can use the videorecorder to record role-playing incidents and to make class presentations. The portable videorecorder can be used to record observations made in the community and on field trips.

Television

When they become 18, most students have spent more time watching television than in classrooms. Eighteen-year-olds have spent an average of 11,000 hours in the classroom and 15,000 watching television.[3] Television is a salient part of most students' lives. You should help students become more critical viewers of television. You should use television as an instructional medium when it is an effective and feasible alternative.

Television is frequently harshly criticized. Its critics claim that its primary purpose is to sell products rather than to inform and entertain, that the quality of most programs is very low, and that it frequently manipulates viewers. Despite the criticisms, there are some excellent programs, on both public and commercial television, that you can use to extend and enrich social studies learning.

Documentaries, historical fiction, and news programs can all be used to extend and enrich the social studies. Alex Haley's *Roots*, shown on commercial television, combined imagination with facts to present a powerful and entertaining saga about blacks in the United States. *Holocaust* and the *Winds of War* were historical novels serialized on commercial television. *Holocaust* gave keen insights into the experiences of Jews during World War II. The *Winds of War* enabled the audience to share the experiences of one American family during World War II. Excellent documentaries are often shown on commercial television. *Vietnam: A Television War History* was a powerful and informative public television documentary.

Programs such as *Roots, Holocaust,* and the *Winds of War* are not aired on commercial television frequently. You should periodically check sources that announce outstanding forthcoming television programs. You need to be aware of the programs in advance in order to give students viewing assignments. Most public television stations provide schedules of their forthcoming programs to subscribers. *Social Education* periodically announces upcoming outstanding television programs and provides its members with viewing guides that can be used with their students. When television viewing assignments are made, their purpose and relationship to the total social studies curriculum should be clear.

Teaching Visual Literacy Skills

The social studies curriculum, as well as the language arts, should help students develop and increase their visual literacy skills. Whether watching a news presentation or a documentary, students should realize that the director of a film, like the author of a book, has biases and a point of view. Most visual presentations present selected perspectives on events and issues while omitting others. Students should be helped to analyze visual media critically just as they are taught to analyze and evaluate the printed word.

Several curriculum projects are designed to help students increase their visual literacy and critical viewing skills. Public television station WNET/13 (New York) developed a text that helps students view television more critically.[4] It states that critical television viewers

1. Analyze what they see and hear on television.
2. Make informed judgments of what they watch.
3. Express their evaluations in discussion, in writing, or in a choice of reading.
4. Distinguish television fiction from life's reality.
5. Understand television's relationship to the printed word.
6. Make judicious use of their viewing time.

Cortés et al. have developed teaching strategies that help students analyze the media.[5] The strategies are

1. Determination of perspective
2. Evaluation of the logic of analysis

3. Analysis of the topic being discussed
4. Analysis of supplementary materials
5. Analysis of connections with other phenomena
6. Projecting into the future
7. Analysis of self

In step 5, students discuss the future implications of the presentation. In the final step, they examine their own beliefs, attitudes, and perceptions.

The techniques developed by WNET and Cortés et al. can help you devise strategies and questions that will enable students to develop and increase their skills in critically analyzing visual media. When students view a film or television presentation they should be asked questions to increase their skills in analyzing the director's point of view and the perspectives from which the presentation is made.

The Computer in the Social Studies

The computer is increasingly becoming a standard part of the hardware in elementary and junior high schools. Most of the computers in the schools are microcomputers. As microcomputers continue to come down in price and as educators begin to use them more and more, the number of microcomputers

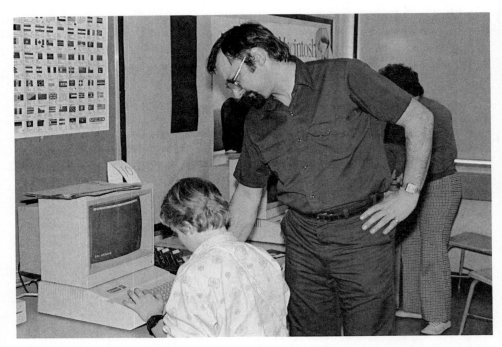

Some teachers use computer software, such as simulations, to enrich social studies lessons and units. (*Source*: Edna Kellman, Seattle Public Schools.)

in elementary and junior high schools will increase. Some students will enter your classroom with rather sophisticated computer literacy and skills, and you will need to have the appropriate computer skills to guide their learning. Since other students will have few computer skills, lessons and activities using the computer will need to be highly individualized.

How you use microcomputers will depend largely on their availability. Some schools have only one or two computers, while others have at least one for each classroom. If there are only a few computers in the school, you can still teach computer awareness and basic literacy skills. Computers placed on mobile units can be moved from classroom to classroom on a fixed schedule. If a computer is available for each classroom, you can establish a computer learning center in one part of your room, and if the computer is assigned to your classroom permanently, then you can go beyond teaching basic literacy and skills. The computer can be used to tutor students, to reinforce skills and concepts, and for simulations and demonstrations. Students can also use the computer to manipulate and analyze data using a computer program such as the *Personal Filing System*.

The teaching of computer literacy and basic computer skills can begin in the primary grades and continue throughout the elementary and junior high school grades. Computer awareness lessons should help students understand the nature of computers, how they follow instructions and manipulate information, and how they help us to solve problems. The students should understand the various parts of the microcomputer and the functions of each part, such as the *keyboard*, the *disk drives*, and the *monitor*. The way information is stored on a *diskette* and how it can be retrieved should also be a part of computer awareness instruction.

Lessons in computer literacy should go beyond computer awareness. They should introduce students to a computer language, teach the concept of programming, and help students develop basic programming skills. The Logo language, which is available commercially in several versions, such as Apple Logo and Terrapin Logo, was designed to be taught to children. Children start learning the language by working with turtle graphics. Children as well as adults find turtle graphics fun and exciting.

Most of the time, you and your students will be using the computer with commercially available programs rather than with programs you have written. Many of these programs provide drill and practice in lower-level skills. Some of the best social studies computer programs involve simulations. These include *Fur Trader*, which simulates a fur trading expedition across Canada by canoe in 1779, *Oregon*, in which students take a trip from Missouri to Oregon by covered wagon in the 1800s, and *Geography Search*, in which students search for a new land and a city of gold.[6]

Selecting appropriate courseware is a difficult and time-consuming task, and one that is not made easier by the paucity of excellent programs and by the fact that courseware made for one kind of computer will not necessarily run on others. Several books contain excellent criteria for selecting courseware.[7] Magazines such as *The Computing Teacher*, *Personal Software*, and *Softalk* periodically review courseware, and *Creative Computing* publishes an annual

Software Buyers Guide. You should make sure that the objectives of the courseware and the objectives of your instructional program are consistent, that the courseware will run on your computer, and that it will interest and motivate your students. It is essential that you actually run any computer program before you buy it.

ROLE-PLAYING, CREATIVE DRAMATICS, AND SIMULATION

Role-playing, creative dramatics, and simulation are techniques that can be used to bring more reality into the social studies classroom. Each of these techniques allows students to experience the feelings, perspectives, and points of view of other people. These techniques can be set in historical or present times.

Role-playing, creative dramatics, and simulation are similar in many ways. However, each technique is also unique. The Shaftels describe role-playing as "a group problem-solving method that enables young people to explore human problems in spontaneous enactments followed by guided discussion."[8] In role-playing situations, several people usually face a problem and are required to make a decision. In their role-playing strategies, the Shaftels present students with a problem story and ask them to identify courses of action and their possible consequences. The students are also asked to make a decision by choosing one of the alternatives. In addition to using open-ended stories, the teacher can use problem situations and dramatic episodes to involve students in role playing.

Students work with a teacher or leader to "create scenes or plays and perform them with improvised dialogue and action" in creative dramatics.[9] Creative dramatics may consist of "creative dramatization of a story told by a leader, . . . creative plays developed to a point where they approach formal plays; and creative dramatics as it is used for tryouts or group scenes in a formal play."[10] Students are allowed to express their feelings and behavior in creative dramatics. They express the thought and feelings of the playwright in formal drama.[11] Students can often develop dramatic presentations that are based on books they read in the social studies. The class that read the *Aeneid* when they studied ancient Rome wrote and produced a play based on the book.

Most of the simulations appropriate for use in social studies classes are *models* of social, economic, or political situations. In simulations, the reality represented is reduced in size so that it is manageable.[12] Only selected aspects of the real situation are included in a simulation. Developers of simulation reduce and simplify reality so students can focus on selected aspects of reality and because of the impossibility of including all of reality in a model or simulation.

There are some excellent commercially available simulations that you can use to extend and reinforce social studies learning. Some creative teachers and their students also develop their own simulations, based on situations, problems, and events they are studying. Simulations can help students to experience realities that other materials cannot. In *Star Power*, students are able to attain wealth by skillfully trading with other players. The group that acquires the most power makes the rules for the game. When the powerful group makes rules to enhance its own power, the powerless groups become increasingly angry and rebel. This simulation enables students to experience what it is like to be powerless.

In *Democracy*, students experience the dilemmas faced by members of Congress when they try to make decisions balancing their values with the values and wishes of their constituents. Students experience some of the problems faced by a community hit by a natural disaster in *Disaster*. The *Market Game* teaches students concepts about a market economy. In *Rafa Rafa*, the participants live with and cope with a different culture. There is a wide range of commercial simulations for use in the social studies.

When you use techniques such as role-playing, creative dramatics, and simulations, every effort should be made to select a technique that is appropriate for a particular lesson or unit and that contributes to the attainment of the unit objectives. These techniques are highly motivating and students usually enjoy them. They are not infrequently used to motivate students when they are not directly related to the unit goals and objectives.

When these techniques are used, a discussion should take place before and after their use. The primary goal of the discussion before the activity is to help the students to see how it relates to the other learning in the unit and to identify its major intended outcomes. The debriefing that follows the use of the technique should summarize and evaluate it.

THE COMMUNITY AS A LEARNING RESOURCE

The community is a rich learning resource that you should not overlook. Institutions and agencies such as factories, museums, zoos, aquariums, newspaper publishers, churches, civil rights organizations, and art galleries are some of the rich resources found in most communities. You can make use of these resources either by taking the students to these institutions (field trips) or by inviting speakers from these institutions to come to the classroom and share their experiences and expertise with the students.

When you decide to make use of a community resource, you will need to determine whether it is more appropriate to take the students to the institution, invite a speaker from the institution to the school, or use some other activity, such as a film, to achieve your objectives. When making this decision, you should consider whether your objectives warrant the time and energy that a field trip involves. Inviting a speaker to the classroom from the institution might accomplish your instructional objectives just as well or more effectively. The decision to take a field trip should be made only when it is the best or only way to achieve instructional objectives. Successful field trips require a great deal of preparation, organization, and energy.

INQUIRY STRATEGY: MAKING DECISIONS IN A ROLE-PLAY SITUATION

Directions

1. Ask the students to carefully read the open-ended story "What Should Arlean Do?"
2. Then ask them to divide into groups of four. One member of the group should serve as the group leader. The other three members of the group should play the roles of

   Arlean Evans, the daughter
   Bruce Evans, the father
   Ruth Evans, the mother

3. The group leader should conduct a discussion with the three role-players so that they will have a clear and definite understanding of their roles. They should understand the points below. The group leader should facilitate the role-play and the discussion that follows.
4. The role-players should forget about their own values, and try to act out the values of the characters in the story as they interpret them from their careful reading of it. The role-players must understand that they are not themselves, but Arlean, Bruce, and Ruth Evans.
5. The primary task in the role-play is to resolve the problem presented in the story.
6. The role-playing should begin where the story ends. In other words, the role-players should assume that they have participated in the events described in the story. Their job in the role-playing situation is to improvise conversation.
7. To end the role-play, the group leader should stop the other members either when a solution has been reached by the role-players, when time is becoming limited, or when the role-playing situation has reached its logical conclusion, even though a solution may not have been attained. The primary function of the role-playing episode is to serve as a springboard for discussion.
8. After the role-playing has ended, each small group should discuss the questions below. The leader of the group should act as a reporter and recorder. She or he should give a brief report of the role play and the discussion in the group when the large group reassembles.

Questions for Discussion

1. What is the main problem in this case? Discuss the main problem rather than ancillary problems.
2. Was the problem resolved in the role-playing situation? If so, is the solution an effective one? Why or why not? If the problem was not resolved, how would you resolve it? What are the possible consequences of the solution you propose?
3. What should Arlean do? Why?

What Should Arlean Do?

Arlean Evans is an attractive, bright, eleventh-grade African-American girl who goes to school at Maplewood High. Arlean is one of a handful of African-

Americans who attend this mainly white school, although about 5 percent of the students are Asians, mostly Japanese and Chinese. Maplewood High is the only high school in the affluent community of Maplewood, which is located in the suburban area of a major city. The Evans family, which consists of Arlean, her brother George, and her parents, have lived in Maplewood all of her life. She attended nearly all-white elementary and junior high schools in Maplewood.

Arlean spends most of her time in her home community. Most of the kids she knows and all of her friends are white. She occasionally visits African-American families in the city, which are her parents' and not her friends. She knows some of their children, but only casually. Once in a while she attends a predominately African-American church in the central city with her parents. Her world, however, is primarily white and middle-class. Arlean feels good about being black and wishes she had more African-American friends.

Arlean is trying to make one of the most difficult decisions of her life: where to go to college. Her best friend, Peggy, has decided to go to State University. Arlean has been accepted there. However, because of her outstanding SAT scores, she has also been accepted at Hamilton, the nation's oldest and most prestigious university. She will receive some financial aid if she goes to Hamilton. Bruce, Arlean's father, is a medical doctor. Members of his family have attended Frederick Douglass University, a highly regarded, predominately black institution, for three generations. He feels strongly that Arlean should go to Frederick Douglass, not only to follow family tradition but, in his words, "to make lifetime friends." He is putting strong pressure on Arlean to go to Frederick Douglass. Because of pressure from her father, Arlean applied to and has been accepted at Frederick Douglass. Ruth, Arlean's mother, is very concerned that, if Arlean does not go to Hamilton, she might miss the educational opportunity of her life. Ruth respects Frederick Douglass and Bruce's family tradition, but believes that Arlean's academic possibilities at Hamilton are more important. Arlean is genuinely conflicted.*

Whenever you decide to make use of a community resource, a great deal of preparation must be made. A speaker must be chosen with extreme care. Speakers should be able to give the students the information they need, communicate effectively with young students, and be acceptable to the school and local community. When you invite speakers to class, you should carefully communicate what you expect from them. You should also inform the principal so that appropriate courtesies can be extended.

You should allow ample time to plan a field trip because careful and extensive planning is required for successful field trips. Here are some guidelines:

1. Visit the institution and find out exactly what experiences the students will have when they arrive.

2. Carefully prepare the students for the trip. Explain why they are taking the trip, how it relates to the other learnings in the unit, and exactly what they will be expected to learn and remember.
3. Prepare a list of questions for the students to answer while on the field trip. Ask only a few good questions. Otherwise the students will spend more time writing answers to questions than looking and listening.
4. Get the principal's permission to take the field trip.
5. Send permission forms to the parents for their signatures.
6. Arrange transportation. While a bus is usually preferable to a carpool, volunteer drivers must be arranged if a carpool is used.
7. Ask several parents to volunteer to go with the class. Having about one adult for every five students will make your job a lot easier. Carefully inform the volunteers of their roles and responsibilities.
8. Check to see what the legal responsibilities are for you and the school prior to taking a field trip and make sure that the school has the appropriate insurance coverage in case of accidents or other problems.
9. Make sure that the students have lunch and restroom facilities during the field trip.
10. Find out what procedures should be followed in the event of an unexpected illness or emergency.

Before a guest speaker or a field trip, the students should discuss the purpose of the activity, the questions they might ask, and how they might use the information collected. The class might be able to get permission to tape the guest lecture or to tape lectures during the field trip and to take pictures. When the guest lecture or the field trip is over, the students should summarize and evaluate the experience. They should carry out the plans for the use of the information they made earlier. The students should also send a thank-you note to the guest speaker or to the institution they visited.

SUMMARY

Students need a wide range of data sources to answer the questions and to solve the problems they study in social studies units and lessons. It is necessary to use a variety of data sources because different sources present diverse perspectives on events, problems, and situations. When a variety of media is used in the social studies, the teacher is able to select the most appropriate media form to teach different concepts and to attain various instructional objectives. No media form is appropriate for all learning situations and for all instructional goals. Some media forms are appropriate for some instructional purposes and not for others. It is also necessary to use a variety of media forms in the social studies because students differ greatly in their learning styles. Different students learn best when different media forms are used.

In this chapter we have described how a variety of media forms can be used in the social studies, including reading materials, and visual, audio, and audiovisual materials. We have described some possible uses for the computer in social studies classrooms. Role-playing, creative dramatics, and simulation are also forms of data; they help students gain feelings, attitudes, and points of view that are difficult to attain from other materials. The community is a rich learning resource. However, like the other forms of information, the community must be used wisely and only after careful and thoughtful preparation.

DISCUSSION QUESTIONS AND EXERCISES

1. Locate a social studies textbook designed for the grade you plan to teach. You will be able to find one in the instructional materials center of your college or university. Select a unit in the book such as "Your Community and State." Develop and write a plan that you can use to update and enrich the unit and make it more meaningful to the students in your community.

2. Choose a social studies unit topic that can be taught at a particular grade level or that you can teach in a class you are student teaching or teaching. Develop a picture file for the topic and cut pictures from newspapers, magazines, and other sources. Develop activities for using these pictures.

3. Develop an assignment requiring students to use reference books. How is the assignment related to the unit objectives? How will you make sure that the students have the skills to complete the assignment?

4. List the units in a social studies textbook. Locate and prepare annotations of five informational and five fiction books that can be used to enrich the units. How can these books best be used to enrich and extend the information in the textbook?

5. Develop a social studies unit plan. Make sure that you include each of the following types of materials in your unit plan. Describe an activity using each type of material:

   a. informational book
   b. fiction book
   c. pictures
   d. recordings or tapes
   e. art (including architecture)
   f. film and/or filmstrip
   g. television
   h. microcomputer
   i. role-playing, creative dramatics, or simulation
   j. guest speaker or field trip

6. Demonstrate your understanding of the following terms by writing or stating brief definitions for each of them. Also tell why each is important.

   a. textbook
   b. reference book
   c. informational book
   d. fictional book
   e. art forms
   f. audiovisual resources
   g. visual literacy
   h. simulation
   i. role-playing
   j. creative dramatics

NOTES

1. Frances FitzGerald, *America Revisited* (New York: Random House, 1979); William E. Patton, "Correcting Sex Stereotypes in Textbooks," in W. E. Patton, Ed., *Improving the Use of Social Studies Textbooks* (Washington, D.C.: National Council for the Social Studies, 1980), pp. 35–48; Nathan Glazer and Reed Ueda, *Ethnic Groups in History Textbooks* (Washington, D.C.: Ethics and Public Policy Center, 1983).

2. James W. Brown, Richard B. Lewis, and Fred F. Harcleroad, *AV Instruction: Technology, Media, and Methods*, 6th ed. (New York: McGraw-Hill, 1983), pp. 69–70.

3. *Critical Television Viewing: A Language Skills Work-a-Text.* Teacher's annotated edition (New York: Cambridge, 1980), p. 8.

4. *Critical Television Viewing.* p. 8.

5. Carlos E. Cortés and Elinor Richardson, "Why in the World: Using Television to Develop Critical Thinking Skills," *Phi Delta Kappan*, Vol. 64 (June 1983), pp. 715–716.

6. Ann Lathrop and Bobby Goodson, *Courseware in the Classroom: Selecting, Organizing, and Using Educational Software* (Menlo Park, CA: Addison-Wesley, 1983).

7. Lathrop and Goodson; Peter Coburn, et al., *Practical Guide to Computers in Education* (Reading, MA: Addison-Wesley, 1982).

8. Fannie R. Shaftel and George Shaftel, *Role Playing in the Curriculum*, 2nd ed. (Englewood Cliffs, NJ: Prentice-Hall, 1982), p. 12.

9. Isabel B. Burger, *Creative Play Acting: Learning Through Drama*, 2nd ed. (New York: The Ronald Press, 1966), p. 6.

10. Burger, p. 6.

11. Burger, p. 6.

12. William A. Nesbitt, *Simulation Games for the Social Studies Classroom*, 2nd ed. (New York: Foreign Policy Association, 1971), p. 4.

FOR FURTHER READING

Budin, Howard, Diane S. Kendall, and James Lengel. *Using Computers in the Social Studies*. New York: Teachers College Press, 1986.

Heinig, Ruth B. *Creative Drama for the Classroom Teacher*, 2nd ed. Englewood Cliffs, NJ: Prentice-Hall, 1981.

Patton, William E., Ed. *Improving the Use of Social Studies Textbooks*. Washington, D.C.: National Council for the Social Studies, 1980.

Schug, Mark C., and R. Berry, Eds. *Community Study: Applications and Opportunities*. Washington, D.C.: National Council for the Social Studies, 1984.

Shaftel, Fannie, and George Shaftel. *Role Playing in the Curriculum*, 2nd ed. Englewood Cliffs, NJ: Prentice-Hall, 1982.

PART _____ III

The Social Science Disciplines: Structure, Concepts, and Strategies

(*Source*: Edna Kellman, Seattle Public Schools.)

While all the social science disciplines study human behavior, each of them views human events and situations from a somewhat unique and different perspective. Each of the social science disciplines also uses research techniques. Each consists of concepts, generalizations, and theories that can make unique and useful contributions to the design and teaching of the social studies in the elementary and junior high school grades.

Part III is designed to acquaint readers with the methods of inquiry and the structures of the various social science disciplines. With this basis they can create learning experiences for students that will enable them to master both the methods and products of social inquiry. *Activities and teaching strategies are an important component of this part of the book.* Activities for teaching each of the key social science concepts discussed in each of the chapters in this part are described. Strategies for teaching key social science generalizations are also found in the last part of each chapter in this section. This part of the book is designed to help readers become more knowledgeable about the social science disciplines and to learn creative ways to teach key social science concepts and generalizations.

9

History: Structure, Concepts, and Strategies

THE TEACHING OF HISTORY

Considerable discussion and debate took place in the 1980s about the role of history in the social studies curriculum and about whether students are learning sufficient historical facts. A number of popular publications indicated that students do not know many of the basic facts about U.S. history and literature.[1] We discussed these works by Hirsch, Cheney, and Ravitch and Finn in Chapter 1. The Bradley Commission on History in Schools, made up of eminent historians and historian-educators, recommended that "the kindergarten though grade six social studies curriculum be history-centered."[2] The History–Social Science Framework for California, issued in 1988, is a history-centered social studies curriculum.[3]

Many of the critics of the teaching of history in the schools, such as Ravitch and Finn,[4] argue that students are not learning historical facts because educators emphasize process rather than basic facts about events, such as the American Revolution or the Civil War, and about major literary figures. However, researchers who have carefully studied what actually goes on in schools, such as Shaver, Davis, and Helburn[5] and Goodlad,[6] point out that most teachers emphasize factual learning rather than thinking processes and higher levels of knowledge, such as concepts and generalizations. Thus, the cure that the critics advocate—the teaching of more facts—is actually a major cause of the problem, say the experts on schools.

Students do need to learn historical facts. However, these facts must be related to concepts, generalizations, and theories if they are to be meaningful to students. People forget a large number of the facts they learn. They tend

This photograph of a farm family listening to a radio in Hood River County, Oregon, on July 20, 1925, can help to enliven history and make it more meaningful to students in the elementary and junior high school grades. (*Source:* The National Archives, Washington, D.C.)

to remember big ideas, like the cause of the American Revolution, rather than factual details. Most people cannot name the capitals of the 50 states in the United States. However, many people can remember that capitals tend to be located in smaller cities within a state rather than in the largest ones. Albany, rather than New York, is the capital of New York; Springfield is the capital of Illinois, not Chicago; Olympia is the capital of Washington, not Seattle. Generalizations about the location and function of state capitals should be emphasized when they are studied, rather than the mastery of the names of the 50 capitals. Students should also know how to quickly locate a state capital when they need to.

We are committed to an interdisciplinary social studies curriculum that includes important concepts, generalizations, and content from history as well as from the other socal science disciplines. Research in history and in the other social sciences is becoming increasingly interdisciplinary. Historians often use concepts and perspectives from anthropology, sociology, and psychology in their research. This makes it easier for teachers to teach from an interdisciplinary perspective.

A social studies curriculum dominated by history may have several unfortunate outcomes. It might become highly nationalistic and focus on the development of blind patriotism. This would be especially unfortunate at a time when the world is increasingly becoming a highly interdependent global community. A history-centered social studies curriculum may also become fact-driven and therefore fail to help students to develop important insights and understandings about the human condition. In the sections below, we focus on the nature of history and describe key concepts and generalizations that can help students to view the human experience from a historical perspective.

WHAT IS HISTORY?

History has at least three separate components. All *past events* can be thought of as history. This part of history is sometimes called history-as-actuality. The *method* used by historians to reconstruct the past is another element of history. The *statements* historians write about past events are also a part of history. Documents, textbooks, and other historical narratives are made up of historical statements.

The views that historians have of the past are influenced by the availability of evidence, their personal biases and purposes for writing, and the society and times in which they live and write. Although history consists largely of accounts of events from particular points of view, it is often taught in school as a body of truth not to be questioned, criticized, or modified. This approach to the teaching of history stems largely from the teacher's confusion about the nature of history and the popular belief that history contributes to the development of patriotism. Much confusion about the nature of history would be eliminated if teachers distinguished historical statements from past events. The historical statement, often referred to as the historical fact, is quite different from the actual event. The event itself has disappeared, never to occur again. An infinite number of "facts" can be stated about any past event.

When future historians try to reconstruct the event in which more than 200 American marines were killed in a suicide bombing in Beirut, Lebanon, in 1983, they will uncover an infinite number of facts. They will find enough facts to fill volumes. However, historians will be neither interested nor able to completely reconstruct the event. Their investigations will be limited by the statements and other evidence recorded by eyewitnesses, newspapers, magazines, radio, television, and other sources. They will not use all of the facts or information they uncover because their purposes, biases, and the times and cultures they live in will determine the statements they will regard as important and valid. American, Israeli, and Lebanese historians might write very different histories of the event.

Historians often encounter conflicting accounts of events when they try to reconstruct the past. On April 9, 1775, shots were fired at Lexington,

Massachusetts, and the American Revolution began. Who fired the first shot, the British or the American colonists, is a problem for historians. Accounts of the Lexington incident written by British commanders and the American colonists often conflict. Historians face similar problems when they try to write accurate descriptions of institutions such as slavery. Accounts written or dictated by slave masters and slaves, and by field slaves and house slaves, often conflict. The historian's problems are complicated by the fact that field slaves on the same plantation often had very different views of slavery.

Since historical sources conflict and historians can never discover all the information about any single event or present all the data they uncover, they must use some *criterion* for selection. Their criteria are highly personal. Current needs and purposes deeply influence historians' interpretations of the past. Becker, the noted historian, writes, "The past is a kind of screen upon which we project our vision of the future; it is . . . a moving picture, borrowing much of its form and color from our fears and aspirations."[7] Historical facts are products of the human mind, since the historian must use sources and artifacts to reconstruct past events.

THE HISTORICAL METHOD

Historians write conflicting accounts of the same events.[8] Historical interpretations of events vary greatly in different times and cultures. Historians debate the extent to which history is a science whose major purpose is to develop generalizations and theories. Historians also disagree about the objectivity of methods of data collection in history.

Historians try to use the method of inquiry used by the behavioral scientist, although they admit that this method must be modified in historical research. Most historians are narrative historians. Narrative historians, such as Arthur Schlesinger, Jr., and Henry Steele Commager, believe that the historical method is to some degree scientific but is at the same time highly personal. Narrative history is a combination of science and art.[9] Gottschalk points out that a clear gap separates past events from written history and that this gap can be filled only by an imaginative process akin to art.[10]

Objective data collection is an ideal and not a reality in each discipline. Historians are keenly aware of the effects of bias on their research. Becker has referred to the researcher's bias as the "personal equation" and argues that it inevitably affects the scientist's conclusions. Becker points out that there is bias in the choice of subject, bias in the selection of material, bias in its organization and presentation, and bias in its interpretation. He argues that historians are "creatures of their time, their race, their faith, their class, their country—creatures, and even prisoners."[11] Perhaps an overstatement, it does emphasize the strong influence of bias on the writing of history.

Sociologists and psychologists attempt to formulate a body of concepts and generalizations that can be tested and verified by other researchers, and thus contribute to building theories. Narrative historians typically study and describe single past events, and approach them in a somewhat personal fashion. Narrative historians describe events rather than attempt to test generalizations and theories. Conflicting findings and interpretations are found more often in narrative history than in the behavioral sciences.

Narrative historians have serious doubts about their ability to formulate scientific generalizations and theories. They regard the reconstruction and description of past events as their primary and proper goal. They also believe that the narratives they write should be interesting and appealing. Some narrative historians believe that history is a branch of literature and that it serves some of the purposes and is governed by some of the principles of literature.[12] Narrative historians are primarily interested in description rather than the formulation of generalizations and theories that explain behavior. They often study specific and unique events rather than a large class of different events having common characteristics.

SCIENTIFIC AND QUANTITATIVE HISTORIANS

While most historians use narrative to imaginatively reconstruct the past, some historians are interested in using quantitative data to test hypotheses and to derive generalizations. These historians are called *scientific* or *social science* historians. Scientific historians often use quantitative data to test hypotheses and to formulate generalizations and theories. Many political and economic historians use quantitative data in their research. Their subfields are known as the "new political history" and the "new economic history."

Scientific historians use quantitative techniques to study such topics as the composition of the British House of Commons, social mobility using census data, public opinion in the past, trade in the Old Northwest, and ethnic groups and voting patterns. Scientific historians such as William O. Adelotte, Lee Benson, and Allyn G. Bogue are optimistic about the contributions scientific and quantitative history makes to historical inquiry and knowledge.[13] However, humanist historians, such as Commager and Schlesinger, believe that many of the most important questions in history must be studied using the approaches and techniques of the humanist rather than those of the scientist.[14] The debate between narrative and scientific historians continues as each group enriches the discipline, which has elements of both science and the humanities.

HISTORY: A MODIFIED SCIENCE

History is scientific because historians try to use the scientific method of inquiry. However, they use it differently from most other researchers. Historical data have large gaps which historians are unable to fill because the events which they study took place in the past and will never occur again. When they study the makeup of Congress or the census in the late 1800s, they

Ethnic history is an important part of the new social history that is now being emphasized by historians. This photograph shows Indians from a Southeastern Idaho reservation in 1897. (*Source*: The National Archives, Washington, D.C.)

1970s. A "new" political history and a "new" economic history emerged. In these two subfields particularly, and in history generally, historians tried to become more analytical, quantitative, and scientific. Many historians "tried harder than ever before to theorize and generalize, but also to respect the particularities of place and time—in sum, not to violate the pastness of the past."[20] Historians tried to be both more analytical and more richly descriptive.[21] Historians also tried to use more quantitative methods and computer technology to answer questions and to test hypotheses.

Historians became less nationally chauvinistic and more inclined toward national self-criticism in their writings during the 1970s. However, they also became more inclined to inject moral positions into their writings and to view history as a moral science. Wrote Gordon Wright, "Our search for truth ought to be quite consciously suffused by a commitment to some deeply held humane values."[22] Historians have heavily borrowed methods, theories, and concepts from other disciplines in recent years. This has enriched history and resulted in more diversity in the discipline. Some historians have borrowed generously from anthropology. Kammen writes, "It is now acceptable for [historians] to plot kinship and child-rearing patterns, analyze festivals and describe idiosyncrasies of village celebrations."[23]

HISTORICAL CONCEPTS

Substantive

The key concepts, generalizations, and theories of a discipline are part of its *structure*. These knowledge components enable the social scientist to view human behavior from restricted perspectives. Student must study these higher levels of knowledge in order to become adept decision-makers and reflective citizen actors. Thus an important goal of the social studies should be to help students learn the key concepts and generalizations within the disciplines. Conceptual approaches to instruction enable students to view behavior from diverse disciplinary perspectives and to understand higher levels of knowledge. Other elements of *structure* are the modes of inquiry used by social scientists to solve problems and to derive concepts, generalizations, and theories. Students must use scientific modes of inquiry to derive higher levels of knowledge.

In Chapter 2 we described the advantages of using conceptual approaches to instruction. However, it is difficult to draw concepts from some of the disciplines for instructional purposes, either because the field's leaders have not focused much attention on their special concepts or, more frequently, because social scientists are unable to agree on what the key concepts within their disciplines are.

Despite the difficulties involved in identifying the key concepts within the disciplines, conceptual approaches are sound. The difficulties involved in identifying key social science concepts indicate the level of scientific development of the social sciences rather than the invalidity of conceptual approaches to instruction. Identifying key concepts in history to guide instructional planning poses special problems. While the behavioral sciences use specialized conceptual frameworks to view human behavior, history's uniqueness stems from the fact that it views behavior that has taken place in the past, and is interested in the totality of the human experience. Because it is concerned with the past, it uses a modified mode of scientific inquiry.

Whereas the sociologist and the political scientist are mainly interested in *socialization* and *power* respectively, the historian may be, and sometimes is, interested in how each of these concepts is exemplified in past human behavior. History, then, is a truly interdisciplinary field since historians, in principle, are interested in all aspects of past human behavior. Thus it is difficult to speak about unique historical concepts. Yet every discipline makes use of the historical perspective and has historical components. When a sociologist studies norms and sanctions in colonial America, and the economist describes how the colonists produced goods and services, they are both studying history.

A quick review of lists of the historical generalizations found in school district and state education departments' curriculum guides will reveal how history uses concepts that originate in other social science disciplines. Note these two examples of historical generalizations prepared by a state department of education:[24]

1. Communities today differ from communities of earlier times.
2. The rate of cultural change varies from one country to another.

The key concepts within these two statements are *communities* and *cultural change*. Community and cultural change are sociological and anthropological concepts, respectively.

Some sources suggest that *change* is a key historical concept. It is true that we cannot verify statements about change without the use of historical data. However, when we speak of change, we must also use some other concept. Change describes the status of concepts at different points in time. Thus change is a relational concept (see Chapter 3). Although change is a historical concept, we must recognize that we can't study change unless we talk about it in concepts usually associated with other disciplines. For example, we can write generalizations about *cultural* change (anthropology), change in *goods* and *services* (economics), or change in *regions* (geography). Both historical data and concepts within other disciplines are necessary to state and test generalizations about change. In the teaching strategies section of this chapter, for example, we describe strategies for teaching change related to the sociological concepts of transportation, schools, entertainment, and the geographical concepts of exploration and regions.

We can show change only by using concepts usually associated with the other social sciences. However, we can make some generalized statements about change that cut across disciplinary lines. We can study, for example, change in transportation, schools, entertainment, exploration, and norms, and make some statements about the factors related to change in general. We can hypothesize that change constantly takes place, that people usually find it more difficult to adjust to social than to technological change, and that change is sometimes abrupt. Statements about generalized change can be called historical since historical data are necessary to test them.

Whereas the behavioral scientist uses specialized conceptual frameworks to view human behavior, the historian can and sometimes does use concepts from different social science disciplines to study the past. *The historical perspective should be concerned with the totality of the human past.* Traditionally, however, many historians have studied the past primarily from a political science perspective. As we point out above, however, more historians are now studying the totality of the human past from different disciplinary perspectives. Social historians study ordinary people. Other historians study political events, leaders, economic events, and institutions.

There is a tremendous lag between historical scholarship and school history. School history textbooks still largely reflect political history. A glance at the table of contents of almost any history textbook will reveal the predominance of political concepts—wars, treaties, revolutions, political leaders, and national movements. However, writers of some history textbooks have been influenced by the new developments in historical scholarship. Today's history textbooks include more information about the lives of ordinary people, families, women, ethnic groups, and factory workers. The more innovative history textbooks often include excerpts from the letters and diaries of ordinary men and women.[25]

The inclusion of new interpretations, social issues, and information about women and ethnic groups in textbooks has evoked criticism. Some writers claim that textbooks have strayed too far from traditional political history or that they overemphasize ethnic perspectives in American history.[26] Other observers believe, however, that the innovations in textbooks have not gone far enough. Some educators believe that the most recent history textbooks are more political, traditional, and factbound than those published in the 1970s. These books, these educators claim, reflect the new conservatism in the nation.

Methodological

The concepts discussed above are related to the content (product) of history. We have noted the difficulty involved in identifying substantive historical concepts. However, history consists of more than its products or conclusions. History is also a process. The mode of inquiry historians use to solve problems and to derive generalizations is also part of the structure of history. While the concepts within history are interdisciplinary, the method used by historians to solve historical problems is unique; historians are the only group of researchers whose research is limited to the reconstruction of past events. Their problem is complicated by the fact that past events have taken place and will never recur. Sociologists can always study a new family situation. Political scientists can observe a future national election.

It is important to teach concepts and generalizations about historical method, as well as concepts related to historical conclusions (products). In the teaching activities that begin on page 283, we state a generalization related to historical research, and describe strategies for teaching it.

The study of historical method (historiography) should constitute a substantial part of a modern historical studies program. A study of the historian's method will enable students to gain an appreciation of the difficulties involved in reconstructing the past, strengthen their inquiry skills, and enable them to become more thoughtful consumers of history.

The concepts used by historians are borrowed from the other social sciences. Historians have written very little about the concepts they use and their place in the social studies curriculum. Fenton, the historian-educator, believes that historians are uncomfortable with concepts. He states that the *analytical questions* that historians ask—rather than key concepts and generalizations—make up the heart of history.[27]

Examples of Concepts

Historians have not written very much about the concepts they use. In a book edited by Edward N. Saveth, a number of historians describe how concepts such as group structure, mobility, social structure, role, leadership, and power can be studied using historical data.[28] Some of the major social science concepts frequently used by authors of history textbooks are described below. Examples of activities that can be used to teach them are also described. Most of these concepts deal with the products (conclusions) of history; one relates to the historical method. Students can be helped to gain historical insights and understanding by studying these concepts using data about past human behavior.

CHANGE

Things in our social and physical environment are constantly becoming different each day, week, and year. It is very important for students to understand the factors that cause change and be able to adjust to and accept change. Historical data must be used to develop this concept effectively, although it is interdisciplinary. You can use concepts from each social science discipline to help students understand the dynamics of social and cultural change.

Activities

1. Ask students to study their childhood pictures at different ages and to tell how they are alike and different.
2. Ask students to state the differences noted in pictures taken in their community recently and those taken 20 years earlier.
3. Compare the roles of women now and in the late 1800s.
4. Compare the culture of the Iroquois today with their culture in the 1840s.

LEADERSHIP

Leadership is the exercise of influence and authority by an individual or group within a social relationship. The democratic leader respects the right of all group members to participate in decision-making and the setting of group goals. The authoritarian leader determines the goals and rules for the group and does not allow other group members to help determine group goals.[29] No leader is entirely democratic or authoritarian. Leaders are more or less democratic or authoritarian.

Activities

1. Study national leaders whose birthdays we celebrate, such as George Washington and Martin Luther King, Jr.
2. Discuss some of the groups the students belong to, such as Blue Birds and the Boy Scouts. List the characteristics of these groups' leaders. Discuss what makes a person or group a leader.
3. Have each child research one American president and discuss ways in which these presidents were alike and different.
4. Interview community leaders and ask several to talk to the class.
5. Study leaders of social movements such as Susan B. Anthony, Cesar Chavez, and Jane Addams. Discuss the extent to which the movements these leaders led were successful.

CONFLICT

Throughout history, disagreements and hostilities have arisen between individuals, groups, and nations when they had divergent goals or different ideas about how similar goals could best be attained. While conflict, like change, is an interdisciplinary concept, historians spend much of their time documenting conflicts and wars. Most past conflicts have had both positive and negative consequences.

Activities

1. Observe disagreements on the playground and note why they occur.
2. Read selections about the American Revolution, the Civil War, and the civil rights movement of the 1960s. Generalize about what causes conflict, its consequences, and ways to resolve conflict.
3. Read about the cultural conflicts experienced by Polish immigrants when they came to the United States near the turn of the century.
4. Identify the major causes of the conflict in the Middle East and explain how it developed.
5. Study the concept *revolution*. A revolution takes place when an existing government is abruptly overthrown, and a different group assumes power. Study the following revolutions and generalize about the causes and sequence of events during a revolution: American (1776), French (1789), Russian (1917), and Algerian (1962).

COOPERATION

Cooperation occurs when individuals or groups work together to achieve the same goals. Students will acquire a skewed view of history if they study about conflict but do not learn about the ways in which individuals and groups have cooperated in the past—and still cooperate today—to solve problems and to bring about social and political change.

Activities

1. List ways families work together to get jobs done around the house.
2. List ways people in the school work together to attain goals.
3. List ways various workers and members of the community work together to improve it.
4. Describe ways the Indians helped the colonists to learn to plant and grow crops in America.
5. Study the history and functions of the United Nations (UN), the North Atlantic Treaty Organization (NATO), and the Organization of American States (OAS) and list ways different nations work together to promote peace and economic development.

NATIONALISM

Nationalism exists when leaders and individuals within a nation take actions intended primarily to strengthen and develop it, and to inculcate loyalty among its citizens. Nationalism is in some ways an ethnocentric doctrine. Nationalists are not very interested in international relations, but primarily in the development of their own nation. In their study of the development of nationalism throughout history, students will be able to conclude that while nationalism is necessary for a nation's development, extreme nationalistic feelings sometimes result in conflict and wars.

Activities

1. Through questioning and discussion, help the students understand how their feelings and attachments to their family, their club, baseball team, or school are similar to feelings that people have toward their nations. Ask them to tell why these kinds of feelings and attachments develop.
2. Read letters, diaries, and other primary sources that reveal why many Southerners experienced a conflict between regional and national loyalties during the Civil War.
3. Identify key events in early United States history indicating that nationalism was developing and the challenges it faced.
4. Describe the role that nationalism played in mobilizing Germany and Japan for participation in World War II.
5. Describe the crisis that American nationalism experienced during and after the Vietnam war.

EXPLORATION

Historians devote a great deal of attention to men who traveled into lands unknown to them. Exploration is a geographical concept. In extolling the virtues of European explorers, historians have sometime distorted or omitted any discussion of the cultures of the people who inhabited the lands before the coming of the Europeans. When using historical data to teach students about exploration, the teacher should help them to view exploration from both the perspectives of those who were exploring as well as from the perspectives of the peoples who inhabited the native lands.

Activities

1. Ask the students to name men and women today who are going to unknown places or discovering new things. Point out that astronauts, archeologists, and scientists are explorers.
2. Read to the students the part of Columbus's diary that describes how he first landed in the West Indies and met the Arawak Indians. Then read them accounts of the Arawak Indians' lives. Ask the students to tell how the Arawaks might have reacted to Columbus's description of them.
3. After the students have studied Cortés's exploration of what is today Mexico, ask them to role play a meeting between Cortés and some Aztec Indians.
4. Study the impact of European exploration into Africa during the fifteenth century.
5. Research the impact of the westward movement in the nineteenth century on American Indian cultures.

HISTORICAL BIAS

No matter how hard they try, historians are unable to completely reconstruct a past event. Many of the sources and artifacts they uncover contain contradictory and inconsistent information. They must judge the accuracy and authenticity of the data. Their data selection is greatly influenced by their personal biases, the nature of the data, their audience, and the culture and times in which they live. Because of the limitations of the historical method, it is very important for students to learn how history is written so that they will be critical readers of the conclusions in their textbooks and in other sources.

Activities

Activities that can be used to teach this concept are in the teaching strategies section of this chapter, beginning on page 283.

HISTORICAL GENERALIZATIONS

Scientific historians are keenly aware of how difficult it is for historians to agree on facts and interpretations. Nevertheless, they believe that historians can agree enough to formulate generalizations. Haskins states that historical generalizations can be formed because "historic events follow the same natural laws as the objects of science."[30]

Most narrative historians distrust generalizations. However, a historian cannot describe a single event or institution without making some kind of

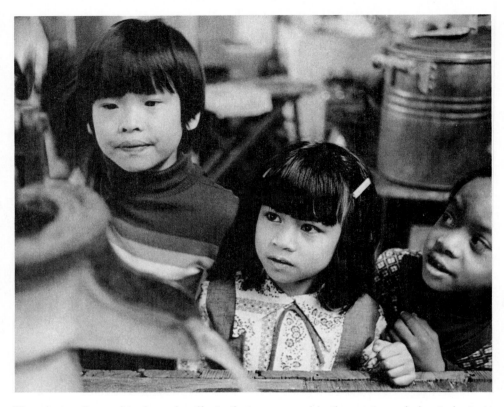

The observations of tools and artifacts that were used in the past can help students to deepen their historical understandings. This photograph shows a group of students observing the type of pump that was used by many farm families in the past to get water from the ground. (*Source*: Seattle Public Schools.)

generalized statements. "The serfs in France were angry" and "The kings of France were arbitrary" are lower-level generalizations about the French Revolution. The second generalization could be written at a higher level if more examples were encompassed within it. It would then read, "The monarchy in eighteenth-century Europe was arbitrary."

Gottschalk, who edited a book on generalizations in history, concluded that all historians make generalizations. However, often historians make generalizations and are not aware that they are making them.[31] Sometimes historians know they are generalizing, but they try to limit generalizations to the event or period they are studying. Scientific historians deliberately try to form generalizations that can apply to a large range of trends and events. They sometimes make generalizations that have implications for future events. During his study of the British, American, French, and Russian revolutions, Crane Brinton derived the generalizations listed below.[32] They not only describe past events, but suggest the nature of future revolutions. Brinton, like other scientific historians, would not argue that these conditions will always emerge whenever and wherever a revolution occurs. However, he does suggest that if a revolution occurred in a society similar to those he studied, the conditions described by these statements will very likely emerge.

Generalizations about Revolutions

In a revolutionary state, vocal critics emerge who create a myth about the coming of a utopian society and decry the evils of the existing regime.

In revolutionary societies, moderate leaders take over after the old regime is overthrown; the moderates are eventually overruled by extremists.

When extremists take control of the government during a revolution, a reign of terror ensues.

Teaching Historical Generalizations

Explicit generalizations are as rare in history textbooks as they are in most narrative histories. Despite the limitations of the historical method and the paucity of historical generalizations, you can help students in elementary and junior high school to generalize using historical data. However, historical generalizations must consist of concepts from other disciplines, such as conflict, exploration, and nationalism. Historical generalizations state how social science concepts were related in the past. Higher-level generalizations are difficult to formulate in history because of the historical method's limitations.[33] While students should be taught to derive and test historical generalizations, they should be keenly aware of their limitations. When students derive statements about the French Revolution, they should realize that a revolution occurring in a society significantly different from France in 1789 may be characterized by a different sequence of events.

Since most history textbooks are organized chronologically and give scant attention to generalizations, you will need to identify the historical generalizations you wish your students to learn during the year, and then to select the appropriate materials and teaching strategies. The generalizations chosen for study may be limited by the topics and content you are required to teach in a particular grade. However, American, state and world history is rich with data that can be used to teach a wide range of generalizations.

You can find lists of historical generalizations in a variety of sources, including conceptual frameworks for basal social studies series, methods books, and school district curriculum guides. You should realize that generalizations on lists can vary widely in quality. Some are of a very low order. Many are not empirical statements at all but are value claims. Others lack empirical support and contain dubious concepts.

Even an excellent list of generalizations is only a list, and should only be used to plan and guide instruction. Students must derive generalizations for themselves if they are to have any meaning. Memorizing meaningless generalizations is not essentially different from memorizing a list of unrelated facts, a practice most educators now publicly criticize. We should not repeat the same kinds of mistakes when teaching students key concepts and generalizations.

INQUIRY STRATEGY: THE WORLD AND YOUR FAMILY

This activity is designed to enable your students to dig into their families' pasts and to determine what was happening in their families when some major U.S. and world events were occurring. Give the students the following list of key events in world and U.S. history. Ask them to interview family members to find how what important events were happening in their families at these times. They might find out such things as where their ancestors (on the mother's side, father's side, or both) were living when the Women's Rights Convention was held in 1848. One student may discover, for example, that, in 1848, her ancestors on her mother's side were living in New York while those on her father's side were in Russia.

Some students will be unable to find out where their families were or what they were doing in some of the years listed. However, almost every student in your class will be able to find out something about his or her family during at least one of those years. Encourage your students to find out such things as where their families were living (such as, in what city, state, and nation), what kinds of jobs they had, and what kinds of positions they took on such events as the civil rights movement of the 1960s and 1970s and the Vietnam War. Also encourage them to find out whether their families experienced any special situations, problems, or good times during the years listed. They should also try to determine if any members of their families took an active part in any of the events listed, such as the civil rights movement or the Vietnam War.

Allow the students to skip any events for which they cannot find information about what their ancestors or families were doing.

Benchmark Events

1848	Women's Rights Convention, Seneca Falls, New York
1917	United States' entry into World War I (The Great War)
1929	The stock market crash, signaling the beginning of the Great Depression
1941	United States' entry into World War II when Japan attacks Pearl Harbor
1954	The *Brown* decision, in which the Supreme Court rules that school segregation is inherently unequal
1955–56	The Montgomery Bus Boycott, which signaled the beginning of the civil rights movement of the 1960s
1963	The March on Washington and Martin Luther King, Jr.'s, "I Have a Dream" speech
1968	With half a million U.S. combat troops in Vietnam, a controversy rages about whether the U.S. should continue to participate in the war. The war ends in 1975 with a communist victory, when Richard Nixon is president. No war since the U.S. Civil War divided the nation so deeply.
1980	Ronald Reagan elected president of the United States

Examples of Historical Generalizations

Because history, in principle, is concerned with the totality of the human past, it is a truly interdisciplinary discipline. It can and sometimes does use concepts from all the social science disciplines to explain the past. We have identified several generalizations below that can be considered historical, and indicated the social science concepts and disciplines to which they are related. This list of historical generalizations can be used to guide the planning of historical studies in the elementary and junior high school grades.

Change (History-Sociology)

Human society is characterized by change.

Conflict (History—Political Science)

Whenever human beings have lived, conflicts between individuals, groups, and nations have arisen. Although conflicts have some negative effects on society, they are often the impetus for effective change.

Cooperation (History-Sociology)

Throughout history, individuals and groups with different cultures and experiences have worked together to achieve common goals, especially when they were threatened by outside forces.

Revolution (History—Political Science)

Revolutions tend to occur in societies where organized groups *perceive* their conditions, which are beginning to improve, as intolerable, public officials as unresponsive to their needs, and legitimate channels for alleviation of grievances as ineffective.

Culture (History-Anthropology)

Wherever humans have lived, they have developed systems of artifacts, beliefs, and behavior patterns that enabled them to satisfy their physical and social needs.

Exploration (History-Geography)

The explorations people made into what were to them strange territories resulted in tremendous cultural exchange as well as conflict between different cultural and ethnic groups. In general, more technologically advanced cultures have assimilated or destroyed cultures that were less technologically developed.

Historical Bias (History)

A historian's view of the past is influenced by the availability of evidence, his or her personal biases and purposes for writing, and the society and times in which he or she lives and writes.

Patriotism and the Teaching of History

Many educators and lawmakers believe that history should be taught in the public schools because it contributes to the development of patriotism and democratic attitudes. Nearly all 50 states require the teaching of United States history because lawmakers believe it helps develop good and patriotic citizens. Some problems have resulted from regarding history instruction primarily as a means to develop patriotic citizens. One serious problem is that there is no public agreement about what kind of patriotism history teaching should develop and about what characteristics patriotic citizens have. Some educators consider patriotism a blind and uncritical acceptance of our nation's past and present.

Because of this notion of patriotism, textbook history has often consisted largely of carefully selected events that show the most positive and harmonious aspects of our nation's past and the most glorious deeds of our national heroes. During the unprecedented quest for human rights in the 1960s and 1970s, many school history books were revised to deal more forthrightly with the problems and value conflicts in our nation. At the same time, they described the tremendous achievements of the American republic and its future prospects. No textbook was without flaws during this period. However, many were substantially improved. Women, ethnic groups, and handicapped citizens appeared in textbooks more than ever before. By the beginning of the 1980s, however, history textbooks were beginning to look more political and traditional. You must supplement history textbooks in order to present your students with a balanced and accurate view of our nation and world.

TEACHING REFLECTIVE PATRIOTISM

The challenging world society in which we live demands a reflective patriotism. To perpetuate democratic ideals and a just national and world society, we need citizens who are not only acutely aware of the characteristics of a democracy, and committed to its ideals, but who are also aware of the inconsistencies between our ideals and behavior. Only then will they be able to help close the gap between the ideals and reality. Citizens who are uncritical and nonreflective will not be able to improve our nation. A patriotic and effective citizen is one who has developed an appreciation for the democratic process by being allowed to use it, who is aware of the struggles, shortcomings, and successes that Americans have experienced to make democracy a reality, and who is willing to act in ways that will maximize democratic opportunities for all the citizens of our nation and world.

When students are saturated with half-truths and sugar-coated success stories about our nation and national heroes, they may conclude that the building and perpetuation of a democracy is an easy job. They need to learn that struggles, pain, agony, and sometimes bloodshed are necessary to build and maintain a democratic and just society. That we have not yet attained this cherished goal should be realized by students. However, they should also know that much progress has been made and that they can help to complete the job. Effectively taught history lessons can help students develop a commitment to democratic values and social change.

Goals for Teaching History

Major public policies in our nation and world are frequently made with little regard for history and often reflect a preoccupation with the present. When a nation pays little attention to its history, it loses much of its capacity to understand its present and to shape its future. Because of the persistent and complex problems that our nation and world face, we need historical insight to help us understand our world. We also need historical insight to shape alternative futures that are rooted in historical realities rather than in myths and illusions.[34] Thus a major goal of history teaching should be to help students develop historical understanding and insight.

Students should not only study the products of history as found in their textbooks and other sources; they should also solve historical problems using the methods of the historian. By using the historical method, students will derive generalizations that help them understand human behavior in the past, present, and future. Historical generalizations will also help students appreciate the pace and extent of change in the modern world.

Helping students to understand and use the methods of the historian should be important objectives of the social studies. We cannot teach what actually happened, but must teach historical accounts from various perspectives. By using this approach to history, you will help your students discover that written history is largely made up of accounts of events from particular points of view. Studying the methods of the historian will also help students realize that there are many ways of looking at identical events and situations. Their own reasoning and critical powers will be used and strengthened. If students are taught to treat history as assured knowledge, they are likely to believe that seeing information in print is sufficient evidence of its credibility.

Learning the method of the historian is also valuable because history is not only an account of the past but a method of inquiry. It develops through a process of asking questions and attempting to find answers. In addition, it involves evaluating the importance and authenticity of artifacts and documents and using them skillfully to understand the past. Just as baseball players cannot become skillful by watching baseball games, students cannot fully understand history by simply reading historical accounts. They must use the historical method. We teach students the historical method so they will learn to appreciate the difficulties involved in reconstructing past events and become more reflective readers of history.

TEACHING STRATEGIES

Generalization: *A historian's view of the past is influenced by the availability of evidence, his or her personal biases and purposes for writing, and the society and times in which he or she lives and works.*

Primary Grades

1. After a class field trip, ask each of the students to summarize in one or two sentences what happened. Write their responses on the board. Ask them how their responses are alike and different, and *why* they are different. Help them to discover that their own personal feelings and experiences shaped their perceptions and memory of the field trip.

2. Ask the students to write or state in one sentence what happened during the art period yesterday, or some other day. Have them compare their responses and see how they are alike and different. Ask them why they wrote or gave *different* versions of what happened.

3. Read the students a story, and ask them to summarize what happened in one or two sentences. Have them compare their responses to see how they are alike and different. Ask them *why* they are different.

4. If the students are in their second year of school, ask them to describe their previous year in one or two sentences. Have the pupils compare their responses, and ask them why, since they were in the same room, they gave different versions of the year's experience.

5. Show the class a picture or a drawing that shows black slaves happy and singing. Show them another in which the slaves are bound in chains and looking sad. A third picture might show slaves being sold on a slave market. As you show each picture, ask questions such as "What is happening in this picture?" "Do these people look happy or sad?" "Why?" When you have finished, ask: "How are all of these pictures alike?" "How are they different?" "Why do you think they are different?" "How can we tell which artist is telling the truth?" The pupils might be asked to write a caption for each of the pictures.

6. Read several short conflicting versions of the life of a person such as Abraham Lincoln or Crispus Attucks. Ask the class why different versions are written about the same person. Ask them which version they think is most nearly correct and why. Ask them to tell how we can go about finding out which version is probably nearest to the truth.

Intermediate Grades

1. Read a short story of the American Revolution to the students. Emphasize the battle of Lexington. Tell the students about the controversy regarding who fired the first shot. Read them some of the conflicting documents that the British and Americans have written about the event. Ask them whether we can determine what really happened, and why or why not.

2. Stage a role-playing situation for the class (using several members of

the class as participants). Ask each student to write what he or she saw happen in the situation. The accounts should be written independently. When the reports have been written, ask the class to compare them to see how they are alike and different. The class should use their accounts to answer these questions:

a. Can different accounts be written about the same event?
b. What does the answer to Question 1 tell us about the writing of history?
c. Are two people who witness an automobile accident likely to give identical reports of it?
d. Are two historians who read the same documents about a particular historical event likely to write identical accounts of the event? Why or why not?
e. Are two people who participate in or observe the same historical event likely to write identical accounts of the event? Why or why not?
f. What are some of the factors that cause historians to write different accounts of the same events?

3. You can help students to better understand bias in history by asking them to compare and constrast accounts of the treatment of events such as the American Revolution, the War of 1812, and World War I in different American textbooks and in British, Canadian, and American textbooks. Many publishers have offices in foreign countries. They are willing to help teachers obtain copies of foreign textbooks for classroom use at regular cost plus air postage. Collecting foreign social studies textbooks for use in the social studies is an interesting and informative project.

Upper Grades

1. Plan a historical investigative unit. Assemble about 10 primary documents related to a specific historical event or institution, such as the life of the slaves, the life of colonial women, the life of colonial children, or the relationship between the first Jamestown colonists and the American Indians. Identify with the class the major questions that can be answered using these documents, such as "What was life like for the slaves?" and "What was the role of women in colonial America?"

    After the students have stated questions and hypotheses related to the problem in the unit, divide the class into four research groups. Assign a leader and a recorder for each group. Give each group a copy of each of the 10 documents. The goal for each group should be to write a brief history, using their primary documents and several library secondary sources. Their brief histories should be in narrative form, should answer the major questions formulated at the beginning of the unit, and should be grouped into subtopics.

When each group has written its history, the four histories should be shared and compared. The class should then discuss why the histories written by each group were similar and different.

2. Researching and writing a community history can help students learn about the difficulties historians have reconstructing the past and how this leads to bias in historical accounts. Divide the class into groups to reconstruct the history of their community. The groups might study these specific topics: the people in the community, the beginnings of the community, the town, business and industry, trade and communication, labor, the professions, education, the arts and crafts, government, and recreation.[35] As the students gather data in their various groups, ask them to identify conflicting information they have uncovered, and to think of ways they can solve the problems that conflicting data cause.

When the students pool their data from the various groups, they should identify consistent and conflicting data and ways to resolve the conflicts. They should also identify gaps in their data. They should discuss how both gaps in data and conflicting data cause problems for historians and how historians try to solve them.

When doing their community history, the students should incorporate ideas from social history and oral history. Social history would require them to work with a broad concept of the community, which encompasses the history of women, children, factory workers, and ethnic groups. They can use oral history techniques by interviewing senior citizens and recording them with an audiotape.

SUMMARY

History consists of three components: (1) the past, (2) statements about the past, and (3) a method of inquiry. It is important for you to understand how these aspects of history differ in order to organize effective lessons in historical studies and to help your students view social problems from the historical perspective. Historians are never able to reconstruct past events totally because of the lack of available data. Furthermore, they are not able to use all the data that they locate. To write a meaningful narrative, they must select from the data they uncover what they regard as most valid and reliable. Their selection of data is influenced by their personal biases, their purposes for writing, and the society and times in which they live and write. Because history is highly influenced by the biases of historians, it is extremely important for students to develop skills in historical inquiry so that they will become more reflective readers of history.

History differs from the other social disciplines in several ways. It includes elements of both science and the humanities. The historians' interest in writing exciting narratives and their tendency to describe unique events relate the discipline closely to the humanities. However, history is "scientific" because historians use the scientific method in modified form, and value objective description. Objectivity is an ideal within the discipline. Thus history is considered a *modified* science in this book.

History is distinguished from the other social sciences not by its special concepts but by its concern for the past and its mode of inquiry. Although the other social sciences are characterized by their tendency to view human behavior from special conceptual frameworks, history, in principle, is concerned with the totality of the human past and thus is in one sense a highly interdisciplinary discipline. While this is the case in principle, in the past historians often used political science concepts. Modern historians, however, are using concepts from the other disciplines more and more frequently to explain the past. This trend will undoubtedly continue as historians become more familiar with concepts in the behavioral sciences. Because historians attempt to reconstruct the past, they experience unique research problems. While all social science disciplines have historical components, history is the only discipline primarily concerned with the past. To help students view problems from the historical perspective, you should teach concepts and generalizations related to the conclusions (products) of history, as well as those that relate to history as a *process*.

DISCUSSION QUESTIONS AND EXERCISES

1. Locate several accounts of controversial historical events, such as the American Revolution, slavery and the Civil War, or the War of 1812, that were written in different periods of history, in different states, and in different countries.[36] After the accounts are located and analyzed, answer these questions: (a) How are the accounts alike? (b) How are they different? (c) Why are they different? (d) What *generalizations* can you make about the controversial historical events(s)? (e) What generalizations can you make about the *nature* and *writing* of history?

2. Obtain a copy of a fifth-grade United States history textbook in your curriculum library. Study the treatment of the American Revolution in it. How would you use this account to help students learn how history is written?

3. Write three lesson plans to teach the following generalization to students at the *primary, intermediate,* and *upper grade* levels:

    A historian's view of the past is influenced by the availability of evidence, his or her personal biases and purpose for writing, and the society and times in which he or she lives and works.

    What difficulties might you encounter in teaching this generalization at these three levels? How might these difficulties be overcome?

4. Study the treatment of women, African-Americans, Chicanos, and Indians in a sample of American history textbooks written for the elementary and junior high school grades. What *generalizations* can you make about the treatment of these groups in the sample of books that you studied? What implications do your generalizations have for teaching history in the elementary and junior high school grades?

5. Carefully study the table of contents of a history textbook and list the major *concepts* discussed and illustrated in the book. After listing the concepts, classify them according to the discipline to which you feel they belong. For example, *revolution* is usually considered a political science concept, *culture* an anthropological concept, and *scarcity* an economic concept. To which discipline do most of the concepts belong? What implications do the results of your investigation have for the teaching of history in the elementary and junior high school grades?

6. Carefully study a chapter on any topic in an elementary or junior high school history book. List the major *generalizations* that the author makes about the topic. Determine the *level* of each of the generalizations. For example, are most of them higher- or lower-order generalizations? (See Chapter 3 if you need to review the levels of generalizations.) Can you use the generalizations you have listed to teach students to generalize at higher levels? Illustrate your response with an actual teaching plan.

7. Demonstrate your understanding of the following key concepts by writing or stating brief definitions for each of them. Also tell why each is important.

    a. history-as-actuality
    b. historical statement
    c. history as process
    d. historical concept
    e. historical generalization
    f. historical bias
    g. historical problem
    h. structure of a discipline
    i. schoolbook history
    j. scientific history
    k. narrative history

NOTES

1. E. D. Hirsch, Jr., *Cultural Literacy: What Every American Needs to Know* (Boston: Houghton Mifflin, 1987); Lynne V. Cheney, *The American Memory: A Report on the Humanities in the Nation's Public Schools* (Washington, D.C.: National Endowment for the Humanities, 1987); Diane Ravitch and Chester E. Finn, Jr., *What Do Our 17-Year-Olds Know? A Report on the First National Assessment of History and Literature* (New York: Harper & Row, 1987).

2. Bradley Commission on History in Schools, *Building a History Curriculum: Guidelines for Teaching History in Schools* (Washington, D.C.: Educational Excellence Network, 1988), p. 7.

3. History–Social Science Curriculum Framework and Criteria Committee, *History–Social Science Framework* (Sacramento: California State Department of Education, 1988).

4. Ravitch and Finn, op. cit.

5. James P. Shaver, O. L. Davis, and Susan W. Helburn, "The Status of Social Studies Education: Impressions from Three NSF Studies," *Social Education*, Vol. 43 (1979), pp. 150–153.

6. John I. Goodlad, *A Place Called School: Prospects for the Future* (New York: McGraw-Hill, 1984).

7. Phil N. Snyder, Ed., *Detachment and the Writing of History: Essays and Letters of Carl L. Becker* (Ithaca, NY: Cornell University Press, 1958), p. 59.

8. Peter S. Bennett, *What Happened at Lexington Green? An Inquiry into the Nature and Methods of History* (Menlo Park, CA: Addison-Wesley, 1970).

9. Arthur Schlesinger, Jr., "The Humanist Looks at Empirical Social Research," in Robert P. Swierenga, Ed., *Quantification in American History: Theory and Research* (New York: Atheneum, 1970), pp. 30–35; Henry S. Commager and Raymond H. Muessig, *The Study and Teaching of History* (Columbus, OH: Merrill, 1980).

10. Louis Gottschalk, Ed., *Generalizations in the Writing of History* (Chicago: University of Chicago Press, 1963).

11. Snyder, op. cit., p. 56.

12. Commager and Muessig, op. cit.

13. William O. Aydelotte, "Quantification in History," in Swierenga, op. cit., pp. 6–24; Lee Benson, "Quantification, Scientific History and Scholarly Innovation," in Swiergena, op. cit., pp. 25–35; Allan G. Bogue, "United States: The 'New' Political History," in Swierenga, op. cit., pp. 36–52.

14. Commager and Muessig, op. cit.; Schlesinger, op. cit.

15. Crane Brinton, *The Anatomy of Revolution* (New York: Vintage Books, 1962).

16. Benson, op. cit.

17. Michael Kammen, "The Historian's Vocation and the State of the Discipline in the United States," in Michael Kammen, Ed., *The Past Before Us: Contemporary Historical Writing in the United States* (Ithaca, NY: Cornell University Press, 1980), p. 35.

18. Peter S. Stern, "Social History and the Teaching of History," in Matthew T. Downey, Ed., *Teaching American History: New Directions* (Washington, D.C.: National Council for the Social Studies), p. 52.

19. Herbert T. Hoover, "Oral History in the United States," in Kammen, op. cit., pp. 391–407; Studs (Louis) Terkel, *Hard Times: An Oral History of the Great Depression* (New York: Avon, 1970); Theodore Rosengarten, *All God's Dangers: The Life of Nate Shaw* (New York: Avon, 1974); John A. Neuenschwander, *Oral History as a Teaching Approach* (Washington, D.C.: National Education Association, 1976).

20. Kammen, op. cit., p. 30.

21. Kammen, op. cit., p. 30.

22. Gordon Wright, "History as a Moral Science," *American Historical Review,* Vol. 81 (1976), pp. 1–11.

23. Kammen, op. cit., p. 41.

24. *A Conceptual Framework for the Social Studies in Wisconsin Schools* (Madison, WI: State Superintendent of Public Instruction, Social Studies Bulletin No. 4, Curriculum Bulletin No. 14), pp. 12–24.

25. James A. Banks (with Sam L. Sebesta), *We Americans: Our History and People,* Vols. I and II (Boston: Allyn & Bacon, 1982); L. Joanne Buggey, et al., *America! America!* (Glenview, IL: Scott, Foresman, 1977).

26. Frances FitzGerald, *America Revisited: History Schoolbooks in the Twentieth Century* (New York: Vintage Books, 1979); Nathan Glazer and Reed Ueda, *Ethnic Groups in History Textbooks* (Washington, D.C.: Ethics and Public Policy Center, 1983).

27. Edwin Fenton, "A Structure of History," in Irving Morrisett, Ed., *Concepts and Structure in the New Social Science Curricula* (New York: Holt, 1967), pp. 52–53.

28. Edward N. Saveth, Ed., *American History and the Social Sciences* (New York: The Free Press, 1964); Robert F. Berkhofer, Jr., *A Behavioral Approach to Historical Analysis* (New York: The Free Press, 1969).

29. George A. Theodorson and Schilles G. Theodorson, *A Modern Dictionary of Sociology* (New York: Barnes & Noble, 1969, pp. 227–228.

30. Ralph W. Haskins, "History," in John U. Michaelis and A. Montgomery Johnston, Eds., *The Social Sciences: Foundations of the Social Studies* (Boston: Allyn & Bacon, 1966), p. 34.

31. Gottschalk, op. cit., p. 113.

32. Brinton, op. cit. These generalizations are adapted, but not quoted from, Brinton's book.

33. See Charles F. Delzell, Ed., *The Future of History* (Nashville: Vanderbilt University Press, 1977); Lee Benson, *Toward the Scientific Study of History* (Philadelphia: Lippincott, 1972).

34. James A. Banks, "Foreword," in Downey, op. cit., pp. ix–xi.

35. Clifford L. Lord, *Teaching History with Community Resources* (New York: Teachers College Press, 1967), pp. 20–28.

36. Donald W. Robinson has edited a book, *As Others See Us: International Views of American History* (New York: Houghton Mifflin, 1969), that contains accounts of such events from textbooks in use throughout the world. A Southern view of slavery can be found in the classical book by Ulrich B. Phillips, *American Negro Slavery* (New York: Appleton, 1918). The following books also contain useful documents for this exercise: John L. Thomas, Ed., *Slavery Attacked: The Abolitionist Crusade* (Englewood Cliffs, NJ: Prentice-Hall, 1965); Eric L. McKitrick, Ed., *Slavery Defended: The Views of the Old South* (Englewood Cliffs, NJ: Prentice-Hall, 1963); David F. Kellum, *American History Through Conflicting Interpretations* (New York: Teachers College Press, 1969); Robert D. Barendsen et al., Compilers, *The American Revolution: Selections from Secondary School History Books of Other Nations* (Washington, D.C.: U.S. Government Printing Office, 1976).

FOR FURTHER READING

Braudel, Fernand. *On History.* Trans. by Sarah Matthews. Chicago: The University of Chicago Press, 1980.

Downey, Matthew T., Ed. *History in the Schools.* Washington, D.C.: National Council for the Social Studies, 1985.

Gifford, Bernard R., Ed. *History in the Schools: What Shall We Teach?* New York: Macmillan, 1988.

Grob, Gerald N., and George Athan Billias, Eds. *Interpretations of American History: Patterns and Perspectives,* Vols. 1 and 2, 5th ed. New York: The Free Press, 1987.

Harris, Robert L., Jr. *Teaching Afro-American History.* Washington, D.C.: American Historical Association, 1985.

Kennedy, Paul. *The Rise and Fall of the Great Powers.* New York: Random House, 1987.

Lerner, Gerda. *The Majority Finds Its Past: Placing Women in History.* New York: Oxford University Press, 1979.

Lerner, Gerda. *Teaching Women's History.* Washington, D.C.: The American Historical Association, 1981.

Marho (The Radical Historians Organization). *Visions of History.* New York: Pantheon Books, 1984.

Meier, August, and Elliott Rudwick. *Black History and the Historical Profession: 1915–1980.* Urbana: University of Illinois Press, 1986.

10

Sociology: Structure, Concepts, and Strategies

THE SOCIOLOGICAL PERSPECTIVE

Sociology is the study of human group life. Sociologists are interested in the interrelationships of human groups, such as institutions, communities, and societies. The largest group studied by sociologists is a *society*, which is a large, permanent, self-sufficient group sharing common values and beliefs. Sociologists try to explain why human activity is characterized by a system of stable social relationships. Sociologists often use the concept *social system*, which exists when two or more people interact, when studying group interactions. Sociologists study the community, institutions such as the family and education, religious and economic institutions, and social movements. Sociologists also study social-category systems such as gender, age, social class, and ethnic groups. Sociologists are also interested in social problems.

Sociologists make several assumptions about the characteristics of groups and their influence on behavior. They assume that individuals need the group for survival, that their behavior is greatly shaped by group norms and sanctions, and that the group helps individuals acquire the behaviors and characteristics needed to adapt to their cultural and physical environments. Sociologists believe that groups have independent characteristics and identities. Groups are more than an aggregate of individuals. Groups have a continuity that transcends the lives of individuals. Sociologists are also interested in the role of individuals in the group and how individuals influence the group.

Sociologists use unique concepts and theories to guide their research and questions. If two sociologists were trying to determine the causes and effects

Sociological concepts can help these students to understand their class as a social system and the appropriate roles for students and teachers in this social system. (*Source*: Edna Kellman, Seattle Public Schools.)

of divorce in U.S. society, they might start by asking what *roles* each spouse is expected to fulfill in marriage, and what *norms* and *values* are associated with these roles. They would also be interested in *sanctions* used to assure fulfillment of role expectations, and the conditions under which these sanctions break down. They might also investigate how modernization has influenced traditional roles, norms, values, and sanctions.

The researchers might also try to determine whether the divorce rate varies in different types of *communities* and within different *social classes*. They would probably be interested in how each spouse is socialized for the marriage role, and the effects of divorce on an individual's *status* in society, as well as on *institutions*. The italicized words are concepts sociologists might use to help them determine what to study about divorce and to some extent how to study it.

Each of the social science disciplines has unique concepts, but often uses concepts from other disciplines. The social science disciplines are becoming increasingly interdisciplinary. Social scientists are discovering they cannot answer all of their important questions by using concepts only within their own disciplines. Historians sometime use concepts from sociology. Sociologists use concepts from psychology, political science, and anthropology. *Culture*, an anthropological concept, is frequently used by sociologists. In introductory college sociology textbooks, an entire chapter is often devoted to culture and socialization.

While each of the social science disciplines uses concepts from other disciplines, there are core concepts each discipline often uses that are traditionally associated with it. Thus a psychologist, an anthropologist, and an economist might use different concepts and ask different questions about divorce. A Freudian psychologist might investigate the extent of *tension* and *aggression* in marriages ending in divorce. An anthropologist might compare the consequences of divorce in different *cultures* throughout the world. An economist might investigate how divorce rates affect the *money* and *wealth* in a society.

THE NATURE OF SOCIOLOGY

Most sociologists accept scientific objectivity as an ideal, but realize the difficulties of attaining complete objectivity when studying human behavior. Sociologists are aware of their bias and try to minimize its effects on their research. Because they are students of socialization, sociologists are keenly aware of how society's values and norms shape an individual's view of social systems and social relationships.

Sociologists believe that, despite the bias that exists in their field, sociology is scientific because its major goal is to build theories that can explain and predict behavior. Sociologists assume, with other behavioral scientists, that human behavior is patterned and systematic and that lawlike statements about human behavior can be discovered. Most sociologists, unlike most narrative historians, are not necessarily interested in single cases and events. While a narrative historian might write a biography of a noted leader, a sociologist is interested in studying a number of leaders in order to form and test generalizations and theories about *leadership*.

The sociologist is primarily interested in studying classes of behaviors and their common characteristics. Sociology is a generalizing discipline. While sociologists sometime use the case study method to study single cities, individuals, and events, they usually try to derive hypotheses from case studies. These hypotheses can later be tested with a larger population.

SOCIOLOGICAL THEORIES

A scientific theory consists of a system of interrelated high-level generalizations (principles or laws) that constitute a deductive system. The development of theory is the major goal of a science. Social science theories can be used to explain and predict behavior. *Grand* or *large* theories are very abstract and inclusive theories that explain most of the facts in a discipline and place most of its general laws and principles into a coherent system. In the older physical sciences, such as physics and chemistry, most of the knowledge in the

PROFILE

Elizabeth G. Cohen

A Sociologist Who Studies Schools

Elizabeth G. Cohen is a Stanford University sociologist who specializes in the study of schools. A member of the Stanford University School of Education faculty, Cohen is especially interested in problems of status and school desegregation. She has published a score of research articles and monographs on these topics. She has written articles on such topics as "The Effects of Desegregation on Race Relations" and "A Multi-Ability Approach to the Integrated Classroom." Her books include *A New Approach to Applied Research: Race and Education* (1979) and *Designing Groupwork: Strategies for Heterogeneous Classrooms* (1986).

In her book *Designing Groupwork*, Cohen uses theory and research to formulate guidelines and principles you can use to structure groupwork in your classroom. She explains how groupwork can help students learn conceptually, improve their language proficiency, and develop more harmonious interracial relations in desegregated classrooms.

discipline is explained by a small number of highly interrelated large theories, such as Sir Isaac Newton's gravitation theory and Albert Einstein's theory of relativity.

A number of factors, including the complexity of human behavior and bias in social science research, have prevented sociologists, as well as other behavioral scientists, from developing large empirical theories that are universally accepted in the discipline. Traditionally, theorists and empirical researchers (data-gatherers) in sociology have been different people and have not worked closely together. The result was that large "armchair" theories were developed by the theorists, but rarely tested in the real world by empiricists. Empiricists, on the other hand, often collected data that did not fit into a theory. This is not as true in sociology today as it has been in the past. Many sociologists today are both theorists and empirical researchers. There are many large theories in sociology. However, many are neither universally accepted in the discipline nor data-based. Some of the major large theories in sociology are functionalism, macrofunctionalism, structuralfunctionalism, social action or Weberianism, conflict and symbolic interactionism, and modern systems.[1]

Sociologists have been more successful in developing empirical *partial* or *small* theories than they have been in developing empirical large ones. Partial theories explain only a part of group behavior, while large theories try to explain all of it. Probably the first empirically tested sociological theory was the theory of suicide developed by Emile Durkheim and presented in his book, *Suicide*, published in 1897. Most sociologists use small or partial theories rather than large ones when they do research. Small theories include role theory, reference group theory, alienation theory, social integration theory, and the theory of cultural and structural assimilation developed by Gordon and summarized below.[2]

1. With regard to *cultural behavior*, differences of social class are more important than differences in ethnic group.
2. With regard to *social participation* in primary groups and primary relationships, people tend to confine these to their own social class segment within their ethnic group, that is, *ethclass*.
3. With a person of the same social class but of a different ethnic group, one shares behavioral similarities but not a sense of peoplehood.
4. With those of the same ethnic group but of a different social class, one shares a sense of *peoplehood* but not behavioral similarities (emphasis added).

SOCIOLOGICAL CONCEPTS

Sociologists, like other social scientists, are still trying to develop concepts that have precise meanings and are universally accepted in the discipline. Concepts such as institutions, social structure, community, and value are rarely defined in identical ways. This can cause research problems. Two sociologists who are studying the *social structure* of middle-class U.S. communities might reach different conclusions if they have different working definitions of social structure.

Although sociological concepts are rarely defined identically by sociologists, there are important similarities in the definitions of key sociological concepts. There is also much consensus within the field about what the major concepts are in sociology. Most sociologists would agree that concepts such as *group, socialization, status, role, institution, society, social stratification, social structure, collective behavior,* and *culture* are among their most important concepts. We will now discuss some of the major sociological concepts and describe ways in which they can be taught in the elementary and junior high school grades. The interrelationship of these concepts is illustrated in Figure 10.1.

Socialization

Sociologists assume that individuals are not born human but are made human by interacting with and learning from the persons in their social groups. Socialization is the process by which individuals become a part of their social group by learning its culture and their roles. Children attain the attitudes,

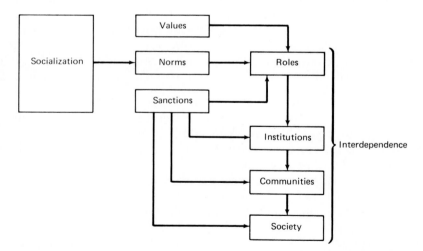

FIGURE 10.1 Concepts in sociology. This figure illustrates the relationships of some of the key concepts in sociology. Through socialization, individuals acquire the values and norms that shape the roles they must fulfill in human groups. Sanctions are used to ensure fulfillment of role responsibilities; they also learn these during socialization. Sets of related roles constitute institutions, such as political, economic, and educational institutions. Institutions exist within communities. Society is the all-encompassing group. All units are guided by norms, values, and sanctions; all are interdependent.

values, and behaviors needed to survive in their communities from other people in their social group. Some sociologists also use socialization to describe the learning of any new role, such as when a child has to learn to become a member of the Girl Scouts or a new teacher has to learn how to function in her role.

Activities

1. Ask the students to name some things they learned from their mother, father, brother, sister, and teacher, such as to tie their shoes, clean the house, and read.
2. Ask the students to name things they have learned from the groups to which they belong, such as the Girl Scouts and the Boy Scouts. Ask them to tell how they learned these things.
3. Study about different religions and identify ways they influence their members' behavior.
4. Examine ways boys and girls in different nations and cultures learn to act differently.
5. Read the story "The Country Mouse and the City Mouse" and discuss ways the city mouse taught the country mouse how to survive in the city.

Roles

Roles are sets of behavior regularly expected of individuals. Each day, almost everyone must function in many different roles. These role often conflict. Elementary school teachers are expected to teach social studies on school days; yet teachers may have family responsibilities in the evening, such as caring for the lawn, cooking, or entertaining, that prevent them from being properly prepared the next morning. A knowledge of the roles people are expected to fulfill will help students to better understand their own roles and obligations.

Activities

1. Ask the students to list some things they are expected to do at home, at school, at church, and in groups to which they belong. Introduce the concept of *role*. Ask the students to state how their roles sometimes conflict.
2. Ask the students to list some things their parents do at home and away from home.
3. Ask the students to name some of the workers in their community and to list what they are expected to do to help the community. Discuss what happens when these workers do not fulfill their role expectations.
4. Compare the roles of women in the United States in the nineteenth century with the roles of women today.

Norms and Sanctions

A *norm* is a standard or code that guides behavior. Norms tell us when our behavior is right or wrong, proper or improper. In our society, people are often expected to dress differently on various occasions and in different social settings. Children are often expected to act and talk in "respectful" ways around adults. Adults are usually expected to act in certain ways around children. Norms vary not only in different times and cultures, but also between different social classes and cultural groups within the same society. Many norms within the United States have changed within the last decade.

Sanctions are rewards and punishments used by groups to ensure that norms are followed and that role expectations are fulfilled. Groups use a variety of pressures and controls to ensure that norms are obeyed. Gossip, embarrassment, and praise are often used as sanctions. Students who get caught cheating on tests are embarrassed when the teacher catches them. Teachers who are popular with parents are usually praised by their principals. We occasionally violate norms, but more often we conform to them because we internalize most of the norms and values of our culture when we are socialized.

Activities

> Activities for teaching norms and sanctions are in the *Teaching Strategies* section of this chapter, beginning on page 306.

Values

Values are aspects of a society or culture to which groups attach a high worth or regard. Individuals acquire the values of their society during the process of socialization. Values are generalized rather than specific and consequently serve as standards for concrete behavior. Human dignity, justice, equality, and freedom of expression are some of the major values expressed in the national documents of the United States, such as the Constitution and the Declaration of Independence. People often agree on general values but disagree about actions that exemplify them. Individuals have different ideas about what constitutes human dignity, equality, and freedom of speech. Values such as freedom of speech and equality often conflict. One individual's freedom of speech might deny equality to another.

Activities

1. Read the "Three Little Pigs" and ask the students to list some things important to each character. Give them at least two examples.
2. Ask the students to make a list of rules they have to follow at home and at school. Ask: Are these rules fair? Why or why not?
3. Discuss the Bill of Rights and list the major values it expresses.
4. Read the following speeches and identify the values each expresses:

Lincoln's Gettysburg address, John F. Kennedy's Inaugural address, and Martin Luther King's "I Have a Dream" speech.
5. Ask the students to name the three persons they most admire and to name the values that each of these individuals exemplifies.

Social Movement

A social movement takes place when large numbers of people organize and try to promote or resist change in a group or society. Sociologists consider social movements a form of *collective* rather than *group* behavior because they do not have the amount and type of interaction and organization that characterize groups. Collective behavior is interrelated but is primarily unstructured. People get together, but interact very little.[3] Social movements sometimes give birth to formal organizations. The social movement that arose during the 1800s to improve conditions for U.S. workers resulted in the

When social movements are studied, the students can examine the important roles played by leaders in such movements, such as the role that Martin Luther King, Jr., played in the emergence and success of the civil rights movement of the 1960s and 1970s. (*Source*: The National Archives, Washington, D.C.)

INQUIRY STRATEGY: VALUES AND NORMS IN CONFLICT

Directions

Read the following story to your class and ask the questions that follow.

Alternative

Read the story to the class. Break the class up into four equal groups. Ask each group to decide what Susan should do. After each group has made a decision, the group decisions are shared with the class. The class then discusses the questions that follow the story.

Susan and Ronald Cortes have been married for nearly 20 years. During most of that time, Susan has strongly supported Ronald and their two children, Kate and Joseph, in whatever they wanted to do. Before their children were born, Susan worked full-time while Ronald completed medical school. She resigned from her junior high school teaching job when Kate, their older child, was born. She wanted to spend more time with Kate and to support Ronald in his efforts to establish a successful medical practice. After Joseph had entered school, Susan enrolled in graduate school with Ronald's encouragement. She completed her master's degree by going to school part-time. However, she was such an outstanding student that she received a doctoral fellowship to study for her Ph.D. degree. With Ronald's strong encouragement and support, Susan completed her Ph.D. degree in sociology after six years of study. Her professors consider her one of the most promising Ph.D. students ever to finish at State University. State University has one of the top-rated sociology departments in the United States.

After two years of trying to find a job teaching sociology at a local college, the best that Susan has been able to find is a part-time job at the community college teaching two courses a year. There is no possibility for a permanent position at the college. Her professors recommended her for a sociology position at one of the nation's best universities. It is located on the East Coast of the United States, about 3000 miles from the Cortes' home on the West Coast. It was tough to get an interview at such a prestigious university. However, Susan was interviewed and has been offered the job.

The Cortes family, which is close-knit, faces a dilemma. Ronald has a well-established medical practice in the city in which they now live. He does not want to start over in a new city. Kate is in her second year of high school and does not want to leave her friends. Joseph is in the sixth grade. While he doesn't want to leave his friends, he is quietly excited about the possibility of living on the East Coast. Susan is strongly committed to her family but wants to pursue her career at a university that will give her opportunities to do research and to realize her promise and talents.

Questions

1. What is the main problem in the case?
2. What values and norms are in conflict?

3. How does this situation challenge traditional norms and values about the roles of men and women in the family?
4. Which of Susan's values are in conflict?
5. What are the choices available to the Cortes family?
6. What are the possible consequences of each choice?
7. Should Susan take the job on the East Coast? Why or why not?

---

establishment of labor unions. The feminist and the civil rights movements of the 1960s and 1970s also gave birth to organizations. During their study of both historical and contemporary events and issues, students in the elementary and junior high school grades will have many fruitful opportunities to study the influence of social movements on society.

Activities

1. View pictures of people who participated in the environmental movement during the 1970s.
2. Interview industrial leaders in the community to determine the extent to which the environmental movement has had an influence on society.
3. Prepare and present a dramatic presentation chronicling the struggles, riots, and mass movements in which workers participated during the 1800s to gain higher wages and better working conditions.
4. Read documents revealing the ways colonists resisted British tax laws during the events leading to the American Revolution.
5. Make a collage showing highlights from the civil rights and feminist movements of the 1960s and 1970s.

Society (Community, Neighborhood, Institution)

The largest unit sociologists study is *society*. A society is an independent unit in the sense that it includes all of the social institutions needed to meet human needs. It is not necessarily economically independent, but is capable of surviving for a long period of time.[4] Societies are made up of communities, neighborhoods, and institutions.

A *community* exists when a group of people frequently interact, live in close geographical proximity, and have a sense of belonging. A sense of a common bond and a shared identity are among the most important characteristics of a community. A community can also exist when a group of people have a shared identity and interests but live in separate geographical areas. The African-American, Jewish, and Mormon communities in the United States are examples of this kind of community. Communities are made up of smaller units called *neighborhoods*, in which people have local ties and face-to-face relationships.

A set of roles organized to attain a specified goal constitutes an *institution*. Education is an institution organized to help children and adults learn. Educational institutions, such as schools, are made up of roles, each having a definite function and expectation. Roles include those of the superintendent, principal, teachers, and students. Sociologists usually study educational institutions, the family, and religious, economic, and political institutions, as well as others.

Activities

1. Ask the students to state what they think a *family* is and what needs families help individuals satisfy.
2. Ask the students to tell what they consider their neighborhoods. Ask them to tell what needs they are able to satisfy in their neighborhoods.
3. Discuss how neighborhoods and communities are alike and different. Name the communities in the region.
4. List institutions in the community and state their functions and their services. Invite community leaders to speak to the class.
5. Discuss how a society differs from a neighborhood, a community, and an institution. Compare and contrast norms, values, and behaviors in the United States and Japan. Discuss how U.S. society and Japanese society are alike and different.

SOCIOLOGICAL GENERALIZATIONS

The following generalizations (and related concepts) can be used to guide sociological studies in the elementary and junior high school grades.[5] The words and phrases in italics are concepts. The statements below them are related generalizations. The learning experiences planned for students are far more important than a list of generalizations. Generalizations should be used to guide instruction. They should not *constitute* it.

Socialization

All characteristically human behavior is learned from other human beings through group interaction.

Groups

People live in social groups of two or more individuals. (These groups help them satisfy their needs.)
The group exerts social control over individual members through the use of sanctions (rewards and punishments).
The group enforces its norms by the use of sanctions.

Social Organization

All societies develop social institutions that may be defined as complex sets of folkways, mores, and laws integrated around the major functions (or needs) of the society.

Group activities and projects can help students understand sociological concepts. (*Source*: Lake Washington School District, Seattle.)

Societies develop specific institutions to carry out their basic functions. Institutions are characterized by division of labor and specialization. Every society consists of smaller social units such as social classes, racial and ethnic groups, communities, clubs, associations, and neighborhoods. Each of these participates in a different way in the total culture.

Social Change

All societies are in constant change.
No society is completely harmonious: Some form of social disorganization is present in all societies.

Conflict

In all societies conflict develops between persons and groups. Controlled conflict sometimes leads to social change that facilitates the attainment of desired goals.

Stratification

> All members of a society are ranked into levels of prestige and power called social classes.

Human Ecology

> People's social relationships and behavior are affected by their spatial distribution in geographic space.

Communication

> Communication is basic to culture and group existence. Individuals and groups communicate in many ways other than by language. However, every type of communication involves symbolism of varying meanings.

Interdependence

> Individuals, families, neighborhoods, communities, organizations, and other groups help each other meet their basic needs.

Discrimination

> Groups are often the victims of discrimination and prejudice because of age, sex, race, religion, or cultural differences.

SOCIOLOGICAL STUDIES IN THE ELEMENTARY SCHOOL

The social science content in the first four grades is primarily sociological. Usually, in kindergarten and first, second, and third grades, institutions such as the home, school, community, and family are studied. These institutions are often taught with a topical rather than a conceptual approach, as recommended in this book. When social studies units are planned in the elementary grades, the teacher identifies the topics (or lower-level concepts) to be taught, such as "Our Family," and then formulates teaching strategies. Too often, the end result is mastery of unrelated and disorganized facts. These are quickly forgotten.

The family is an institution that can be analyzed and studied from diverse perspectives. Psychologists look at it very differently than do sociologists. More effective units are structured when teachers identify *key* or *organizing* concepts and generalizations that they want the students to master before they select content, lower-level concepts, materials, and teaching strategies. This procedure allows teachers to freely select content samples meaningful to students, and also timely, diverse, and more appropriate for a greater variety of ability levels. If, for example, third-grade students are expected to study *norms*, you can use a variety of content samples to illustrate how norms are formed and how they shape behavior. Norms in such institutions as the family, school, and community could be examined.

This ideal way to plan instruction often is not practical for many teachers. In designated grades the teacher is frequently required to plan units dealing with specific topics and lower-level concepts, perhaps the home and school in kindergarten, and the family in first grade. If you find yourself in this situation, you should carefully study the required content, and identify key concepts and generalizations that the content can be used to illustrate. Higher-order or organizing concepts, such as *norms* and *values*, can be illustrated with a wider variety of content than can lower-level concepts such as "Our Town," which is referred to above as a topic. (See Chapter 3 for a discussion of concept levels.)

The social studies program should be sequential, but scope and sequence should be based on the development of central, organizing concepts and generalizations rather than on topics or lower-level ideas. A conceptual approach to the study of institutions, such as the family and community, will help militate against the superficial way that they are often presented in the primary grades. When you try to help pupils master the concept *role*, you can use materials on families from many different groups to increase students' understanding. You can use a variety of content samples to help students discover that the roles of the mother in homes with one and with two parents working outside the home might be quite different.

Since any content can be studied from many different perspectives, you should select organizing concepts from several disciplines when planning social studies units. However, one discipline may be emphasized more than others in a particular unit. When studying the family, for example, sociological concepts may be stressed, since sociology is the study of human groups (the family is a group). However, economic and political science concepts will also help students to understand important aspects of family life. Chapter 2 discusses effective ways to plan interdisciplinary units. The point emphasized here is that you should have key, organizing concepts and generalizations in mind when you plan and teach units even if you are required to work within the limits of previously identified content. As we noted before, the conceptual approach to social studies instruction greatly facilitates comprehension, transfer, and mastery of content.

Sociology is rich with concepts and generalizations that can be used throughout the elementary and junior high social studies program to help students better grasp traditional subjects, understand their social environment, and make decisions on important social issues. A study of institutions, such as the family and school, can help young children understand essential aspects of *socialization*, a key sociological concept. These institutions can also be used to teach such concepts as *values*, *norms*, and *sanctions*, since roles in all institutions are guided by norms and sanctions. A sound unit on community helpers can help pupils to understand such central sociological concepts as *institution*, *status*, and *role*. *Society* can be taught when intermediate and upper grade pupils study the United States and various nations of the Eastern and Western hemispheres.

TEACHING STRATEGIES

Generalization: *The group enforces its norms by the use of sanctions.*

Primary Grades

Read the following situation to the class and ask the questions that follow:

> During recess, the boys in Miss Jones's class hurried outside to play with the big, red ball that Miss Jones had just bought for her pupils. Miss Jones had wanted the boys to play a game with the girls that morning, but the boys, led by Joe, had begged her to let them play with the big, shining ball. When she pulled the ball out of the closet, Joe and Johnny grabbed it. They ran toward the large play area, which was a distance from where Miss Jones usually stood to watch the children play. Joe and Johnny threw the ball to each other and to their friends. Carl, who was not too well liked by some of the leaders in the crowd, didn't get a chance to catch the ball very often. When Carl and Joe were struggling for the ball, it rolled out of the playground into the street. It was crushed by a speeding car. Stu ran and told Miss Jones exactly what had happened.

1. Did Joe and Johnny treat Carl in a way that would have been approved by Miss Jones? Why or why not?
2. When children are playing, what are some ways that adults expect them to act? (List statements [norms] on the board or butcher paper.)
3. Did Stu act in a way that the other boys would approve? Why or why not?
4. When children are playing, what are some things that they expect each other to do and not to do? (List norms on board or butcher paper.)
5. What are some things that Miss Jones might do to make Joe and Johnny treat Carl differently? (List *sanctions* on board.)
6. What might the other boys do to make Joe and Johnny treat Carl differently? (List *sanctions* on board.)
7. What might the boys do to stop Stu from tattling? (List *sanctions* on board.)

Intermediate Grades

1. Read the students the story of Joan of Arc. Ask them to state the kinds of behavior and belief she exemplified that those in authority would not tolerate. The concept of *mores* could be introduced. Mores are protected by very strong sanctions, some as extreme as death. Ask the students whether they can identify some mores we have today.
2. Have the students read novels and accounts of the Salem witch trials in colonial America.[6] Help them to identify why some people were

called witches, and why they were persecuted. Ask the class: "What behavior codes (norms) did people called 'witches' violate? What punishments (sanctions) did the group give 'witches'?"

3. During a study of the Middle Ages, read the class selections dealing with the many aspects of chivalry. Help the students identify the kinds of behavior expected of men and women during those times, and the sanctions that were used to enforce them.

4. Have the class read books and selections dealing with life in America during the settlement of the West. Ask them such questions as "What did the community probably think of women who went to taverns? Why? Of women who carried guns? Why? What would the people have said about a woman who wanted to run for public office?"

Upper Grades

Read the following case and ask the questions that follow;

Albert Roberts's parents live in a beautiful, large house in one of New York City's most exclusive suburbs. Mr. Roberts, his father, is a very successful lawyer who drives to and from the city every day. Mrs. Roberts is a psychologist and a Sunday school teacher. Albert was a straight "A" student in elementary and high school. He was able to get most of the things he wanted from his parents. When he left home to attend Green University, his parents gave him a new car. When Albert came home for Christmas vacation, his hair was longer than his sister's. He was smoking strange cigarettes that had a peculiar odor. His clothes were dirty and ragged. His parents were very upset when they saw him. They told him that he could not stay at home during the vacation period unless he cleaned up, cut his hair, and stopped smoking the strange cigarettes.

1. What did Albert do that his parents did not think a young man should do? (Solicit norms.)
2. How did they show their disapproval? (Solicit sanctions.)
3. Have you ever done anything of which your parents strongly disapproved?
4. What did they do to show their disapproval?

Ask the students to list:

1. The kinds of behavior they usually expect of:

a. parents	f. store clerks	j. neighbors
b. teachers	g. the letter carrier	k. close friends
c. brothers	h. the principal	l. strangers
d. sisters	i. senior citizens	m. relatives
e. ministers		

2. The kinds of behavior they do not expect of the individuals and groups named above.
3. The kinds of behavior they display to show disapproval of unexpected behavior from the persons and groups named above.
4. The kinds of behavior that the individuals and groups named above expect of them.
5. The kinds of behavior that the persons and groups named above would display to show disapproval of the students' unexpected behavior.

SUMMARY

Sociological concepts and generalizations can help students in the elementary and junior high school grades to make decisions related to social problems and to better understand the groups in which they live. Sociology is primarily concerned with group influences on individual behavior, and the relationships between different groups. Students must understand the structure of human groups and the interrelationships between groups in order to make reflective decisions on social issues. They must also be familiar with the ways their own behavior is shaped by their social groups.

Students can be introduced to sociological concepts and generalizations in the earliest grades; these key ideas can be developed and expanded in later grades. There are many opportunities for the teacher in the primary grades to introduce sociological concepts, because the topics traditionally studied in these grades are primarily sociological. The family, community, school, and neighborhood are usually studied in primary grade social studies. You can help your students understand these institutions by organizing your units around key sociological concepts. When students study an institution such as the family, they can be introduced to such key concepts as *socialization, role, norm, sanction,* and *values.*

The family plays a major role in socializing individuals and in preparing them to satisfy their societal needs. Each individual within a family has roles he or she is expected to fulfill. Norms tell people whether they are performing their roles properly, and sanctions are used to reward individuals for properly fulfilling their role expectations and to punish them when they fail. Both norms and sanctions reflect the values found in institutions such as the family. Although key concepts such as *socialization, role, norm, sanction* and *values* can be introduced in the primary grades, these ideas can be developed at a more sophisticated level in the higher grades, with different content samples. When students study such topics as large urban centers, our state, United States history, and the Eastern and Western Hemispheres, they can learn key sociological concepts. When they study large urban centers, students can compare or contrast the ways in which socialization in the city family differs from that in the rural or less urbanized areas. The roles, norms, and sanctions present in urban institutions can also be examined.

When studying the history of the United States and regions such as the Eastern and Western Hemispheres, students can determine the ways in which roles, norms, and values differ within various periods of U.S. history, and the many ways in which individuals are socialized in different parts of a region.

While certain units during the year might emphasize concepts from various disciplines, every unit should contain sociological concepts because of sociology's focus on group interactions and the ways in which the group influences an individual's behavior. Students must often view human behavior from the perspective of sociology in order to understand the complexity of human relationships.

DISCUSSION QUESTIONS AND EXERCISES

1. Examine an introductory sociology college textbook and make a list of these knowledge forms discussed in it: (1) key *concepts*, (2) key *generalizations*, and (3) key *theories*. Make a lesson plan for teaching one of the key concepts and several related generalizations to a group of students in one of the following grade levels: (a) primary grades, (b) intermediate grades, or (c) upper grades.

2. What is the unique nature of sociology? How does it differ from the other social sciences, such as anthropology, political science, and economics? What implications does the unique nature of sociology have for planning an elementary and junior high school social studies program?

3. Examine several primary units in the curriculum library of your college dealing with such topics as the family, the community, the neighborhood, and the school. What key sociological concepts are stated in these units? Are the concepts accurate? Will the activities contained in the unit develop the concepts supposedly taught? What key sociological concepts could you add to the unit to enable students to gain a better perspective of the ways in which groups influence the behavior of individuals? What teaching strategies would you use to develop the key concepts that you would add to the unit?

4. Structure a unit on the family for the primary grades and plan teaching strategies to teach the concepts *socialization, role, norm, sanction* and *values*. Which of these concepts is easiest for young children to understand? Which is the most difficult for them to understand? What special methods will you use to ensure that the students will gain an understanding of the most difficult concepts?

5. What do you think should be the primary goal(s) of sociological studies in the elementary and junior high school grades? How can the unique nature of sociology facilitate the attainment of this goal(s)?

6. Select a current social problem dealing with an issue such as race relations, the environment, war, or poverty. Illustrate, with a teaching plan, how students could use sociological concepts to better understand the situation and make decisions regarding the issue. While completing this exercise, review the decision-making model presented in Chapter 1.

7. Demonstrate your understanding of the following key concepts by writing or stating a brief definition for each of them. Also tell why each is significant:

a.	grand or large theory	g.	values
b.	partial or small theory	h.	social movement
c.	socialization	i.	community
d.	roles	j.	neighborhood
e.	norms	k.	institution
f.	sanctions	l.	society

NOTES

1. Leon H. Warshay, *The Current State of Sociological Theory: A Critical Interpretation* (New York: David McKay, 1975), pp. 3–5. See also Robert K. Merton, *Social Theory and Social Structure*, enlarged ed. (New York: Free Press, 1968); Lewis A. Coser, *Masters of Sociological Thought*, 2nd ed. (New York: Harcourt Brace Jovanovich, 1971); Edward Shils, *The Calling of Sociology and Other Essays on the Pursuit of Learning* (Chicago: University of Chicago Press, 1980); Thomas S. Kuhn, *The Structure of Scientific Revolutions*, 2nd ed., enlarged (Chicago: University of Chicago Press, 1970).

2. Milton M. Gordon, *Assimilation in American Life* (New York: Oxford University Press, 1964), pp. 52–53.

3. Neil J. Smelser, *Theory of Collective Behavior* (New York: Free Press, 1963); James A. Kitchens and Raymond Muessig, *The Study and Teaching of Sociology* (Columbus, OH: Merrill, 1980).

4. George A. Theodorson and Achilles G. Theodorson, *A Modern Dictionary of Sociology* (New York: Barnes & Noble, 1969).

5. All of the generalizations on pp. 302–304, except the ones noted here, were taken from the Advisory Committee on the Social Studies, *A Guide for Concept Development in the Social Studies* (Denver: Colorado Department of Education, 1967), "Sociology" insert. Used with permission. The generalizations on the concepts of *conflict*, *interdependence*, and *discrimination* were written by the author. The generalization for the concept of *communication* is from John U. Michaelis and A. Montgomery Johnson, *The Social Sciences: Foundations of the Social Studies* (Boston: Allyn & Bacon, 1965), p. 334.

6. One source is Elizabeth G. Speare, *Witch of Blackbird Pond* (Boston: Houghton Mifflin, 1958).

FOR FURTHER READING

Alba, Richard D., Ed. *Ethnicity and Race in the U.S.A.: Towards the Twenty-First Century*. New York: Routledge, 1988.

Banks, James A., and Cherry A. McGee Banks, Eds. *Multicultural Education: Issues and Perspectives*. Boston: Allyn & Bacon, 1989.

Bellah, Robert N., Richard Madsen, William M. Sullivan, Ann Swidler, and Steven M. Tipton. *Habits of the Heart: Individualism and Commitment in American Life*. New York: Harper & Row, 1985.

Blalock, Hubert M., Jr. *Basic Dilemmas in the Social Sciences*. Beverly Hills, CA: Sage Publications, 1984.

Boulding, Elise. *Building a Global Civil Culture: Education for an Interdependent World*. New York: Teachers College Press, 1988.

Gouldner, Alvin W. *The Coming Crisis in Western Sociology*. New York: Basic Books, 1970.

Kitchens, James A., and Raymond H. Muessig. *The Study and Teaching of Sociology*. Columbus, OH: Merrill, 1980.

11

Anthropology: Structure, Concepts, and Strategies

THE ANTHROPOLOGICAL PERSPECTIVE

Anthropology literally means the science (logos) of man (anthropos). Human behavior is studied in all of the social sciences. However, anthropology is concerned with people's behavior and their physical traits. Anthropology's interest in the relationship between culture and human biological traits is unique. Humans' long period of dependence, bipedal locomotion, large brain, and ability to symbolize are among the biological traits that enable them to create and acquire culture.

All of the concepts, generalizations, and theories in anthropology are related to those activities, artifacts, and belief systems that anthropologists call *culture*.[1] Although many animals are social and live in groups, people are the only animals that have culture. The dominant interest in the concept of culture and the "holistic" method of studying it also distinguish anthropology from the other behavioral sciences. Anthropologists use a holistic approach when studying culture; they study all parts of a cultural system. Culture, they assume, is an integrated whole. Therefore, cultural traits cannot be understood in isolation from the whole. When anthropologists study a society, they collect data on all its aspects, including history, religion, geography, economy, technology, and language. To derive valid generalizations about a cultural complex, such as marriage, anthropologists feel that they must be familiar with all of society's other institutions.

The comparative approach to culture and affinity with history and the humanities are more important to anthropology than to any of the other behavioral sciences. In the past most anthropologists were interested in study-

"Now that we've learned to talk, what's the meaning of it all?" (*Source*: Herbert Goldberg. Used with permission.)

ing nonliterate rather than modernized societies. They concentrated their work on nonliterate societies because it was easier to study whole cultures in small homogeneous societies than in complex, modern ones. Also, anthropologists wanted to test their generalizations in cultures very different from their own. Isolated, nonliterate societies served as laboratories for most earlier anthropologists. The interests of today's anthropologists extend far beyond nonliterate societies. Most modern anthropologists view their discipline as a general biocultural study.[2] They study nonliterate as well as highly modernized societies and the institutions within them. Themes in Japanese culture, the culture of the U.S. school, and African American culture in the United States are among the kinds of cultures and subcultures that anthropologists study in Westernized societies.

A number of important ethnographies of schools have been conducted since the 1970s. These include Ray Rist's study of a newly desegregated school in Portland, Oregon, John U. Ogbu's study of education in an urban neighborhood, and Susan Philips's study of communication in classroom and community on the Warm Springs Indian Reservation.[3] George Spindler, an educational anthropologist, has edited an important book that includes a number of school ethnographies.[4]

The formulation of the concept of culture and the study of nonliterate societies are two of the most significant contributions that anthropology has made to social science and the modern world.[5] Many of the traits and characteristics that had been considered "human nature" were reexamined when anthropologists such as Ruth Benedict and Margaret Mead found that these traits and characteristics were not always the same in nonliterate and modernized societies. As a result of the work of anthropologists such as Benedict and Mead, social scientists began to understand better the cultural influences on human behavior.[6]

In the 1980s, however, the research assumptions and methods of anthropologists such as Benedict and Mead were seriously questioned by anthropologists who believe their research methods were not sufficiently rigorous. In a controversial and highly publicized book, *Margaret Mead and Samoa: The Making and Unmaking of an Anthropological Myth*, Derek Freeman refutes the conclusion Mead reached in her book *Coming of Age in Samoa*, published in 1928.[7] In her book, Mead concludes that adolescence is not a universally traumatic period as social scientists claim, because the adolescent period in Samoa is tranquil.[8] Freeman argues that Mead's conclusion is invalid because she went to Samoa to reinforce her environmental biases, was given inaccurate information by her informants (because they gave her the information she wanted rather than facts), and because Mead did not sufficiently understand the language and culture of Samoa. Despite the criticisms that have been made of earlier anthropologists such as Benedict and Mead, their important contributions to the study of culture and to anthropology are widely recognized and appreciated by most social scientists.

Historical approaches and elements are probably more important in anthropology than in any of the other behavioral sciences. Throughout the brief history of the discipline, anthropologists have shown a keen interest in the historical origins of cultural traits, and later a concern for unique and particular cultural elements. One area of anthropology, archeology or prehistory, is devoted exclusively to reconstructing early human history. Anthropology is also closely akin to the humanities. Books such as Benedict's *Patterns of Culture*, Mead's *Coming of Age in Samoa*, and Marvin Harris' *Cows, Pigs, Wars and Witches: The Riddles of Culture* are interesting, engrossing, and informative.[9]

THE FIELDS OF ANTHROPOLOGY

Because of the broad scope of the discipline, anthropologists usually specialize in one of the subfields of anthropology. Although most of the areas are closely related, some are linked primarily by their common interest in humans. *Physical* anthropologists, who study the evolution of humans and their relationships with other animals, particularly other primates, are more akin to biologists than to social scientists. However, social and cultural anthropologists depend on physical anthropologists for information regarding the unique biological traits of humans, which are essential for the formation of culture. Weston LaBarre, in *The Human Animal*, argues that biological drives and needs are the basis for many human institutions, such as the family.[10] Physical anthropologists are also interested in the concept of race and have devised various schemes for classifying and identifying races.[11]

Anthropological concepts can help students to understand the range of cultures in U.S. classrooms. The students in this photograph are proudly participating in a cultural event. (*Source*: Edna Kellman, Seattle Public Schools.)

Cultural anthropology is often considered the main area of the discipline because it is concerned with the study of whole cultures, including cultural change, acculturation, and diffusion.

An area called *social anthropology* has also emerged, primarily in England. Social structure rather than culture is the key concept in social anthropology. Its leaders refer to it as "comparative sociology" and contend that social anthropology searches for laws and generalizations while cultural anthropology is concerned primarily with tracing the history of cultural traits.[12] They regard cultural anthropology as primarily historical and social anthropology as mainly explanatory.

Other areas of anthropology include *ethnography*, the accurate description of living cultures, and *ethnology*, which is mainly concerned with comparing and explaining the similarities and differences in cultural systems. *Linguistics* is devoted to the description and analysis of languages. Anthropologists have discovered that the language systems of cultures reveal much about their beliefs, ideology, and behavioral patterns.

Archeologists, or prehistorians, attempt to reconstruct the history of peoples without a written history by digging up artifacts and other cultural elements. Elementary and junior high school students will find the techniques and methods used by the archeologist interesting as well as revealing. In recent years, archeologists have used a number of chemical processes both to locate artifacts and to determine their age. When applications of these processes revealed how very old our earth is, the archeologists made a significant contribution to scientific knowledge.

RESEARCH METHODS IN ANTHROPOLOGY

The two most frequently used methods in anthropology are *participant observation* and *interviewing*, which are used when anthropologists do field work.[13] When anthropologists study a culture, they live with the people, learn their language, and take an active part in the daily affairs of the community. They cook with the women, go hunting with the men, participate in the ritual ceremonies, and help with the harvest. They take field notes while actively participating in the culture. Anthropologists face a number of problems when trying to keep their methods of data collecting objective. Sometimes anthropologists must take notes several hours after they have observed or participated in an event. While other social scientists usually select their subjects for an interview randomly, anthropologists interview persons with whom they can establish rapport, or persons from whom they feel they can get accurate and detailed information. The accounts they receive from different subjects are often conflicting and contradictory. Anthropologists attempt to minimize errors in their data by observing as well as by interviewing, and by making cross-checks with other informants when they detect contradictory information. In the past, anthropologists made little use of the written questionnaire, largely because most of their subjects were not literate.

Data collection in anthropology tends to be more exploratory and personal than in the other behavioral sciences. Some of the difficulties anthropologists face in collecting data are inherent in the discipline itself; others reflect a tradition in anthropology that tends to regard suspiciously data-gathering procedures preventing anthropologists from directly observing the wholeness of cultures.

Anthropologists are concerned about the claim by some social scientists that ethnographic studies are often not objective. In recent years, they have tried to make their research methods more objective and rigorous without "abandoning altogether the informal and personalized methods that have been the hallmark of fieldwork."[14] A number of anthropologists have combined such techniques as random sampling, structured interviews, and quantitative methods with traditional ethnographic field work. Anthropologists also use cameras, videotapes, and other research equipment to improve the objectivity of their data collecting methods.

One development that has helped to foster objectivity in anthropology, as well as to save many hours of fieldwork, is the Human Relations Area Files,

PROFILE

Johnnetta B. Cole

An Anthropologist Who Heads a Distinguished College

Johnnetta B. Cole is an anthropologist who specializes in the study of race and gender. She writes, "The issues of race and gender have been central in my life, in my work as an anthropologist, and in my community activities. There is a fundamental question at the base of the anthropology I do: how can people of color, poor people, and women become full, productive, and equal members of the society in which they live?" Her scholarship centers on cultural anthropology, African-American studies, and women's studies. Her books include *All American Women: Lines That Divide, Ties That Bind* (1986), *Anthropology for the Eighties: Introductory Readings* (1982), and *Anthropology for the Nineties* (1988).

A former professor of anthropology at Hunter College of the City University of New York, in 1987 Cole became the first African-American woman president of Spelman College, the prestigious predominantly black college for women in Atlanta, Georgia. Cole is using her anthropological insights and perspectives to lead the 107-year-old liberal arts college. She is working to make Spelman a renowned center for scholarship on African-American women.

which include a large range of data on a variety of topics about cultures throughout the world. By using these files, the anthropologist can randomly select samples from many cultures and test hypotheses dealing with such topics as child-rearing practices, magic and religion, and marriage rites. Some anthropologists, however, feel that this procedure is invalid because it does not permit them to study whole cultures.

THEORIES IN ANTHROPOLOGY

In Chapter 3 we defined a theory as a set of interrelated statements (propositions) or laws that can be tested. In Chapter 10 we discussed two kinds of theories: partial (or small) and grand (or large). Partial or small theories explain only a part of behavior. Large or grand theories attempt to explain most of the findings in a discipline. Cultural anthropology is primarily historical and descriptive rather than theoretical. In this respect, anthropology is akin to history. Anthropologists devote most of their time to the description and comparison of cultures rather than to building generalizations and theories. However, anthropologists such as Marvin Harris and Clifford Geertz are interested in formulating generalizations and theories about culture.[15] Anthropologists have formulated a number of important generalizations about culture that can be incorporated into the elementary and junior high school grades.

Empirical partial theories are as scarce in anthropology as they are in history. However, during its brief history, a number of grand theories, schools of thought, and approaches have been developed in anthropology. These are referred to as theories in the anthropological literature and are summarized in Table 11.1 on pp. 320–321.

ANTHROPOLOGICAL CONCEPTS

As in history and sociology, the concepts in anthropology tend to be broadly defined, and used differently by various anthropologists. Anthropological concepts are more standardized than historical concepts, but less refined than those in sociology. We find less agreement among anthropologists than among sociologists about what the key concepts in their discipline are and what they mean. However, cultural anthropologists do agree that *culture* is the most important concept in the discipline, although there is considerably less agreement about what culture means. After surveying the literature, Kroeber and Kluckhohn found 164 different definitions of culture. They defined culture as the "patterns, explicit and implicit, of and for behavior, acquired and transmitted by symbols, constituting the distinctive achievement of human groups, including their embodiments in artifacts. . . ."[16]

Some anthropologists point out that, while the development of well-defined concepts is a goal in the discipline, anthropology lacks standardized concepts because of the newness of the field. Writes Keesing, "No two anthropologists think exactly alike, or use precisely the same operating concepts or symbols. The science is too new, and the struggle to give sharp meanings to what are usually everyday terms still too wide open. . . ."[17] Although anthropologists often define the same concepts differently, there is usually some degree of similarity in their meanings. We discuss some of the key concepts in anthropology below and describe activities that can be used to teach them to elementary and junior high school students.

Culture

Culture comprises the behavior patterns, belief systems, artifacts, and other human-made components of a society. It includes the foods people eat, the tools they use, their clothing, myths, religion, and language. It consists of those elements humans use to adjust to their physical and social environments. It is their solution to the problem of survival. The unique biological structure of humans and their ability to symbolize make them the only animals able to create and acquire culture.

Since culture is human-made, students will be able to conclude that cultures vary greatly in different parts of the world, in different societies, and among different peoples. Students should be helped to discover that a culture system is an organized whole. Any drastic external or internal changes are likely to disrupt it. Culture is the key concept in cultural anthropology. Since all the other concepts are related to it, culture should be given special attention and focus in anthropological studies in the elementary and junior high school.

When teaching the concept of culture, you may find it helpful to introduce three closely related concepts: *culture element* (trait), *culture complex*, and *enculturation*. A culture element is the smallest unit of culture. A tool such as an ax, a custom such as tipping the hat when greeting a person, and a word such as house are all culture traits. A set of functionally interrelated traits is a culture complex. The marriage complex in U.S. society usually consists of a period of courtship, a formal engagement, and an elaborate ceremony. Often culture traits are in the form of complexes when they spread from one culture area to another. Enculturation is the process by which individuals learn to participate in the culture of their society. Sociologists use the term socialization to describe this process.

You can also introduce the concepts *macroculture* and *microculture* when teaching about culture. A macroculture is a large culture. United States culture and Japanese culture are examples. Microcultures are subcultures that are part of a large or macroculture. Ethnic cultures such as the Italian-American, African-American, and Japanese-American, and religious cultures such as the Appalachian and Mormon are examples of microcultures in the United States.

TABLE 11.1. The Development of Anthropological Theories

Theory	Description	Leaders	Major Contributions to Anthropology
Evolutionism	An evolutionary theory of cultural development. All human cultures had experienced the same developmental stages; each higher phase represented more progress. Preliterate cultures typified the earliest stages of human cultural development. Western European civilization was the highest stage of culture that people had attained. Formulated in the 1800s.	Edward B. Taylor Lewis H. Morgan Sir James Frazer	Formulated the concept of culture. Stimulated research by others.
Historicism	Produced ethnographies indicating that the development of culture traits had not been uniform and unilinear. Within the same culture area could be found traits associated with each of Morgan's developmental levels. Advocated studying the historical origin of each culture trait through extensive fieldwork.	Franz Boas	Started the tradition of empirical fieldwork in anthropology.
Diffusionism	Cultural traits and elements had been invented in only a few areas of the world and had spread from these areas to all other culture regions.		Emphasized the importance of borrowing in the formation of cultures.
Functionalism	Each element in a culture exists to fulfill the needs of individuals. Every cultural system is an integrated whole, and each culture element fulfills definite functions. All cultures must meet three kinds of needs: Primary or biological needs, derived or instrumental needs, and integrative or synthetic needs.	Bronislaw Malinowski A. R. Radcliffe-Brown	Stimulated discussion and debate in anthropology.
Configuration-alism	Cultures do not consist of separate elements but are organized wholes. Cultures as wholes can be characterized according to the dominant ideologies, values, and ideas embraced by the individuals	Ruth Benedict	Introduced the idea that cultures may have themes or patterns.

TABLE 11.1. (*continued*)

Theory	Description	Leaders	Major Contributions to Anthropology
	within them. These dominant ideologies and ideas are called "themes" of cultures.		
Psychological approaches (culture and personality)	A basic personality emerges within a culture because of the commonality of early childhood experiences. This basic personality is manifested in all of the culture's institutions, such as religion, magic, and mythology.	Margaret Mead Abram Kardiner	Pointed out how culture shapes the personality of the individual.
Cultural materialism	A major goal of these theorists is to explain the differences and similarities in human groups. They feel that the differences and similarities in cultures can best be explained by the material constraints found in human environments. When trying to satisfy their basic needs for food, shelter, and tools, human groups encounter material constraints. The variations in the mental and spiritual parts of human life are caused largely by variations in the material constraints affecting the way groups satisfy their basic needs.	Marvin Harris	Pointed out the importance of material constraints on the development of human culture.

Activities

1. Show the students symbols such as a flag, a cross, and a stop sign. Ask them to tell what each of these symbols means. Point out that they are all examples of culture because they represent ideas that humans use to communicate.
2. Read the students descriptions of life in different subcultures in the United States, such as on a farm in Texas, in Appalachia, and in New York City. Ask them to identify ways in which life in these various places are alike and different.
3. Study the various cultures of Indian groups in the United States and describe ways in which they are alike and different.
4. Compare and contrast the life of children in the United States with

Students can compare this photograph of a family with a covered wagon on the great westward migration with modes of transportation today. This will help them to understand cultural continuity and cultural change. (*Source*: The National Archives, Washington, D.C.)

the life of children in nations such as the United Kingdom, Nigeria, Japan, and Lebanon.

5. Divide into groups and make lists of what each group thinks makes up U.S. culture. Pool the ideas of each group and make a master list of what the class thinks constitutes U.S. culture.

Diffusion

A culture area is a geographical region that shares a number of culture traits and complexes. Anthropologists have identified the following culture areas for American Indian cultures: the Eskimo, the Pacific Northwest coast, the Plains, and the Southwest. The spreading of culture traits from one culture area to another is called diffusion. A concept related to diffusion is invention, the process of independently developing a new cultural trait or artifact.

INQUIRY STRATEGY: AN ARCHEOLOGICAL CULTURAL ODYSSEY

Directions

Read the following scenario to the students. Then give them the items described in the "artifacts" list that follows the scenario.

It is 1000 years from now. You have landed in an unknown land and are conducting an archeological dig. You know nothing about the people who lived in this land a thousand years ago except what you can detect from the following items that you find on the dig. This unknown land is the United States.

Your task is to try to describe the *culture* of the United States in 1990 as revealed in the items listed below. For example, on the front side of the one dollar bill is found a photograph of George Washington. On the back, the seal of the United States appears. It includes an eagle and the words *E Pluribus Unum*. Also on the back of the one dollar bill are the words "In God We Trust." What do these symbols and words, as well as those in the other items in this activity, tell you about the culture of the United States?

Break up into groups of five to complete this activity. Appoint a leader and a recorder for each group. Each group will independently make a list describing what these items reveal about the culture of the United States.

Each person in each group should also draw a circle or a box and make a personal "seal." The seal should contain words and/or symbols that reveal what is most important to you personally and to your cultural/ethnic group.

When these two steps have been completed, assemble in a large group. Ask the recorder from each small group to share the list it developed and the highlights from the group's discussion about the personal "seal."

Artifacts

1. Photograph of a one dollar bill, showing details of both the front and back. (Actual one dollar bills may also be used.)
2. Photograph of a U.S. postage stamp that shows a famous American or a symbol about American society. (Actual postage stamps can also be used.)
3. The following excerpt from the Declaration of Independence (1776):

We hold these truths to be self-evident, that all men are created equal, that they are endowed by their Creator with certain unalienable rights, that among these are life, liberty, and the pursuit of happiness. That, to secure these rights, governments are instituted among men, deriving their just powers from the consent of the governed. That, whenever any form of government becomes destructive of these ends, it is the right of the people to alter or abolish it, and to institute new government, laying its foundation on such principles, and organizing its powers in such form, as to them shall seem most likely to effect their safety and happiness.

4. The poem, "I Too, Sing America" by Langston Hughes, in Langston Hughes and Arna Bontemps, Eds., *The Poetry of the Negro, 1746–1970* (Garden City, NY: Doubleday, 1970), p. 182.
5. Excerpts from Martin Luther King, "I Have a Dream," in *The Annals of America, Volume 18, 1961–1968* (Chicago: Encyclopedia Britannica, Inc., 1968), pp. 156–159.

Anthropologists have discovered that most of the traits that make up a culture were borrowed, not invented. However, all cultures have made independent inventions. Many of the words, customs, behavior patterns, and artifacts that are very important components of United States culture were invented in other culture areas. Culture traits may spread from one microculture to another within the same macroculture, as well as from one macroculture to another.

Activities

1. Study the origins of words in U.S. English that came from other nations, such as *enchilada, pizza,* and *bon voyage.*
2. Study the invention and spread of architectural forms to various nations, such as the post and lintel construction, the dome, and the Doric, Ionic, and Corinthian orders.
3. Research the evolution, domestication, and uses of the horse and how the horse spread to and was used by various cultures.
4. Research the factors that gave rise to French Impressionism and its influence on art in various Western nations.
5. Ask the students to list the major values stated in the United States Declaration of Independence and the Constitution. Help them to identify the European writers and philosophers that strongly influenced the ideas of the founding fathers in the United States.

Tradition

A social custom, behavior pattern, or belief that has been part of a culture for a long period of time is a tradition. Folkways, mores, and myths are part of the traditions of a society. Traditions in the United States include decorating a tree for the Christmas season, eating turkey on Thanksgiving Day, and wearing a ring to indicate marital status. Traditions help a society to maintain stability and to socialize children. However, as Durkin points out, "Societies and the groups and individuals within them tend to retain many traditional ways of living and dealing with current problems, whether or not that behavior is appropriate."[18]

Activities

1. Study the origins of holidays such as Christmas, Chanukah, New Year's Day, and St. Valentine's Day.
2. Compare and contrast the ways in which nations such as Colombia, Brazil, Canada, the United Kingdom, and the United States celebrate Christmas.

3. Study U.S. traditions that originated within, and are celebrated primarily by, ethnic groups within the United States, such as Jewish Passover, Yom Kippur, and Black History Month.
4. Students can learn how difficult it is to start a new national holiday by studying the history of the development of Labor Day and Martin Luther King's Birthday as national holidays. Ask them to identify the major factors involved when a day is made into a national holiday.
5. Ask the students to make a list of special traditions that exist in their families, such as having a family reunion every five years or going to grandmother's house for Christmas.

Acculturation

The cultural exchange that takes place when two unlike cultures experience extended contact is called acculturation. Acculturation often takes place when powerful groups capture or subjugate less powerful ones. Much cultural exchange took place when the American colonists invaded the areas inhabited by the American Indians. It is extremely important for students to understand that acculturation is a two-way process. While most Americans are aware of how the Indian cultures were affected by Anglo-Saxon culture, our great cultural debt to the Indians is less well-known and less acknowledged.

Acculturation is a selective process; cultures accept only those elements from a foreign culture that blend with their own cultural elements. When they use traits from another culture, they modify them. Forced cultural change can disrupt a culture, since cultures are organized wholes. Many of the forced cultural changes that the Indians experienced had a profoundly negative effect on their life-style. If you and your students make extensive use of this concept in the early grades, when they are learning about Indian and Eskimo groups, the study of these peoples will be less superficial and ethnocentric than it currently is in many classrooms.

Activities

1. Study ways in which the Indian cultures changed after the arrival of the English colonists.
2. List the things that the Indians taught the early colonists that enabled them to survive the harsh winters in New England.
3. Research ways Black culture has influenced mainstream American culture, especially in music and the arts.
4. Identify the ways foods in the United States have been influenced by other nations.
5. Examine the ways United States culture has influenced other nations.

Ethnocentrism

Every group tends to think its culture is superior to all others. Writes Spain, "Many groups . . . refer to themselves by using names which translate as 'true humans' or 'people,' while the names for 'others' are the equivalent of such words as 'savage,' 'barbarian,' or other more descriptive indications of their distinctive and inhuman qualities such as 'the-ones-who-walk-on-their heads.' "[19] A knowledge of this concept will help elementary and junior high school students to better understand the pervasive ethnocentrism in the modern world.

Activities

1. Ask the students to list epithets they have heard used to refer to various cultural, ethnic, and religious groups. Discuss why people use such negative terms to refer to outside groups.
2. Read documents written by various European explorers to the Americas and discuss words they used to describe the American Indians. Discuss why they used these words.
3. View drawings of American Indians that were done by Europeans in the nineteenth century and discuss ways in which they exemplify ethnocentrism.
4. View pictures of Africa in textbooks and other sources and list ways that they show ethnocentrism.
5. Study the role ethnocentrism played in leading Japan and Germany to World War II.

Cultural Relativism

Cultural relativism means we can gain a full understanding of the behavior within a group only if we look at it from the perspective of that group's culture. Many cultural practices, such as water witching, the vision quest among the Plains Indians, and the revival meetings of southern fundamentalist Baptists, often seem strange and perplexing to outsiders unless they view them from the perspectives of the cultures in which they are practiced.

Cultural relativism is often interpreted to be a moral position which indicates that cultures should not be judged with others cultures' criteria. However, as Swartz and Jordan point out, cultural relativism need not be an ethical concept. They write, "Being able to understand the forces that influence behavior is one thing and evaluating that behavior is quite another. Cultural relativism, seen as an intellectual tool, is very different from cultural relativism as an instrument of moral judgment."[20]

When interpreted as an ethical concept, cultural relativism can be abused. It can be used to justify the destruction and exploitation of human lives. However, students should be aware of this concept since it can help them to see that behavior in other cultures that they may consider bizarre is often quite meaningful and useful to the people who practice it. They should also be aware of the limitations of cultural relativism when used in an ethical context.

Activities

1. Identify current practices and customs in American society, such as beliefs about ghosts, the four-leaf clover, and the rabbit's foot, and explain how these customs emerged and why people believe in them.
2. Do a survey to find out how many modern office buildings in your community do not have a thirteenth floor, and find out why.
3. Read about the customs related to witches in American colonial society and discuss why they ended.
4. Read about customs in traditional Indian and Eskimo cultures that are perplexing to most Americans and explain what they meant to the people who practiced them.
5. Identify some of the customs in several of the major world religions, such as Christianity, Judaism, and Islam, and discuss why these practices are perplexing to outsiders and what they mean to those who practice them.

Rite of Passage

A rite of passage is a ceremony marking an important change in an individual's life. The individual moves from one status to another. Ceremonies related to birth, puberty, marriage, and death are rites of passage. Rites of passage are important to individuals because they clearly mark important changes in their lives and provide them with emotional support.

Activities

1. Make a list of the ways the students celebrate their birthdays.
2. Share pictures of important events in the students' lives, such as birthdays and baptisms.
3. Read about the Jewish bar mitzvah and bas mitzvah ceremonies and identify their nature and major purposes.
4. Do research to find out ways in which marriage ceremonies are similar and different in various cultures.
5. Do research to find out ways in which death ceremonies are similar and different within various United States subcultures and within different nations.

ANTHROPOLOGICAL GENERALIZATIONS

Most anthropological generalizations are based on cross-cultural samples and deal with the discipline's key concept, culture. A number are also interdisciplinary, because anthropologists study many problems of interest to other behavioral scientists. The following generalizations can be used to guide anthropological instruction in the elementary and junior high school grades. The generalizations are grouped under major concepts.

Culture

>   Every society consists of a human-made system of artifacts, beliefs, and behavior patterns, called culture. Culture enables individuals within it to meet their needs according to their physical and social environment.
>   Because of their unique biological traits, humans are the only animals able to create and acquire culture.
>   Culture is an integrated whole. Changes in one part are reflected in nearly all other components.
>   Cultures use a diversity of means to attain similar ends and to satisfy common human needs.

Symbols

>   Making and using symbols is an essential component of every culture.

Diffusion

>   Every culture consists of a variety of borrowed cultural elements. However, cultures are selective in the traits they borrow. Societies adapt borrowed cultural elements to their own particular life-styles.

Acculturation

>   Cultural exchange takes place when groups with diverse cultures come into prolonged contact. Cultural change may disrupt a society.

Magic and Religion

>   In all human societies, magical and religious practices arise to help individuals explain perplexing phenomena in the universe, and to attain a sense of control over their environment.

Rites of Passage

>   All societies have traditional ceremonies and rituals to signal and mark important status changes in a person's life.

Traditions

>   All societies have a set of traditions that help to maintain group solidarity and identity.

ANTHROPOLOGY IN THE ELEMENTARY AND JUNIOR HIGH SCHOOL

Many units in the primary and intermediate grades have content dealing with preliterate societies that can be profitably studied from an anthropological perspective. When students are taught about Eskimos, Indians, and Africans, the exotic and strange behavior of these peoples are often emphasized. As a result, students often conclude these groups are not very human. They seem very different from the students, and they do many things that seem inhuman or absurd, such as sending the aged into subzero weather to freeze to death or dancing to make it rain. Most young children think that behavior very different from their own is bizarre. Too often social studies units reinforce students' misconceptions about other cultures, rather than help them to understand the meaning of the "puzzling" behavior to the people who practice it.

Social studies units on groups such as Indians and Africans often include songs, dances, and materials that reinforce stereotypes of Indian and African cultures. Units on Indians often present the stereotypic image of Plains Indians. Rarely is the tremendous diversity among Indian tribes accurately described in social studies units for young children. Africa is often presented in the curriculum as a land that consists only of preliterate cultures. The modernized cities in Africa and the tremendous diversity of the peoples and cultures that make up Africa are rarely described in elementary school units. Units on Africans and Indians often describe traditional cultures without indicating the tremendous ways in which these cultures have changed as a result of modernization. Units on Indians and Africans should be taught from anthropological perspectives and help students understand the tremendous diversity both within and across Indian and African cultures.

Units on Indians and Eskimos, if approached from an anthropological perspective, can help students broaden their understanding of what it means to be *human*, and enable them to better understand their own culture and life-style. Students should be helped to discover that although people are born with the physical capacity to become human, individuals become human only by learning the culture of their group. Anthropologists call this learning process *enculturation*. Since cultures are human-made, there are many ways of being human. Our middle-class American life-style is one way; the Navajo Indian culture represents another. Studying these important anthropological generalizations helps students to appreciate humankind's great capacity to create a diversity of life-styles and to adapt to a variety of environments.

During their study of preliterate cultures, students can learn that although human beings have many of the same basic needs—such as love, protection, and food—different cultures have devised a great variety of means to satisfy them. The rain dances of the Hopi Indians, the Shaman among some African groups, and water witching in the United States all represent attempts by humans to control and manipulate their environment.

Once students understand preliterate people's behavior, they will be less likely to consider it exotic and bizarre. With understanding may come tolerance.

While you should help students see and understand differences, you should also make them aware of the many ways in which all human groups are alike. For example, all human societies have families, a system of government, the incest taboo, and divisions between male and female roles. However, these institutions often take diverse forms. Nevertheless, you should not emphasize differences to the neglect of important similarities. Students should know how closely they are related to all human groups—both biologically and culturally. Anthropologists call the many ways in which all human cultures are alike *culture universals.*

Anthropology can also help students better understand their own culture. By studying about other ways of being and living, students will see how bound they are by their own values and prejudices. The fact that most Americans think romantic love is the most important part of marriage indicates how much we are creatures of our culture. Individuals in some cultures would be shocked by the idea that marriage could be based on such flimsy grounds. Kluckhohn writes, "Studying preliterates enables us to see ourselves better. Ordinarily we are unaware of the special lens through which we look at life. . . . *Anthropology holds up a great mirror to man and lets him look at himself in his infinite variety.*"[21]

You can use a conceptual approach to the study of preliterate societies to militate against perpetuating stereotypes and misconceptions. You can begin by identifying a number of key anthropological concepts that will serve as an organizing framework for your units. Once you have identified a number of organizing concepts such as *culture, tradition, acculturation,* and *diffusion,* you should select several generalizations related to these concepts, such as "Cultures employ a diversity of means to attain similar ends and to satisfy common human needs" and "Culture exchange takes place when groups with diverse cultures come into prolonged contact." After key concepts and generalizations are identified, you can select teaching materials and devise appropriate teaching strategies.

If you select the first generalization named above, you could identify three cultures for content samples, such as the Navajo Indians, the Iroquois Indians, and the Netsilik Eskimos, or you could select one of these groups and use mainstream U.S. culture as a comparison group. Selecting a small number of cultures and covering them in depth is better than selecting a large number of cultures and covering them superficially. Selection of content samples should be based primarily on the materials available, interests of the students, recommendations in the district curriculum guide, teacher competency and interests, and the prior experiences of the students. If the students studied the Navajo Indians in a previous year, it would be better to select the Iroquois for the new unit.

When teaching the generalization "Cultures employ a diversity of means to attain similar ends and to satisfy common human needs," you could construct, with the pupils' help, a data retrieval chart similar to the one illus-

TABLE 11.2. Data Retrieval Chart: Comparison of Cultures

Concepts and Related Questions	Navajo	Iroquois	Netsilik Eskimo
Food What foods are eaten? How are they obtained?			
Protection What kinds of shelter exist? How are they made?			
Recreation What do people do for fun?			
Esteem How do people gain recognition?			

trated in Table 11.2. You could begin by asking the students to name some needs that all human beings have. Their responses may include food, protection from extreme weather, love, esteem, recreation, and a need to explain the origin of the universe and people's place in it. Their responses could be used to structure categories on universal human needs. Once these categories are structured, the class can identify a number of questions related to the categories that can be asked about each of the cultures studied. The names of the cultures should be listed on the chart. The students should participate in a variety of activities—such as reading, role playing, and viewing films and filmstrips—in order to gain the information needed to complete the chart. Once the chart is complete, the students will be able to derive the generalization stated above.

TEACHING STRATEGIES

Generalization: *The making and use of symbols is an essential component of every culture.*

Primary Grades

Show the class these symbols. Then ask the questions that follow.

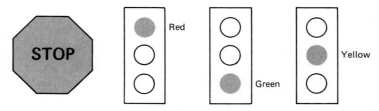

1. Look at these signs. Have you ever seen them before? Where? What does each mean? Can you think of other signs? (Recalling meanings of specific symbols.)
2. Did you always know what the first sign means? How did you find out what it means? (Cultures pass on meanings of symbols.)
3. Do these signs help people? How? (Symbols help people adjust to their environment.)
4. What would happen if we didn't have these signs?

Ask the following questions:

1. Did anyone ever tell you that you were a little monkey? Why would anyone call you a little monkey? Would you like to be called by that name? Why or why not? (Example of a symbol.)
2. Draw a line between the animal and the thing it stands for. (Matching symbols with meaning.)

mouse	courageous, brave
lion	quiet, tiny
elephant	clever
fox	good memory

3. Isn't it funny that we think of animals in these ways? Do you think a mouse is really quiet? Think about the other animals and the words we use to describe them. Do these words and animals fit? (Questioning the relationship between the symbol and its meaning.)
4. Did you ever hear a story about a house where "nothing was stirring, not even a mouse"? Why don't we say, "where nothing was stirring, not even a horse"? Which phrase makes the house seem quieter? Why? Does it help to use animal names to tell about things? How? (Examining the use of symbols in descriptions.)

Read the class a story about Indians or Eskimos that tells about totem poles and includes characters that have animal names such as Running Bear or Crazy Horse. Then ask the children to write a story in which they use animal names to describe characteristics of people and things. (Application: Using symbols.)

Ask the following questions: Do you ever pretend to be a driver of a car or a fisherman in a boat? Do you sometimes walk around the house in your mother's or father's shoes? Do you ever pretend to ride horses or drive trucks and trains? Why? (Identifying feelings that are symbolized in action.)

Tell the class: England is a country that is on the other side of the Atlantic Ocean. (Show on a globe.) There, when a person is old enough, he or she *gets the key*. The boy (or girl) is given the key to his or her house when he or she is big enough.

Ask the following questions: Would you like to be big and have a key to your house? Would your parents give a key to a one-year-old child? Why not?

Say: We would call the key a symbol of being big because you get one only when you are old enough to take good care of a key and will not lose it. You get a key when you are big. (Determining the reason for particular meaning of symbol.)

Ask: Can you think of other symbols of being big? If we had no symbols of being big, would you ever know if you were grown up? (Remembering, predicting, and hypothesizing result of loss of symbols.)

Ask the children to act out, tell a story about, draw pictures of, or write about someone's acting in a way that shows or symbolizes what he or she would like to be. (Applying knowledge.)

Intermediate Grades

Tell the class:

> Every year in Mexico, as in many other countries, there is a retelling of the story of Jesus' birth. In a symbolic journey, a girl and a boy, representing Mary and Joseph, walk each night for nine days. On the last day an innkeeper gives them shelter and Jesus is born.

Ask the following questions:

1. Is Jesus really born each time the boy and girl walk through the journey in the story? (Recognition of symbolic nature of the action.)
2. What do people in other countries do to symbolize the birth of Jesus? (Memory; comparison of similar symbols.)
3. Why do you suppose the people have this festival every year? (Determining meaning of symbolic tradition.)
4. Have you ever seen a cross? What does a cross mean? Why do some people wear a cross? (Analyzing a concrete symbol.)

Ask the following questions:

1. In scouting, Boy Scouts, Girl Scouts, and Campfire Girls receive emblems for each skill attained and demonstrated. How is this practice similar to the markings of the Indians? How is it different? (Comparing symbol systems.)
2. Military organizations also use symbols to designate achievement levels. How are military symbols similar to the ones we have discussed? How are they different? (Comparing symbols.)

Ask the students to complete the following activities:

1. Select flags from three African nations. Investigate the meanings or symbolism behind each color used and also the meanings of the

designs on the flags. (Identifying symbolic meanings.) Each student will discuss with the class the flags he or she selected, indicating all symbols involved.

2. Discuss things to which you could feel loyal, like your family, friends, class, city, state, religion, and country. What other things could you feel loyal to? What could be symbols of the things you named? (Identifying feelings, creating symbols.)

3. Select something to which you feel you are loyal and create a flag, using symbols to express important aspects of it. (Identifying feelings, creating symbols.)

Tell the class: Before you had money to buy some of the things you wanted, you could collect things and trade them for items that you didn't have.

Ask: What things could you collect when you were smaller? What could you trade them for?

Upper Grades

Read the class the following summary of an Eskimo anthropologist's report of one aspect of American life:

> Many peoples in the world pay close attention to time, but none more than Americans. Though it might be denied, time seems sacred in the United States.
>
> This is apparent from the American language. It is generally regarded as sinful to "waste time." One of the greatest American philosophers has said: "Dost thou love life? Then do not squander time, for that is the stuff life is made of."
>
> But to be specific. Nearly all Americans carry idols that represent time. Larger idols that show time are displayed throughout American igloos and in public places.
>
> Even when busy, Americans often gaze at such idols and regulate their lives according to them. They start when they get up in the morning, and they hardly stop until they go to bed. Many students and workers seem more interested in the time idol than they are in their tasks.
>
> If time worship can be considered a religion, Americans may be the most religious people on earth.[22]

Ask these questions:

1. What did the Eskimo anthropologist say about Americans and time? (Memory.)

2. Do Americans worship idols of time? Why or why not? (Analyzing symbolism about time.)

3. Do you agree with the Eskimo anthropologist? Why or why not? (Evaluating the interpretation of symbols.)

4. What does this selection tell you in regard to making assumptions about other people? (Evaluating method of interpretation.)

Say to the class: Words are symbols. They stand for ideas and values that people have. Ask your parents and your grandparents what words they used to describe things they liked when they were your age. What words do people your age use for things they like? Are they the same as they were when you were five years younger? Why or why not? Do you think that you will use different symbols or words for things you like when you are five years older? Why or why not? (Changing of symbols through time.)

Find out how people from different countries greet each other. We greet each other with "Hello," "Hi," "How are you?"; in parting we may say "Goodbye," "Peace," or "Take it easy." The Navajo say "Ya ta hey"; it is used to say "Goodbye" or "Peace." The Jewish people may say "Shalom," which means "Peace be with you," or also "Hello" or "Goodbye." The Chinese say "Ni Hâu Ma" for "How are you?"

Ask: How are these symbols alike? Different? What would we do without them? (Comparing symbolic systems.)

Ask the class the following questions:

1. Have you ever heard of someone holding up a black fist? (Recall of symbol.) What does a black fist mean today? Has it always meant what it means today? Why or why not? (Identification of meaning through time and changes with time.)
2. Have you ever seen an Afro (or natural) hair style? What do you think that it symbolizes or means to the person who wears it? What does it mean to you? Has it always meant what it means today? Why or why not? (Same as above; also distinguishes meaning of the same symbol for two different people.)
3. There has been a change through time in the symbols for peace. Indians had a few peace symbols. Can you name one? (Pipe and broken arrow.) Can you name three symbols for peace used later in this country? (Dove, eagle with olive branches, ☮ , and two fingers making a V.) Find out ways in which peace is symbolized in other societies. Create your own symbol of peace. (Identification of meaning, recall of symbols, comparison of symbols with same meaning; and application of knowledge by creating a new symbol.)

SUMMARY

Anthropology is distinguished from the other social sciences because of its focus on *culture*—the behavior patterns, belief systems, artifacts, and other human-made components of a society. Anthropologists use a "holistic" approach when they study culture; they believe that valid generalizations can be made only when all the elements of a cultural system are studied as an integrated whole. The comparative study of preliterate cultures is also a unique characteristic of anthropology. The main research method used in the discipline is participant observation. Anthropologists live in the cultures they study. Because of the nature of the discipline and its traditions, anthropological research is more exploratory than research in the behavioral sciences like sociology and psychology. Most anthropologists are more interested in describing particular cultures than they are in formulating empirical theories about many different cultures. Anthropological generalizations are often interpretive judgments rather than empirical statements. The participant observation method does not facilitate the making of hard generalizations. Thus anthropology is akin to both the humanities and history. Theory development has been retarded in the discipline because of its research aims and methods and a nonempirical tradition involving the search for single-factor theories to explain the emergence of individual cultures.

Despite the scientific status of anthropology, its focus on *culture* and its concern for preliterate cultures make it an excellent vehicle for helping students to broaden their conception of what it means to be human and understand how bound they are by their own cultures, prejudices, and biases. In all societies, people tend to think that their way of doing things is the right way or the only way. Such chauvinistic ethnocentrism is especially detrimental in our increasingly small and interdependent world, where peoples of many different cultures, races, and ideologies must learn to live together if the human race is going to survive the challenges of the twenty-first century. Anthropology can help students to learn that there are other ways of living and being that are just as valid as the ways with which they are familiar. With understanding, tolerance sometimes comes. Anthropology merits a special place in the schools because it gives students a unique lens to view other humans—and themselves.

DISCUSSION QUESTIONS AND EXERCISES

1. Why is anthropology considered a social *science*? In what ways is anthropology scientific? In what ways is it nonscientific?
2. What characteristics distinguish anthropology from the other social sciences? What special contribution can anthropology make to helping students become effective decision-makers and citizen actors?
3. What is the "holistic" approach to studying culture? Find and summarize a study in anthropology that is an example of the holistic approach to studying culture. What are the advantages of this approach? What are its limitations? What implications does the holistic approach have for teaching *culture* in the elementary and junior high grades?
4. Read one of the classic books in anthropology, such as *Mirror for Man* by Clyde Kluckhohn, *Patterns of Culture* by Ruth Benedict, or *Coming of Age in Samoa* by Margaret Mead, or a more recent book or ethnography, such as

Marvin Harris, *Cows, Pigs, Wars and Witches: The Riddles of Culture,* Clifford Geertz, "Deep Play: Notes on a Balinese Cockfight," in *The Interpretation of Cultures,* and answer the following questions:

a. What key concepts and generalizations are discussed in the book or ethnography?

b. What kinds of data are used to support the generalizations made by the author?

c. What methods of research were used to gather the data discussed by the author?

d. How does the writing style of the book or ethnography compare with that in studies you have read in other disciplines? (For example, is the book or ethnography more interesting than books that you have read in other subject areas?)

e. What were the major strengths and limitations of the book or ethnography?

f. In what ways can the information reported in the book or ethnography help you to plan and organize a unit on *culture* for students in the elementary and junior high school grades?

5. Examine a primary grade social studies unit in your curriculum library, dealing with the cultures of preliterate groups, such as some American Indian, Eskimo, or African societies. What key concepts and generalizations are developed within the unit? Are the concepts and generalizations accurate? If not, in what ways are they inaccurate? Are the facts used to teach the concepts and generalizations accurate? Are the activities designed to teach the concepts and generalizations effective? What concepts and generalizations would you add or take out of the unit in order to make it more effective? What learning activities would you add or take out of the unit to make it more effective?

6. Select one of the following generalizations and write a series of activities (similar to the ones in this chapter) that can be used to teach it to students in the (1) primary grades, (2) middle grades, and (3) upper grades.

a. The making and use of symbols is an essential component of every culture.

b. Cultures use a diversity of means to attain similar ends and to satisfy common human needs.

c. Cultural exchange takes place when groups with diverse cultures come into prolonged contact. Cultural change may disrupt a society.

d. All societies have traditional ceremonies and rituals to signal and mark important status changes in an individual's life.

7. Examine an introductory college textbook in anthropology and list the key concepts and generalizations within it that could serve as a guide to a social studies curriculum committee.

8. Assume that you are an anthropologist who is studying a primary grade classroom.

a. State the key concepts you would use to guide your analysis of the culture within the classroom.

b. List key questions related to the concepts you would raise.

c. State related hypotheses.

d. Indicate how you would test your hypotheses.

e. If possible, carry out the study.

Can students in the upper elementary grades implement an anthropological study of their classroom, school, or community? If you think that they can, tell how. If you feel that they cannot, state why.

9. Demonstrate your understanding of the following key concepts by writing or stating brief definitions for each of them. Also tell why each is significant.

a.	holistic method	m.	culture
b.	comparative approach	n.	culture element
c.	cultural anthropology	o.	culture complex
d.	ethnology	p.	enculturation
e.	ethnography	q.	culture area
f.	evolutionism	r.	diffusion
g.	historicism	s.	acculturation
h.	diffusionism	t.	ethnocentrism
i.	functionalism	u.	tradition
j.	configurationalism	v.	culture relativism
k.	psychological approaches	w.	rite of passage
l.	cultural materialism		

NOTES

1. Muriel Dimen-Schein, *The Anthropological Imagination* (New York: McGraw-Hall, 1977); Marvin Harris, *Culture, People, Nature: An Introduction to General Anthropology*, 3rd ed. (New York: Harper & Row, 1980).

2. Pertti J. Pelto and Raymond H. Muessig, *The Study and Teaching of Anthropology* (Columbus, OH: Merrill, 1980), p. 4.

3. Ray Rist, *The Invisible Children: School Integration in American Society* (Cambridge, MA.: Harvard University Press, 1978); John U. Ogbu, *The Next Generation: An Ethnography of Education in an Urban Neighborhood* (New York: Academic Press, 1974); Susan U. Philips, *The Invisible Culture* (New York: Longman, 1983).

4. George Spindler, Ed., *Doing the Ethnography of Schooling* (New York: Holt Rinehart and Winston, 1982).

5. Clifford Geertz, *The Interpretation of Cultures* (New York: Basic Books, 1973); Clifford Geertz, *Local Knowledge: Further Essays in Interpretive Anthropology* (New York: Basic Books, 1983).

6. Ruth Benedict, *Patterns of Culture* (Boston: Houghton Mifflin, 1934); Margaret Mead, *Coming of Age in Samoa* (New York: Mentor Books, 1928, 1949).

7. Derek Freeman, *Margaret Mead and Samoa: The Making and Unmaking of an Anthropological Myth* (Cambridge, MA: Harvard University Press, 1983).

8. Mead, op. cit.

9. Benedict, op. cit.; Mead, op. cit.; Marvin Harris, *Cows, Pigs, Wars and Witches: The Riddles of Culture* (New York: Vintage Books, 1974).

10. Weston LaBarr, *The Human Animal* (Chicago: University of Chicago Press, 1954).

11. Ashley Montagu, *Man's Most Dangerous Myth: The Fallacy of Race*, 5th ed. (New York: Oxford University Press, 1974).

12. Marvin Harris, *The Rise of Anthropological Theory: A History of Theories of Culture* (New York: Crowell, 1968), pp. 514–567.

13. Pertti J. Pelto and Gretel H. Pelto, *Anthropological Research: The Structure of Inquiry*, 2nd ed. (New York: Cambridge University Press, 1978).

14. Pelto and Muessig, op. cit., p. 42.

15. Marvin Harris, *Cultural Materialism: The Struggle for a Science of Culture* (New York: Vintage Books, 1980); Clifford Geertz, *Local Knowledge*.

16. Alfred L. Kroeber and Clyde Kluckhohn, *Culture: A Critical Review of Concepts* (New York: Vintage Books, 1963), p. 357. (First published in 1952.)

17. Felix M. Keesing, *Cultural Anthropology: The Science of Custom* (New York: Holt Rinehart and Winston, 1958), p. 152.

18. Mary C. Durkin, *The Taba Social Studies Curriculum (Grade 5: United States and Canada)* (Menlo Park, CA: Addison-Wesley, 1969), p. vi.

19. David H. Spain, Ed., *The Human Experience: Readings in Sociocultural Anthropology* (Homewood, IL: Dorsey Press, 1975), p. 5.

20. Marc J. Swartz and David K. Jordan, *Anthropology: Perspectives on Humanity* (New York: John Wiley, 1976), p. 71.

21. Clyde Kluckhohn, *Mirror for Man* (Greenwich, CT.: Fawcett, 1965), p. 19.

22. *Anthropology in Today's World: Case Studies of Peoples and Cultures* (Middletown, CT: American Education Publications Units Book, 1965), p. 7.

FOR FURTHER READING

Bateson, Mary Catherine. *With a Daughter's Eye: A Memoir of Margaret Mead and Gregory Bateson.* New York: Pocket Books, 1984.

Benedict, Ruth. *Patterns of Culture.* Boston: Houghton Mifflin, 1959. There are more recent and many different editions of this classic book.

Cole, Johnnetta, Ed. *Anthropology for the Nineties: Introductory Readings.* New York: The Free Press, 1988.

Cole, Johnnetta, Ed. *All American Women: Lines that Divide, Ties that Bind.* New York: Free Press, 1986.

Dimen-Schein, Muriel. *The Anthropological Imagination.* New York: McGraw-Hill, 1977.

Hall, Edward T. *Beyond Culture.* Garden City, NY: Doubleday, 1977.

Harris, Marvin. Cows, *Pigs, Wars and Witches: The Riddles of Culture.* New York: Random House, 1974.

Mead, Margaret. *Coming of Age in Samoa.* New York: Mentor Books, 1949 edition. There are more recent and many different editions of this classic book.

Modell, Judith. *Ruth Benedict: Patterns of a Life.* London: The Hogarth Press, 1984.

Ogbu, John U. *The Next Generation: An Ethnography of Education in an Urban Neighborhood.* New York: Academic Press, 1974.

Pelto, Pertti J., and Raymond H. Muessig. *The Study and Teaching of Anthropology.* Columbus, OH: Merrill, 1980.

Philips, Susan U. *The Invisible Culture: Communication in Classroom and Community on the Warm Spring Indian Reservation.* New York: Longman, 1983.

Simonson, Rick, and Scott Walker, Eds. *Multicultural Literacy.* St. Paul, MN: Graywolf Press, 1988.

12

Political Science: Structure, Concepts, and Strategies

THE NATURE OF POLITICAL SCIENCE

We described sociology as the study of human groups and anthropology as the study of culture. However, it is difficult to briefly define political science because there are many different types of political scientists. They ask very different kinds of questions, have different research aims, and use many different concepts and approaches.

Political scientists' views of their discipline vary as much as the approaches within it. Some political scientists define the discipline as the study of the legal government of the state. Other political scientists consider this view too narrow. They point out that it does not reflect the study of the many informal groups and processes that are not part of legal government. These include interest groups, lobbying, bargaining, and logrolling. The first view of political science is also problematic because there are many different definitions of state. One author reports that he found 145 such definitions.[1]

Some political scientists define the discipline as the study of the struggle of competing groups for power. Like state, power has many different definitions. Consequently, it does not clearly define the boundaries of political science. Some political scientists cannot accept the power definition because they believe it does not specify unique behavior for them to study. They point out that power exists in all institutions, including a gang, a family, and a church. While the power definition is in one sense too inclusive, it is too restrictive in another. Political behavior is not limited to a struggle for power.[2] The power definition of the discipline is not accepted by some political scientists because of these problems. However, it is a very popular definition that is accepted by many political scientists.

David Easton, a leading political scientist, defines political science as the "study of the authoritative allocation of values for a society." [3] He points out that people have competing values, demands, and aspirations that they would like to become part of public policy and enforced in society. The political system is the process by which people decide which demands and goals will become public policy. This system prevents disruptive struggles among competing individuals and groups. Some citizens of the United States, for example, are strongly opposed to nuclear weapons, while others feel strongly that the United States needs to build more nuclear weapons in order to defend itself against a possible attack from the Soviet Union. The American political system, which provides for the election of representatives to Congress, makes possible a representative means for deciding which nuclear weapons policy the nation will implement. Individuals who are dissatisfied with existing national policies toward nuclear weapons can work to elect members of Congress whose views are consistent with their own.

Easton's definition specifies the boundaries of political science more clearly than do the state and power definitions. Political scientists study all the processes by which the goals and demands of competing groups become public policy when they use Easton's definitions. They do not study just legal government and formal institutions. If political scientists were trying to determine how the bill supporting the MX missile was passed in 1983, they would not merely study the formal ways by which the bill became law. They would also study the informal acts that influenced its passage—lobbying, logrolling, filibustering, and the speeches by President Reagan, which were designed to influence public opinion. Easton's definition is more precise than the power definition. It does not suggest that political scientists study all competing goals and values within a society, only those that are enforced by legitimate public authorities. Despite its strengths, some political scientists find Easton's definition unclear. Others disagree about what it means.[4]

We have discussed three definitions of political science: the study of the

"Just because he deals in abstractions doesn't make him any wiser than us." (*Source*: Herbert Goldberg. Used with permission.)

legal government of the state, the struggle for power, and the authoritative allocation of values for a society. They reflect the diversity of methods and approaches within the discipline. While all the definitions have competed for acceptance within political science, each has been only partially accepted. Each of them has a place within the discipline, but none reigns supreme. What Sorauf has said about approaches to the study of politics is also true of definitions of political science: ". . . in the skirmishes within political science there have been neither victors nor vanquished. As new approaches have appeared, they have been absorbed into the discipline without expelling or displacing any of the older traditions or approaches. Consequently, political science became a [mixture] of different and often conflicting approaches to the study of politics."[5]

APPROACHES IN POLITICAL SCIENCE

The Normative Approach

The first political scientists were armchair theorists who were primarily concerned with describing the ideal political system—one that would result in the best possible life for people. These theorists were mainly interested in value questions, such as "What should be the proper political system?" rather than scientific questions. They considered themselves philosophers and tried to advise political leaders and to influence public policy. Political philosophy (as this approach is sometimes called) is still an important part of modern political science.[6] Political thinkers such as Aristotle, Plato, Locke, and Marx are often studied by political theorists in order to develop ideas about the best type of political system.

Normative political theorists are very critical of the more scientific trends in the discipline. They feel that such approaches tend to ignore value questions—the most important questions facing people—and to study trivial, narrow questions whose answers will not contribute to the improvement of human life. Scientific political scientists contend that they do not ignore value questions, but study values instead by describing them, just as they do other behavior. They try to avoid advocating values or forms of government best for society.

The Legal-Institutional Approach

The first professors of political science were members of law faculties; thus a strong legal tradition has existed within the discipline since it first emerged. In this approach, an attempt is made to understand a political system primarily by describing and analyzing the laws, codes, constitutions, and other documents that are a part of legal government. The legalist studies the U.S. Constitution to discover the functions of the legislative, executive, and judicial branches of American government.

PROFILE

Jennifer L. Hochschild

A Political Scientist Who Studies Public Policy

Jennifer L. Hochschild, a professor of politics and public affairs at Princeton University, studies and influences public policy that fosters racial equality and justice. Her books and monographs include *The New American Dilemma: Liberal Democracy and School Desegregation, What's Fair: American Beliefs about Distributive Justice,* and *Thirty Years after Brown.* Hochschild is especially interested in school desegregation. Her paper "Equal Opportunity and the Estranged Poor" appeared in *Annals of the American Academy of Political and Social Science* (January 1989).

In *The New American Dilemma,* she challenges incremental and participatory methods used to desegregate schools. These methods, she argues, result in pain for blacks and whites and few gains for both groups. School desegregation succeeds when rapid and extensive change is imposed by nonelected officials without citizen involvement.

The institutional approach, closely related to the legal method, focuses on describing the functions of various governmental bodies and officials, such as the roles of judges, jurors, and congresses. The roles of formal institutions are described in great detail. However, little attention is given to the individual voter, the personalities of leaders, or to informal political institutions, such as interest groups and other organized lobbyists.

While many insights can be gained about a political system by studying its legal codes and formal institutions, the information that can be gained from this approach is greatly limited. Laws are interpreted variously by different authorities and in different time periods. The effect on the political system of informal groups and the personalities of political leaders is as great—if not greater—than the effect of formal codes and institutions. The legal powers of the president were no different in the 1930s than they were in the 1950s, yet Franklin D. Roosevelt exercised much more power than Dwight D. Eisenhower. An approach that largely ignores the role of individuals and personalities in the shaping of public policy—as this approach does—cannot provide keen insights into how a political system actually works.

The legal-institutional approach has traditionally dominated American political science. It has retarded the theoretical development of political science because it focuses on the accurate description of laws and formal institutions rather than on the development of generalizations and theories about political behavior.

Closely related to the legal-institutional approach is the historical tradition. When political science first emerged, it was primarily political history. The historical tradition—with a focus on particulars and unique events—shaped the development of political theory much as it influenced the growth of theory in history and anthropology. Most school and college textbooks are heavily influenced by the legal-institutional approach to the study of political behavior.

The Behavioral Approach

In the years following World War II, a protest movement developed within political science that caused sweeping changes within the field. It started a bitter struggle between the newly trained political scientists and those more traditional (those who endorsed the approaches described above). The protest movement emerged because a significant number of young political scientists, such as Harold Lasswell, David Easton, and Robert A. Dahl, were very dissatisfied with the scientific status of the discipline. They were unhappy about its research goals, methods, and the body of accumulated knowledege.

The new group of political scientists wanted the discipline to become more scientific and less concerned with trying to describe the "best" political system or the "good life." They argued that these goals were not scientific. They wanted political scientists to study less about values, legal documents, and institutions. They wanted the discipline to focus on the study of the behavior of people in a political system, to use rigorous research methods, and to make scientific theory development its major goal.

This new movement is known as the *behavioral approach* because its leaders are primarily interested in studying the behavior of political actors, rather than legal codes and institutions.[7] While they are not uninterested in the legal duties of the president and of senators, they are primarily concerned with developing scientific generalizations about their behavior. Behaviorists believe that "It is the activity within and the behavior around the political institution which should be the main concern of the political scientist."[8]

Behaviorists can also be distinguished by their research methods and strategies. They often use techniques such as opinion surveys, content analysis, case studies, and experimental studies. Behaviorists also frequently quantify data and use sophisticated statistical techniques. Most of their field research consists of voting studies. Behaviorists also try to unite political scientists more closely to the other behavioral sciences. They use many of the key concepts, theories, and research methods from psychology, sociology, and anthropology. Subfields such as *political sociology* and *political psychology* reflect the interdisciplinary nature of behaviorism.[9] The behaviorists have also tried to make political science concepts more precise, measurable, and meaningful.

The behavioral orientation has won a place within the discipline, but it has neither escaped harsh criticism nor displaced the more traditional legal-institutional, historical, and normative approaches. However, behaviorism nearly dominated political science during the 1960s. It also polarized and created more reform and soul-searching within the discipline than any other previous movement. The attacks on it have been severe. Sometimes they are sound, but just as often they are shortsighted and subjective. Behaviorism has its shortcomings, as its leaders are keenly aware. In their zest for information about political actors, behaviorists have not always appreciated the contributions that legal, institutional, and historical approaches can make to the development of political generalizations. The emphasis on the individual political actor has sometimes prevented full consideration of the political group and the political system.

The most serious attack on the behaviorists has come from normative political theorists, who believe that the discipline's primary goal should be to improve human life by searching for the best possible political system and recommending it to policy makers. These theorists accuse the behaviorists of neglecting values, and therefore of avoiding the most important questions that face humankind.

BEHAVIORISM: THE SYSTEMS APPROACH

Some behaviorists have tried to focus their research in the discipline by conceptualizing the political process as an interrelated system. The political system is conceptualized as one of a number of interrelated but somewhat independent social systems that make up society. The orientation of this approach is essentially scientific. It is more inclusive than a behavioral approach that focuses primarily on individual political actors. It not only attempts to develop generalizations about individual political actors, but also tries to explain how organized pressure groups influence the making of public policy. Systems theorists focus on developing generalizations about how the competing demands and inputs of political actors become public policy or outputs. David Easton, a leading systems theorist, believes that the major research task of the approach is to ". . . identify the inputs and the forces that shape and change them, to trace the processes through which they are transformed into outputs, to describe the general conditions under which such processes can be maintained, and to establish the relationship between outputs and succeeding inputs of the system."[10]

Figure 12.1 illustrates the relationships among the central concepts in Easton's systems theory.

The Postbehavioral Movement

The tremendous social changes within U.S. society during the 1960s and 1970s deeply affected many political scientists and gave birth to a new movement within the discipline. This movement arose as a reaction against the strong behavioralism that had gripped the discipline by the late 1960s and as a response to the major problems that the nation faced.[11] These included a controversial war in Vietnam that deeply divided the nation, the quest for civil rights by minority groups and women, and a new awareness about the wide gap dividing the rich from the poor in the United States.

The postbehaviorists argued that the behaviorists, by devoting almost all of their attention to research methods and theory, were showing no concern for the value conflicts and problems that were threatening the nation. The postbehaviorists believe that social scientists have a moral responsibility to use their knowledge and expertise to help solve human problems. They said that political science had become too removed from human affairs in the 1970s and that political science research was conservative and supported the status quo.

The postbehavioral call for political scientists to become more involved in value issues and in public policy created tremendous debate and conflict within the discipline.[12] The movement had a significant impact on many political scientists. David Easton, one of the leaders of the behaviorist movement, discussed the postbehaviorists in his presidential address to the Ameri-

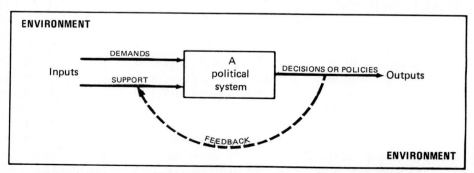

FIGURE 12.1 Easton's System Theory. (*Source:* Reprinted from David Easton, "An Approach to the Analysis of Political Systems," *World Politics* 9 [3]: 384 [April 1957]. Reprinted by permission of Princeton University Press.)

can Political Science Association in 1969.[13] He urged political scientists to heed the call of the new revolutionaries within the discipline. He agreed that political scientists needed to pay more attention to their value assumptions, to get more involved in the urgent social problems of the day, and to play an important role in the formation and implementation of public policy. At the same time, however, Easton urged political scientists to continue to do research aimed at building theory. He believes that the discipline should both respond to the concerns of the postbehaviorists and continue to pursue its traditional goals. The postbehavioral movement has enriched the diversity of political science. Like the movements before it, it will find a place within political science but will not replace the discipline's other approaches and traditions. Table 12.1 summarizes the major approaches within political science.

THEORY AND RESEARCH IN POLITICAL SCIENCE

The goal of science is the building of theory that can be used to explain, predict, and understand behavior. The building of scientific theory is not the goal in any of the more traditional approaches within political science. The aim of political philosophy is to describe the ideal political system. The legal-institutionalists regard the accurate descriptions of legal codes and formal institutions as their primary goal. The emphasis is on describing unique

TABLE 12.1. Approaches in Political Science

Approach	Description	Major Goals
Normative	Focuses on the examination of the ideas of such political theorists as Plato, Locke, and Marx.	To describe the ideal political system and how it can be attained.
Legal-institutional	Focuses on description and analysis of legal documents and the functions of governmental bodies and officials.	To accurately describe legal institutions and the roles within them.
Behavioral	Primarily interested in studying the behavior of political actors.	The development of theory about political behavior that can be used to predict and control behavior.
Systems	Focuses on organized political behavior and its effects on the political system.	To develop generalizations and theories about the competing demands and inputs that are parts of the political process within a political system.
Postbehavioral	Focuses on public policy, issues, and social problems.	To use political science knowledge to help solve social problems and improve the human condition.

codes and institutions, and not on developing high level generalizations about them. Many traditional political scientists do not believe that high level political science generalizations can be developed because of the complexity of human behavior.

Only in the newer approaches to political science—the behavioral and systems orientations—is the expressed goal the building of scientific theory. While the newer approaches have theory building as their goal, the discipline is largely void of tested theories. However, attempts have been made, and are still being made, to formulate and test partial theories. Easton writes, "By and large, students in political science have not considered it worthwhile to allocate even a small part of their collective energies to systematic theory. . . ."[14] A major challenge facing the discipline is the clarification of goals, that is, whether political science will become a scientific discipline whose major goal is to build theory, a discipline that will have major policy goals and make prescriptions for society, or whether it will try to accommodate each of these orientations.

POLITICAL SCIENCE CONCEPTS

The concepts within all of the political science approaches tend to be vague rather than precise. Such terms as *state* and *government*, which are central to traditional approaches, and such concepts as *power, legitimacy,* and *authority,* essential to newer approaches, are often defined differently. However, the behaviorists make concerted efforts to make their concepts precise and to operationalize them for measurement purposes.

Any attempt to identify the key concepts in political science is destined to be futile because of the variety of approaches within the discipline. Each approach, to some extent, uses a unique set of concepts. The concept of natural law is important in political philosophy but foreign to the systems approach.

A selected list of concepts from each of the orientations within political science should be an integral part of the social studies curriculum for the elementary and junior high school grades. However, although some concepts from the traditional approaches should be taught (such as *constitution*), you should select most of the concepts you teach from the more modern approaches for two reasons: (1) These approaches build scientific generalizations about political behavior, and (2) traditional approaches are easily abused by teachers. When teachers use traditional approaches, the emphasis easily shifts to requiring students to memorize the duties and powers of various offices, and away from helping them derive generalizations about political behavior. The normative approach permits teachers to moralize, without evidence, about the merits of particular institutions—the values of which are not fully demonstrated. It also places undue emphasis on the views of authorities, whether classic (Plato, Aquinas, Crotius, or Locke) or more contemporary (Lippmann, Lasswell, or Hyneman).

Participation in group activities and projects can help students to better understand political science concepts such as power. (*Source*: Tacoma [Washington] School District.)

We describe some key political science concepts, and activities that can be used to teach them, below.

Power

Power is the ability of one individual or group to influence, change, modify, or in some other way affect the behavior of others. Power may be attained in a variety of ways. An individual or group may have formal authority over others. Political leaders have authority when they are able to make decisions and laws that are legally binding for the individuals within a political system. They may be elected by the people, appointed by leaders, or take authority by force, as during a *coup d'etat* or revolution. However, for a political system to function smoothly, it is necessary for authority to be legitimate. A government is regarded as legitimate when the individuals affected by its policy accepts its authority as valid. If an authority is not viewed as legitimate, authorities have to expend a great deal of energy enforcing their decisions.

Activities

1. List examples of the individuals who exercise power in the family. Discuss the source of their authority.
2. Discuss why and how authorities exercise power in the school and why.
3. Investigate how European kings used the concept of "divine right" to legitimize their authority.
4. Ask the students to investigate ways in which the governor and the state legislature try to exercise power over each other.
5. Study the ways in which the states' power made the federal government weak during the early federal period in U.S. history and why.

Social Control

Social control is the regulation of human behavior by outside social forces. It is maintained by laws and rules that emerge within every society and institution. Every institution must have ways to control the behavior of its members in order to attain its goals and to maintain an environment in which individuals and groups can satisfy their wants and needs. The laws that govern behavior within a society are usually found in written documents, such as legal codes and constitutions. Laws reflect the norms and values of a society. Norms that are very important to a society usually become laws, and the violators of these norms are punished by the state.

Activities

1. Ask the students to list some of the rules they have at home and to tell why their families have them. Ask the students to tell what they think of these rules.
2. List the rules at school and discuss whether the school should have them and why or why not.
3. Make a list of county and state laws and discuss why they were made.
4. Make a list of federal laws and discuss why they were made and whether they are helpful.
5. Compare federal laws in the United States with federal laws in other Western nations, such as Germany, the United Kingdom, and France.

State

The concept of *state* is central to traditional approaches in political science. Political science is often defined by traditionalists as the study of the legal government of the state. Although this concept has been defined in many different ways, it is sometimes defined as the institution that has ultimate responsibility for maintaining social order, usually within a geographically and legally defined territory. Closely related to the concept of state is the concept of *government*. Government is an agency of the state, and is used by it to maintain social control. Deutsch defines state as "the organized machinery for the making and carrying out of political decisions and for the enforcing of the laws and rules of government."[15]

Activities

1. Introduce the concept of *nation* and point out that when political scientists use the term *state* they are usually referring to the nation-state.
2. Discuss the relationship among the federal, state, county, and city governments in the United States.
3. List the duties and functions of the *executive, legislative,* and *judicial* branches of the United States federal government.
4. Role play a session of the United States Senate and discuss how the Senate makes decisions.
5. Visit the state capitol and observe a session of the state legislature.

Interest Group

An *interest group* is a collection of individuals who share common concerns and goals; they organize in order to more effectively attain those goals. Individuals with similar goals join interest groups to influence political bodies because they realize that they are more likely to influence public policy when working in groups than when working alone. Interest groups are sometimes called special interest groups or pressure groups.

Activities

1. Form an interest group and work to get a school levy passed.
2. Identify a current bill before Congress or the state legislature and role play a situation in which various interest groups try to persuade the legislative body.
3. Interview a lobbyist who works in the state capitol and represents an interest group, such as the state education association, farmers, or the state medical association.
4. Interview members of the city council or the state legislature about how they are influenced by lobbyists and interest groups when they vote and make decisions.
5. Read and discuss the section from President Carter's biography, *Keeping Faith: Memories of a President*, which describes the interest groups that lobbied against the passage of the Panama Canal treaties in 1978.

INQUIRY STRATEGY: AN EQUAL RIGHTS AMENDMENT SIMULATION

Congress passed the Equal Rights Amendment (ERA) in 1972. To become law, it was required that the ERA be ratified by 38 states by 1979. A total of 35 states had ratified the ERA by 1977. Ratification was needed in only three other states to make the amendment a part of the Constitution. However, the ratification process remained locked at 35 states. Supporters of ERA were able to get the House of Representatives to extend the deadline to June 30, 1982, which was constitutionally questionable. Another constitutionally questionable development occurred when Idaho, Kentucky, Nebraska, and Tennessee rescinded approval of the ERA.

Despite the extension of the deadline, the following 15 states did not ratify the ERA: Mississippi, Alabama, Arkansas, Georgia, Louisiana, Missouri, Utah, Nevada, North Carolina, Arizona, Virginia, South Carolina, Oklahoma, Florida, and Illinois.

The ratifying states were (in order of ratification) Hawaii, New Hampshire, Delaware, Iowa, Idaho, Kansas, Nebraska, Texas, Tennessee, Alaska, Rhode Island, New Jersey, Colorado, West Virginia, Wisconsin, New York, Michigan, Maryland, Massachusetts, Kentucky, Pennsylvania, California, Wyoming, South Dakota, Oregon, Minnesota, New Mexico, Vermont, Connecticut, Washington, Maine, Montana, Ohio, North Dakota, and Indiana.

The Text of the ERA

Section 1: Equality of rights under the law shall not be denied or abridged by the United States or by any State on account of sex.

Section 2: The Congress shall have the power to enforce, by appropriate legislation, the provisions of this article.

Section 3: The amendment shall take effect two years after the date of ratification.

Directions for Simulation

1. Write the name of each of the 50 states on a 3 × 5″ index card, indicating whether the state ratified or did not ratify the ERA (use the lists above). Distribute the cards to your students in a way that proportionately represents the percentage of states that ratified and failed to ratify the ERA. Slightly less than two-thirds of the students should have cards for states that ratified the ERA. The other students should have cards for states that did not ratify the ERA.
2. Each student should develop a set of arguments, to be presented in a simulated "meeting of the states," defending the position on the ERA taken by the state he or she represents in the meeting. Prior to this meeting, the students should be given time in the library to research positions taken on the ERA. During the meeting, each student will give a one-minute statement defending the position taken by his or her state.
3. After the one-minute statements are completed, the students should be given a ten-minute persuasion period. During this period, each student will try to persuade other state representatives to accept his or her state's position. After the persuasion period, a roll call will be taken, during which each state will indicate whether it has decided to ratify or not ratify the ERA. The passage of the ERA will require a two-thirds majority vote by the students. When deciding how to

vote, encourage your students to consider not only the wishes of their states, but also consider their own personal feelings about the ERA.

4. After the vote by the students, they will discuss why their vote was similar to or different from the actual votes taken by the state legislatures between 1972 and 1982. They should also discuss the future prospects for the ERA and these questions:

    a. What characteristics are shared by the states that ratified the ERA? Those that did not ratify it?

    b. Did the states located in the "Bible Belt" ratify the ERA? What are those states? Why do you think they failed to ratify the ERA?

    c. Why do you think ERA advocates were very hopeful that Florida and Illinois would ratify the ERA? Why do you think these states failed to ratify it?

    d. Utah and Nevada are heavily populated by Mormons. Do you think the religious characteristic of these states is related to the failure of the ERA? Why or why not?

References for This Inquiry Strategy

Berry, Mary Frances. *Why ERA Failed: Politics, Women's Rights and the Process of Amending the Constitution*. Bloomington: Indiana University Press, 1986.

Feinberg, Renee, Compiler. *The Equal Rights Amendment: An Annotated Bibliography of the Issues, 1976–1985*. New York: Greenwood Press, 1986.

Political Socialization

The process by which individuals acquire their attitudes, beliefs, and perceptions of the political system is called *political socialization*. Behavioral political scientists have shown a great deal of interest in this concept. Their research suggests that, of the many institutions affecting the child's attitudes toward the political system, the family is the most important. People are usually members of the same political party as their parents. Research indicates that children's basic political attitudes are formed during their early years—when they are between the ages of three and thirteen.

Activities

1. Sing "America the Beautiful" and "The Star-Spangled Banner" and discuss the attitudes and beliefs these songs help children develop toward the U.S. political system.

2. Recite the Pledge of Allegiance to the flag and discuss the ideas it expresses about U.S. democracy. Discuss the extent to which these ideals are realities in the United States.

3. Discuss the ways citizens in the United States celebrate national holidays, such as Washington's Birthday and Independence Day. Identify ways in which the celebration of these days develops and reinforces loyalty to the United States.

4. Research and present reports on ways nations with communist governments, such as the Soviet Union, Cuba, and the People's Republic of China, develop loyalty in schoolchildren.

5. Conduct a survey to find out whether students have political beliefs that are similar to their brothers, sisters, and parents.

Political Participation

Political participation is the "actions of private citizens by which they seek to influence or to support government and politics."[16] Political scientists conceptualize political participation to include not only voting and lobbying, but activities such as campaigning, attending political meetings, and running for office. Political scientists often do research to determine which personal, social, and economic factors are most closely related to political involvement.

Activities

1. Vote on some decisions that need to be made in the classroom and discuss the factors that influenced the way individuals voted.
2. Send a class letter to a member of Congress or to a state legislator, expressing an opinion on an important bill that is up for a vote.
3. Run for election in a student government election and present points of view in speeches and on posters.
4. Work in a campaign headquarters during an election and describe the experience to the class.
5. Make a class visit to the state legislature or city council to present views on a bill that will soon be up for a vote.

POLITICAL SCIENCE GENERALIZATIONS

Much of what we have said about political science concepts is also true of political generalizations, since generalizations state relationships between concepts. Generalizations in political science, like those in the other behavioral sciences, vary greatly in the extent to which they can be applied to help us understand behavior. In selecting generalizations to guide political studies in the elementary and junior high school grades, you should only select scientific statements. Many lists of political science generalizations in state and school district curriculum guides contain a large number of value statements such as these: "Young people respect and obey parents and teachers"; "Autocracy, or similar centralization of power in one man or body, develops when citizens shirk their responsibilities."

Below is a list of political science generalizations that can be taught in the elementary and junior high school grades. They are grouped under concepts related to them.

Social Control

In every society and institution, regulations and laws are formed to govern the behavior of individuals; individuals usually experience some form of punishment when authorities catch them breaking laws.

Rules and laws reflect the basic values of a society or institution.

Government

Within every society, some individual or group is authorized to make binding decisions and to allocate values.

Many different types of political systems are used in various societies to determine public policy and to regulate behavior.

Interest Groups

Organized interest groups attempt to influence the making of public policy when they believe that such policy will affect their goals.

Individuals are more likely to influence public policy when working in groups than when working alone.

Individuals and groups resort to extreme methods to change public policy when they believe that authorities are unresponsive to their needs or that legitimate channels for the alleviation of grievances are ineffective.

Authority

Authorities may be violently replaced if they remain unresponsive to the demands of the citizens in their state.

When authorities feel that the basic ideology and well-being of their political system is threatened, they may take extreme action against individuals and groups, denying them the basic rights guaranteed under the laws of the state.

Authorities tend to resist any change they feel will reduce their power and influence.

Authorities attempt to legitimize their power in order to maintain control (i.e., convince their constituency that they have a right to rule because of divine right, the constitution, etc.) and to ensure a stable political system.

Leadership

Leaders emerge when individuals are able to articulate and personify the wishes and goals of groups; leaders lose their power and influence when groups perceive their goals as different from those of the leaders.

POLITICAL STUDIES IN THE SCHOOLS

Political studies are usually either ignored or treated superficially in the early and middle grades, and taught with the historical and legal-institutional approaches in junior high school. Political studies are neglected or poorly taught largely because the goals of political education are unclear, confusing, and conflicting.

The most often stated goal of political studies is to develop patriotic citizens, loyal to the nation and committed to American democracy. However, *patriotic citizen* is rarely defined clearly. In order to perpetuate its dominant values and system of government, every nation-state must socialize its citizens in such a way that it inculcates its prevailing ideology. Thus, developing loyal and patriotic citizens is a sound goal of political education.

However, political studies are often taught poorly because of the way teachers and textbook authors interpret *patriotic*. A patriotic citizen is often regarded as one who votes regularly, obeys the laws, respects the flag, and rarely criticizes our political leaders and national policies. Teachers and text-book authors often emphasize the strengths of the United States and the problems of other nations when trying to help students become patriotic citizens with strong national loyalties.

The major goal of political education should be to help students develop a reflective patriotism and become thoughtful citizen actors. Citizens with reflective patriotism are committed to American democratic ideals, are aware of the gap between ideals and realities in our nation, and are committed to taking action to help close the gap. To develop reflective citizens, we must teach students about the ideals of American democracy, the extent to which these ideals have been attained, and the work that must still be done to fully realize them. To attain this goal, the curriculum must teach about the hopes and promises of U.S. democracy, as well as about the problems the nation faces. The quest for civil rights by minorities and women, the challenges posed by the nuclear threat, and the problems that plague American cities should be an important part of a political education curriculum. A sound political education curriculum should also have an important global dimension. Students should realize that the most complex problems facing humankind today can only be solved by nations working together.

Political studies in the elementary and junior high school should also emphasize *political behavior* rather than the description of legal documents and institutions. In the legal-institutional approach to civic education, students spend a great deal of time memorizing the legal powers and responsibilities of various political posts and the functions of the different branches of government. The emphasis is on memorizing facts and giving them back to teachers.

A focus on documents and institutions will give students a misconception of the political system. To understand how a bill is actually passed, one cannot merely study the Constitution, but must know how competing pressure groups work to influence the making of public policy. Simulation games such as *Democracy* and *Napoli* can help students understand informal political processes, such as bargaining, logrolling, pledging support in return for another's support on other issues, wheeling and dealing, compromising, welching on promises, misleading others, and other political tactics. We must help students learn about the realities of political life, while at the same time helping them develop a commitment to American democratic values and ideals. This is a challenging task since these goals often conflict.

TEACHING STRATEGIES

Generalization: *Conflict arises within a political system when individuals or groups have competing goals and/or interpret the meaning of laws differently; rules and laws reflect the basic values of a society or institution.*

Primary Grades

Ask the students: "What are some of the rules you have at home for going to bed, for eating, and for playing?" Responses might include "Be in bed by 8:00, be in bed by 9:00, eat everything on your plate, eat everything you serve yourself, take at least one bite of everything on your plate, play in your own yard, no playing after dinner." List the responses on the board in the categories indicated and any additional ones that student responses suggest. Ask the following questions:

1. Why were there different times listed for going to bed?
2. Why are there rules for eating?
3. Why are there rules for playing?
4. What sentence could we write that would be true of rules in all our families? Rephrase the question as necessary to solicit the response, "While all families have rules, each family has different ideas about them."
5. What do these rules tell us about the importance of children to their parents? (Rephrase the question as necessary to solicit the response that reflects the idea that taking good care of children is an important value in our society.)

Ask the students: "What are some rules at school that the principal and teachers think are important, but you feel are unimportant?" Write the responses on a chart such as the following:

School Rules Not Important to Me   Why

_____   _____

_____   _____

_____   _____

_____   _____

_____   _____

After the responses are recorded, ask the students why they think these rules are unimportant. Write their responses under the "Why" column. A sample response might be "Don't talk in the hall." "Why?" "Because I like to talk to my friend and can never talk to him in class." You might plan and carry out an experiment related to some of the rules the children have identified as unimportant. The following activity, relating to talking in the corridors, could be planned and carried out with another teacher and his or her class.

Have the students from another class walk by your classroom and talk loudly while your students are taking a spelling test. Afterward, ask each of your students to record whether or not the noise made by the other students affected his or her performance on the spelling test. On another day, the classes should switch roles. Have your class make loud noises near the door of the other class while the students in it are taking a test. Put together the observations made by both classes. Discuss the results and how the students feel about the school rule after the experiment.

The following activity will help students discover how conflict may arise when individuals interpret the meanings of rules differently. Ask several students to role play a classroom situation that has the agreed-upon rule that no one should talk during the daily math test. The rule also states the punishment. The test paper of the person who is caught talking is automatically torn up by the teacher. While he is taking his math test one morning, Johnny breaks the lead in his pencil. He quietly asks Sue for an extra pencil. After the test, some members of the class insist that Johnny's test paper be torn up. However, Johnny becomes upset and argues that the rule does not apply to him because he was not talking but was just asking for a pencil that he badly needed to complete his test. After the role-playing situation, ask each member of the class to tell whether he or she thinks Johnny's paper should be torn up. Help the students to derive the generalization that even though we may have laws to govern behavior, conflict often arises when individuals interpret those laws differently.

Discuss with the students the idea of freedom of speech as set forth in the First Amendment to the Constitution. Write the phrase "freedom of speech" on the board. Ask the following questions:

1. What is speech?
2. What is freedom? Give some examples. (A possible response might be "Doing anything you want to.")
3. Let's put the ideas of these two words together. What does "freedom of speech" mean? (List responses on the board.)
4. What are some things the idea of freedom of speech does *not* mean? (An example, such as the following, may be necessary here.)

Boys and girls, if you are having trouble answering this question, listen to this story. Jane is in the first grade. She told all the children in her class that Sam always steals things from her desk, that she saw him take a banana from her lunch, that he stole her library book from the coat room, and that he even stole some candy from Mr. Jones's store. Soon the children were saying to Sam, "You are a robber." "I'm not going to play with you." "You can't touch my things, Sam." "You are a thief." Jane's teacher found out that Jane was lying. Is Jane's use of speech an example of what is meant by "freedom of speech"? Why or why not?

Pair the students and give to each pair some pictures torn from magazines. Have them group these pages into examples of "freedom of speech" and "nonfreedom of speech." The discrimination made between pictures representing freedom and nonfreedom of speech will depend on individual interpretations of the pictures. Encourage the students to talk about this as they make their judgments. An example of nonfreedom of speech might show a father scolding his child without giving him a chance to defend himself. An example of freedom of speech might show a politician making a speech in a public forum. The students can cut out the pictures from the pages and glue them onto two labeled charts to develop collages representing the two categories discussed.

Intermediate Grades

Select six students from the class and divide them into two equal groups. Give Card 1 to one group and Card 2 to the other. Direct the students to read the cards and follow the directions written on them.

Card 1. George is accused of stealing a typewriter from the school office and selling it to a pawnshop in order to buy a new football of special design, which his parents told him that he could not have. George is an "A" student and is on the student council. He is also captain of the baseball team and a real leader. Most of the boys and girls in his class respect him highly. George is known to be a friend to everyone and is always helping out the other guy. His parents are well known in the community; his father is a doctor. George says he is not guilty. Prepare a statement to present to the class on why George should or should not be charged with the crime.

Card 2. Joe is accused of stealing an adding machine from the school office and selling it to a pawnshop in order to buy Christmas presents for his family. Joe is a very poor student who gets mostly D's and sometimes C's. He is often in the office for being late to school, not paying attention in class, and fighting on the playground. He is a sloppy dresser, wears dirty clothes, and doesn't participate in sports. His only friend is Mike, who lives in the same run-down apartment building in a poor neighborhood. Joe's father works in the flour mill. Joe says he is not guilty. Prepare a statement to present to the class on why Joe should or should not be charged with the crime.

Have each group read the case descriptions and present their arguments to the class. Have the class vote on the following:

1. George should be charged with the crime and brought before the appropriate authorities. Yes _____ No _____
2. Joe should be charged with the crime and brought before the appropriate authorities. Yes _____ No _____

Tape record the session, and save the tape and results of the class vote for the next day's lesson.

Play yesterday's tape directing students to listen for the facts and assumptions that supported or rejected charging each boy with the crime. These observations should be listed on a chart similar to Table 12.2. Stop the tape after each case presentation to make suggested notations.

Display a chart on which Section 1 of the Fourteenth Amendment to the Constitution of the United States is written, and ask the following questions.

> *Section 1.* All persons born or naturalized in the United States, and subject to the jurisdiction thereof, are citizens of the United States and of the State wherein they reside. No State shall make or enforce any law which shall abridge the privileges or immunities of citizens of the United States; nor shall any State deprive any person of life, liberty, or property, without due process of law; nor deny any person within its jurisdiction the equal protection of the laws.

1. How do the data collected relate to this Amendment?
2. Did our actions yesterday violate this Amendment? Why or why not?
3. Were the assumptions made justified? Why or why not?
4. Why did yesterday's vote turn out as it did?
5. How does this vote reflect our value systems?

Write the First Amendment to the Constitution of the United States on the board:

> Congress shall make no law respecting an establishment of religion, or prohibiting the free exercise thereof; or abridging the freedom of speech, or of the press; or the right of the people peaceably to assemble, and to petition the Government for a redress of grievances.

Divide your class into research groups of five students each. Direct each group to formulate an interpretation of the meaning of this statement that reflects a unanimous decision of the group. In this interpretative statement they should give examples of what they think citizens can and cannot do

TABLE 12.2.

Supporting Facts	Assumptions Made from Facts
George:	
Joe:	

Rejecting Facts	Assumptions Made from Facts
George:	
Joe:	

without violating this Amendment. After the students have completed this task, ask these questions:

1. What problems occurred in your groups when you were trying to reach a unanimous decision? Why?
2. What was the source of your problems?
3. If no problems occurred, why?

Type the data collected, and mimeograph the material so each student can have a copy. Direct students to read all the reports and prepare for a discussion on the similarities and differences in interpretations. During a class discussion, ask the students to explain the differences and similarities in interpretations.

Ask your students to read the newspapers for a week and collect examples of articles that relate to the First Amendment. Have students mount these articles on construction paper and write a one-sentence heading for the article saying "In this article the First Amendment is interpreted to mean that. . . ." Display these articles on a bulletin board. Direct students to read them as they are displayed. After numerous articles are collected, discuss them and ask the students whether they agree or disagree with the various interpretations of the Amendment demonstrated in the articles, and why. Ask: "What in your life experience causes you to make that judgment?"

Upper Grades

Have a group of three students collect and research the current laws in your state concerning drug usage, and duplicate their findings for the entire class. Discuss the laws within the following framework: (1) statement of the laws themselves, (2) legal interpretation of the laws, (3) student interpretations of the laws, (4) society's behavior toward the laws, (5) reasons for society's behavior, (6) resulting conflicts, (7) possible ways to resolve conflicts, (8) values the laws represent, and (9) values that conflict with the laws.

Have students research forced busing as a method of attaining school desegregation. Direct them to find five examples of methods used to carry out busing in five different states. Then divide the class into debating teams, one for busing and one against busing. The rules for the debate are (1) All debating must be done from a legal base, from the laws and governing documents at the national and state level; (2) the debaters should state the laws and then tell how they either support or outlaw busing; and (3) students should point out when local and national laws conflict.

After the research is carried out, have the groups select formal spokespersons to direct the presentation of the material collected. Audiotape or videotape the presentations if possible. After the debates, discuss the following questions:

1. What were the major differences in interpretations? (List on board).
2. Why did the differences occur? (Rephrase this question as necessary

to solicit responses focusing on the conflicting values within our society.)

3. Why does conflict occur in instances such as these?
4. What ways can you suggest to resolve some of these conflicts?

Activity for the Next Day. Give each of the students a sheet of paper listing the laws and part of the governing documents that the students used to support their ideas. Leave room on these sheets so that during the debate, while they listen to the tape replay, the students can write notes on the various interpretations made of these laws. The tape replay on the following day serves several purposes: (1) It can be replayed to check points, and (2) it allows students to focus on the variety of interpretations of the laws during a session, separate from the debate itself. The emotional reactions generated during the debate should have cooled so that the students can discuss the laws objectively. Discuss the student observations of each law.

1. How do the interpretations relate to the Declaration of Independence and the Constitution? Are they consistent with these documents? Why or why not?
2. How can we explain the differences in interpretations?
3. How can these differences be resolved?

Have students research several current controversial legal cases. Direct students to consider the following points in their research:

1. With what laws have these persons come in conflict? Find the specific laws and their source.
2. How do these laws relate to the First Amendment of the United States Constitution?
3. What were the circumstances surrounding the conflict in which these people found themselves?

After research has been completed, discuss:

1. What do these cases have in common?
2. How are they different? Chart the responses:

             Alike   Different

_____   _____

_____   _____

_____   _____

_____   _____

_____   _____

3.   On the basis of your research and the First Amendment, under what conditions is it legal to demonstrate and speak out on controversial subjects?

Have the students vote on the case for which they would most like to role play a mock trial. Guide the students in determining the roles that should be included in the trial, such as judge, jury, defense attorney, prosecuting attorney, witnesses, and research teams. After each role has been determined, give the students time to research their role, in the trial and prepare for their performance. Then carry out the trial in its entirety.

SUMMARY

Political science is a discipline with many different structures and traditions. It has been defined as the study of the legal government of the state, the struggle of competing groups for power, and the "study of the authoritative allocation of values for a society."[17] The latter definition is accepted by many political scientists because it defines the boundaries and sets a focus for the discipline.

The earliest political scientists were normative theorists who felt that their main goal should be to describe the ideal state and the means by which it could be attained. The legal-institutional approach, another tradition within the discipline, focuses on describing political laws and institutions. In the period after World War II, a new tradition, known as the behavioral approach, emerged within political science. It emerged as a protest against the normative and legal-institutional approaches. The behaviorists regard theory construction as their primary goal, and believe that political scientists should focus their study on political *behavior*, and not on laws and institutions. They feel that the legal-institutional approach is inadequate because it focuses on the description of particular institutions and not on the development of scientific statements and theory. The behaviorists reject the normative tradition because they believe it is antithetical to the development of an empirical science. The behaviorist movement has initiated intense soul-searching within political science, and has to some extent polarized the discipline's various factions. While the movement has profoundly affected political science, it has not been a victor. It was seriously challenged by the postbehavioral movement during the late 1960s and the early 1970s. Although political science is becoming more theoretical and empirical, the older traditions are very much alive within the field today.

Each of the traditions within political science has concepts and generalizations that can be profitably incorporated into the elementary and junior high school social studies program. However, the normative tradition, with its emphasis on values, can best be used when students are studying valuing and decision-making problems. The legal-institutional approach has dominated the discipline as well as those components of political science that are studied in the schools. Although students should be familiar with the legal codes and constitutions that affect political actors, the emphasis in school political studies should be on political *behavior*. Without a focus on behavior, students will get an unrealistic view of the ways our political system actually works, because laws are interpreted variously by different public officials and citizens.

Students should be introduced to political science concepts in the earliest grades, and they should gradually develop a better understanding of them in successive grades. To assure that students acquire political literacy in a sequential and developmental fashion, you should identify the political science concepts and generalizations you regard as essential for students to learn and choose appropriate content samples, teaching strategies, and materials to develop those understandings at the beginning of the year or when a curriculum guide is structured. Without such deliberate and early planning, the teaching of political understandings will be incidental and ineffective.

DISCUSSION QUESTIONS AND EXERCISES

1. What is the unique nature of political science? How does the political science "perspective" differ from the ways in which other social scientists view human behavior? What implications does your response have for planning political studies in the elementary and junior high school grades?
2. How has political science been defined by different political scientists? Why do you think political scientists define their discipline differently? Which of the definitions of political science reviewed in this chapter do you think is the most useful? Why? Which do you feel is the least useful? Why? How might the definition of political science that teachers endorse affect their planning of political studies for elementary and junior high school students?
3. Name the various approaches and traditions within political science. How are these approaches alike and different, in terms of goals and research methods? Which tradition has most heavily influenced political studies in the elementary and junior high school grades? Why? Which approach do you feel is most promising? Why? What implications does your last response have for planning political studies in the elementary and junior high school grades?
4. Analyze several junior high school civics textbooks. Tell whether the books represent the normative, legal-institutional, behavioral, systems, or postbehavioral approach. Document your response with excerpts from the books. Assume that you are teaching in a school in which one of these texts was adopted. Illustrate, with a lesson plan, how you would teach with the text and yet help students learn concepts and generalizations that the text does not illustrate or discuss.
5. Structure a lesson plan illustrating how middle grade students can implement a community study to derive generalizations about the political attitudes and voting patterns of citizens in their community. What problems might students encounter in implementing such a study? How might these problems best be resolved?
6. Select one of the following generalizations and devise a series of activities

(similar to the ones in this chapter) that can be used to teach it to students in the (a) primary grades, (b) middle grades, and (c) upper grades.

   a. In every society and institution, regulations and laws emerge to govern the behavior of individuals; individuals usually experience some form of punishment when authorities catch them breaking laws.

   b. Within every society, an individual or some group is authorized to make binding decisions and to allocate values.

   c. Many different types of political systems are used in various societies to determine public policy and to regulate behavior.

   d. Individuals are more likely to influence public policy when working in groups than when working alone.

7. Research a current or historical legal case that is taking place or took place in your local community or elsewhere in the United States. Share your research with your class and ask the students to act out the trial but reach their own verdict. Ask different students to play the roles of defendant, judge, jury, and defending and prosecuting attorneys.

8. Demonstrate your understanding of the following key concepts by writing or stating brief definitions for each of them. Also tell why each is important.

a. normative approach	g. government
b. legal-institutional approach	h. power
c. systems approach	i. interest group
d. behavioral approach	j. political socialization
e. postbehavioral movement	k. political participation
f. state	l. social control

NOTES

1. David Easton, *The Political System: An Inquiry into the State of Political Science*, 2nd ed. (Chicago: University of Chicago Press, 1971), p. 107.

2. Easton, op. cit., p. 117.

3. Easton, op. cit., p. 129.

4. Dwight Waldo, "Political Science: Tradition, Discipline, Profession, Science, Enterprise," in Fred I. Greenstein and Nelson W. Polsby, Eds., *Handbook of Political Science, Vol. 1, Political Science: Scope and Theory* (Reading, MA: Addison-Wesley, 1975), pp. 1–130.

5. Francis J. Sorauf, *Political Science: An Informal Overview* (Columbus, OH: Merrill, 1965), p. 10.

6. Dante Germino, "The Contemporary Relevance of the Classics of Political Philosophy," in Greenstein and Polsby, op. cit., pp. 229–281.

7. John A. Straayer and Raymond H. Muessig, *The Study and Teaching of Political Science* (Columbus, OH: Merrill, 1980), p. 6.

8. Alan C. Isaak, *Scope and Method of Political Science* (Homewood, IL: Dorsey, 1969), p. 27.

9. Tom Bottomore, *Political Sociology* (New York: Harper & Row, 1979).

10. David Easton, "An Approach to the Analysis of Political Systems," in Martin Feldman and Eli Seifman, Eds., *The Social Studies: Structure, Models, and Strategies* (Englewood Cliffs, NJ: Prentice-Hall, 1969), p. 140.

11. George J. Graham and George W. Carey, Eds. *The Post-Behavioral Era: Perspectives in Political Science* (New York: McKay, 1972).

12. Waldo, op. cit., p. 13.

13. David Easton, "The New Revolution in Political Science," *The American Political Science Review*, Vol. 63 (December 1969).

14. Easton, *The Political System*, p. 65.

15. Karl W. Deutsch, *Politics and Government: How People Decide Their Fate*, 3rd ed. (Boston: Houghton Mifflin, 1980).

16. Lester W. Milbrath and M. L. Goel, *Political Participation: How and Why Do People Get Involved in Politics*, 2nd ed. (Washington, D.C.: University Press of America, 1977).

17. Easton, p. 2.

FOR FURTHER READING

"Afro-Americans and the Evolution of a Living Constitution," *Update on Law-Related Education*, Vol. 12 (Fall 1988). This special issue includes articles by Mary Frances Berry, John Hope Franklin, and Derrick Bell.

Berry, Mary F. *Black Resistance/White Law: A History of Constitutional Racism in America*. Englewood Cliffs, NJ: Prentice-Hall, 1971.

Domhoff, G. William. *Who Rules America Now? A View for the '80s*. New York: Simon & Schuster, 1983.

Flexner, Eleanor. *A Century of Struggle: The Woman's Rights Movement in the United States*. New York: Atheneum, 1968.

Gardner, John W. *In Common Cause: Citizen Action and How It Works*. New York: Norton, 1972.

Kegley, Charles W., Jr., and Eugene R. Wittkopf. *American Foreign Policy: Pattern and Process*, 2nd ed. New York: St. Martin's Press, 1982.

Keller, Clair W., and Denny Schillings, Eds. *Teaching about the Constitution*. Washington, D.C.: National Council for the Social Studies, 1987.

Redman, Eric. *The Dance of Legislation*. New York: Simon & Schuster, 1973.

Rutland, Robert A. *The American Solution: Origins of the United States Constitution*. Washington, D.C.: U.S. Government Printing Office, 1987.

Shafritz, Jay M. *The Dorsey Dictionary of American Government and Politics*. Chicago: The Dorsey Press, 1988.

Straayer, John A., and Raymond D. Muessig. *The Study and Teaching of Political Science*. Columbus, OH: Merrill, 1980.

13

Economics: Structure, Concepts, and Strategies

THE ECONOMIC PERSPECTIVE

Human behavior is viewed from different perspectives within each of the social sciences. A historian, sociologist, and political scientist would view the problems related to world hunger and poverty in a different manner. Each of the social sciences provides us with a lens through which we can view the human drama; each enhances our insights and understandings. Economics, too, enables us to see human behavior from a unique perspective. The key concept in this discipline is *scarcity*, and the science focuses primarily on how people try to satisfy their unlimited wants with limited resources. The major principle of the discipline is that there are not enough natural and human resources to satisfy all of people's wants. (See Figure 13.1.) Economists study how people use limited resources to *produce, exchange*, and *consume goods and services*.

THE PRODUCTION-POSSIBILITIES CONCEPT

Economists often use a hypothetical production-possibilities example to show how a society must make hard choices when determining what goods and services to produce with its limited resources. We will use such an example here to illustrate this important economic principle.

Society X has the resources and technological expertise necessary to produce a maximum of five bales of cotton *or* 16 bushels of corn. To produce five bales of cotton or 16 bushels of corn, society X must maintain full

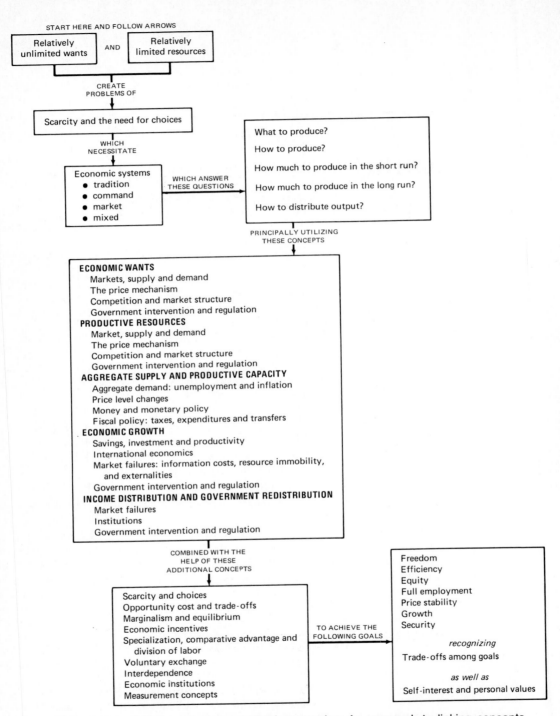

Relatively unlimited wants AND Relatively limited resources

CREATE PROBLEMS OF

Scarcity and the need for choices

WHICH NECESSITATE

Economic systems
● tradition
● command
● market
● mixed

WHICH ANSWER THESE QUESTIONS

What to produce?

How to produce?

How much to produce in the short run?

How much to produce in the long run?

How to distribute output?

PRINCIPALLY UTILIZING THESE CONCEPTS

ECONOMIC WANTS
Markets, supply and demand
The price mechanism
Competition and market structure
Government intervention and regulation
PRODUCTIVE RESOURCES
Market, supply and demand
The price mechanism
Competition and market structure
Government intervention and regulation
AGGREGATE SUPPLY AND PRODUCTIVE CAPACITY
Aggregate demand: unemployment and inflation
Price level changes
Money and monetary policy
Fiscal policy: taxes, expenditures and transfers
ECONOMIC GROWTH
Savings, investment and productivity
International economics
Market failures: information costs, resource immobility, and externalities
Government intervention and regulation
INCOME DISTRIBUTION AND GOVERNMENT REDISTRIBUTION
Market failures
Institutions
Government intervention and regulation

COMBINED WITH THE HELP OF THESE ADDITIONAL CONCEPTS

Scarcity and choices
Opportunity cost and trade-offs
Marginalism and equilibrium
Economic incentives
Specialization, comparative advantage and division of labor
Voluntary exchange
Interdependence
Economic institutions
Measurement concepts

TO ACHIEVE THE FOLLOWING GOALS

Freedom
Efficiency
Equity
Full employment
Price stability
Growth
Security

recognizing

Trade-offs among goals

as well as

Self-interest and personal values

FIGURE 13.1 A Schematic framework of economics: An approach to linking concepts
(*Source*: Reprinted from W. Lee Hansen, et al, *A Framework for Teaching Economics: Basic Concepts.* New York: Joint Council on Economic Education, 1977, pp. 28–29. Used with permission of the Joint Council on Economic Education.)

A study of the work done by women during World War I can help students to better understand their contribution to the U.S. economy at different periods of American history. This photograph shows a woman assembling gas masks during World War I. (*Source*: The National Archives, Washington, D.C.)

employment at its current level of technology. It does not have the resources needed to produce *both* five bales of cotton and 16 bushels of corn. If it decides to raise both cotton and corn, the quantities of each product must be less than the maximum amounts that could be produced if only one crop was raised. Table 13.1 illustrates the various combinations of cotton and corn that

TABLE 13.1. The Production Possibilities of Cotton and Corn in Society X

Production Possibilities	Cotton (in Bales)	Corn (in Bushels)
A	0	16
B	1	15
C	2	13
D	3	10
E	4	6
F	5	0

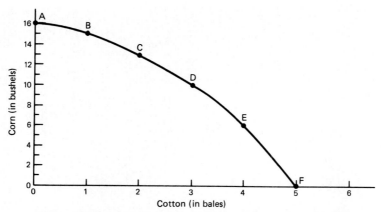

FIGURE 13.2 Production possibilities graphically illustrated.

society X can produce. The table indicates that as the amount of one product increases, the amount of the other decreases. If one bale of cotton is produced, 15 bushels of corn can be produced; if five bales of cotton are produced, no corn can be produced. Likewise, when 16 bushels of corn are produced, no cotton can be raised.

Our table suggests that a society must sacrifice some products in order to produce others because of the limitations of both human and nonhuman resources. As one economist has stated, "Society cannot have its cake and eat it too . . . there's no such thing as a 'free lunch.' This is the essence of the economizing problem."[1] Figure 13.2 graphically illustrates the production possibilities of cotton and corn in our hypothetical society. If society X experiences some unexpected catastrophe, such as a destructive wind storm, extreme rainfalls, or prolonged unemployment, or if its present level of technology declines, it will not be able to produce the maximum quantities of either cotton or corn.

THE ECONOMIC PROBLEM

The basic economic problem faced by every society is how to best use its limited resources to satisfy its wants and to assure its existence. Every human society must solve three related economic problems: *What goods and services shall we produce and in what amounts? How shall they be produced? And for whom shall they be produced?*

Throughout history, people have used different methods to solve these problems. In determining what to produce and how to produce it, some societies have relied heavily on tradition.[2] Among the Hopi Indians of North America, corn was the most important crop, largely because traditionally corn had been raised and to some extent even venerated. In the past, cotton was the dominant crop in many of our southern states, because of the "cotton"

PROFILE

Andrew F. Brimmer

An Economist Who Advises the Government and Businesses on Economic Trends

Andrew F. Brimmer is President of Brimmer and Company, Inc., a firm that conducts research and advises clients concerning trends for economic activity and prospects, developments affecting financial institutions, and interest rates in money and capital markets—with special emphasis on Federal Reserve monetary policy.

President Lyndon B. Johnson appointed Dr. Brimmer to the Board of Governors of the Federal Reserve System, a capacity he served in from 1966 to 1974. In a letter to President Gerald Ford on December 20, 1974, Dr. Brimmer originated the suggestion of a 10 percent rebate of 1974 personal income taxes to stimulate the economy and to help end the 1973–75 recession. After modification, Congress enacted the provision, which accounted for $8.1 billion of the $22.8 billion tax reduction passed early in 1975. Author of a number of books and monographs, Dr. Brimmer is a frequent contributor to *Black Enterprise* magazine. He has taught at Harvard, Michigan State, and the Wharton School, University of Pennsylvania.

tradition in the South. Since the 1960s, with the growth of southern technology and the recognition by southerners of the disadvantages of a one-crop economy, farmers have diversified their crops. Every society to some extent relies on tradition to solve the three basic economic problems. Heilbroner notes how tradition can negatively influence an economy: "*Its solution to the problems of production and distribution is a static one.* A society which follows the path of tradition in its regulation of economic affairs does so at the expense of large-scale rapid social and economic change."[3]

In some societies, public authorities determine what goods and services are produced.[4] Dictators such as Castro, Hitler, and Franco not only exercised political control within their nations, but to a great extent determined which goods and services would be produced and for whom they would be produced. Government control over the economy is more prevalent in communist countries than in the United States. However, as Heilbroner correctly points out, in every society the government influences what goods and services are produced as well as how they are distributed. He cites as an example our taxes or ". . . the preemption of part of our income by the public authorities for public purposes."[5] The degree of government influence varies among different nations.

THE MARKET ECONOMY

In the same year the Declaration of Independence was signed (1776), a book was published in Europe that signaled a revolution in the economic world. Adam Smith, the "father of economics," published *The Wealth of Nations.* Prior to the publication of this classic, the status of economic systems in the Western world had been largely shaped by a group of European writers known as the mercantilists. They felt that a sound economic system had to be tightly controlled by centralized authorities. Without such control within an economy, they believed, the results would be confusion, depression, and chaos. Adam Smith's seminal book challenged the ideas of these influential writers.

Smith believed that the best type of economic system resulted when the government maintained a "laissez-faire" or "hands-off" policy. Manufacturers would be forced to produce the goods consumers wanted; otherwise they would fold because of lack of sales. Only those goods that satisfied customers would remain on the market. Competition between producers and manufacturers would assure that prices would not become too high. Merchants who charged too much for their goods would go out of business because consumers would buy goods at stores with reasonable prices. The government could best help the economy, Smith argued, by leaving it alone.

Smith's ideas are embodied in the market economy, which is the economic system (in modified form) used in the United States and in most Western nations.[6] In a market economy, consumers largely determine what goods and services are produced, and the quantities in which they are produced. During the 1970s and 1980s, the sales of Japanese cars in the United

States and in other Western nations soared. Consumer demand for American-made cars dropped sharply. Consumers were increasingly buying Japanese cars because they believed they were more competitively priced, more fuel-efficient, and a better buy in general than many American cars. *However, the U.S. economy is not a pure market economy. It is a mixed one.*

THE MIXED ECONOMY

The federal government plays a large role in determining what goods and services are produced and sold in the United States. As American car manufacturers faced increasingly stiff competition from makers of Japanese cars in the 1980s, the U.S. government put pressure on Japan to reduce the number of cars it was exporting to the United States. The U.S. Senate gave the Chrysler Corporation, a major U.S. car manufacturer, loan guarantees of $1.5 billion to enable the company to stay in business. The federal government intervenes in the economy to protect consumers from items it considers harmful, such as diet drinks containing harmful chemicals, and unsafe toys.

Every reader of this book must know how heavily subtle and often deceptive television, radio, and other advertising influences the wants of U.S. consumers. Many consumers in the 1950s used only a small number of basic detergents and soaps for household chores. However, the average middle-class household today uses a number of "specialized" cleaners and spot removers. The soaps used to clean the bathroom, the oven, woodwork, and to wash dishes are often different. These specialized desires and "needs" have been largely shaped by television commercials that many of today's shoppers spend hundreds of hours watching each year. The strong impact that the antismoking commercials had on smokers during the 1960s and 1970s is another example of how consumer wants are shaped by the mass media. Thus, consumers, the government, and the producers themselves all play a role in determining *what* goods and services are produced in the U.S. mixed economy.

Business firms largely determine *how* goods and services are produced in the U.S. economy. Their main goal is to produce the largest amount of goods and services for the smallest outlay of resources. Most large industries specialize in the products they make, and have a division of labor within their plants. By producing only a few kinds of items and using a production-line technique to manufacture them, firms make maximum use of their resources. The U.S. federal government, as well as labor unions, to some extent influence *how* goods and services are produced. The government sets minimum safety standards and regulates the use of dangerous machines. Strongly organized unions, which are becoming less influential in U.S. society, demand specific kinds of working conditions, hours, and salaries.

How do we determine *who* within a market economy will get the goods and services produced? To a great extent, the persons who contribute most to the production of goods and services also consume or use most of them. Two persons with similar training and experience who do identical work at an automobile plant usually earn a comparable salary. They can buy about the same amount of goods and services each month. In principle, this is what happens in a pure market economy; the goods and services that individuals receive are roughly comparable to the contribution they make to the total production of goods and services for the society.

Often this does not happen in a mixed economy, but to some extent it does. The salaries of workers in an automobile plant might be determined as much by the strength of their union as by the contribution they make to the production of society's goods and services. Consumers may be willing to pay very high salaries to some workers, such as sports and movie stars, whose contributions to the production of society's goods and services are not very important in a tangible or measureable sense. Experience, level of education, and how much consumers are willing to pay for a particular good or service might heavily influence a worker's salary.

Because of certain societal values, the U.S. federal government often intervenes to upset the "natural" working of the market economy. Disabled individuals, retired workers, public officials, unwed mothers, and unemployed workers often receive a share of society's production pie even though they may contribute very little or nothing to the production of the goods and services they consume. Federal legislation also prevents children from working in industry. Children are perhaps the largest single segment of nonproductive consumers in the United States.

THE DEATH OF ADAM SMITH'S DREAM

Smith urged the government to keep its hands off the economy. He felt that, if left alone, the market system would result in a balanced, efficient, and just economy. When free market economies developed within Western societies, it was not long before it was fairly clear that Smith's ideas were overly optimistic. Because merchants tried to make the highest profits with the least amount of resources, their interests were often contrary to those of consumers. And because they were, merchants often used devious methods to get and keep sales; consumers often didn't have the choices Smith thought they would have. Monopolies emerged and merchants conspired to raise prices and to "beat the consumer." In the United States, railroads were among the first large monopolies. Federal antitrust laws unsuccessfully attempted to shatter such seats of power.

The government gradually assumed greater and greater responsibilities in the economic realm. The stock market crash of 1929 and the publication of John Maynard Keynes's *The General Theory of Employment, Interest and Money* in 1936 were two significant events that helped to legitimize government intervention. The Depression of the 1930s painfully revealed the ills that could plague a market economy. Keynes's book suggested that because of the tremendous freedom that customers and businessmen have in a market system, "the total demand for new goods and services will sometimes be too large and sometimes too small to keep us at full employment." Thus, from time to time the government needed to intervene in order to spike up the economy. Even though Malthus and a few other writers had challenged Smith's laissez-faire theory prior to the 1930s, it had survived all criticisms with the help of such influential writers as David Ricardo and John Stuart Mill. But the tragic fate of Smith's powerful legacy was inevitable. The free market economy was gradually replaced by a highly mixed one.

The roles that the federal and state governments play in the United States economy have increased greatly in recent years. In 1920, less than 10 percent of goods and services in the United States was bought by the government. In 1980, that figure was over 20 percent.[7] Big increases in spending for defense, education, and roads account for most of the large jump. The welfare expenditures of the federal government have also grown greatly. The percentage of the gross national product (GNP) redistributed by the federal government as transfer payments increased from less than 1 percent in 1929 to about 10 percent in 1982.[8] The number of federal agencies regulating different parts of the economy has also increased by leaps and bounds. They range from the Food and Drug Administration, which regulates drugs and foods, to the Environmental Protection Agency, which administers antipollution legislation.

RESEARCH METHODS IN ECONOMICS

The Intellectual Experiment: a Public Method

Unlike most other social scientists, who make extensive use of the laboratory experiment and the structured interview, economists cannot conduct laboratory experiments, and the interview technique is not a major research strategy within the discipline. The most frequently used method in economics is the *intellectual experiment*.[9]

Economists test hypotheses by *assuming* that all the variables are constant (or equal) except the variable whose effect they are trying to determine (the independent variable). Let's study an example. Professor Jones, an economist at State University, studies this problem: "What is the most important factor influencing consumer demand for compact cars?" She concludes that the *price* of compact cars is the most important factor. She bases her conclusion on the analysis of statistics that show the cost of compact cars and the number purchased within each of the last 10 years. What factors did Professor Jones assume to be equal or constant? She assumed that the income of consumers, the quality of compact cars, and the price of larger cars were constant variables. *In other words, she assumed that of all the other factors that might influence consumer demand for compact cars, only the price varied.*

In the real world (which the economist *simplifies* for research purposes) other factors often do not remain constant. In applying her generalization,

Professor Jones may find that even though the price of compact cars increased significantly the following year, the number bought also increased. Several new American compact cars hit the market, and the hourly wages of consumers reached a new peak. These factors brought about an unexpected increase in the number of compact cars purchased.

In determining the production possibilities of cotton and corn in society X earlier in this chapter, we *assumed* that society X would not experience any natural catastrophes, that all workers would remain employed, and that its level of technology would remain constant. Because economic research is based on such shaky assumptions, economic generalizations are often tentative and not applicable under some conditions.

Economists often show the relationship between economic concepts with mathematical and graphic models. The production-possibilities example in this chapter is a highly simplified model. The *intellectual experiment* procedure is a *public* method because economists usually state the variables they assume will remain constant or equal.

This photograph of a street view of a town in Utah in 1859 can be used to help students to formulate hypotheses about what goods and services were produced and exchanged in this Western town. What kinds of stores can the viewer of the photograph see? (*Source*: The National Archives, Washington, D.C.)

NATURE OF ECONOMIC CONCEPTS

Economic concepts are probably more precise than those in any of the other social sciences. The meanings of such concepts as *scarcity*, *production*, and *exchange* are rather standard in the discipline.[10] This can easily be seen by examining one of the several dictionaries of economics. There is also a great deal of consensus about what the key economic concepts and generalizations are. The tables of contents in most introductory economics textbooks look very similar.

OBJECTIVITY IN ECONOMICS

Since most economic data are quantitative (such as the prices of goods, the number of hours that employees work, and hourly wage rates), data collection within the discipline tends to be more objective than in the other social sciences. Much of the data used by economists is compiled by such agencies as various departments of the federal government. Because of the use of models and the quantitative nature of economic research, statistics are often used to analyze data as well as to control variables that economists would otherwise be unable to control or hold constant. The quantitative nature of the data, the preciseness of the concepts, and the intellectual experiment method make it possible for one economist to replicate studies done by others.

ECONOMIC ANALYSIS
AND POLICY ECONOMICS

Economists usually distinguish between two major approaches within the discipline. One approach is called *economic analysis* or positive economics. Its main goal is the development of scientific theory. High-level generalizations about the *law of supply and demand*, the *law of diminishing returns*, and the *law of scarcity* are examples of the products of this method of inquiry. The other approach is known as *policy economics* or normative economics. The goal of policy economics is to use the generalizations and theories developed in economic analysis to solve social problems that are largely economic in nature. This approach deals with such problems as "Should we reduce income taxes in order to stimulate the economy?" and "How can we best manage the economy so that we have sound welfare programs?" Bach has outlined the steps in policy economics: "*[1] . . . define the problem . . . [2] map out the main alternative ways of achieving the desired goals . . . [3] analyze carefully the alternative policies outlined in step two . . . [4] check your solution—both against flaws in your own analysis resulting from fallacies or blind spots, and against past experience. . . .*"[11]

Economics is both a science and an applied discipline. *Economic analysis is* scientific because the goal is to develop scientific theory. *Policy economics* is an applied field because it deals with *value* questions as well as with scientific knowledge. In order to determine the goals of an economy (such as in Bach's step 2), we must make one value choice instead of another. *Thus value inquiry is an essential part of policy economics.*

There are difficulties when a discipline that has both scientific and policy aspects. When economists make statements or recommendations, it is often not clear whether they are speaking as scientists, that is, basing their statements on scientific knowledge alone, or whether the statements are derived from a combination scientific-valuing process, that is, whether they reflect economists' personal biases. The dual nature of the field is largely responsible for the reputation economists have for disagreeing among themselves. Someone once said, "If you laid all the economists in the world end to end, they would still not reach a conclusion." Although there is actually a great deal of agreement among economists about the nature of the discipline and its key concepts and principles, they have different values and ideas about what the proper goals of an economy should be, and they often, as is to be expected, disagree about policy issues. The public does not often make this distinction, largely because economists rarely make it themselves when they make public statements. When teaching economic studies in the elementary and junior high school grades, you should help students discover how economic analysis can help policy makers determine the possible consequences of different courses of action, but emphasize that citizens, not economists, should determine the goals of the U.S. economy.

LEVELS OF ECONOMIC ANALYSIS

Economists derive generalizations about economic behavior at two levels. *Macroeconomics* focuses on large units, such as the economy as a whole or major divisions within it, "such as government, households, and businesses."[12] *Microeconomics*

> is concerned with *specific* economic units and a detailed consideration of the behavior of these individual units. Here we talk in terms of an individual industry, firm, or household and concentrate upon such magnitudes as the output of a *specific* product, the number of workers employed by a single firm, the revenue or income of a particular firm or household, [or] the price of a particular product. In microeconomics we examine the trees, not the forest.[13]

Generalizations that are valid in macroeconomics are not necessarily valid on a small scale of analysis. For example, the *fallacy of composition*, a common fallacy made when citizens talk about economic problems, is assuming that what is true for the part is also true for the whole. A small manufacturer who lowered his prices might increase his sales and therefore his profit because consumers tend to buy more goods when prices decrease. However, if all the manufacturers within an economic system lowered their prices, their sales would not necessarily increase. Total input into the circular flow of income would be lowered and wages would be lowered as a consequence. People tend to buy less when they make less money. Our example illustrates the importance of distinguishing between these two levels of analysis.

ECONOMIC CONCEPTS

There is a lot of agreement about what the key concepts in economics are. Their definitions are also highly standardized. Almost any economist would regard the law of *supply and demand* and the law of *diminishing returns* as key economic ideas, and would define them in much the same way as other economists. We define some of the key economic concepts below, and describe activities that can be used to teach them to elementary and junior high school students. A list of basic economic concepts, developed by the Joint Council on Economic Education, appears in Table 13.2.

Scarcity

Just as *culture* is the main concept in anthropology, and *group* is the key concept in sociology, *scarcity* is the most important concept in economics. All other economic principles and theories are related to it. The essence of this concept is that, while people have unlimited wants, the amount of resources within any society are limited.[14] Thus there are never enough goods and services to satisfy all wants. Consequently, people must make some hard choices when they decide what goods and services they will produce with their limited resources, how they will be produced, and how they will be distributed. When a society becomes wealthier and develops a higher level of technology, it is able to create more and better goods and services. However, scarcity continues because citizens' wants also increase.

Activities

1. Ask the students to make a list of all the things they would like for their birthdays or for another special occasion, such as Christmas or Chanukah. Ask them to narrow the list to the things they can realistically expect to get. Discuss why the two lists are different.
2. Interview parents about how family budgets are planned and managed.
3. Interview public officials in the community about community services they would like to see and the extent to which they are limited by the amount of *taxes* citizens are willing to pay.
4. Role play a session of the state legislature in which budget allocations are made for such services as education, health, transportation, welfare, and crime prevention. Discuss ways the state legislature solves

the problems that result from demands by citizens for increased services *and* fewer taxes.

5. Role play a session of the United States Congress. The session is faced with a budget deficit of $200 million in one year. Develop a plan to greatly reduce or to eliminate the deficit. Discuss the effects of such a large deficit on the nation's economy.

TABLE 13.2. Basic Concepts in Economics

Fundamental Economic Concepts

1. Scarcity
2. Opportunity Cost and Trade-offs
3. Productivity
4. Economic Systems
5. Economic Institutions and Incentives
6. Exchange, Money, and Interdependence

Microeconomic Concepts

7. Markets and Prices
8. Supply and Demand
9. Competition and Market Structure
10. Income Distribution
11. Market Failures
12. The Role of Government

Macroeconomic Concepts

13. Gross National Product
14. Aggregate Supply
15. Aggregate Demand
16. Unemployment
17. Inflation and Deflation
18. Monetary Policy
19. Fiscal Policy

International Economic Concepts

20. Absolute and Comparative Advantage and Barriers to Trade
21. Balance of Payments and Exchange Rates
22. International Aspects of Growth and Stability

Measurement Concepts and Methods

Tables
Charts and Graphs
Ratios and Percentages
Percentage Changes
Index Numbers
Real vs. Nominal Values
Averages and Distributions Around the Average

SOURCE: Reprinted with permission from Philip Saunders (Chair), G.L. Bach, James D. Calderwood, and W. Lee Hansen, *A Framework for Teaching the Basic Concepts* (Master Curriculum Guide in Economics), 2nd ed. (New York: Joint Council on Economic Education, 1984), p. 11.

Production

Production is the process of creating goods and services to satisfy human wants. The farmer who grows cotton and corn, the worker who works on an automobile assembly line, and the spouse who cooks and sews for a family are all producers. Workers who produce services, such as doctors, teachers, and service station attendants, are also producers.

When teaching about production, you can introduce these concepts: *goods, services,* and *consumers.* Goods are products that satisfy consumer wants. A service is work done that satisfies consumer wants. Books, food, toys, and automobiles are examples of goods. Teaching, washing windows, and nursing are examples of services. Consumers use goods and services to satisfy their wants and needs. Students should realize that every human being, in order to survive, must consume goods and services, and that these goods and services must either be produced by themselves or someone else.

Activities

1. Make a list of the goods and services all human beings need to survive, such as food, shelter, and water. Discuss how these goods and services are obtained in your community.
2. List and discuss services the students produce, such as washing the dishes, mowing the lawn, cleaning the car, and selling newspapers.
3. Make a list of the goods and services the students consume. Compare the goods and services they consume with the ones they produce.
4. Make a list of the goods and services produced by the city, county, state, and federal governments. Make a list of citizens who consume these goods and services and discuss how they are supported.
5. Do research to determine how societies with the following kinds of economic systems determine what goods and services to produce, how to produce them, and who will receive them: *traditional, command,* and *market.*

Interdependence

When an economic system is characterized by specialization and exchange, it is highly *interdependent.*[15] Interdependence is relying on other producers for the goods and services needed to satisfy one's wants, and helping others to satisfy their wants by participating in the production of goods and services consumed. In colonial America, and in many preliterate societies, families were highly independent because they produced their own food and most of the other goods and services they needed. Early American farm mothers made many home remedies to treat their children's diseases and canned most of the family's foods. Sometimes members of families delivered the babies. Because workers in highly technological societies are so specialized, most families, communities, cities, regions, and nations cannot exist without relying on the goods and services produced by other workers and economic units.

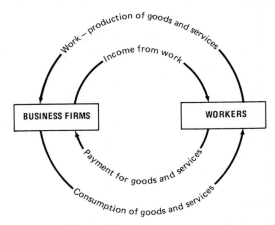

FIGURE 13.3   The circular flow of income.

The circular flow of income diagram (see Figure 13.3) illustrates both interdependence and the structure of a market economy. Money flows from business firms to workers. When workers produce goods and services for business firms, they are paid for their work. When they buy goods and services, the money they earn as salary is paid to the firms or to markets selling goods. Thus income continuously flows, and the people who produce goods and services also consume them.

Activities

1. Do a survey to find out what major goods and services are produced in the community and where the major markets are for these goods and services. Discuss how the goods and services produced in the community help other communities, the nation, and the world.
2. Survey the foods served one day at home to discover where they were grown, packaged, and marketed. Share this information at school during a discussion of how interdependent communities, cities, and nations are.
3. Ask the students to pretend that the following goods and services were cut off from their homes for one week and to describe what life would be like: electricity, phone, gas, transportation, food.
4. Ask the students to pretend that the nations in the Middle East decided suddenly to stop the supply of oil to the Western nations. Ask them to describe the effects on the economies and ways of life in the Western nations.
5. Ask the students to describe how a group of them might survive if they were in a plane crash that landed in the middle of the woods in an unknown land.

Specialization and Division of Labor

Specialization occurs when an economic unit, such as an individual, a business, a region, or a country, produces a narrower range of goods and services than it consumes. *Comparative advantage* results from specialization when economic units produce those goods and services that they can produce most efficiently.[16]

Division of labor is based on the principle of comparative advantage. It consists of dividing the production of goods and services into smaller parts so that each worker does a specific and specialized job. This process often involves an *assembly line* technique. Usually each person who helps to manufacture an automobile makes or attaches only one part. Division of labor, or specialization, has both advantages and disadvantages. With specialization, goods are usually produced more quickly and efficiently. Workers also develop greater skills at performing their particular tasks because they practice the skills frequently. However, workers often have low morale and little pride in their work. If a large number of workers help to make a product, it is difficult for any one of them to gain a great deal of satisfaction from its production. With increased specialization, pride in workmanship tends to fade.

Activities

1. Divide the class into four equal groups. In two of the groups, make a sugar cookie using division of labor. In the other two groups, make the cookie without using division of labor. The class should keep time to determine which group makes the cookie in the least time.
2. Interview workers about job satisfaction. Interview those who produce their products working primarily alone, such as writers and artists, and workers who produce their products working closely with others, such as workers in an automobile plant. Compare the responses of the two types of workers.
3. Visit an automobile plant or another kind of factory where an assembly line is used. Discuss the observations in class.
4. View a film or filmstrip which shows the large number of workers involved in producing one type of goods, such as an airplane, car, or computer.
5. Debate the pros and cons of division of labor and specialization, including its effects on the workers' morale and the quality of products.

Voluntary Exchange

In a specialized market economy, individuals and other economic units produce more of a particular good or service than they can use or consume. To meet their needs for other goods and services, they must exchange the goods and services they produce with other workers. A worker who makes computers needs other goods and services—medical care, food, and shelter. A farmer who grows food might need a computer to help him on the farm. The computer worker and the farmer need each other's products. They could directly exchange a computer for food. This kind of exchange, called *barter,* was often used in traditional societies before forms of money were developed. Since bartering is both awkward and inefficient, money was developed to make the exchange between workers easier and more efficient. Buyers and sellers make their exchanges in a *market.*

Activities

1. Have a county fair. Ask the students to make items in their art and shop classes and trade them for items made by others during the fair. The students should try to make the best possible items with as few resources as possible, and market them at the highest possible prices.
2. Ask the students to bring some stickers or other items to class to trade with other students. Discuss some of the major observations they made about trading during this activity.
3. Ask the class to investigate whether there is a good or service needed or wanted by the students in the school that is not available and that they could provide by starting a business. If there is, work with the students to start a small business that sells goods such as paper, pencils, stickers, and notebooks.
4. Role play to demonstrate ways in which barter has been used in traditional and preliterate societies.
5. Do research to determine what money means in a market economy and how policies regarding its printing and distribution are made.

ECONOMIC GENERALIZATIONS

Since the key concepts in economics can be readily identified, it is not difficult to find generalizations showing the relationship between economic concepts. Generalizations that can be used to guide economic studies in the elementary and junior high school grades are found in economics textbooks, in professional books on the teaching of the social studies, and in many curriculum guides in school systems throughout the nation. The following generalizations are representative of the types you can use to guide the planning of economic studies.[17]

Scarcity

A conflict between unlimited wants and limited resources creates the need for decision making.
Choices are based on the individual's value system, but the value systems are to a large extent culturally derived. Needs and wants are therefore culturally derived.

Interdependence

All families and family members in a community are dependent upon one another. Division of labor refers to the separation of production into various jobs.

The growth of interdependence increases the problems of adjustment for the individual in the society, and it also increases the need for coordination through organization-managerial direction, and market mechanisms.

Voluntary Exchange

Individual producers of goods and services exchange with others to get the goods and services they need to satisfy their basic wants.

Individuals who contribute to the production process receive a share of the goods and services produced.

Price is a measure of the relative scarcity and need for goods, services, or resources.

Money is an institution to facilitate the operation of an exchange economy.

Market Economy

Consumers determine what is produced in a free economy, considering all the available alternatives. Advertising and the mass media often influence choices.

Government has increasingly become a participant in the market economy. It is a competitor and also a creator of economic opportunities.

Table 13.3 contains a *summary of economic content* that you will find helpful when teaching economic concepts and generalizations.

TABLE 13.3. A Summary of Economic Content

1. Economics is the science that investigates the conditions and laws affecting the production, distribution, and consumption of wealth or materials to satisfy human desires.
2. Scarcity is the condition created by not having sufficient resources to produce all the goods and services we could desire. Scarcity is the basic economic problem.
3. The lack of resources relative to our wants forces us to economize. Decisions must be made at the individual and societal levels to obtain maximum satisfaction from available resources.
4. The economic system is the system through which we collectively make decisions relating to how scarce resources will be allocated to supply goods and services.
5. The three basic questions that every economic system must answer are
   a. What goods and services will be produced?
   b. How will these goods and services be produced?
   c. Who will receive the goods and services that are produced?   (Cont'd)

TABLE 13.2. (continued)

6. The three basic types of productive resources or factors of production are human resources, natural resources, and capital resources.

7. Human resources refers to all the workers in the human resource pool and their abilities. As the labor force becomes better educated and more energetic, it will create a more productive economic system.

8. Division of labor refers to specialization in skills or tasks. Through specialization, workers have to depend on each other to complete the entire production process.

9. Able managers make specialization possible by directing and bringing together the factors of production and by making decisions about what products should be made and how these should be distributed.

10. People make the economic system work; without their talents, energies, imagination, and desire, our economic system could not function.

11. Natural resources refers to the basic gifts of nature—above, on, or below the surface of the earth.

12. The real value of any natural resource depends largely on the people's knowledge of its potential usefulness, allocation, and utilization.

13. Capital resources are those resources which have been created by human effort and saved to be used to produce goods or services. They are very important in determining the wealth of a nation and its economic growth.

14. Capital formation is the process of saving productive resources to create capital resources, instead of producing consumer goods and services.

15. To make our society productive and to take advantage of technological advances, the economy requires a tremendous amount of capital goods. The savings of individuals and businesses provide the funds for the purchase of these capital goods.

16. The traditional system, the command system, and the market system are the three economic systems which have been developed to deal with the allocation of scarce productive resources.

17. In the traditional system, economic decisions are formulated by the customs and traditions of the society.

18. In the command system, the economic decisions are formulated by central decision makers, usually working within the government.

19. In the market system, the economic decisions are made by individuals and institutions, guided by their own self-interest, in a free market process with a minimum of government intervention.

SOURCE: Ronald A. Banaszak and Dennis C. Brennan, *Teaching Economics: Content and Strategies* (Menlo Park, CA: Addison-Wesley, 1983), pp. 16–17. Reprinted with permission.

ECONOMIC EDUCATION IN THE SCHOOLS

The Need for Economic Understanding

Economic problems and issues within a society divide large segments of the population. Part of our inability to find viable solutions to complex economic problems results from economic illiteracy on the part of both citizens and public officials. Because of their confusion about economic issues and prob-

INQUIRY STRATEGY: BUYING AND SELLING STOCKS

1. Explain what stocks are to your students and show them the stock exchange page from a daily newspaper, such as *The New York Times* or *The Wall Street Journal*.
2. Show the students how to read the New York Stock Exchange page. Explain these columns in the stock exchange page: 52-week high and low, stock, dividend, yield percent, price/earnings ratio, sales 100s, high, low, last, change. You might invite an investment broker to class to talk about stocks and to help explain the stock exchange page to your students. A book by Louis Engel, in collaboration with Peter Wyckoff, called *How to Buy Stocks* (New York: Bantam, 1977) is also helpful.
3. Give each student a voucher that is "worth" $4000 for buying and selling stock in class. Ask two of the students to serve as stockbrokers who will buy and sell stocks for the students and keep a record of all stock transactions made in class.
4. Ask each student to identify about $4000 worth of stocks they will "buy" from the two "stockbrokers." They should pay a 1-percent commission each time they buy and sell their stocks.
5. For three months the students should monitor their stocks each day. They may buy and sell each week on Friday morning.
6. The student or students who make the most from their stocks during the three-month period should be given an award, such as cash from a PTA fund or a book. The two students who serve as class stockbrokers should also be given an award.

lems, citizens often vote for candidates who make grand and unrealistic promises about economic reform. Candidates often make such promises out of ignorance, but just as often they make them merely to get votes and do not consider how they might deliver the promised reforms. Promising no new taxes is a campaign strategy often used by politicians to get votes.

To be able to judge the soundness of proposals for economic reforms, citizens must have a clear understanding of the nature of a mixed economy, and an awareness of the complexity of modern economic systems. Because many students end their formal education when they leave the public schools, the schools must implement sound programs in economics education if future citizens are to intelligently influence economic policy and participate effectively in our political system.[18] Almost all the social issues that societies face have economic aspects, and the economic perspective will help us to resolve them.

Although the economic point of view can help us to solve problems, economics cannot tell us whether we should have a guaranteed annual income for all families, or whether income taxes should be reduced or increased. However, economic concepts and principles can help us to *predict* the possible consequences of a guaranteed annual income or of an increase in income taxes. The discipline cannot tell us what the consequences of these actions *will be;* as we have suggested, economic principles, in common with other social science principles, depend on many variables. Nevertheless, even tentative knowledge can help us to make decisions on complex economic problems by revealing the probable consequences of different courses of action.

Economics education is complicated by the fact that students, like adults, have many misconceptions about the economic system. Often journalists, equally ignorant about economic matters, reinforce the common myths about the economy. Almost everyone is a self-styled economic expert. Economics and education probably have more experts than any other disciplines. For example, a common fallacy is the assumption that what is good for their individual situation is also good for the economy as as a whole. When our economy is depressed, citizens often argue that the economy would recover if the government would simply stop spending money. Individuals can often improve their economic situation by saving a significant portion of their incomes, but much unemployment results when the government limits spending, because many people have government-related jobs. In some cases, it is necessary for the federal government to *increase* spending in order to stimulate a troubled economy.

Because money is such an important part of our lives (it is often said that money, not love, makes the world go 'round), reasoning on economic issues tends to become clouded by emotion. Citizens are often opposed to increasing taxes, yet keep demanding more efficient and extensive services from the city or federal government. Students should be helped to understand that more extensive public services mean higher taxes. The *scarcity* concept will help them to discover that you can't have your cake and eat it too. Citizens should demand honesty on the part of public officials and the most efficient services possible from the funds spent. However, expecting something for nothing and demanding efficient use of scarce resources are separate matters; the study of economics will help students to make this distinction.

A Sequential Program in Economics Education

The need for economic understanding is too important to be left to chance. While many gifted teachers help students view social studies content from an economic perspective, we can be assured that all students gain economic understanding only if we plan a specific program of instruction. This does not mean that a separate economics program should be implemented. We do not recommend this approach to economics instruction in the elementary and junior high school. Rather, the social studies staff or teacher should identify a number of key economic concepts and related generalizations that can be taught with the content that constitutes the core of the social studies program. *Economics is not specialized content, but a unique way of viewing the content that presently constitutes the social studies curriculum.* The key concepts and generalizations identified should be introduced in the earliest grades and further developed in other grades. Students will gain an increasing depth of understanding as they study economic concepts in successive grades in a spiraling fashion.

There are many opportunities for you to introduce and extend economic concepts with content that constitutes the traditional social studies curriculum. Let's consider how the concept of *scarcity* and a related generalization, "Every individual and society faces a conflict between unlimited wants and limited resources," might be introduced in kindergarten and further developed in successive grades. You could introduce this concept in kindergarten with a role-playing situation. In the situation, Mother and Father are trying to decide whether they should take a trip next summer or add a needed room to the house. They do not have enough money to do both. You could ask the students such questions as "What is the problem in this situation?" "Why is there a problem?" "Why do you think Mother and Father can't do both things?" " Have you ever had to make a choice between two things?" "What did you decide to do?" "Why?" "What helped you to decide?" "If you were Mother and Father, what would you do?" "Why?"

The study of *community helpers* in the next grade could extend this concept. You could ask the students to name the services that the community provides (you might start by showing them pictures of the helpers in the community), to hypothesize about why more services are not provided, and to think of ways in which the present services could be extended and improved. You could then ask them *why* current services are not better or more extensive. You should help the students discover that a community has limited funds (derived from taxes), and that it cannot provide unlimited services, such as more street sweeping, more fire stations, or more police.

Topics such as food, clothing, transportation, and our state, traditionally parts of elementary social studies, also contain content that can further develop this concept. Investigating how people must make choices when buying clothing and why public transportation systems are inefficient in many of our cities, and becoming aware of the continuous search by state officials for additional funds to provide needed public services, will extend the concept of *scarcity* in later grades.

Production, goods, services, consumption, exchange, and *interdependence* are economic concepts that should also be built into the social studies program. To facilitate the teaching of these concepts and to extend students' understanding of an economic system, you can pose the three basic economic problems: What goods and services shall we produce and in what amounts? How shall they be produced? For whom shall they be produced? You can also help the students determine, through their inquiries, how the problems are solved by different kinds of societies. You should select societies that have different kinds of economies so that the students can derive the generalization that all human groups have solved these basic economic problems and have invented a wide variety of ways to solve them.

TEACHING STRATEGIES

Generalization: *All members of a society are economically interdependent; individual producers of goods and services exchange with others to get the goods and services to satisfy their basic wants and needs.*

Primary Grades

Have students compare the self-sufficiency of pioneers living on farms with the interdependence of people in today's society. Research the following questions: What was the source and process of obtaining butter in pioneer days? What is it today?

Lead the students into a discussion about how pioneer farmers obtained butter. Bring out the points that they would milk the cow, set the milk in a cool place to allow the cream to separate from the milk, and then place the cream in a churn and mix it until butter appeared. After churning, the butter was removed, washed, salted, and shaped. It was then used for eating and cooking. If it is possible to obtain whole unprocessed milk in your area, bring some to school so that the students can see how the cream and milk separate. Then have students skim the cream from the top of the milk and place in an old-fashioned churn if one is available, and churn the butter. If whole unprocessed milk and a churn are not available, purchase thick cream from the grocery store and place it in a jar. Students can take turns shaking it until butter is obtained.

Next show a film, filmstrip, or a series of pictures that illustrate how butter gets from cows to the pupils' morning toast. If there is a dairy or creamery accessible, plan visits to these places. After the students have seen a visual presentation illustrating how milk is produced and have taken a field trip, have them develop a pictograph for the bulletin board showing the people and processes involved in the journey of butter to their tables.

The students can also make a pictograph illustrating the processing and consumption of butter during pioneer days and compare the production of butter during these two periods.

Discuss the following questions:

1. Are more people involved in processing butter now or were there more during the pioneer period?
2. How do they help one another?
3. How would people in a pioneer town obtain butter?
4. How would we obtain butter if the plant workers who process it went on strike?
5. Is butter today better? Why or why not?

Have your students engage in a block-building contest. Obtain two sets of blocks. One student will work with one set of blocks and two students with the other set. The rest of the class will observe the two teams to see which team can build a structure more quickly using all the blocks. Before they begin building, have the observers make predictions regarding which team will be finished first and why. Repeat the contest several times to see whether their predictions are verified each time. If the student who is working alone wins, ask the students why this happened. A possible response might be that the two people were not working well together. Ask the students what they observed as advantages and disadvantages of working alone and with a partner.

Show a film, filmstrip, or a series of pictures depicting the construction of a modern-day house. Next put a large picture of a new house in the center of a bulletin board. Have the students list and discuss the kinds of workers who would be needed to build the new house. After these have been listed, have students draw pictures of these workers, label them, and place them on the bulletin board around the house.

Use the homemaking corner of your classroom to illustrate the interdependence of family members. If you don't have a homemaking corner, assemble some appropriate props for the following role-playing situation. Have students role play a working father, a working mother, a new baby, and a school-age child. While the rest of the class observes, have the students act out their parts in the homemaking corner according to their own interpretations.

Ask the following questions and list responses on the board:

1. What jobs does each member of the family carry out?
2. How does each family member help the others?
3. Which family members do the most work? Why?
4. Are there other family members who could do more work? Who are they and what kind of work could they do?

Next, change the composition of the family by eliminating the father role. Discuss how the jobs of the mother and children might expand as a result of the elimination of the father role.

1. What additional work will the mother have to do?
2. What other jobs might the child do at home to help the family?

Have students role play this family situation. Observers will list their observations, as in the first role-playing situation.

Change the composition of the family a third time by eliminating the mother role and reinstating the father role. Discuss the same questions, and have the students act out their new family roles. The pupils will list their observations of jobs done by family members and how each member helps the others.

Discuss the similarities and differences among the different lists of family services. Ask, "What could we say was true of each family situation?" Rephrase the question as necessary to solicit responses indicating that the students recognize the interdependence of family members for services.

Have your students plan a town to be constructed in your room. In the planning stages:

1. Pretend that you as a family are going to construct a town. What will you need in this town so that your family can live there and get along?
2. What kinds of businesses and services are needed? As the students begin to suggest businesses, guide their planning so that they include

those services considered necessary for the existence of a town—a grocery store, clothing or variety store, post office, telephone service, gas station, and some sort of delivery service for getting the goods to the town. Divide your class into groups representing the businesses listed. Have each business group make a chart illustrating the source of their supplies and the means of delivery. Ask, "What occupations would you want represented in your town?" (Responses might include a doctor, dentist, teacher, and police officer.)

After you and the students have planned and discussed what you want your town to consist of, name the town and put it into operation in your room. Have students role play the roles necessary for their plans. Develop role-playing situations. For example, Johnny Brown broke his arm playing in the park. His mother took him to the doctor who is out of supplies for fixing broken arms. To whom should the doctor go for help?

Develop other situations in which the interaction of town members can be demonstrated, and have the students role play the situations. After each role-playing situation, have students list the people called on for services. Discuss how members of a city work together to help provide other members with the services and goods they need.

Intermediate Grades

A number of the goods and services needed by modern-day families are more easily obtained when families get together to pay for them. These goods and services are usually paid for with tax monies or when the people use them. Such services might include providing water, roads, electricity, schools, fire protection, street cleaning, police protection, health facilities, parks, street repair, stop lights, and bus services.

Have your students interview their parents to find out how many and what kinds of goods and services mentioned above are used by their families. Have students also find out what percentage of their family's taxes go for what items and which services are paid for directly when used.

After students have collected this information, pool the information, chart it as indicated here, and answer the questions that follow.

Goods and Services	Source of Revenue	Amount of Revenue
Electricity	Direct payment, according to amount of kilowatts used	
Schools	Taxes	20%
.	.	.
.	.	.
.	.	.

1. Why is it to the mutual benefit of the people in the community to pay for these goods and services together?

2. Are there some goods or services listed that are no longer useful to the community as a whole, and that should be dropped or replaced? Support your answer with facts.

3. Are there some goods or services not listed that should be added and paid for by the entire community? Support your answer with facts.

4. In some communities a service that has been paid for directly upon use has had difficulty maintaining itself financially. Tax support has been proposed and added in some cases. Thus the service is both tax-supported and paid for directly. One such example is the transit system in Seattle, Washington. A city transit tax of 50¢ was added to the city electric light bill. The city made riding the bus more attractive by adding several Blue Streak Lines, which provided rapid service for those who work in the city. Have students examine their chart to determine whether there have been similar problems in their community. Then determine how the community solved the problem to the mutual benefit of most of its members. Research on this problem may require some exploration of the newspapers to determine what kinds of problems have existed and what action was taken. There may be a problem for which the solution is currently being sought. If this is the case, have your students research it and make proposals for its solution.

Present your students with the following situation:

Here are three men, each of whom has a problem. Mr. Cline owns a grocery store on the corner. It is just a small store, so he does all the work required to run it. The man who regularly delivers fresh vegetables to his store is ill, and the big delivery companies won't take his order because it is too small. He will lose customers if he doesn't do something, because fresh vegetables of good quality are one of the main reasons why people shop at his store. Mr. Cline calls his friend Mr. Hoboken, who owns his own truck, and asks for his help. Mr. Hoboken says that he can't help because his truck is broken down, and he probably won't be able to get it fixed for several weeks. The next day Mr. Hoboken's neighbor, Mr. Glass, comes to visit and says he lost his job as a mechanic two weeks ago. He hasn't yet been able to find new work. He has run out of funds and wonders whether Mr. Hoboken would be willing to let him have food on credit.

Ask the students to think about how these three men could solve their problems without using money. Then have three students dramatize the roles of the men in the story, and show how they solved their problems.

Discuss the following questions:

1. Why were the men unable to solve their problems alone?
2. Was the solution acted out by the three players a logical one?
3. How does the solution illustrate the interdependence of workers?
4. What are some other examples of interdependence you can think of?

Read the following situation to your students:

> At the beginning of summer vacation, Charles Abernathy built a new dog-house for his dog, Rags. His neighbor, Mr. Herman, liked it and asked Charles to build a similar one for his spaniel, Freckles. He told Charles he would pay him $10. Charles was very excited about this because he wanted to earn money for summer camp and maybe even enough to buy a Stingray bike. Before Charles completed the house for Freckles, another friend came by and asked Charles to build a dog house for his spaniel, too. Then Mr. Hildreth dropped by and asked Charles to build a house for his Great Dane that would be twice the size of the others he had built. Mr. Hildreth offered to pay him $20 for the job. Before long Charles had orders for 25 dog-houses: 20 regular-sized ones and 5 double-sized ones. He began to worry then, because it had taken him about a week to make the first one, including the sanding and painting. How would he ever be able to build 25 doghouses by himself!

After presenting the situation to the students, divide the class into four groups. Direct the groups to devise a very detailed solution to Charles's problem. The solution must be one that allows him to keep his commitment for building the doghouses and possibly to handle some more orders. After the groups have decided on their solutions, have a spokesperson from each group present his or her group's plan to the class. Discuss the merits of each plan and have the students vote for the one that would work best. Be sure the students support their arguments for and against the various proposals with good reasons.

Upper Grades

Have the students plan a car wash in order to earn money for a cause that is important to them or in order to sponsor some event at your school. Planning should include the following points:

1. What would be the best location for the car wash? Why? (Students may need to investigate the parts of town in which people would be most likely to need their cars washed.)
2. What points will need to be considered regarding the selection of the place to hold the car wash?
3. Would it be better to have several locations? Why or why not? If so, what should those locations be?
4. What would be the most efficient way for the responsibilities to be shared? Why? Why not just have each individual have a car wash in the area around his or her home?
5. What are the best sources of the supplies necessary for carrying out the car wash?
6. What would be the best price to charge for the service?
7. What would be the most effective kind of advertising?

8. Where should the advertising be distributed?
9. How long in advance of the sale should advertising be out?
10. Develop a chart representing the interdependence of the operation and the services provided.

Tell your students that they will be playing a game in which half of them will be working in buying teams of two for the Vroom Airplane Company. They will be buying the following items: aluminum, engines, tires, and electrical wiring. They will be negotiating with representatives, teams of two, of other companies in the United States and in other countries.

Each company team selling a product will have a standard price per unit of measure for their goods. Each company team will have a recommended bargaining procedure. The major bargaining device is the promise to buy a certain number of planes. The company teams may negotiate within a range of $3–$10 for the cost per unit of measure and may promise to buy from 0–25 planes. The following are the standard prices and recommended bargaining procedures suggested by company presidents to their sales representatives.

1. Aluminum
   a. Adanac: $7 per unit of measure
      If you buy from this foreign country, you receive an extra point because you will be furthering the international balance of payments.
      President of the company recommends you order 15 new Vroom planes.
   b. Lubeck Aluminum, U.S.: $5 per unit of measure
      If you buy their aluminum, they will give you a bonus of aluminum serving trays for food service use on your planes.
2. Engines
   a. Jolyes Joyce: $100,000 per unit measure
      President of the country in which this company is located will purchase 13 Vroom planes if you buy their engines.
   b. Standard Electric: $98,785 per unit of measure
      Will guarantee a sale of 15 planes, if you also purchase their wiring.
3. Tires and related rubber components
   a. Goodday: $2 per unit of measure
   b. F. B. Richgood: $3 per unit of measure
4. Electrical wiring
   a. Standard Electric: $10 per unit of measure
   b. Housevesting: $11 per unit of measure
      Their subsidiary, Ajax Airlines, will buy 5 planes.

Give the students an opportunity to get the constraints of their roles well in mind. Direct each buying team and selling team to keep very careful and accurate records, subject to audit, in order to substantiate their business negotiations. Designate four areas of the room with signs of the four negotiating companies. The Vroom teams will travel to the "offices" of the selling teams for conferences. After all the teams have made their purchases and sales, have each Vroom buying team present their business deal to the class, which will vote for the winning team. The team that obtains the lowest *total* cost per unit, therefore the lowest cost of production, and sells the most planes is the winner.

If there is a major industry or business in the area you live in, have your students write and/or visit it. Interview some of its representatives to determine some of the major supplies they use in production. Have the students ask:

1. Which supplies do employees of the company produce themselves?
2. Which supplies does the company order? From whom?
3. Where does the company get the materials for those items it makes itself?
4. Where do the suppliers get their raw materials?

When the students have collected this information, have them develop a large bulletin board illustrating the chain of goods and services that goes into the making of that product.

Have the students assume the roles of members of the population of a growing town, Dorado. Several members of the town council have been trying to persuade the rest of the members to work to get rail transportation into the town. Several members, however, are opposed. One of the reasons for their opposition is that the town will then become more dependent on outside sources for many goods and services. The council members in favor of rail transportation believe that Dorado has some products that are needed in other areas, and other towns have some products that are needed by Dorado to expand business and production. The chairman of the council has called a town meeting. The council members will debate the issue. Then there will be questions from the general citizenry. A vote of all town members in attendance will be taken at the conclusion of the debate.

Lead the class in a general discussion, getting the students to define the distinguishing characteristics of this imaginary town. Have them include the following information:

1. Geographical location and influences.
2. Major businesses and industries of Dorado.
3. Major businesses and industries in surrounding towns that would profit from the rail connection.
4. Actual population.
5. Growth projection.
6. Kind of work force available for the new jobs that would be created.

Then have the students select and research their roles, carry out the debate, and vote on the issue.

SUMMARY

Economics is primarily concerned with how people attempt to satisfy their unlimited wants with limited resources. The key concept in the discipline is *scarcity;* one of its major principles is that there are not enough resources for us to satisfy all of our wants. The production, exchange, and consumption of goods and services are also dominant concerns of the discipline. In their study of scarcity, economists try to determine how each society solves the three basic economic problems: What goods and services shall be produced and in what amounts? How shall they be produced? And for whom shall they be produced?

The major research method used in economics is the *intellectual experiment.* In using this strategy, economists assume that all the variables are constant except those whose effect they are trying to ascertain. Economic concepts are probably more precise than those in any of the other social sciences. Not only is there a great deal of agreement about what the key concepts in economics are, but the definitions of economic concepts are highly standardized. The nature of economic concepts considerably facilitates the job of curriculum builders when they try to identify economic concepts for inclusion in the social studies curriculum. Furthermore, economic research tends to be more objective than research in any of the other social sciences; most economic data are quantitative. Highly statistical techniques are often used to analyze data in the discipline. We can identify two major approaches within the discipline, *economic analysis* and *policy economics.* The goal of economic analysis is to develop scientific generalizations and theory. The objective of policy economics is to use generalizations and theory to solve the economic problems that society faces. While economists usually agree on their scientific generalizations, they often make highly conflicting recommendations in the policy area, because they have different values and ideas about what the proper economic goals of society should be.

Because of the complex nature of society, there is a tremendous need for schools to help students develop economic literacy and understanding. Almost all the social problems pervasive in our society have economic aspects. Students will be able to make much more reflective decisions about political candidates, referenda, and economic proposals if they understand the general principles of our economic system.

Students should have experiences in the earliest grades that will help them to gain some understanding of economics. All the topics traditionally covered in social studies can be viewed from an economic perspective because economics does not consist of specific content, but of a unique way of looking at human behavior. When students consider the family, the community, the state, and the world, they can be helped to view the problems from an economic perspective. Economic concepts and generalizations can also help students to understand more clearly many of the experiences that they have each day.

DISCUSSION QUESTIONS AND EXERCISES

1. What is the economic perspective? What key concepts do economists use in studying human behavior? How does the economic perspective differ from the conceptual tools used by other social scientists to study human behavior?

2. What are the three basic economic problems that must be solved by all societies? Illustrate, with a teaching plan, how students in the elementary grades can use a data retrieval chart to derive generalizations related to these three basic problems.

3. How did the ideas of Adam Smith differ from those of the mercantilists? In what ways were Smith's ideas overly optimistic?

4. What was the central argument set forth in Keynes's *The General Theory of Employment, Interest and Money?* Compare and contrast the ideas of the mercantilists, Smith, and Keynes. To what extent does the U.S. economy reflect the ideas of the mercantilists, Smith, and Keynes?

5. What is the *intellectual experiment?* Give examples of how an economist uses this method to study a problem. What are the advantages of this method? Disadvantages? Illustrate, with a teaching plan, how you would help students to understand this method of research.

6. Compare and contrast *economic analysis* and *policy economics* in terms of goals and research methods. Why is it important to distinguish these two components of the discipline? What contributions can each make to the social studies curriculum?

7. Analyze a teaching unit in your curriculum library. What economic concepts and generalizations does the unit contain? What economic concepts and generalizations would you add to or delete from the unit in order to make it more effective? How else would you change the unit to increase its quality?

8. Select one of the following generalizations and design a series of activities (similar to the ones in this chapter) that can be used to teach it to students in the (a) primary grades, (b) middle grades, and (c) upper grades:
    a. All members of a society are economically interdependent; individual producers exchange goods and services with others to get what they require to satisfy their basic wants and needs.
    b. The conflict between unlimited wants and limited resources means that individuals and societies must make difficult decisions about the utilization of scarce resources.

9. Demonstrate your understanding of the following key concepts by writing or stating brief definitions for each of them. Also tell why each is significant.

a. production-possibilities concept	d. scarcity
b. market economy	e. production
c. fallacy of composition	f. goods
	g. services

h. consumption
i. interdependent
j. specialization and division of labor
k. exchange
l. circular flow of income

m. mixed economy
n. microeconomics
o. macroeconomics
p. comparative advantage

NOTES

1. Campbell R. McConnell, *Economics: Principles, Problems, Policies,* 6th ed. (New York: McGraw-Hill, 1975), p. 27.

2. Roman F. Warmke and Raymond H. Muessig, *The Study and Teaching of Economics* (Columbus, OH: Merrill, 1980), p. 4; Ronald A. Banaszak and Dennis C. Brennan, *Teaching Economics: Content and Strategies* (Menlo Park, CA: Addison-Wesley, 1983), p. 15.

3. Robert L. Heilbroner, *The Economic Problem* (Englewood Cliffs, NJ: Prentice-Hall, 1968), p. 17.

4. Heilbroner, op. cit., p. 18.

5. Heilbroner, op. cit., p. 18.

6. Robert Heilbroner and Lester Thurow, *Economics Explained* (Englewood Cliffs, NJ: Prentice-Hall, 1982), pp. 17–23.

7. Heilbroner and Thurow, op. cit., p. 56.

8. Heilbroner and Thurow, op. cit., p. 56.

9. Lloyd G. Reynolds, *Economics: A General Introduction* (Homewood, IL: Richard D. Irwin, 1966), p. 8.

10. Paul A. Samuelson, and William D. Nordhaus, *Economics,* 13th ed. (New York: McGraw-Hill, 1989).

11. George L. Bach, *Economics: An Introduction to Analysis and Policy,* 11th ed. (Englewood Cliffs, NJ: Prentice-Hall, 1987).

12. McConnell, op. cit., p. 14.

13. McConnell, op. cit., pp. 14–15.

14. Marilyn L. Kourilsky, *Understanding Economics: Overview for Teachers, Experiences for Students* (Menlo Park, CA: Addison-Wesley, 1980), pp. 1–10.

15. Philip Saunders (Chair), G.G. Bach, James D. Calderwood, and W. Lee Hansen, *A Framework for Teaching the Basic Concepts* (Master Curriculum Guide in Economics), 2nd ed. (New York: Joint Council on Economic Education, 1984).

16. Saunders et al., op. cit.

17. The Colorado Advisory Committee on the Social Studies, *A Guide to Concept Development in the Social Studies* (Denver: Colorado Department of Education, 1967), p. 14.

18. Donald W. Wentworth, W. Lee Hansen, and Sharryl H. Hawke, Eds. *Perspectives on Economic Education* (Boulder, CO: Social Science Education Consortium, 1977); S. Stowell Symmes, Ed., *Economic Education: Links to the Social Studies* (Washington, D.C.: National Council for the Social Studies, 1981).

FOR FURTHER READING

Banaszak, Ronald A., and Dennis C. Brennan. *Teaching Economics: Content and Strategies*. Menlo Park, CA: Addison-Wesley, 1983.

Children in the Marketplace: Lessons Plans in Economics for Grades 3 and 4, 2nd ed. New York: Joint Council on Economic Education, 1986.

Davis, James E. *Teaching Economics to Young Adolescents: A Research-Based Rationale*. San Francisco: Foundation for Teaching Economics, 1987.

Galbraith, John Kenneth. *The Age of Uncertainty: A History of Economic Ideas and Their Consequences*. Boston: Houghton Mifflin, 1977.

Heilbroner, Robert L. *The Worldly Philosophers: The Lives, Times and Ideas of the Great Economic Thinkers*, 6th ed. New York: Touchstone, 1987.

Kourilsky, Marilyn L. *Understanding Economics: Overview for Teachers, Experiences for Students*. Menlo Park, CA: Addision-Wesley, 1983.

Miller, Steven L. *Economic Education for Citizenship*. Bloomington, IN: Social Science Education Consortium, 1988.

Saunders, Philip (Chair), G. G. Bach, James D. Calderwood, and W. Lee Hansen. *A Framework for Teaching the Basic Concepts* (Master Curriculum Guide in Economics), 2nd ed. New York: Joint Council on Economic Education, 1984.

Warmke, Roman F., Raymond H. Muessig, and Steve I. Miller. *The Study and Teaching of Economics*. Columbus, OH: Merrill, 1980.

Wenthorth, Donald R., and Kenneth E. Leonard. *Teaching Strategies: International Trade (Secondary)*. New York: Joint Council on Economic Education, 1988.

14

Geography: Structure, Concepts, and Strategies

THE GEOGRAPHIC PERSPECTIVE

Geography is one of the oldest social sciences. It dates back to the time of the ancient Greeks. The term *geography* comes from the Greek words meaning "to write about the earth." Geographers have a unique concern for place: mountains, valleys, cities, river systems, barren deserts, dense jungles, and icy polar regions. Geographers are interested in the climate of those places, the movement of people in and out of them, the growth and decline of cities, the use people make of the resources available to them, and the patterns of highways, railroad, and airline routes. More specifically, geographers are interested in the features that give a place its special character and differentiate it from other places. They are also concerned with the relationship between places and the factors that serve as connecting links (or barriers) in the space between places. In short, geographers strive to develop descriptions and explanations that carefully integrate people and the place and space in which they live.

FIVE TRADITIONS

As we have noted in previous chapters, most of the social sciences are comparatively new; they emerged as distinct disciplines or fields of knowledge only within the past century. Geography, however, has a very long history. The ancient Greeks and Egyptians carefully observed the course of the sun and the stars, accurately charted the dimensions of their world around the

Students can use a comprehensive atlas to explore many parts of the world and to increase their geographic understandings and skills. (*Source*: Seattle Public Schools.)

Mediterranean, and recorded descriptions brought back by traders and travelers of the lands and people beyond their borders. Out of this long tradition of careful observation and study of the earth have come five different perspectives, or research interests, shared by many geographers. While each is somewhat different in its approach to the study of *place* and *space*, they are recognized and accepted by most geographers as being well within the mainstream of the discipline. Taken together, these five traditions reflect the broad scope of the field and the varied approaches used by geographers. Elements of each of these traditions may be found in the geography components of the social studies curriculum in the schools.[1]

Physical Geography *or* the Earth Science Tradition

The study of the surface of the earth, particularly the arrangement and function of natural features, is physical geography. This study includes physical features, such as plains, valleys, mountains, and rivers; the weather and climate of the atmosphere (meteorology); the action of waves, tides, and currents (oceanography); and the vegetation and animal life of the earth. This approach has always been a strong one among geographers, particularly as they sought to collect and systematize the rapidly expanding knowledge of the world brought back by travelers and explorers. In large measure, these early studies and reports were descriptive.

Regional Geography *or* the Area Studies Tradition

Regional geographers study an area or region of the earth's surface that is homogeneous in terms of some specific criteria such as location, manufacturing, land forms, climate, economic activity, cultural trait, or ethnic origin of the people. The regional geographer asks: "What are the key features that give the region its character?" "How are these key features or criteria related to other features in the same or adjacent areas?" Thus, the regional geographer attempts to present as comprehensive a description and analysis of an area as possible. The regional approach is widely used in the elementary and junior high schools. Three types of regions are most commonly studied: *physical regions*, in which the land features are basically alike; *cultural regions*, in which some aspect of culture or level of technology predominates; and *political regions*, which are grouped along the lines of territorial boundaries.

Cultural Geography *or* the Human–Land Tradition

Cultural geographers study the relationships between people and the environment. With this approach, sometimes called human geography or ecological geography, the geographer is specifically interested in the interrelations of cultural development and environmental conditions. The importance or use that we make of the physical and biotic features of the earth is a function of the attitudes, objectives, and technical skills of our culture. Thus, coal could be considered a "valuable natural resource" only when we had discovered it, learned what to do with it, and had the technology to produce it in usable quantities.

Spatial Geography *or* the Location Theory Tradition

Spatial geography centers on the location of places and the patterns of distribution. This tradition seeks to explain why features such as cities, mountains, or human populations are arranged as they are on the earth's surface, and why there are differences in the densities, dispersions, and patterns. Another major part of this tradition is the geometry of the earth's surface, which includes the study of maps and the design of map projections (cartography), and the precise location and mapping of places and surfaces of the earth (geodesy and geodetic survey).

In recent years, spatial geography has tended to concentrate on developing theories of location. Spatial geographers have studied the central location of towns, the spatial interaction or movements of trade, people, and ideas, and the spatial structure of urban areas and their relation to surrounding areas. In marked contrast to the regional or cultural geographer, the spatial geographer is more likely to use quantified data and statistical methods to determine the interaction of a cluster of variables relating to economic activities. Perhaps more than any of the other geographic traditions described above, spatial geographers have attempted to develop high-order generalizations and to weave these into comprehensive theories about the location of place and space.

The Historical Geography Tradition

This is the study of the geographic change of a region as it has occurred over time. In contrast to the four approaches already described, historical geographers use time as the main dimension for studying spatial distributions and patterns on the earth's surface. They are chiefly concerned with how various features of the landscape appeared in the past and with the physical and human patterns that have combined to bring about a change in that landscape. Thus, the geographer shares with the historian the dimension of time—but in quite a different way. For example, a historian might consider the return of Lenin from exile as a key event in the Bolshevik Revolution of 1917, whereas a geographer might consider the elimination of private land-holdings and the establishment of collective farms during the 1920s as marking a significant change in the geography of Russia.

In summary, these five traditions or approaches to geography—*physical*, *regional*, *cultural*, *spatial*, and *historical*—represent a broad range of research interests and methods of investigation within geography. Elements of each are used in the social studies curriculum at various grade levels; each helps provide a balanced approach to the study of geography. Given these rich and varied traditions, there is little reason for teachers to rely so heavily upon the memorization of place names, capital cities, and lists of products as the exclusive approach to geography.

THE DEVELOPMENT OF GEOGRAPHIC THEORY

Geographers tend to be more concerned with developing maximum understanding of individual areas rather than with the formulation of broad universal laws and principles. Consequently, there has been comparatively little growth in the formation of theory that systematizes sets of high-order generalizations or principles into a comprehensive explanation of complex phenomena. In this section we will briefly describe three prominent theories in geography: (1) location theory, (2) central place theory, and (3) spatial structure theory.

Location Theory

How can we explain why things are located where they are? Is there some relationship, for example, between the location of cattle grazing lands and the distance to a meat packing center? Or if we wanted to locate a new branch of a business or a manufacturing plant, could we determine an optimal location? These questions are the concern of geographers (and economists, too), who are now able to turn to a rather well-developed body of knowledge, called *location theory*, for appropriate answers or ways of finding answers.

Location theory has at various times been a rather broad umbrella for studies derived from the related fields of economics, urban studies, and transportation studies. Essentially, it is the study of the geography of economic activities. Put more broadly, it is the study of the effects of place and space on the organization of economic activities.

Central Place Theory

Central place theory has played a key role in studying the location of towns and cities in urban geography. Based on a study of the agricultural towns in south Germany, Christaller[2] discovered that small villages tended to cluster about larger towns or cities in a rather hexagonal pattern. These larger towns served as the center for many important marketing, social, and cultural activities. The development of the railroad and, more recently, the interstate network of freeways and airways has greatly changed the growth and importance of many towns and cities, thus making Christaller's earlier concept of hexagonal trade patterns obsolete. Although many modifications have been made in central place theory, it remains an important component in the study of urban geography.[3]

Spatial Structure Theory

A third theory in geography that has considerable importance, especially in urban geography, is the spatial structure theory. In many ways this is an outgrowth of the central place theory. It conceives of space on the earth's surface as being ordered in a hierarchy of use and function. An expansion of the central place theory is that cities and towns are arranged in a functional hierarchy of ascending order, from the smallest hamlet through the town, the city, and finally to the large metropolitan center. Such theoretical patterns provide useful methods of examining and determining the ordered use of land and the patterns of various land usage.

Each of the three major theories—*location*, *central place*, and *spatial structure*—plays a useful role in describing, explaining, and predicting the complex events of the organization and interaction of place and space, especially as they relate to the field of urban geography. We will now discuss a number of the concepts that are central to the work of the geographer, ones that can serve as organizers for planning units in the elementary and junior high schools.

GEOGRAPHIC CONCEPTS

The broad areas of location theory and spatial interaction, urban spatial patterns, cultural diffusion, and environmental perception represent some of the more prominent geographic emphases in the social studies curriculum. Central to them are a number of key social science concepts and related subconcepts such as *location, spatial interaction, urban spatial patterns, internal structure of a city, cultural diffusion*, and *environmental perception*. Each of these is discussed below. Examples of how each concept might be taught at various school levels are given.

Location

One of the most essential tasks of the geographer is the location or identification of place and space. From earliest times, geographers have been concerned with the precise location of towns and rivers, great bodies of land or water, and other features. Systems of latitude and longitude, the distance between places expressed in miles, and measures of area all help to define or identify the location of particular places or spaces on the earth's surface. But the concept of *location* also includes several other closely related subconcepts that greatly extend the rather narrow meaning of precise location described above. These are *site, situation*, and *environment*.

Site refers to the location of a place in terms of its local internal features and resources. This may be the presence of a number of steep hills in a town, a winding river, sheltering hillsides, or the juncture of two main railroad lines. Such internal features are often key factors in studying the growth of a city, or related phenomena such as settlement patterns and the development of industry.

Situation refers to the larger context of a site. Thus, *situation* might refer to the location of a town within a valley and its surrounding hilly or mountainous country, or to the location of a larger city and its relation to the network of rail, air, and waterways that connect it to many other surrounding places. Thus, whereas *site* deals with the *internal* features of a place, *situation* deals with the *external relations* of the place and its interaction with other places.

The term *environment* is used to refer to the totality of both *site* and *situation*. In its broadest context, this includes the physical, biotic, and cultural features of the landscape and their interactions. Current usage of the term *environment* in the context of pollution and conservation of natural resources is too restricted and limited a use of the term. Students should use the term in its broadest meaning. *Cultural development* and *technological growth* are part of the total picture of the earth's surface.

Activities

1. In primary grades students can locate their school in terms of its *site*: for example, at the corner of Northfield Road and Clarkwood Street; near a lot of trees; close to the Granada apartments where I live.
2. Older students can use a map to identify the *situation* of their town: for example, surrounded on all sides by other small towns; a large freeway goes close by; the land is flat as far as you can see; part of Cuyahoga County that includes the city of Cleveland.
3. Use town maps with simple grid systems (letters along the top and bottom and numbers along the sides) to locate familiar landmarks: streets, schools, shopping centers, and so forth. Be sure students can use the system in both ways. They should be able to locate a street listed on the map index as Northfield Road, D-4, as well as to define the coordinates of a shopping center by tracing with their fingers (and later eyes alone) to the coordinates J-6.
4. In upper grades, ask students to describe the location of a city in terms of its *environment*. Cleveland, for example, might be described as being a major port city on Lake Erie with shipping links to the upper Midwest, Canada, and the Atlantic Ocean; rail, air, and highway connections to Chicago, St. Louis, and New York; steel mills and auto assembly plants; large and diverse ethnic populations; and an outstanding symphony orchestra and art museum.
5. With older students, use the latitude and longitude system of coordinates on the globe to teach the precise location of places (see Chapter 5). Locate New York, San Francisco, London, Canberra, Tokyo. (Note the many related concepts needed for a full understanding: hemisphere, Prime or Greenwich Meridian, east and west longitude, equator, north and south latitude and degrees of a circle [actually a half-circle] around the earth.)

Spatial Interaction

Very few places on earth exist entirely alone, isolated, or wholly independent from one another. Instead, people form relationships with other places as they move from one place to another, engage in economic trade, provide services, or transmit ideas, learning, and culture. Geographers use the term *spatial interaction* to refer to the relationship of one place to another within the surrounding space and to the varying degrees of mutual dependence that may exist between places. Chicago, for example, is the hub of a great metropolis with links to a ring of surrounding cities in other states including Milwaukee, Rockford, Indianapolis, and Toledo. Thus, the relationship between these cities and the hub city, Chicago, is called *spatial interaction*. Geographers look for the links that aid or hamper the movement of people, trade, or ideas between these cities and for the pattern these movements create. They use the subconcepts *circulation* and *access* to help describe the relationships in spatial interaction.

Circulation refers to the patterns of movement between places. Valleys, mountain passes, interstate highways, rivers, canals, and airways are types of geographic features serving as paths for the circulation of people or trade. In contrast, deserts, lakes, mountains, large swamps, and jungle areas are surface features that may at one time have been barriers to the easy movement of people and goods. Modern technology now provides the means for overcoming them. Yet curiously, it is the same technology which now creates new barriers to circulation. Major freeways bypass whole areas of the countryside or the crowded cities. Many smaller towns and cities now find themselves almost cut off entirely from the movement of goods, people, and ideas by freeways that skirt around them to provide high-speed movement, uninterrupted by the flow of local traffic.

Access deals with the easy entry into and exit from the circulation patterns. Cities that are intermediate stops along a main railroad or airline route, that have port facilities on a river or seacoast, or that have entry/exit cloverleaves along a superhighway are all examples of places with good *access* to the circulation pattern. In contrast, many island areas have only limited ferry service to the mainland and people in vast, remote areas such as Alaska and parts of Australia are connected to the "outside" only by the irregular flights of local bush pilots. In addition, it is not uncommon for people whose towns have been bypassed by freeways to have to drive 20 or 30 miles to enter or leave a modern highway. Lastly, as these same modern, "limited access" freeways cut across large cities, they create great concrete walls that divide traditional neighborhoods, force a major rearrangement of social patterns and often lead to urban decay. Thus, the modern technology that has helped us overcome some of the *circulation* limits of mountains and deserts presents new problems of *access* for small towns and inner-city urban areas.

Activities

1. Ask younger students to name cities or large towns near their homes where they go with their parents to shop, to go to movies or a museum, or to visit relatives. Ask them to describe how they get there and how long it takes. The teacher can draw a simple outline map on a wall chart to show direction flow and pattern of movement (circulation).

2. Is there a large interstate highway nearby? Ask older students where it goes and what cities are along its route. How close (or far away) is the nearest entry (access)?

3. Using markers and plastic overlays, trace on a map the various connecting links to major cities in your area (highways, railroads, airlines). Are there some links that are seldom used or no longer exist? Why?

4. Using the same maps as in activity 3, trace the linkage for ideas and communications. Where is the nearest regional postal center which sorts, distributes, and forwards all mail? Plot the network of towns

and local post offices that are served by the regional postal center. Where are the major and local television stations that serve your area located? Where are local and metropolitan newspapers published? How close or far away are these places?

5. Examine a map of your state or region that shows large interstate freeways. Are there bypassed towns or cities? Explain why and what is likely to happen to them in the future.

6. Have students interview parents or local merchants about how they were affected when a large freeway was built near or through their city or town.

7. Using a topographical or relief map, ask students to locate deserts, swamps, mountains, or large lakes. Investigate how these have been overcome or whether they still remain barriers today. Explain why.

Urban Spatial Patterns

The urban areas of the world provide geographers with an excellent opportunity to study the basic concept of *space* and how it is used. The concept *city*, for example, means a place providing many centralized and specialized services for itself and the surrounding area. The space or distance that people travel to work or shop in the city or to spend their leisure time there is called the city's *sphere of influence*. Put more specifically, what is the average distance a person drives or commutes to work in the city; the maximum distance? Conversely, this same concept applies to the space or distance that newspapers are delivered regularly from the city to outlying areas, that goods (both wholesale and retail) are normally delivered by trucks from city businesses, and by the distance of phone calls made regularly to and from the city. In short, how far beyond the corporate limits of the city does its influence extend? The space within the *sphere of influence* is variously known as the hinterland, the trade area, the supporting area, or the tributary area.

Another concept of key importance to the urban geographer is that of the town or city as a *central place*. Viewed as a kind of common marketplace, the town is organized to provide a variety of goods and services centralized within a single area. People will come a considerable distance to buy in this market what they cannot buy at a local cluster of convenience stores. Cities are much the same as towns, but only on a much larger scale. But the distance people are willing to travel is proportionate to both the time and cost of the journey and the cost and availability of goods or specialized services. At some point, however, people decide to purchase locally or to travel to some other town where goods are available at a lower cost in terms of time and money.

The growth of large shopping malls over the past 30 years, however, has brought about a major change in the geography of cities and has challenged the concept of the city as a *central place*. Built in outlying suburban areas with easy access to interstate freeways, the shopping malls are virtually small towns under one large roof with a year-round comfortable "climate." When a number of malls surround a city, they form a network of competing economic centers. Many people now do all their major shopping at a mall, and seldom if ever go downtown to the older *central business district*. As a result, many downtown stores and businesses moved out of the cities, often to new, more convenient locations in the shopping malls. This has been a major factor in the decay of older cities. For urban renewal planners, the pressing question is how to revitalize the inner core of the cities to attract people to come downtown once again for shopping, professional services, commercial transactions, recreation, and the like.

A development known as *gentrification* is contributing to the revitalization of the central cities. This process consists of the purchase and renovation of houses and stores in deteriorating inner-city communities by middle- and upper-class people. Gentrification, however, has some unfortunate social consequences. The lower-class individuals and small businesses who occupied the older, replaced housing and stores are displaced because they cannot afford to buy or rent the new and expensive properties. Despite its social costs, gentrification does attract young, affluent families, sometimes called *Yuppies*, to the central cities.

Not every city fits the model of a central place. Some cities do not have a central location nor do they provide centralized services. However, they may have a special feature around which an urban area has developed. They are referred to as *special place* locations. Such examples of *special place* locations are recreational centers such as Vail, Las Vegas, and Monte Carlo; mining centers such as Butte and Anaconda; and capital cities such as Olympia, Washington, Washington, D.C., and Brasilia.

Finally, there is the concept of *urban sprawl*. This refers to the gradual growth of a city from urban to suburban to rural areas, and the buildup of the areas in between. It is the outward extension of the city through a series of concentric rings. Current efforts at urban renewal suggest some reversal of the outward movement pattern and a trend of return to the central area of a city, closer to the central business district. Town houses are seen by some as a desirable alternative to the long, congested commuting trip from the suburbs.

What happens when urban growth becomes so great that the *urban sprawl* from one city gradually merges with that of another large city, and there is almost a continuous belt of urban development stretching many miles? Such a combination of large metropolitan areas is called a *megalopolis*. A gigantic urban sprawl stretches for more than 600 miles from southern New Hampshire to northern Virginia, and includes the cities of Boston, New York, Philadelphia, Baltimore, and Washington, D.C. This is the largest *megalopolis* in the world. Although the area involved represents only 1.8 percent of the United States, it contained 50 million people in 1980, or about 31 percent of the entire population of the United States. *Megalopolis*, therefore, is the *urban area* or *city* on the grandest scale imaginable.

Activities

1. Have students look at local newspaper stands. What newspapers are carried regularly? What paper comes from the city farthest away? Why do you think the store carries that newspaper? Compare the difference in amount and variety of advertising in the local paper and one from a large city. Explain the difference in the two papers.

2. Look in the front pages of a city telephone directory and study the map of local telephone exchanges. From how far out can you make a local call? At what point do the calls become long-distance?

3. Look at the advertisements of several major department stores in newspapers of a large city. How far will they normally deliver purchases such as a sofa or a refrigerator?

4. Examine the map of a nearby city's metropolitan transit authority. How far out from the city do the commuter bus lines extend? Rail or subway lines? At what point do major expressways begin to get crowded with inbound commuter traffic heading toward a city?

5. Take a walking tour of a nearby town (or a driving tour of a large city). Jot down in a notebook evidence of centralized facilities or services—for example, large warehouses, grain elevators, railroad yards, large department stores, oil storage tanks, airports (including air cargo terminals). What smaller communities do these facilities serve?

6. Drive along a major highway leading out of a city. How can you tell when you have left the major urban area and entered the suburban residential area? Is there a clear boundary or a gradual transition? How far do you go until you reach a clearly rural area? Or do you begin to reach another urban area? Mark off these different areas on a local road map.

7. Study the classified advertisements in the Sunday paper from a nearby city. Are there any housing ads designed to encourage suburbanites to move back into the city? What special attractions do they offer? Would you move? Explain why?

Internal Structure of a City

So far we have discussed the location of cities and their external relations with other cities. Let us consider briefly several concepts related to the city itself. The *internal structure* of a city comprises the arrangement of the parts of the city and the function of those parts. The basic pattern of the streets of the city, its *layout*, refers to the grid pattern of the streets, as in Denver; or the radiating spokes, as in Washington, D.C., or Paris; or to the riverine pattern of Nashville, Tennessee. One of the most useful concepts is the *central business district (CBD)*, which is the area marked by the convergence of transportation and commerce linkages. It is the major market center, the trade or business district. It is often referred to as *downtown* in contrast to the less commercial and more residential area often called *uptown*. In recent years huge suburban shopping centers have competed with the CBD. These malls mark the outward expansion of the city and serve as nuclei for the urbanization of residential areas.

The *circulation network* consists of major streets or rapid transit lines (buses, streetcars, subways, elevated trains, and so forth) into, out of, and around the city. New freeways provide fast and easy access to the suburbs and beyond, but also block off and isolate parts of the city by huge moats of concrete. Helicopters and air-taxis sometimes provide entirely new routes in the circulation network of the largest cities.

Another important concept for analyzing the internal structure of a city is its *land use patterns*. Most cities have clearly identifiable zones or sectors of differentiated use, such as the industrial area, the wholesale districts, the theater district, residential areas, the port or terminal transfer area, the retail sales–banking–office area, and the like. The location of these sectors often depends on the location of transportation facilities for the movement of people, goods, and services to and from the area. The change from fixed means of transportation, such as railroads or streetcars, to the more mobile cars, buses, and trucks has produced a series of newer sectors. The older ones have been left to decay; the result is the growth of slums.

Finally, there is the *social variation* in the internal structure of a city. In cities all over the world, minority groups of differing national origins, color, or religion can be found set apart from the rest of the populace in distinctive ethnic communities. Whether they congregate willingly, for reasons of social and cultural identity, or because of discrimination, different ethnic cultures and traditions or use of a language other than English may characterize a neighborhood for several generations. These districts are often among the poorest in the city. Color, however, has been a far more insidious barrier to movement within or out of the city than religion, language, or national origin has ever been. The restriction of Blacks to certain areas of the cities by a variety of legal, economic, and social pressures has created one of our most urgent social problems.

Another aspect of social variation is the level of wealth or income that clearly divides residential areas into upper-, middle-, and lower-income home districts, each with different levels of density, availability of living space, provision of public services, etc. Similarly, the retail trade area falls into districts based on the wealth or purchasing ability of its clientele. High-fashion shops tend to be uptown, whereas stores carrying low-cost goods, pawn shops, and secondhand stores tend to be in the older, decaying parts of the city. In recent years gentrification has affected the kinds of houses, stores, restaurants, and other types of businesses located in the central cities. The central areas of many cities are being renovated and revitalized. The huge and unfortunate growth in the rate of homelessness in the United States in recent years may result in part from the large number of poor people who have been displaced from their central city apartments and homes by gentrification.

Activities

1. Put a plastic overlay on a large map of a nearby city. Trace the main streets with colored pens. Is there a well-defined pattern to the arrangement of streets? How would you describe it?
2. Using a different overlay on the same map, mark off the main streets that contain most of the business offices and retail stores in a city or large town. This is the *central business district (CBD)*.
3. Observe the flow of traffic in a large city or town, particularly during a commuter rush hour. What are the streets that carry most of the traffic into, out of, or across the city at various points? A map showing the routes of buses and the rail lines of a metropolitan transit system will also demonstrate the circulation network of a city.
4. Using the map you made of the CBD in activity 2 above, outline areas or zones of different *land use patterns* in different colors. For example, outline manufacturing areas, grain or oil storage areas, theater districts, or residential areas.
5. Can you locate various ethnic or cultural neighborhoods on a map? A good clue to look for as you drive around a city is the location of churches, community centers such as a Polish-American club, or ethnic food stores or restaurants. The Yellow Pages in a phone directory may also give some clues.
6. Make a walking (or driving) tour of the residential area of a nearby city. What characteristics of the houses or of the neighborhood distinguish higher-income areas from lower-income ones?

Cultural Diffusion

An important anthropological concept used by geographers and often neglected in school geography is *cultural diffusion*. It refers to the distribution of some cultural trait such as language, education, ethnic origin, religion, or technological development within a particular area. The geographer interested in cultural diffusion asks: Where are such traits found? What is their dispersion? What is their density? Is the pattern of movement relatively fixed or highly mobile over time and space? What features of the earth's surface appear to be related to the diffusion (or restriction) of a particular cultural trait?

Many studies have traced the immigration and settlement patterns of French-Canadian and Scotch-Irish mill workers in New England, or of German and Scandinavian farmers in the Midwest. Others have traced the concentration or the spread of religious groups, the clustering of elderly citizens in certain areas, and the diffusion of rock music. While avoiding invidious

The study of the diverse cultures that make up U.S. society should be an integral part of geographical studies in the elementary and junior high school grades. (*Source*: Edna Kellman, Seattle Public Schools.)

comparisons, the alert and sensitive teacher can easily help students in the middle and upper grades to identify neighborhoods in which a different language is spoken, to plot the circulation range of a Spanish edition of a newspaper, to study the changing patterns of participation in such recreational areas as skiing, soccer, or camping, or to analyze the incidence of serious crime.

Activities

1. Locate areas of a city where other languages are spoken, such as Spanish, Greek, or Arabic. (A phone call to the Board of Education offices might quickly tell you which schools hold bilingual classes for children or which hold classes in English for adults.)
2. Check in the phone directory or on the newsstands for a foreign language newspaper. Where is it sold locally? Is it written and published in that local community or is it printed somewhere else and distributed nationally by mail to a network of ethnic communities? How long has the paper been in existence? (Your local library may also have copies of old foreign language newspapers that were once very popular in your city but are no longer published or sold there.)

3. Some sports, such as skiing, soccer, and gymnastics, have become increasingly more popular. Social geographers can trace the movement of such cultural changes. Check with the owner of a local sports store or a high school physical education department to find out where centers for such sports are located, who are the old hands and the newcomers at these sports, and how new interest was aroused and sustained. What part do various ethnic groups in the community play in supporting these sports?

4. Are senior citizens clustered in one or more distinct areas of your city? Visit a community planning agency for local census data that will show age, income levels, and type of housing for various census districts in your city.

5. Have students visit a home for elderly citizens where there are residents who come from different ethnic or cultural backgrounds. Interview residents to discover when and how they came to the city, where they lived, went to school, the jobs they held, and how things have changed (or remained the same) in their old neighborhoods.

Environmental Perception

The renewed concern of geographers for a better understanding of people and the environment has brought them into close contact with similar interests among psychologists and sociologists. Each has been concerned with the broad question "How do people view the world around them?" The feelings, attitudes, images, or ideas that result from cognitive structuring of physical and social environment are referred to as *environmental perception*. Geographers are especially interested in the differences in perception that different groups have of the same environmental area and in the distribution of such perceptions over space.[4] For example, the perceptions of resource *managers* (city planners, zoning commissioners, conservationists, forest wardens, etc.) are often quite different from those of the resource *users*, the people most immediately concerned. Note that the common restrictions on the uses of watershed areas and water systems are often viewed quite differently by campers, naturalists, boaters, hunters, industrialists, loggers, and those officials responsible for the reservoir and waterworks. Similar problems exist when parts of the land, especially urban areas, are perceived differently by various groups of people: the rich, the poor, Blacks, whites, and various other ethnic groups. Terms such as "across the tracks," "silk stocking neighborhood," and "snob hill" are common in our language and usually have negative connotations. Many towns and cities have sections in which particular ethnic groups have located. These areas are often referred to in a derogatory way as "coontown," "Jewtown," and the like. Mayors who are eager to drum up tourist trade may describe their city as an "exciting, fun city" but residents concerned with an alarming increase in crime may describe the same city as a "frightening jungle." A new group of geographers, called social geographers, has recently given considerable attention to how different groups of people, such as ethnic minorities, new residents, children, elderly people, and hospital patients, view their environmental surroundings and how these views may change as people move from place to place over time.

Activities

1. In many areas local school buildings are being closed because of declining enrollment. What new uses are being suggested for the buildings or the land? How do various community groups perceive these new uses?

2. Boating is becoming an increasingly popular recreation on our lakes, rivers, and oceans. However, many state and federal agencies raise concerns about human safety, increased pollution, danger to fish and wildlife, disruption of the natural ecology, and the uncontrolled growth of resort areas. Role play a public meeting where the conflicting claims of increased recreational use of public waterways are debated against the public interest concerns of governmental officials.

3. Have students interview various members of a community (e.g., residents, merchants, city officials, and so forth) for their perceptions about various parts of the city. Is there an upper-crust section, a tough area, a fashionable, stylish, or chic section, or a neighborhood that is referred to as "down and out" or "across the tracks"? How do they describe the downtown area (CBD) during the daytime? At night? Are there some areas where people are afraid to walk alone at night? Where they feel perfectly free and safe at any time? Are derogatory words used to describe some neighborhoods? Do city officials describe an area in one way, but residents or shop owners describe it quite differently? How would you account for such differences?

GENERALIZATIONS IN GEOGRAPHY

Geography has traditionally been more concerned with the development of descriptive and explanatory studies than with the formulation of empirical generalizations of wide universality. While there has been no lack of concepts within the discipline, they have served principally as organizing elements for analytical studies.

The generalizations which follow are directly related to the concepts discussed above. While some are predictive, most are descriptive or explanatory. Nevertheless, they represent appropriate end points for student learning in concept-oriented studies in geography. That is, classroom teaching should focus upon a variety of student activities and content examples so that students may formulate the generalizations (or some approximations in their own words). They can then test their applicability to a number of other similar situations.

For teachers, generalizations such as these represent convenient starting points for planning and organizing instruction, gathering appropriate materials, and devising activities to engage students in direct learning experiences. Many textbooks and school district curricula developed in recent years use generalizations as organizing principles or themes to provide for a coherent and integrated sequence of geographic learning from grade to grade.

Location

> Cities are located at places where there is easy access to one or more major routes of transportation.
> As knowledge of science and technology increased, people were able to locate and map places on the globe with greatly increased accuracy.

Spatial Interaction

> A variety of relationships exist between a city and the smaller towns surrounding it. These relationships are based on the exchange of trade, services, or ideas.
> Technological change tends to alter the established relationships between cities and towns and to affect the movement of people, trade, and services.

Urban Spatial Patterns

> A city's economic influence extends outward, to a wide area of the surrounding hinterland, and greatly affects the livelihood of many people.
> Cities provide a centrally located trading place and a ready supply of goods and services not available in the surrounding area.

Internal Structure of a City

> The transportation, commercial, and financial linkages of a city converge at one place to form a central trade or business district (CBD).
> The change from fixed means of transportation, such as railroads or streetcars, to more mobile cars, buses, and trucks results in the growth of new sectors of the city and the eventual deterioration of older sectors, resulting in slums.
> When immigrant or minority groups move into a city, they tend to congregate in clearly defined sections of the city in order to retain social or cultural identity and because of economic or social pressures.

Cultural Diffusion

> The movement of people with culturally different traits is facilitated by improved transportation and changes in technology.
> The interactions between an ethnically or culturally different group and the members of other groups in a community result in the gradual movement and exchange of cultural traits from place to place.

Geographical features of the earth such as oceans, mountains, and swamps tend to isolate certain people and cultural groups until they develop technological changes that permit them to conquer these barriers.

Environmental Perception

Groups of people view the environment differently, depending upon the value or worth they place upon its use.

The social conditions of a community will affect how its members or visitors perceive it.

Racial or ethnic biases affect how a person feels about or perceives a neighborhood where culturally different people live.

GEOGRAPHY IN THE SCHOOL

Geography has long been a part of the elementary school curriculum. Together with history, it was the mainstay of the social studies program. Geography has been taught in a variety of ways: as a separate discipline with its own textbook and separate content matter, as part of a multidisciplinary approach with special emphasis on geography at one or more grade levels, and as related knowledge in a broad, interdisciplinary study.

Trends in teaching geography in recent years have reflected an integrated social science approach, focused around broad themes or major social issues. Certain geographic topics have typically received major emphasis at a particular grade level. For example, students usually study their town or city in grade 2, their state or region in grade 4, a regional or cultural approach to Europe, Asia, or Africa in grade 6, and urban geography and physical geography in grades 7–8. At other times, geographic content is integrated when the curriculum focuses more directly upon history, as in the growth of the American nation in grade 5. Modern textbooks reflect these trends and organize content around relevant concepts and generalizations of geography. In a few places, geography is taught as a separate discipline. A separate geography textbook is used and the curriculum content is not integrated into a broader social science curriculum.

The National Council for Geographic Education and the Association of American Geographers have developed a set of guidelines for geographic education.[5] They have proposed a set of five fundamental themes or concepts in geography that should serve as the central core of all geographic studies in elementary grades. These are

1. *Location:* position on the earth's surface
2. *Place:* physical and human characteristics
3. *Relationships within places:* Humans and environments
4. *Movement:* Humans interacting on the earth
5. *Regions:* How they form and change

TABLE 14.1. Geography in the Elementary School

Kindergarten through Second Grade

1. Self in space
   Location
   Characteristics of place
2. Homes and schools in different places
   Relative location
   Characteristics of microenvironments
3. Neighborhoods—Small places in larger communities
   Location
   Place
   Environmental change
   Interdependence across space
   Interactions within and between neighborhoods
   Neighborhoods as regions with similarities and differences

Grades Three and Four

1. Community—Sharing space with others
   Relative location
   Characteristics of landscapes
   Environmental relationships
   Interdependence and interaction with community
   Community as a region
2. The State, nation, and world
   Location
   Nature and characteristics of places
   Interaction of human and physical environments
   Human interactions within and between state, nation, and world.
   Global interdependence
   The nature of regions

Grades Five and Six

3. United States, Canada, Mexico
   Location
   Comparative analysis of places
   Quality of life
   Human interaction in U.S. with Canada and Mexico
   Physical and cultural regions of U.S., Canada, and Mexico
4. Latin America, Europe, USSR, Middle East, Asia, Africa
   Location
   Physical and cultural geographic characteristics
   Human-environmental interactions
   Spatial interrelationships
   Regions and subregions of the world

SOURCE: Adapted from *Guidelines for Geographic Education: Elementary and Secondary Schools.* Prepared by the Joint Committee on Geographic Education of the National Council for Geographic Education and the Association of American Geographers, Washington, D.C.: 1984. Reprinted with permission of the publishers.

These concepts are used as the central themes for the study of geography in grades K–6 as shown in Table 14.1. They have been extended, and several alternative curriculum models have been developed that can be used in most school settings.[6]

SOME PERSISTENT ERRORS

While the teaching of geography has improved greatly in the last two decades—largely because of the interest and involvement of professional geographers in textbook writing and teacher training—old errors and misconceptions still persist. Outdated textbooks often convey a notion of geography as "exotic lands and strange people." We still find statements such as "geographic features determine how people make a living," a long-outmoded geographic determinism that fails to take into account people's ability to adapt or modify the environment through new technological developments. And nineteenth-century concepts of British colonialism still lock us into inaccurate and misleading terms, such as *Middle East* and *Far East*, which presume London is the center of the imperial world. Lastly, most classroom maps still use outdated Mercator projections that badly distort many parts of the earth, rather than some of the newer map projections, which are based on far more accurate photographs made from satellites orbiting in space.

TEACHING STRATEGIES

Generalization: *Regions can be distinguished according to physical features.*
Concepts: *Region; physical features.*

Primary Grades

The teacher begins by arousing interest with large colorful pictures of various geographic regions: tropical rain forests, deserts, tundra, marine climates, plains, Alpine mountains.

The teacher asks: "What are we looking at? Are these all the same? What is the same? What is different? What are the differences?" (Children might reply: hot, cold, dry, wet, plants, no plants, big mountains, and so on.)

After considerable discussion of similarities and differences, the teacher asks: "Could we put some of these pictures together in groups? Which ones seem to belong together?" Students get up and begin to move pictures to tables in different parts of the room. They sort and resort the piles of pictures, discussing similarities and differences, until they seem satisfied with each of the different piles of pictures.

The teacher asks: "What name could we call these different piles of pictures?" Children might reply: different kinds of places. Places that are different but that have the same kinds of things in them.

Teacher seeks to clarify: "What do you mean, different kinds of *things?*" Children reply: "Some places have lots of rocks; some have no rocks; some are all flat; some have lots of trees; that picture looks like a big jungle."

The teacher is satisfied that children have actually identified different geographic features to distinguish among the various groups of pictures they put together. The teacher instructs the class to call these different piles of pictures "different places that have the same kinds of things in them."

At various times during the next few days the children play with the pictures, challenging one another to sort and resort them into appropriate piles. Some children bring pictures from magazines into class and set up their own piles of "different places that have the same kinds of things in them." The teacher allows them to continue to use the awkward but correct title for groupings.

After several days or more, when the teacher is sure that all the children understand the process of sorting, grouping, and labeling the piles, the teacher asks: "Would you like to learn a special word that we use to name these 'different places that have the same kinds of things in them'? We call these different places *regions*, and we call the same kinds of things *physical features*." The teacher repeats and practices the new words with the class. They seem proud to show off their new vocabulary (though a few still continue to stick with the phrase they learned first.)

Intermediate Grades

Regional studies are typically found in the intermediate grades, frequently grade 4. The students learned to form the basic concept of *region* in the primary grades and to distinguish common physical features as a criterion for the concept. Here we shall use the case study approach, so that students will see the region as a totality and will establish relationships between its many other features.

The teacher selects one example of a wet tropical forest area for which materials are available, for example, Amazon rain forest, portions of the Hawaiian Islands, or other tropical islands.

The teacher shows a picture of one specific wet tropical region, such as the Amazon area, and asks, "What can we tell about this place from its picture?" (It probably rains a lot, it has a lot of plants and trees; there are probably only a few people there; there might be a big river there.) The teacher asks each student his or her reason for thinking that the idea is true and records the idea on the board.

After they have done as much research and inferring as they can from the picture and from other sources such as reference books, letters from people in the area, and stories about the area, the teacher asks, "What are the specific and special things that work together to make the Amazon region what it is?"

The study of an entire region is designed to help students perceive the totality of one particular place, people, or time, as opposed to the analytic approach, in which students focus on one aspect—land forms, or cultural adoptions. It is a geographic case study of a region. This case study could be focused on one point in time or it could focus on one region throughout time.

Upper Grades

This strategy is designed for use with students in upper grades, who may be studying urban geography and who may already have some historical knowledge of the westward movement in the United States. The purpose of this activity is to focus on one specific region and observe the role of its river in influencing where people settle. The teacher can use Memphis, Minneapolis, St. Louis, Detroit, Pittsburgh, or a similar city.

In focusing on a river town, the students will observe how people can get goods and services more easily because of the river. They will observe the complete integration of the lives of the people and their needs with the role of the river.

1. *Concept Diagnosis.* The first objective for the students is to determine topics on which they want information about the city in question. The teacher might ask, "What kinds of information do you think you should have about the city, based on what you know about cities in general and about this city in particular?" These categories of knowledge can function as areas for committee research and for labels on a data retrieval chart to be constructed (see Table 14.2).
2. *Data Collection.* The teacher can then help the students record their data on a chart so that they can use it in generating hypotheses about the way in which the parts of the city are integrated.
3. *Generalizing.* The third stage of this investigation is the discussion of patterns that seem to appear in the data retrieval chart. The teacher asks whether the students see any patterns in the way things work together, and the whole class evaluates the possibility of patterns and the implications each pattern might have for the whole city or for individual parts of it. In free-flowing ways they can explore the values involved in the pattern.
4. *Definition of Problem.* This strategy follows quite naturally from gathering data regarding one particular city and from observing the relationships among people, goods, services, and regions. The purpose here, as it is in geography in general, is to understand the interactions of people, space, and time. In this instance the teacher may present the class with a specific problem. The problem may be related to the way people value the existing relationships of people and space and time. For example, the problem could be "Given that people have overcome their dependence on river transportation and considering the level of technology that exists today, what are the best ways in which we can plan locations of future cities?"

TABLE 14.2. The Influence of a River upon a City

Concepts	Memphis	St. Louis	Pittsburgh
Location			
Place			
Spatial Interactions			
Internal Structure			
Cultural Diffusion			
Impact of Technology			

5. *Proposing Solutions—Value Clarification.* Once the problem has been defined, the teacher can form groups, or can allow the class to form its own structure for tackling the problem. By the upper grades, if the valuing process has been used before by the teacher, the students can go through the steps on their own and only later resume in a larger group to discuss their chosen solutions. For classes going through this process for the first time, the teacher could ask, "What are the possible alternatives available?" These could be listed vertically under the label: "Alternatives." The teacher could then ask, "What would the consequences be for each alternative suggested?" and some beginning ideas could be sketched out.

This kind of problem is open enough so that each student can approach it on an appropriate level of sophistication. Some pupils might want to research carefully the alternatives and probable consequences; others might wish to use whatever information they have available at the time. The only requirement is that the individual think through alternatives and consequences, and be able to provide a rationale for his or her choice or lack of choice.

SUMMARY

In this chapter we considered the role of the geographer and the five traditions of the discipline: physical, spatial, cultural, regional, and historical. We examined the place of geography among the social sciences and saw that it ranged widely in the continuum, close to the physical sciences at one end, and close to the humanities at the other. The regional method was seen as the principal research method of the geographer. It was approached in two quite different ways: the broad area study and the topical or systematic approach. In practice, however, the geographer actually uses both approaches. Quantitative methods and the use of maps, globes, and special cartographic projections constitute the special techniques and tools of research.

In discussing geography as a generalizing discipline, we pointed out that the geographer, perhaps because of the nature of the discipline, has tended to concentrate more on individual studies than on the development of general laws or theory. Out of these extensive studies on individual regions of the earth have come a large body of concepts, a group of generalizations of somewhat restricted application (mostly at the regional level), and a comparatively small body of theory. Three of these theories were discussed briefly: location theory, central place theory, and spatial structure and organization. A large number of concepts selected from the general area of urban geography were discussed in detail. Activities and strategies for teaching selected geographic concepts and generalizations were described.

DISCUSSION QUESTIONS AND EXERCISES

1. Summarize briefly each of the five traditions in the discipline of geography, and show how each contributes to the study of place and space. How can each tradition be reflected in elementary and junior high school geography?
2. Compared with the other social science disciplines, geography has many concepts, comparatively few high-order generalizations, and only a very limited body of theory. How can you explain this situation?
3. Examine a social studies curriculum in a local school district. Does it reflect evidence of some of the newer trends in the development of geography education described in this chapter? In what areas is it deficient?
4. Look over a sampling of social studies textbooks from a local school district. What place is given to geography? What emphasis within geography does it reflect? To what extent does it provide materials for social inquiry, valuing, and decision-making as described in Chapter 1 of this book?
5. Demonstrate your understanding of the following key concepts by writing or stating brief definitions for each of them. Also tell why each is significant.

   a. physical geography
   b. regional geography
   c. cultural geography
   d. human–land tradition
   e. spatial geography
   f. historical geography
   g. the regional method
   h. megalopolis
   i. location theory
   j. central place theory

   k. environment
   l. spatial interaction
   m. circulation
   n. sphere of influence
   o. urban spatial patterns
   p. central business district (CBD)
   q. cultural diffusion
   r. ecological system
   s. environmental perception

NOTES

1. Jan O. M. Broek et al., *The Study and Teaching of Geography* (Columbus, OH: Merrill, 1980).

2. Walter Christaller, *Central Places in Southern Germany* (Englewood Cliffs, NJ: Prentice-Hall, 1966).

3. Robert A. Harper and Theodore H. Schmuddle, *Between Two Worlds: An Introduction to Geography*, 2nd ed. (Boston: Houghton Mifflin, 1978).

4. Thomas F. Saarinen, "Environmental Perception," in Phillip Bacon, Ed., *Focus on Geography: Key Concepts and Teaching Strategies*, 40th Yearbook (Washington, D.C.: National Council for the Social Studies, 1970), pp. 63–99.

5. *Guidelines for Geographic Education: Elementary and Secondary Schools* (Washington, D.C.: Joint Committee on Geographic Education of the National Council for Geographic Education and the Association of American Geographers, 1984).

6. Natoli, Salvatore J., Ed., *Strengthening Geography in the Social Studies*, Bulletin No. 81 (Washington, D.C.: National Council for the Social Studies, 1988).

FOR FURTHER READING

Guidelines for Geographic Education: Elementary and Secondary Schools Washington, D.C.: Joint Committee on Geographic Education of the National Council for Geographic Education and the Association of American Geographers, 1984.

Natoli, Salvatore J., Ed. *Strengthening Geography in the Social Studies*, Bulletin No. 81. Washington, D.C.: National Council for the Social Studies, 1988.

PART _____ IV

Value Inquiry, Decision-Making, Citizen Action, and Evaluation Strategies

(*Source*: The National Archives, Washington, D.C.)

In previous chapters, we pointed out why higher-level scientific knowledge is essential for sound decision-making. However, knowledge in itself is not sufficient. Citizen actors must also be able to identify and clarify their values before they can take effective action to solve personal problems or influence public policy. Values deeply influence human behavior. The first part of

Chapter 15 sets forth a rationale for value education, reviews several policy-making and valuing models, and presents a value-inquiry model that you can use to help students to identify and clarify their values. Valuing activities are also described.

Once decision-makers have gained higher-level knowledge and clarified their values, they must synthesize their knowledge and values in order to determine their courses of action. The second part of Chapter 15 focuses on how decision-makers relate their derived knowledge to their values in order to make decisions and to determine courses of action on social issues. This part of Chapter 15 illustrates how skills and knowledge components discussed in earlier chapters can be applied to help citizen actors make reflective decisions and intelligently influence public policy. Activities and strategies that can help students gain proficiency in valuing and decision-making skills constitute an important part of Chapter 15.

To assure that the skills constituting decision-making and citizen action are mastered by your students, you must have effective ways to evaluate student achievement. Chapter 16 presents a number of techniques you can use to evaluate student behavior. While evaluation should be a continuous process in teaching, we focus on the topic here to emphasize its importance.

15

Valuing, Decision-Making, and Citizen Action

VALUE INQUIRY: NATURE AND APPROACHES

The Value Component of Decision-Making

While knowledge is an essential component of decision-making, it is not sufficient. To make reflective decisions, citizen actors must identify and clarify their values, and relate them to the knowledge they have derived. The valuing component is a very important part of the decision-making process; values often determine what knowledge an individual will accept or reject. Value confusion often results in contradictory and confused citizen action.

The Nature of Values

A universally agreed upon definition of value does not exist in either the social sciences or philosophy. Rokeach defines value as a ". . . type of belief, centrally located within one's total belief system, about how one ought or ought not to behave, or about some end-state of existence worth or not worth attaining."[1] Values, unlike attitudes and other beliefs, are not related to any specific things, persons, or groups, but are very general and influence a person's behavior toward a large class of objects or persons. A value is also a standard for determining whether something is good or bad, and for judging one's own behavior. People learn their values, as they do most other beliefs and attitudes, from the persons in their social environment. Most values are not reflectively and independently derived. The social origin of values explains why most people socialized within the same culture, subculture, or social system are likely to have similar values.

Value Conflicts in Individuals and in Society

Most individuals socialized within modernized societies do not attain a set of clarified values but inculcate values that are contradictory and at odds with each other. This creates value confusion and value problems. Conflicting values are found within individuals as well as within the larger society. Both freedom and equality are part of the American creed, yet in practice these values often conflict. Landlords who want the freedom to rent to whomever they please may not rent to nontraditional families or to couples with young children, thus denying these individuals equality. Shaver and Strong comment on the inherent conflicts in American creed values, such as equality, justice, and freedom. "Extensions of freedom of speech are likely to encroach on domestic tranquility; greater equality for some—the outcome of the civil rights movement—results in limitations on the liberty of others. In no instance is any one value likely to be fully realized as the society struggles toward the ultimate ideal of dignity for all."[2]

The value problems faced by youths in modernized democratic societies are especially acute. Much more than youths in traditional societies, they are faced with an infinite number of value alternatives from which they must choose, many of which are contradictory. The mass media and the tremen-

Value inquiry should help students to clarify their values and to make decisions of which they are proud. (*Source*: Robb Mitchell, Lake Washington School District, Seattle.)

dous mobility within modern society expose today's youths to a wide variety of life-styles and belief systems. Their problems are complicated by the fact that they are expected to move from childhood to adulthood within a short span of time, and therefore to live by two different sets of standards. Young people often become cynical when adults fail to live up to the ideals they expound. They interpret the failure of adults to live up to certain ideals as the absence of the ideals themselves. As Shaver and Strong point out, people can hold ideals, such as equality and honesty, without always living up to them.[3] However, this is often difficult for young people to understand and appreciate.

Value Education in the Schools

Because the social and personal problems within modern society are rooted in value confusion, the school should play an important role in helping students to identify and clarify their values, and to make value choices intelligently. However, many teachers fail to help students deal with moral issues intelligently.[4]

Some teachers treat value problems like invisible people. They deny their existence. They assume that if students get all of the facts correct, they can solve important social problems. These teachers practice the cult of false objectivity. Other teachers use an evasion strategy. When value problems arise in the classroom, they try to change to a safer topic. When issues such as genetic screening, gay rights, and political scandals come up in the classroom, they are quickly and forcefully dismissed by teachers who use the evasion strategy.

Probably the most frequently used approach to value education in the elementary and junior high school is the indoctrination of values considered correct by adults. Such values as justice, truth, freedom, honesty, and equality are taught along with legendary heroes, stories, rituals, and patriotic songs. A major goal of value inquiry in U.S. schools should be to help students develop a commitment to American creed values such as equality and human dignity. However, we cannot use an indoctrination approach when trying to help students develop a reflective commitment to democratic values. An indoctrination approach violates democratic values and does not help students develop a method for deriving and clarifying their own values.

The didactic inculcation of values is also unsound because it assumes that most value conflicts and problems result because students are unable to distinguish "good" from "bad" values. However, this is not the case. Students can rather easily distinguish good from bad. Most value problems result because students must often choose between two goods. For example, if a student's friend asked his opinion of a very poor drawing, he must decide whether to be honest or courteous. To be honest would hurt his friend's feelings, and he would therefore not be courteous. When teachers use didactic methods to teach students contradictory but equally "good" values, such conflicts are intensified.

Didactic methods are also unsound because they deny students freedom of choice and do not teach students how to derive, clarify, and justify their moral choices. While we should require students to defend their moral choices within the context of societal values such as human dignity and equality, each generation must have the opportunity to define the meanings of these idealized values. We cannot expect standards to guide a person's life unless those standards have been freely chosen from alternatives, and after thoughtful consideration of the consequences of the alternatives. Individuals must also be proud of the standards that guide their behavior.[5] If teachers and other adults force values on students, students will not prize the values. The forced standards will have little influence on their behavior when they are out of the presence of authorities.

The Goals of Value Education

The major goal of value education should be to help students to develop a set of consistent, clarified values that can guide purposeful and reflective citizen action. This goal can best be attained by teaching students a method or process for deriving their values within a democratic classroom atmosphere. In this kind of democratic classroom, students must be free to express their values choices, determine how those choices conflict, examine alternative values, consider the consequences of different value choices, make value choices, and defend their moral choices within the context of human dignity and other American creed values. Students must be given an opportunity to reflectively derive their own values in order to develop a commitment to human dignity, equality, and to other democratic values. They must be given an opportunity to reflect upon value choices within a democratic atmosphere in order to internalize values. Values must be freely chosen from alternatives, and after thoughtful consideration of the consequences of each alternative, before they can be internalized.[6]

VALUING: MODES OF INQUIRY AND APPROACHES

We have suggested that teachers should help students develop a method or process for clarifying and deriving their own values rather than teach values didactically. This is the only approach to value education that is consistent with a democratic ideology and that is pedagogically sound. While no standardized value-inquiry model exists within social science or philosophy, several models have been developed that emphasize uncoerced choice. Important models have been developed by Hunt and Metcalf, Oliver and Shaver, Newmann, and Kohlberg.[7] The Hunt and Metcalf model is designed to help students analyze value problems related to what they call the "problematic areas of culture," such as social class, religion and morality, and race and minority-group relations. Using this model, the students define value concepts, project consequences, appraise consequences using set criteria, and attempt to justify the criteria used to evaluate the consequences.

FIGURE 15.1 Newmann's approach to the analysis of policy issues. (*Source*: Reprinted with permission from Fred N. Newmann [with the assistance of Donald W. Oliver], *Clarifying Public Controversy: An Approach to Teaching Social Studies* [Boston: Little, Brown and Company, 1970], p. 43.)

Oliver and Shaver and Newmann have structured policy-making and valuing strategies that are based on the assumption that most Americans are committed to values in the American creed, such as justice, equality, and human dignity. In their view, public controversy results primarily from conflicting values in the American creed and diverse interpretations of these values. Some values within the creed are more important than others. *Human dignity* is the most basic American value. Write Shaver and Strong, "This belief that each individual has worth and deserves consideration because he is human—and equal to anyone else in that sense, if not in wealth, intellect, or physical prowess—is, we believe, central to democracy. Its essence is captured in the phrase human dignity."[8] Oliver and Shaver and Newmann propose methods whereby public controversy can be resolved through rational discussion. Newmann suggests that policy issues involve three components: (1) a moral issue, (2) a definitional issue, (3) a fact-explanation issue.[9] (See Figure 15.1.)

Kohlberg developed a theory of moral development heavily influenced by Piaget's theory of cognitive development. Briefly, it states that an individual's ability to reason morally develops sequentially, in a series of definite steps or stages. Kohlberg identified three levels of moral development: (1) *the preconventional*, (2) *the conventional*, and (3) *the postconventional*.[10] These levels consist of six stages (see Table 15.1). The six stages constitute a hierarchy; each higher stage is a more sophisticated and rational form of moral reasoning. At stage 1, moral reasoning is influenced mainly by a desire to avoid punishment and a deference to power and authority. This stage contrasts strikingly with stage 6. At stage 6, moral reasoning is influenced by universal ethical principles such as justice, equality, and the sanctity of human life.

Kohlberg determined the levels of moral reasoning of individuals by analyzing their responses to story problems that presented moral dilemmas. They were asked to state what actions the main character in the story should take and to give reasons for their choice. Kohlberg believed that there is a relationship, but not a direct one, between chronological age and level of moral development. Very young children tend to reason at the lower stages. As individuals grow older they tend to reason at higher stages.

The notion that moral education must be based on the students' level of

TABLE 15.1. A Brief Characterization of Kohlberg's Six Stages

I. Preconventional Level

At this level the child is responsive to cultural rules and labels of good and bad, right or wrong, but interprets these labels either in terms of the physical or the hedonistic consequences of action (punishment, reward, exchange of favors) or in terms of the physical power of those who enunciate the rules and labels. The level is divided into the following two stages:

Stage 1: *The punishment-and-obedience orientation.* The physical consequences of action determine its goodness or badness regardless of the human meaning or value of these consequences. Avoidance of punishment and unquestioning deference to power are valued in their own right, not in terms of respect for an underlying moral order supported by punishment and authority (the latter being stage 4)

Stage 2: *The instrumental-relativist orientation.* Right action consists of that which instrumentally satisfies one's own needs and occasionally the needs of others. Human relations are viewed in terms like those of the market place. Elements of fairness, of reciprocity, and of equal sharing are present, but they are always interpreted in a physical pragmatic way. Reciprocity is a matter of "you scratch my back and I'll scratch yours," not of loyalty, gratitude, or justice.

II. Conventional Level

At this level, maintaining the expectations of the individual's family, group, or nation is perceived as valuable in its own right, regardless of immediate and obvious consequences. The attitude is not only one of *conformity* to personal expectations and social order, but of loyalty to it, of actively *maintaining,* supporting, and justifying the order, and of identifying with the persons or group involved in it. At this level, there are the following two stages:

Stage 3: *The interpersonal concordance or "good boy–nice girl" orientation.* Good behavior is that which pleases or helps others and is approved by them. There is much conformity to stereotypical images of what is majority or "natural" behavior. Behavior is frequently judged by intention—"he means well" becomes important for the first time. One earns approval by being "nice."

Stage 4: *The "law and order" orientation.* There is orientation toward authority, fixed rules, and the maintenance of the social order. Right behavior consists of doing one's duty, showing respect for authority, and maintaining the given social order for its own sake.

III. Postconventional, Autonomous, or Principled Level

At this level, there is a clear effort to define moral values and principles that have validity and application apart from the authority of the groups or persons holding these principles and apart from the individual's own identification with these groups. This level again has two stages:

Stage 5: *The social contract, legalistic orientation*, generally with utilitarian overtones. Right action tends to be defined in terms of general individual rights, and standards which have been critically examined and agreed upon by the whole society. There is a clear awareness of the relativism of personal values and opinions and a corresponding emphasis upon procedural rules for reaching consensus. Aside from what is constitutionally and democratically agreed upon, the right is a matter of personal "values" and "opinion." The result is an emphasis upon the "legal point of view," but with an emphasis upon the possibility of changing law in terms of rational considerations of social utility (rather than freezing it in terms of stage 4 "law and order"). Outside the legal realm, free agreement and contract is the binding element of obligation. This is the "official" morality of the American government and constitution.

Stage 6: *The universal-ethical-principle orientation.* Right is defined by

TABLE 15.1. (continued)

the decision of conscience in accord with self-chosen *ethical principles* appealing to logical comprehensiveness, universality, and consistency. These principles are abstract and ethical (the Golden Rule, the categorical imperative); they are not	concrete moral rules like the Ten Commandments. At heart, these are universal principles of *justice*, of the *reciprocity* and *equality* of human *rights*, and of respect for the dignity of human beings as *individual persons.*

SOURCE: Lawrence Kohlberg, "The Claim to Moral Adequacy of a Highest Stage of Moral Judgment," *The Journal of Philosophy 70* (18):631–632 (25 October 1973). Reprinted with permission.

moral development and that students will be unable to understand levels of moral reasoning more than one stage higher than their own is central to Kohlberg's theory.[11] A related assumption is that instruction below the students' stage of moral development will not stimulate their moral growth. Another basic assumption of Kohlberg's theory is that an individual must proceed through the stages sequentially and that none can be skipped. Kohlberg's research indicated that when individuals participate in discussions of real moral dilemmas and are asked questions that require them to reason at one stage above their own, moral growth is stimulated. Such discussions and dilemmas can help individuals to move to, but not beyond, the next higher stage of moral development. Kohlberg believed that the major aim of moral education should be to stimulate students so that they might move to the next higher stage.

A VALUE INQUIRY MODEL

We have discussed the nature of values, presented and defended a position regarding value education that emphasizes reflective inquiry and uncoerced choice, and reviewed several approaches to moral education. The major approaches, as summarized by Superka et al., are presented in Table 15.2. It is now appropriate to present a valuing model consistent with the theory of social studies education presented in this book and one that you can use when teaching value lessons or giving students opportunities to increase their proficiency in decision-making skills.

Our valuing model is consistent with the position of value education defended above. It is a model that enables students to identify the sources of their values and those of others, to determine how values conflict, to identify value alternatives, to predict the consequences of alternative values, to freely choose from the values that they can identify, and to justify their moral choices in terms of American creed values such as equality and human dignity. To successfully implement this valuing strategy in the classroom, you must have a firm commitment to the belief that students must freely choose their own values. At the same time, students should be helped to discover the consequences of different values, be consistent in their value choices, be required to defend and justify their moral choices in terms of *human dignity*, and be willing to accept the consequences of and to act on their beliefs.

PROFILE

Carol Gilligan

A Different Voice in Moral Development

Carol Gilligan, a professor in the Graduate School of Education at Harvard, is an influential and different voice in moral development. She has contributed to our understanding of the ways in which the concepts and interpretations used to study moral development are human constructions and has deepened our insights into the moral development of women. In her important and best-selling book, *In a Different Voice: Psychological Theory and Women's Development*, she challenges the way male psychologists have conceptualized as mere weaknesses some of the moral characteristics of women. She writes, "Sensitivity to the needs of others and the assumption of responsibility for taking care lead women to attend to voices other than their own and to include in their judgment other points of view. Women's moral weakness, manifest in an apparent diffusion and confusion of judgment, is thus inseparable from women's moral strength, an overriding concern with relationships and responsibilities [p. 17]."

Role-playing and dramatic activities are excellent vehicles for helping students to analyze their values and beliefs. (*Source*: Edna Kellman, Seattle Public Schools.)

When you develop value inquiry lessons, you should consider seriously the age and developmental levels of your students. Students should not be required to reason morally beyond their stage of moral development. Most primary grade children will be unable to reason about complicated moral issues that involve high-level ethical principles. However, they can understand simple stories and dilemmas that involve values such as honesty, truth, and loyalty. Sensitive teachers will carefully tune value lessons to their students' levels of moral and cognitive development.

1. Defining and Recognizing Value Problems: Observation-Discrimination

To intelligently reflect on values and to resolve issues, students must be able to recognize the value components of decision-problems, and to distinguish definitional, value, and scientific problems. You can use case studies, incidents from novels and stories, factual information, and open-ended stories to teach students to recognize the value components of decision-problems.

To help students develop skills in defining and recognizing value prob-

TABLE 15.2. Overview of Typology of Value Education Approaches

Approaches	Purposes	Methods	Examples of Materials	
			Title	Developers
Inculcation	To instill or internalize certain values in students. To change the values of students so they more nearly reflect certain desired values.	Modeling; positive and negative reinforcement; mocking; nagging, manipulating alternatives; providing incomplete or biased data; games and simulations; role playing; discovery learning	*Human Values Series* *Coronado Plan: Teacher's Guides*	Blanchette et al. (1970) Bensley (1974)
Moral development	To help students develop more complex moral reasoning patterns based on a higher set of values. To urge students to discuss the reasons for their value choices and positions, not merely to share with others, but to foster change in the stages of reasoning of students.	Moral dilemma episodes with small-group discussion relatively structured and argumentative	*First Things: Values* "Teaching Strategies for Moral Dilemmas"	Kohlberg and Selman (1970) Galbraith and Jones (1975)
Analysis	To help students use logical thinking and scientific investigation to decide value issues and questions. To help students use rational,	Structured rational discussion that demands application of reasons as well as evidence; testing principles; analyzing	*Public Issues Series* *Analysis of Public Issues Program* *Values Education*	Oliver and Newmann (1967–72) Shaver and Larkins (1973) Metcalf (1971)

TABLE 15.2. (*continued*)

Approaches	Purposes	Methods	Examples of Materials	
			Title	**Developers**
	analytical processes in interrelating and conceptu-alizing their values.	analogous cases; debate; research		
Clarification	To help students become aware of and identify their own values and those of others. To help students communicate openly and honestly with others about their values. To help students use both rational thinking and emotional awareness to examine their personal feelings, values, and behavior patterns.	Role-playing games; simulations; contrived or real value-laden situa-tions; in-depth self-analysis exercises; sensitivity activities; out-of-class activities; small group discussion	*Decision and Outcomes* *Values and Teaching* *Values Clarification* *Values in Action* Scholastic *Contact* Series A Probe into Values	Gelatt et al. (1973) Raths et al. (1966) Simon et al. (1972) Shaftel and Shaftel (1970) Goody-Koontz (1968–74) Church (1973)
Action learning	Those purposes listed for analysis and clarification. To provide students with opportunities for personal and social action based on their views. To encourage students to view them-selves as personal-	The methods listed for analysis and clarification as well as action projects within the school and commu-nity and skill practice in group organiz-ing and interpersonal relations	*Finding Community* *Social Action*	Jones (1971) Newmann (1972)

(*continued*)

TABLE 15.2. *(continued)*

| | | | Examples of Materials | |
Approaches	Purposes	Methods	Title	Developers
	social interac-tive beings, not fully autonomous, but members of a commu-nity or social system.			

SOURCE: Douglas P. Superka, Christine Ahrens, Judith E. Hedstrom, with Luther J. Ford and Patricia L. Johnson, *Values Education Sourcebook: Conceptual Approaches, Materials Analyses, and an Annotated Bibliography* (Boulder, CO: ERIC Clearinghouse for Social Studies/Social Science Education, 1976). Reprinted by permission of the Social Science Education Consortium.

lems, you can read an open-ended story such as "Finders Weepers"[12] and ask such questions as What is the problem in this situation? What things are important to the individuals in this story?

Finders Weepers

In "Finders Weepers," an open-ended story by the Shaftels, Eddie, Pete, and Tom are visiting Eddie's uncle for a week. Uncle Ross told the boys to have fun and to enjoy the big lake but not to use the boat. While Eddie and Tom were swimming, Pete ignored his promise to Uncle Ross and rowed the boat into the lake. While Eddie scolded Pete, all of the boys enjoyed using the boat. On the last day of their visit, the boat was missing. When they found it a mile away it was badly damaged. It will take $30 to repair the boat. The boys have only $11 more than their bus fare home. In the bus station they find a wallet that contains $22 in cash and a check for $292. Pete argues strongly that they should keep the money and turn the check and the wallet in at the Lost and Found office at the bus station. Eddie argues just as strongly that they should not keep the money and should turn the wallet with the money and the check in at the Lost and Found office. They decide to vote on the matter. Tom must cast the deciding vote.

2. Describing Value-Relevant Behavior: Description-Discrimination

In this phase of value inquiry, the student names the behavior of the individuals in the problem story, event, or situation. Not every action or gesture needs to be described; only the behavior central to the problem under discussion. If the class is discussing an open-ended story such as "Finders Weepers," the students should briefly describe the behavior of the characters: Uncle Ross, Pete, Eddie, and Tom. They should not describe every word said by each character, but should try to summarize their behavior in one or two sentences. They might describe Pete's behavior in this way: "Pete was the first to use the boat. He wanted to take the money out of the wallet before turning it in at the Lost and Found office at the bus station." You can ask questions to help students accurately describe the relevant behavior in a problem situation: "What did Pete do?" "What did Eddie and Tom do?" When the students are describing behavior, they should make as few inferences as possible. Students should be taught to clearly distinguish *observation*, *inferences*, and *value judgments* during this phase of value inquiry.[13]

3. Naming Values Exemplified by Behavior Described: Identification-Description, Hypothesizing

In this phase of value inquiry, the students try to name the values evidenced by the behavior described in step 2. To facilitate this phase of inquiry, you can list the behavior on the board in one column, and related values next to the behavior in another column. During this process, the students will make inferences, and will not necessarily always agree on the values they see in the behavior described. While you should encourage independent thinking at this point, you should require the students to give reasons for the values they identify. This phase of inquiry requires the relating of behavior and values to be as accurate as possible even though the pupils may have limited information about the individuals in the problem situation.

In discussing the open-ended story "Finders Weepers," you can ask these questions during this phase of value inquiry: "What does the behavior of Pete tell us about what is important to him?" "What was more important to Pete, honesty or getting out of trouble?" "What was most important to Eddie?" "What was most important to Uncle Ross?" "In our role play of the story, what was most important to Tom?"

4. Determining Conflicting Values in Behavior Described: Identification-Analysis

To help students discover that there are many value conflicts within our society as well as within individuals, you can ask the students to name conflicting values exemplified by particular individuals and evident in the behavior of different persons. When the class is studying "Finders Weepers," you can ask questions that help the students to describe Eddie's conflicting values. He did not want his Uncle Ross to get angry at him for using the boat. Yet he wanted to have fun. When Pete started using the boat, both he and Tom participated and enjoyed using the boat with Eddie. Eddie wanted both to have fun with the boat and to please his uncle. These desires were conflicting.

You can help middle-grade students to develop skills in identifying conflicting values by studying major historical decisions and the value conflicts experienced by past leaders. President McKinley anguished about whether to give the Philippines independence after the Spanish-American War in 1898 or to annex that nation to the United States. In an interesting and revealing document, he tells a church group how he walked the floor of the White House night after night and prayed before he decided to annex the Philippines to the United States. When studying this important decision, students can analyze the political, cultural, and ethical factors that influenced McKinley's decision. Some Americans were very unhappy with McKinley's decision. Samuel Clemens (Mark Twain) was one of them. The students could discuss ways in which the values of McKinley and Twain, in this situation, conflicted.

5. Hypothesizing about the Sources of Values Analyzed: Hypothesizing

During this phase of value inquiry, the students state hypotheses about the sources of the values they identified in step 3. As with all hypothesizing, you should require the students to give reasons for their statements. Hypotheses should be based on reason and evidence, and should not be ignorant guesses. This part of the inquiry process is designed to help pupils discover that most of our values are "caught" from persons within our environment and are not independently or reflectively derived. Once students are aware of the sources of their own values as well as those of other persons, they can more easily evaluate the soundness and appropriateness of these values in various situations.

When discussing "Finders Weepers," the students can hypothesize why Uncle Ross, Pete, and Eddie had different values. They can also hypothesize about why President McKinley and Mark Twain had different values related to the annexation of the Philippines, and why they consequently made different decisions. When students state hypotheses about the sources of values, they should give examples and evidence to support their ideas.

6. Naming Alternative Values to Those Exemplified by Behavior Observed: Recalling

Students should know that within our society there are many value alternatives from which to choose. If they are to derive their own values and be proud of the choices they make, they must be aware of a wide range of alternatives. Without alternatives an individual cannot make choices. This phase of value inquiry is designed to help students discover value alternatives. When the students role play "Finders Weepers," you can ask questions to help them identify value alternatives: "Eddie valued having fun and staying out of trouble more than some other things. What are some other things Eddie could have valued?" When the class is studying McKinley's decision regarding the Philippines, you could say: "We have said that McKinley highly valued giving the Filipino people the American way of life and maintaining American military strength in the Pacific region. What are some other things he could have valued?"

7. Hypothesizing about the Possible Consequences of Values Analyzed: Predicting, Comparing, and Contrasting

The following are important goals of value inquiry: (1) help students see that different values result in different consequences, (2) help students learn to accept the consequences of the values they hold, and (3) help students consider the consequences of different beliefs. During a discussion of "Finders Weepers," the students can discuss the possible consequences of Pete, Eddie and Tom's keeping the money but turning the check and wallet in at the Lost and Found. One possibility is that they may face criminal charges when the wallet is returned to the owner. If they return the wallet with the money and the check, they may have to get loans from their parents to pay for the boat. They could possibly get part-time jobs to earn the money to pay off their loan. When discussing McKinley's decision about annexing the Philippines, the students could discuss the actual consequences of his decision (one consequence was a revolt against the United States) and hypothesize about what might have happened if McKinley had decided to support independence for the Philippines.

A case study about Jackie Robinson, who faced blatant racial discrimination when he entered major league baseball, can evoke stimulating value-inquiry questions and discussion. (*Source*: The National Archives, Washington, D.C.)

8. Declaring Value Preferences: Choosing

After the students have described the behavior of the individuals in the stories, cases, and situations studied, identified the values involved, determined how they conflict, and predicted the possible consequences, they should be asked to declare their personal value preferences. This phase of value inquiry is extremely important and should be handled sensitively.

During this phase of value inquiry, you should be careful not to condemn values inconsistent with your beliefs. This is not to suggest that you should remain neutral on value issues, but rather that you should not declare value preferences until the students have expressed their own choices. Unless you create a classroom atmosphere that allows and encourages students to express their true beliefs, value inquiry will become a game in which students will try to guess what responses you want them to make. However, once they are out of the classroom and among friends, they will act out and freely express their true beliefs. If your students know that you think that Pete, Eddie, and Tom should return the wallet, the money, and the check, you will be unable to teach a useful value inquiry lesson with "Finders Weepers." Value preferences must be freely made within a democratic classroom atmosphere, and after the student has thought reflectively about the consequences of different value positions.

9. Stating Reasons, Sources, and Possible Consequences of Value Choices: Justifying, Hypothesizing, and Predicting

While you are obligated to help students derive their values within a democratic classroom atmosphere, you also have a responsibility to help them determine the sources of their values, the reasons they embrace them, their possible consequences, and to defend their moral choices in terms of American creed values such as equality, justice, and human dignity. Reflective citizen actors have clarified values, know why they embrace their beliefs, and are aware of the sources and consequences of their values. Once students are keenly aware of both the sources and consequences of their values, they are more likely to consider embracing other beliefs and to act on those they hold. We also hypothesize that they are more likely to endorse such American creed values as justice and human dignity.

You can use questioning strategies to help students declare value preferences and defend their moral choices. During a study of "Finders Weepers," you can ask different students: "What do you think Pete, Eddie, and Tom should do with the wallet? Why? What did you consider in making your decision? What does your decision indicate you think is most important in this situation? Would you be willing to act on your decision? Is your decision a fair decision? Why or why not?" You have to be very careful when asking questions like these so they will not, in any way, abuse the students or punish them for freely expressing their beliefs and values. *Students must be able to express their attitudes, beliefs, and values freely in order for value inquiry to take place.*

TABLE 15.3. Banks's Value-Inquiry Model

1. Defining and recognizing value problems: Observation-discrimination
2. Describing value-relevant behavior: Description-discrimination
3. Naming values exemplified by behavior described: Identification-description, hypothesizing.
4. Determining conflicting values in behavior described: Identification-analysis
5. Hypothesizing about sources of values analyzed: Hypothesizing (citing data to support hypotheses)
6. Naming alternative values to those exemplified by behavior observed: Recalling
7. Hypothesizing about the possible consequences of the values analyzed: Predicting, comparing, contrasting
8. Declaring value preference: Choosing
9. Stating reasons, sources, and possible consequences of value choice: Justifying, hypothesizing, predicting

Value Analysis and Clarification

The operations that comprise the valuing model we have discussed are summarized in Table 15.3 and Figure 15.2. You can use this model to teach students a process for valuing, to help them identify and clarify their values, and to justify their moral choices. Although the steps within this model are discussed separately, in practice they will not be clearly divided—they will be highly interrelated. For example, you may ask a student to describe value-relevant behavior and to name the values it exemplifies at the same time. However, we have separated these operations in our model to emphasize the

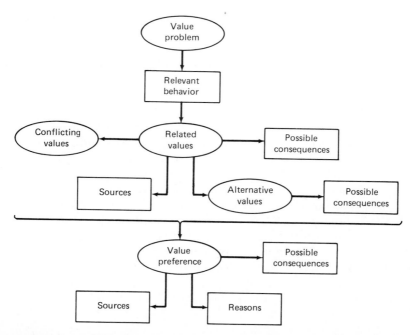

FIGURE 15.2 Operations of value-inquiry model, graphically illustrated.

contribution that each can make to the clarification and derivation of values. While students should be given practice in all the operations of the model, within a particular valuing lesson you may decide to deal with one or several of the processes. The operations can be taught separately or as a unit. We believe that students need both types of practice in order to develop proficiency in value inquiry skills.

VALUING STRATEGIES

You can use a variety of materials to give students practice in using the operations comprising our value inquiry model. Descriptive content in the social sciences, historical events, classroom and playground incidents, literature, art, photographs, open-ended stories, role playing, short films, and news stories are among the diverse materials that can be used. Below is a list of valuing strategies, grouped by grade levels, you can use to help students increase their value inquiry skills. These strategies are examples only. You will think of many others equally appropriate for teaching value analysis and clarification skills.

Primary Grades

1. Students sometimes experience a dilemma about what to do when they find a stray animal, such as a cat or a dog. Discuss this incident with the class: Jerry was taking his dog for a walk when a little puppy came running up to him whimpering for affection. Jerry's own dog was very concerned about the puppy; his interest was shown by sniffing and licking the puppy. Jerry didn't want to leave the dog outside alone. However, he knew that his mother did not want the family to own more pets. It was obvious that the stray puppy did not have a home. What should Jerry do?

2. Susie has been trying to save enough money to buy a Polaroid camera for almost a year. Although she saves a part of her small allowance each week, it doesn't seem as if she is ever going to save the $14 more needed to buy the camera. She would especially like the camera for her birthday party in two weeks. The bell that ends the school day had just rung when Susie saw the crisp new $20 bill on the playground. She picked it up quickly and hid it in her hand. What should Susie do?

3. Joe was looking at Kay when she copied from Carol's paper during the science test last Friday. On Monday Mr. Hinkle, the teacher, announced that because Kay had gotten the highest score on the science test he had chosen her to represent their class in the schoolwide science fair. Should Joe tell Mr. Hinkle about Kay's cheating last Friday?

4. Read to the class "Three Little Pigs". Ask them to name the values of the first little pig, the second little pig, the third little pig, and the wolf. Write these values on the board or butcher paper. Ask them to list the results of each set of values, as described in the story. Are these results realistic? Why or why not? Ask the students to act out or describe different endings for the story. Ask them to name the values of the characters in the story as they changed it in their descriptions or role play.

Intermediate Grades

1. To help students identify values, pictures without captions can be used. Choose pictures that portray a value position. For example, a picture of a group carrying signs and picketing indicates that the group values public demonstration as a form of protest. Some of the protests against the war in Vietnam were violent. Show photographs of both peaceful and violent protests. Have the students identify the value positions of (1) the people protesting and (2) of those they are protesting against. Either current or historical photographs can be used.

2. Ask the students to read arguments by leaders who say we need to increase our defense spending and by those who say we are spending too much money on defense and too little on domestic problems. Ask the students to identify the values of the various leaders and the possible consequences of their values. Ask the students to take a position on the defense spending controversy and defend it.

3. Lumber is an example of a quickly depleted natural resource. Ask the students to identify on a continuum the positions an individual might take regarding the appropriate use of trees and forest products. For example, one end of the continuum would indicate the total use of present lumber supplies for housebuilding, furniture, paper manufacture, and the use of logs in fireplaces. The other end of the continuum would indicate the conservationist position—favoring leaving all trees on the land, reforesting all places where forest fires and logging have depleted tree growth, and finding synthetic materials for all products now made of wood.

4. During their study of United States history, ask the students to read about Lincoln's decision to issue the Emancipation Proclamation in 1863. The Proclamation freed all the slaves in the states that were in rebellion against the Union. What were the major factors that influenced Lincoln's decision? To what extent was his decision political? To what extent was it ethical? Also ask the students to examine the moral and political factors that influenced President Andrew Jackson's decision to support the Indian Resettlement Act of 1830, President Truman's decision to authorize the dropping of the atomic

bomb on Japan in 1945, and President Kennedy's decision to support an attempt to overthrow the Castro government in Cuba in 1961.

Upper Grades

1. Read the following situation to the class. A group of three students are in a field or out-of-the-way place smoking cigarettes. They are obviously experimenting to find the proper way to hold a cigarette. Inhaling the cigarette is difficult for them; they cough a great deal. They attempt to affect the casual air of experienced smokers. Later, one of the three students arrives home and is greeted by his father. The student casually walks into the house, but doesn't get past his father's scrutiny. His father immediately notices the smell of smoke on the boy's clothes. The father asks the boy whether he has been smoking. Ask the students to role play an ending to this situation and to discuss the value issues it raises.

2. During the early 1980s, capital punishment reemerged as a major national issue. It surfaced in large part as a response to the high crime rate in the United States. Several states reenacted the death penalty. At least one state began to execute the prisoners who had been sentenced to death in previous years. Ask the students to examine the arguments for and against the death penalty and to identify the moral, political, and social issues involved in the debate. Ask the students to take and defend a position on the issue.

3. The attempts by women's rights groups to add an Equal Rights Amendment to the United States Constitution had not succeeded by 1989. The proposed Amendment continued to be highly controversial. Ask the students to examine the various issues and values involved in this debate. They should also take and defend a position on the issue. Their position should be based largely on their values, which they will delineate.

4. Most of the cases that come to the United States Supreme Court involve competing value claims. Ask the students to identify some major historical and current cases that have come before the Court, the values that were in conflict, and the values the Court upheld. They should also examine the dissenting opinions in each case and identify the values exemplified in the dissents. Three examples of race relations cases that the students might study are (1) The *Plessy* v. *Ferguson* case (1896), in which the Court ruled that "separate but equal" facilities were constitutional; (2) the *Brown* v. *Board of Education* case (1954), in which the Court ruled that school segregation was "inherently unequal," thus reversing its own *Plessy* decision; and (3) the *Regents of the University of California* v. *Bakke* case (1978), in which the Court upheld the idea of affirmative action but ruled against strict racial quotas.

DECISION-MAKING AND CITIZEN ACTION STRATEGIES

Sequencing the Development of Decision-Making Skills

Students must be able to derive interdisciplinary knowledge using an inquiry process, and form and clarify their values, in order to make reflective decisions and to shape public policy. We will consider how a teacher or curriculum designer may plan the development of these skills, and the related decision-making skills—synthesis, prediction, and the affirmation of a course of action.

Teachers' development of these skills depends greatly on the social studies curriculum within their districts, their own interests, the resources available, and their students' backgrounds. Many teachers will find themselves in school districts where only social science inquiry units are part of the approved curriculum. Other teachers will feel that, while valuing and decision-making skills are important, social science inquiry should constitute the bulk of their social studies program. This book is designed to help teachers and curriculum designers with different points of view about the social studies curriculum.

Readers who are primarily interested in social science inquiry will find Chapters 9 through 14 of most interest. However, value inquiry and decision-making skills can be taught within the context of social science inquiry units and with social science and historical content. For example, while students are studying the American Revolution, you can ask the following kinds of questions:

Valuing Questions

1. What does the behavior of the British and the colonists tell us about what was important to them?
2. How were the things important to the British different from the things important to the colonists?
3. What were other things that the British and the colonists could have regarded as important?

Decision-making

1. What were the alternatives open to the colonists?
2. What were the possible consequences of each alternative in question 1?
3. What evidence can you give to support your belief that the alternatives you state were possible?

Thus one approach you can take to developing inquiry, valuing and decision-making skills is to teach these skills within the context of social science inquiry units. Another approach is to identify a number of vital social problems or issues, list social science concepts related to the issues, and plan separate units to teach the concepts and the analysis of the issues related to the concepts.

The students could apply the knowledge they learned during the inquiry units when they decide on social issues. During the social issues units, they would develop proficiency in valuing and decision-making skills. Citizen action and participation projects could also be planned and implemented during the analysis of social issues, so that the students could take action on some of the decisions they make. For example, you may decide to teach conceptual units that will help students to decide on social issues related to the nuclear arms race, a current war or international conflict, race relations in the community, and erosion of the ozone layer of the atmosphere. Concepts will be taught in the social science inquiry units that will enable students to make reflective decisions and to take citizen action to help resolve these problems.

Once you have identified the social issues you plan to teach during the year, you should use the criteria for the selection of concepts found in Chapter 2. These criteria suggest that concepts should be accurate, have the power to organize a great deal of information and data, and be suitable for the students. While these criteria should be exercised, the relationship of the concepts to the social issues to be studied should be the most important criterion. This relationship will give students the knowledge they need to make decisions and take action on social issues. Such concepts as *power*, *international law*, *authority*, and *scarcity* might be developed to help the students analyze a current war or international conflict. By studying the concepts of power and authority, the students will be able to determine who has the authority to declare and lead us into war, and how citizens can exercise power to influence public policy regarding war. The concept of international law will help students discover how international laws are made, and their usual consequences. Materials and activities related to the concept of scarcity will illuminate the way wars often affect the economy of a nation. For example, the students may discover that wars often increase prosperity and that the termination of wars often results in widespread unemployment.

We have discussed two major ways you might plan units to teach inquiry, valuing, and decision-making skills. These skills may be developed with deliberate questioning strategies within the framework of social science inquiry units. An alternative plan is to identify a number of social issues, structure conceptual units to give students the knowledge needed to make reflective decisions regarding them, and to teach decision-making units related to the social issues at different points in the year.

Although both these plans have certain advantages or may be the only plans feasible for many teachers, we will propose another alternative. We believe this third alternative is the most effective way to structure learning experiences that enable students to develop proficiency in social science inquiry, value inquiry, decision-making, and citizen action skills. Although we will discuss this organizational plan separately, you should realize that it is highly related to the other plans discussed, and that its strategies can be used within the previously discussed plans. You will be able to adapt these procedures and our decision-making model to your own unique teaching situation, or you can use the procedures exactly as we describe them. We believe that the most effective organizational plan is the approach outlined below.

IDENTIFYING IMPORTANT SOCIAL ISSUES AND PROBLEMS

The first step in planning decision-making units, using the method we consider most effective, is to identify *social issues* that are of concern to the students and that are unresolved in the local community and the larger society.[14] The issues should be pervasive and of enduring interest. Decision-making units should not be built around problems that are narrow or of only temporary concern. You can determine the pervasive social issues within a society by carefully studying the news media over a period of time, by being generally aware of the events within the community and society, and by listening to the students' conversations and class comments about their social and political worlds.

You can also use questionnaires and essays to determine what social issues are most important to your students and the community. Although social issues frequently vary within different time periods, some have been of enduring concern in modern society. These include political alienation, poverty, racial and gender inequality, pollution, and in recent years, concern about the nuclear arms race.

Teaching Decision-Problem Units

IDENTIFYING THE DECISION-PROBLEM

We will illustrate how a class may study a social issue, and through a decision-making process, decide what action to take regarding it. In a medium-sized industrial community called Riverdale, racial conflict has developed between blacks and whites. During the previous summer, a black family moved into the predominantly white Riverdale neighborhood, and a racial confrontation occurred in which several persons were injured, including two white policemen. A number of citizens formed a group to campaign for an open-housing bill, but to date support for the movement has been meager. Race relations within the city are tense.

In response to federal legislation, a movement to integrate the public schools by cross-busing began, but an anti-school-integration movement emerged to defeat the attempts for integration and to recall the school board. The students in the sixth-grade class at Abraham Lincoln, an all-white school on the fringes of Riverdale, pose this problem, "What action should we take regarding race relations in our community?"

SOCIAL SCIENCE INQUIRY (RELATED KNOWLEDGE)

Since scientific knowledge is one essential component of the decision-making process, the teacher identifies social science concepts and related generalizations to help the students make reflective decisions about the issue. The teacher selects these concepts: *discrimination* from sociology, *conflict* from history, *culture* from anthropology, *specialization* from economics, and *power* from political science. Organizing generalizations related to the concepts are identified, and subideas related to the organizing generalizations and to black-white relations in the United States are stated. The key generalization and subideas for one of the key concepts follows.

Concept: Discrimination

Organizing Generalization: Groups are often the victims of discrimination because of age, sex, race, religion, and cultural differences.

Subideas:

1.   Black slavery was a form of discrimination.
2.   African-Americans have experienced discrimination in legal matters. The slave codes and laws such as the grandfather clause are examples.
3.   African-Americans have experienced discrimination in the administration of justice. The widespread lynching in the early 1900s is an example.
4.   African-Americans experience discrimination in the areas of voting and government.
5.   African-Americans experience discrimination in employment.

ORGANIZING FOR INSTRUCTION

You should identify the key concepts related to the social issue you wish the class to decide on, and state the organizing generalizations and related subideas. Then you are ready to formulate the teaching strategies and specify the instructional materials for the social science phase of the decision-problem unit. The concepts and materials should also be organized in a logical fashion.

In our example, you may wish to start the unit with the first key concept (discrimination), because the subideas related to this concept deal with the earliest period of black-white relations in America. While decision-problem units need not be chronological, they should have some kind of logical organization. Another teacher using the concepts in our example may wish to start with the key concept *power*, and discuss the civil rights movement of the 1950s and 1960s. When organizing social issues units, you should consider the interests of the students, the availability of materials, your own interests,

TABLE 15.4.

Key Ideas	Activities
Concept: Discrimination *Organizing generalization*: Groups are often the victims of discrimination because of age, sex, race, religion, and cultural differences. *Subidea*: Blacks have experienced much discrimination in all phases of American life, including education, the administration of justice, and employment.	1. Read selections from *South Town, North Town,* and *Whose Town?* by Lorenz Graham. 2. View a filmstrip on black slavery and list ways in which it was a form of discrimination. 3. Find copies of such documents as the slave codes and the grandfather clause, and role play how they affected the lives of blacks. 4. Compile statistics on the number of blacks who were lynched during the early years of the 1900s. 5. Read and discuss accounts of the discrimination that blacks experience in employment, school, and in the administration of justice today.

the relationships of the concepts, the content to be studied, and the social issue to be analyzed.

We illustrated in Chapter 2 how you can organize social science inquiry units. The same form of organization is appropriate for the social science phase of social issues units. You can divide a sheet of paper in half and write the key concepts and generalizations on one side of the paper, and the activities designed to develop the ideas on the other half, as illustrated in Table 15.4.

VALUE INQUIRY

After the students have had an opportunity to derive social science generalizations related to their decision-problem, they should undertake lessons that will enable them to identify, analyze, and clarify their values. For value inquiry exercises, you may use case studies clipped from newspapers and magazines, open-ended stories, photographs, role-playing activities, or moral dilemmas that the students and you write. Much of the factual material, which is covered during the social science phase of the unit, may also be used to help the students to form and clarify values related to the problem or issue being studied.

When teaching a decision-problem or social issue, you should use valuing strategies directly related to the issue under consideration. In our example unit, it would be inappropriate for you to ask the students value questions about such issues as water pollution and a current international conflict unless these issues were directly related to black-white relations in the United States or to black-white relations in the students' local community.

Appropriate valuing activities for our sample unit would include

1. Reading and discussing selections from the novels *South Town, North Town,* and *Whose Town?* by Lorenz Graham. This trilogy describes the problems, hopes, and dreams of a black family that migrated from the South to the North in search of the American dream. These novels include many selections that are rich in value conflicts and dilemmas.
2. Reading about and discussing the moral crisis that surfaced during the Civil War. Speeches by the abolitionists and their opponents will highlight the moral crisis that the Civil War brought to national consciousness.
3. Reading and discussing the moral issues raised in Martin Luther King, Jr.'s, "Letter from a Birmingham Jail" (April 16, 1963), in which he responds to charges that he was an outside agitator in that city and defends his passive resistance tactics.
4. Reading and discussing the moral issues raised in Martin Luther King, Jr.'s, "I Have a Dream" speech, delivered on August 28, 1963, during the March for Jobs and Freedom, in Washington, D.C.
5. Militant Black leaders, such as Malcolm X and Stokley Carmichael, became increasingly impatient with King's nonviolent tactics. Read speeches and documents by King, Malcolm X, and Carmichael and discuss the ways their values were alike and different.
6. Role playing and discussing the integration of an all-white school.
7. Viewing and discussing pictures of nonviolent civil rights demonstrations during the 1960s.
8. Reading and discussing a news story about a race problem in the local community.
9. Reading about and discussing the value conflicts which surfaced when federal and state institutions implemented "affirmative action" plans to help eliminate job discrimination in the 1970s and 1980s.

DECISION-MAKING AND CITIZEN ACTION

After the students have derived social science generalizations and clarified their values regarding the social issue, you should ask them to list all the possible actions they could take regarding race relations in their community, and to predict the consequences of each alternative.

It is imperative that the alternatives and consequences be realistic and based on the knowledge students have mastered during the scientific phase of the unit. Alternatives and consequences should be intelligent predictive statements and not ignorant guesses or wishful thinking. You should require students to give data and reasons to support the alternatives and consequences they formulate. For example, a student who states that his or her class can solve racial problems in the community by going from door to door telling residents about the problems would obviously be dreaming. This state-

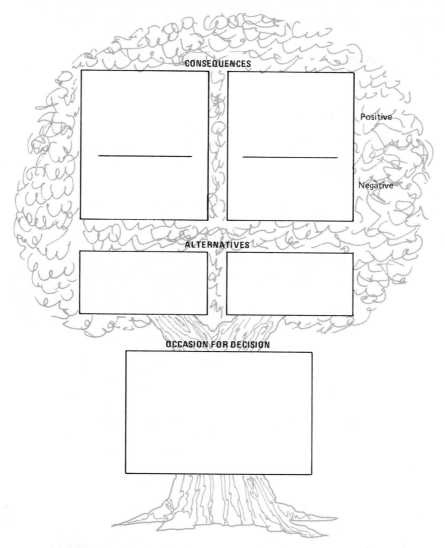

CONSEQUENCES

Positive

Negative

ALTERNATIVES

OCCASION FOR DECISION

FIGURE 15.3 Decision Tree. (*Source*: Reprinted with permission from Roger La Raus and Richard C. Remy, *Citizenship Decision-Making: Skill Activities and Materials*. [Reading, MA: Addison-Wesley, 1978], p. 57.)

ment is not meant to suggest that information would not contribute to the problem's resolution. In our example, it would be impossible for the students to think of actions that would *solve* the racial problems in their community. However, they might be able to take action that will help to improve their own racial attitudes.

The students can identify alternatives and possible consequences in chart form, as illustrated in Table 15.5, or list them on the decision tree developed by La Raus and Remy. (See Figure 15.3.)

TABLE 15.5. Alternative Actions and Possible Consequences

Alternative Action Regarding Race Relations in Our Community	Possible Consequences
1. Take no group action.	1. More hostilities may occur. 2. More persons may be injured in racial violence. 3. Blacks and whites may further separate and form separate societies. 4. Our own school may become involved in a racial conflict over school integration. 5. We will not be criticized by conservative factions in the school and wider community. 6. Blacks may be denied more rights in our community.
2. Take group action to improve racial feelings in our classroom and school.	1. We may encounter hostility from administrators, other students, and teachers. 2. If we proceed carefully, we may improve race relations in our school, but they will not necessarily improve in the wider community. 3. We may interest other students and teachers in working to help improve race relations in the school or wider community.
3. Take group action to improve race relations in the wider community.	1. We might encounter hostility from community groups. 2. We might inflame racial feelings from such groups. 3. Unless we win the cooperation of our parents, they may work against or not support our efforts. 4. By working carefully and wisely with civic and religious groups, we might be able to positively influence racial feelings in the community.
4. Take no group action, but individually act to improve race relations.	1. Such action may have little effect on the racial problems in our community, but it may make us feel better because we may be acting in ways more consistent with our values than before. 2. Our individual actions may influence the action of other individuals, and thus our efforts would have more influence.

DETERMINING A COURSE OF ACTION

After naming alternatives, predicting their consequences, and identifying the knowledge supporting the alternatives and consequences, the students should then order the alternatives according to their hierarchy of values. The decision-making process is illustrated in Figure 15.4.

The students should pose and answer this question: Which course of action is most consistent with my most important values? The students should identify their values and order them into a hierarchy during the valuing phase of the social issues unit. A group of students may decide that they value the worth and dignity of the individual above all else, and that their next most important value is equality. They should try to define their values operationally and relate them to the alternative courses of action they have stated. They must resolve such problems as: Is taking no action at all when blacks are experiencing discrimination in our community consistent with our

FIGURE 15.4 The decision-making process.

values about the worth and dignity of the individual? Are we not denying the worth and dignity of the individual when we deny people equal opportunities under the law, in employment, and in education? How can we act in ways consistent with the values we hold?

Another group of students may conclude that they value majority rule above all else. Since the majority of whites in the community do not think that blacks should have certain jobs or live in certain neighborhoods, taking no action about the situation would be consistent with their values. These students studied the results of a recent community racial attitude survey.

If a group of students reaches this conclusion after thoughtful reflection, your role is to help the students reanalyze the sources of their values, determine how they may conflict with other values they hold or with American creed values such as equality and human dignity, and help them to identify the possible consequences of their beliefs. You should also help the students determine whether they can live with and be proud of the possible consequences of their value choices. *To implement our theory of moral education, students must be allowed to make uncoerced decisions within a democratic classroom atmosphere.* It is not an easy theory to implement. However, it is consistent with a democratic ideology and a commitment to human dignity, values which we endorse and on which our theory is based.

Students should be encouraged to make their own decisions, to accept responsibility for them and not to rely on others, including teachers, to make decisions for them. While students should be encouraged to think independently about social issues, there will be situations in which students should and will make group decisions. Practice in group decision-making is desirable. In real-life situations, the individual must often participate in group decision-making. Skillful group decision-making is essential for civic competency in a democratic, pluralistic society. Also, if citizen action projects are to be planned and implemented, they will usually be undertaken in groups, although some individuals may decide to take independent action on some of the social issues the class studies.

PROVIDING OPPORTUNITIES FOR CITIZEN ACTION AND PARTICIPATION

After students have made decisions on important social issues, we should, whenever possible and practical, provide opportunities for them to participate in action and participation projects to implement their decisions. Participation gives students a greater sense of personal, social and civic efficacy. Knowledge is of little value if it is not used to help solve human problems— especially in a period of our history when personal and societal problems loom large. While you will not be able to provide opportunities for students to act on all or perhaps most of the decisions they make (this would be neither possible nor desirable), the school, by cooperating with public and private agencies, can provide opportunities for students to act on some of their decisions. Traditionally, the social studies has educated students for civic apathy rather than for efficacy and action.

Citizen action and participation projects may take different forms. They may consist of volunteer services in the community, community studies having an action component, community research projects, internships, and citizen action designed to influence public policy at the regional, state, national or international level.[15] The age and grade level of the students will be major factors to be considered when citizen action and participation projects are planned. Internships in private and public agencies are usually not appropriate for students in the elementary and junior high school grades. There are a number of successful internship projects, however, in many high schools. Elementary and junior high school students can and do often participate in community service and research projects.

Students in the elementary and junior high school cannot solve the major societal problems that very competent adults have been unable to solve. However, they can take some actions related to major social problems. These actions will contribute in small ways to the improvement of their classrooms, schools, and communities. More importantly, however, such actions can help them to develop greater personal, social, and civic efficacy. *Helping students to develop a greater sense of personal, social, and civic efficacy, and to develop greater skills in influencing their social and civic environments, should be the major goals of citizen action and participation projects and activities.* Services to their communities should be an important but secondary consideration.

Citizen Action in the Community and School   When a social issue has divided a community, such as race relations in our example, it is probably best for students to confine their actions to their classroom, school, or to local situations (such as a club or church) where they do not run the risk of being publicly abused or ostracized. If a group of students becomes involved in a heated racial controversy in a sharply divided community, the school and the students may become vulnerable to severe attacks from extremist groups. Some students may independently decide to become involved in such a social issue in the community. However, they should act as individuals and not as agents of the school. Because the public school is so vulnerable in our society, it will be severely criticized if teachers and administrators do not exercise sound judgment in planning action and participation projects for students.

The most reasonable course of action for the students to take in our exemplary decision-problem unit may be to formulate a race relations program or ethnic studies lessons in their own school. They could start by working jointly with the principal, teachers, parents, and other persons in the school and neighborhood. The PTA may give the students needed help and support. Although the class, as a group, may decide on a course of action, no students should be forced to participate in a citizen action project or activity that they feel is contrary to their values and beliefs.

Since the school is a social institution with problems mirroring those of the larger society, students can practice shaping public policy by working to help eliminate problems in their classroom, school, or school district. They might start by studying and analyzing the problems within their classroom.

To help students develop a sense of personal, social, and civic competency, you and your principal must be committed to the belief that students should participate in the making of school and other public policies.

Unless teachers and principals are willing to give students a role in the making of classroom and school policies, student action projects cannot be successfully implemented. Students who lack personal, social, and civic efficacy in their own school will be ineffective in shaping public policy and contributing to the solution of social problems in the wider community. Obviously, there are school policies that students cannot and should not be allowed to make or influence. School administrators and teachers must also conform to rules and laws made by higher authorities. However, when issues and problems such as discipline, dress codes, school assemblies, cafeteria food selection, fights on the playground, sexism, and racism arise in the school, student participation in the development of policy can help solve these problems—as well as help students develop a greater sense of personal, social, and civic efficacy. The nature and extent of student participation in school policy should be determined by the issue or problem, and by the maturity, knowledge, and interest that students have in the issue or problem.

Teachers who want to help students develop proficiency in citizen action skills should provide them with ample opportunities to clarify their policy goals and to learn how to exercise civic skills successfully. In a useful model (see Figure 15.5), Newmann identifies several essential components of an effective citizen action curriculum. It should help students to develop skills in (a) formulating policy goals, (b) working to rally support for those goals,

FIGURE 15.5 Areas of competence required to exert influence in public affairs. (*Source*: *Education for Citizen Action: Challenge for Secondary Curriculum* by Fred N. Newmann. © 1975, published by McCutchan Publishing Corporation. Reprinted by permission of the publisher.)

and (c) resolving psycho-philosophic concerns.[16] When students formulate policy goals using this model, they articulate and justify the moral choices involved in their policy and carry out policy research related to it. They explore and experiment with ways of exercising civic power when they work to rally support for their goal. Citizen action may cause philosophical and psychological dilemmas for individuals. Hence the need for the citizen action curriculum to help students to resolve psychological and philosophical concerns.

Guidelines for citizen action and participation are presented in Table 15.6. Examples of citizen action and participation projects, grouped by grade levels, are presented below.

TABLE 15.6. Guidelines for Citizen Action Projects

1. The activities should be *meaningful* experiences, not merely projects in which students become involved just to say that they are participating in citizen action projects.

2. The *primary* goal of citizen action projects should be to provide experiences for the students whereby they can attain a sense of political effectiveness, and not just serve the community. However, the most effective projects contribute to the attainment of both goals.

3. Charity and other kinds of community help experiences are legitimate and potentially meaningful activities, although the projects should, as often as possible, help students to gain a sense of political effectiveness.

4. Students should participate in citizen action activities only after they have studied the related issue from the perspectives of the social sciences, analyzed and clarified their values regarding it, identified the possible consequences of their actions, and expressed a willingness to accept those consequences.

5. When problems within the school can be resolved through student action, participation in school activities should have priority over participation in projects in the wider community.

6. While group decision-making is legitimate and often desirable, no individual student should be required to participate in an action project that he or she feels is contrary to his or her values and beliefs.

7. The experience and age of the students should be considered when action projects are planned and implemented. Young children should confine their actions to their classroom, school, and family, or to other primary groups or secondary institutions that they feel secure in and that are supportive of their actions.

8. When citizen action projects are planned, the support of other teachers, students, school administrators, related community agencies, and members of the community should be solicited.

9. Students who wish to participate in citizen action projects should be allowed to have schedules conducive to such participation. The concept of the school should be broadened; activities needn't necessarily take place within the four walls of the school room.

10. When a community is seriously divided over a social issue and feelings within the community are intense, action projects should be confined to the classroom, school, family, or to other supportive institutions in which students feel secure.

(continued)

TABLE 15.6. (continued)

11. Citizen action projects planned by students should not violate the laws and mores of a community.

12. Citizen action projects planned within the school should be consistent with American creed values and human dignity.

13. When citizen action projects are planned, the teacher should make every effort to help the students identify all the possible consequences of their actions, especially those actions that may have adverse consequences, either for the individual or the group.

14. Students who wish to engage in individual projects should not be discouraged, but should be helped to realize the fact that group action is usually more politically effective than individual action.

15. When citizen action projects are planned, the teacher should make every effort to minimize any physical, emotional, or psychological damage to the students. This can be accomplished largely by soliciting the cooperation of other persons in the school and wider community, and by carefully considering the possible consequences of different courses of action.

16. Citizen action projects in the social studies program should be nonpartisan. Although groups of students may decide to campaign for a particular candidate or issue, students with other beliefs and goals should have the option to plan parallel projects to support their beliefs and political choices.

CITIZEN ACTION PROJECTS

Primary Grades

1. During a unit on the family, the children interviewed their parents and grandparents about what life was like when they grew up. Working with their teacher, the students developed a set of questions that each of them used in interviewing their parents and grandparents. The children who had grandparents who lived in another city conducted phone interviews.

2. When the children were studying about their community, they learned that pollution was a major problem. They decided they wanted to take some action about the problem. They saved all of the aluminum cans used in their homes and asked some of their neighbors to save those they did not want. They sold the aluminum cans to the Department of Ecology in their state for 17¢ per pound, and used the money to buy plants and shrubs for their school yard.

3. A unit on the community in a second-grade class dealt in part with senior citizens in the community. The children became interested in the problems of senior citizens and raised the question: What can we do to help the senior citizens in our community? They decided to visit a senior-citizen home during the holiday season. They took gifts and sang holiday carols.

4. A third-grade class studied their city and learned that some people,

in some parts of the city, often did not have enough food. There was a food bank that solicited donations of food for them. Each student saved a part of his or her allowance for several months to contribute money for a class food-bank donation. The class also chose the items it donated to the food bank.

5. A class studying family life in Colombia, South America, became concerned about poverty in other nations. The class decided that it wanted to make a donation to an agency that helped families in Latin America. They investigated different organizations and decided which would be the most appropriate to receive their donation. They raised the money for their donation by sponsoring a Walk-A-Thon at school. They asked neighbors to pledge 20¢ for each mile they walked.

Intermediate Grades

1. A class studying American history learned about the role of the United States in world affairs. They became interested and concerned about the nuclear arms race. They conducted a survey in their school about awareness of and concern about the nuclear buildup. They presented a school assembly program, depicting both sides of the nuclear debate and the results of their survey.

2. While they were studying an economics unit, the students pointed out that they always had trouble finding the specific brands of school supplies their teachers requested each September. They worked with their teacher and established and ran a school supply store in a vacant room in their school. They learned about wholesale prices, retail prices, customer satisfaction, and so on. They also provided a needed service for their school.

3. A class that wanted to take a trip to their state capitol raised money with a series of car washes in their community. They observed their state legislature in action, talked to some of its members, and prepared a written report to share with the whole school.

4. A class wanted some new social studies software for use with the computers in their school. They raised money to buy it by selling spices to the people in their community.

5. A class conducted a comprehensive historical study of their community by interviewing senior residents and visiting museums, cemeteries, and other institutions. They wrote their findings in the form of a narrative history and shared it with the other classes in the school.

Upper Grades

1. When the school district faced a major budget problem, the students developed a campaign leaflet asking neighbors to vote for a special levy. They went to homes in their neighborhoods to distribute the

       leaflets and to ask citizens to support the special levy.

2. After studying a unit on the role of women in American life, the students in one class met and talked with the principal and the teachers about ways that the entire curriculum could include more content about women.

3. A group of students formed a Tutorial Club. The members of the club stayed one hour after school on designated days to tutor students who came to their Tutorial Center.

4. After studying the Bill of Rights and the Constitution, the students in one class sponsored a number of activities to promote the rights of students, including an assembly, a debate, and a guest lecture.

5. When the city was considering a proposal to name a street after Martin Luther King, Jr., a class visited the City Council to present their support for the proposed legislation.

SUMMARY

Both scientific knowledge and clarified, reflectively examined values are necessary for citizen actors to make thoughtful decisions that will help to solve personal, social, and civic problems. Because of the conflicting and confused values in modern societies, schools need to help students develop clarified values consistent with American creed values, such as equality and human dignity. Students need to be taught a process for deriving and clarifying their values. We cannot expect people to affirm and to act on values that they have not chosen from alternatives within a democratic classroom atmosphere. In the first part of this chapter, we reviewed several value inquiry models that can be used to teach students a process for deriving and clarifying their values. A theory of value education and strategies for implementing it were also presented.

    While valuing is essential in the decision-making process, citizen actors must also synthesize knowledge and values, and decide on a course of action consistent with their value choices. The second part of this chapter presents a rationale for decision-making and citizen action, an example of a decision-making unit, and examples of citizen action and participation activities. The major goal of citizen action and participation should be to help students to develop greater personal, social, and civic efficacy. Students will not be able to take action on many of the decisions they make in social studies classes. However, by working cooperatively with public and private agencies, you can provide students with some rich opportunities to implement a few of their decisions. While citizen action and participation activities undertaken by students may make only small contributions to improving life in the community and solving social problems, they can contribute greatly to helping students acquire the attitudes and skills needed to influence their personal, social, and civic worlds.

DISCUSSION QUESTIONS AND EXERCISES

1. Locate a case study in a recent publication about an individual or group facing a decision-problem that has value components. The case may involve a white couple who are trying to decide whether to allow their children to be bused to an integrated school, a young person who is trying to decide whether he or she should experiment with illegal drugs, or an organization that is trying to decide whether it should support an urban renewal project that will displace slum residents but result in a badly needed freeway. Using the author's valuing model, develop a valuing lesson plan around the case to teach to a group of students.

2. Pictures without captions are excellent tools for teaching value inquiry. Locate, in current magazines, a number of pictures that can evoke value questions. Mount the pictures and develop a series of questions (based on the value inquiry model presented in this chapter) that you can ask students in order to develop their value inquiry skills.

3. Descriptive social science data can evoke value questions. Articles and accounts of the American Revolution, slavery, the Civil War, the Vietnam War and contemporary social problems have much potential for value inquiry. Identify a selection in a social studies textbook and illustrate, with a teaching plan, how the selection can be used to help students to increase their value inquiry skills.

4. In your curriculum library, examine several social studies curriculum guides and textbooks and evaluate their value components. Do the materials include value inquiry objectives? Are the strategies for developing the objectives sound? In what ways would you modify the value components of these materials in order to make them more effective?

5. What role do values play in decision-making? What are the implications of your response for teaching decision-making skills?

6. What alternate unit plans can you use to help students gain proficiency in decision-making skills? Which plan do you think is most effective? Why? Most practical? Why?

7. Identify a current social issue and construct a decision-making unit for students in the elementary or junior high school grades. Include key concepts and generalizations related to the issue from the following disciplines: history, sociology, anthropology, geography, political science, economics, and psychology. Plan strategies for teaching value inquiry. Also include strategies for teaching pupils how to relate the key ideas to their values in order to make decisions. List possible courses of action that students might take on the issue, and their possible consequences.

8. Demonstrate your understanding of the following terms by writing or stating brief definitions for each. Also tell why each is important.

   a. values
   b. value inquiry
   c. value conflict
   d. value clarification
   e. didactic strategies
   f. Kohlberg's cognitive-developmental approach to moral education
   g. decision-making

   h. decision-problem
   i. enduring social issue
   j. personal efficacy
   k. social efficacy
   l. civic efficacy
   m. Banks's value inquiry model

NOTES

1. Milton Rokeach, *Beliefs, Attitudes and Values* (San Francisco: Jossey-Bass, 1969), p. 124.

2. James P. Shaver and William Strong, *Facing Value Decisions: Rationale-Building for Teachers* (Belmont, CA: Wadsworth, 1976), p. 57.

3. Shaver and Strong, op. cit., p. 57.

4. Louis E. Raths, Merrill Harmin, and Sidney B. Simon, *Values and Teaching: Working with Values in the Classroom*, 2nd ed. (Columbus, OH: Merrill, 1978).

5. Raths et al., op cit.

6. Raths et al., op cit.

7. Hunt and Metcalf, op. cit.; Donald W. Oliver and James P. Shaver, *Teaching Public Issues in the High School* (Boston: Houghton Mifflin, 1966); Fred M. Newmann (with the assistance of Donald W. Oliver), *Clarifying Public Controversy: An Approach to Teaching Social Studies* (Boston: Little, Brown, 1970); Lawrence Kohlberg and Elliot Turiel, "Moral Development and Moral Education," in Gerald S. Lesser, Ed., *Psychology and Educational Practice* (Glenview, IL: Scott, Foresman, 1971).

8. Shaver and Strong, op. cit., p. 43.

9. Newmann (with Oliver), op. cit., p. 43.

10. Kohlberg and Turiel, op. cit.

11. Kohlberg and Turiel, op. cit.

12. Fannie R. Shaftel and George Shaftel, *Role Playing in the Curriculum*, 2nd ed. (Englewood Cliffs, NJ: Prentice-Hall, 1982), pp. 157–159.

13. Ronald Lippitt, Robert Fox, and Lucille Schaible, *Social Science Laboratory Units: Teachers Guide* (Chicago: Science Research Associates, Inc., 1969).

14. Shirley H. Engle and Anna S. Ochoa, *Education for Democratic Citizenship: Decision Making in the Social Studies* (New York: Teachers College Press, 1988).

15. Fred N. Newmann, *Education for Citizen Action: Challenge for Secondary Curriculum* (Berkeley: McCutchan, 1975).

16. Newmann, op. cit.

FOR FURTHER READING

Belenky, Mary F., Blythe M. Clinchy, Nancy R. Goldberger, and Jill M. Tarule. *Women's Ways of Knowing: The Development of Self, Voice, and Mind.* New York: Basic Books, 1986.

Brown, Lester, et al. *State of the World.* New York: Norton, 1989.

Engle, Shirley H., and Anna S. Ochoa. *Education for Democratic Citizenship: Decision Making in the Social Studies.* New York: Teachers College Press, 1988.

Gilligan, Carol. *In a Different Voice: Psychological Theory and Women's Development.* Cambridge: Harvard University Press, 1982.

Greene, Maxine. *The Dialectic of Freedom.* New York: Teachers College Press, 1988.

Metcalf, Lawrence E., Ed. *Values Education: Rationale, Strategies and Procedures.* Washington, D.C.: National Council for the Social Studies, 1971.

Shaver, James P., and William Strong. *Facing Value Decisions: Rationale-Building for Teachers*, 2nd ed. New York: Teachers College Press, 1982.

Simonson, Rick, and Walker Scott, Eds. *Multicultural Literacy*. St. Paul, MN: Graywolf Press, 1988.

"Values, Resources, and Politics in America's Schools," *Daedalus*, Vol. 113, No. 4 (Fall 1984). Special Issue.

16

Evaluation Strategies

How well have the students accomplished the important goals of social studies? What progress have Chris, Rob, and Sonya made? Have Jane and Alexandra improved in their ability to form concepts and to propose hypotheses? Questions such as these are the concern of *evaluation* of social studies instruction.

Evaluation is a technical aspect of teaching. Its purpose is to develop as much precise and objective information about the instructional process as possible in order to (1) assess the effectiveness of instruction; (2) determine whether or not instructional goals have been accomplished; and (3) provide feedback to students about their performance. Evaluation also provides information on which important decisions can be made about students' progress in school, providing reports to parents, modifying instructional goals, or making changes in the curriculum.

There are many techniques and devices that can be used in evaluation. Some are informal teacher-made measures; others are formal methods or standardized tests. Some examples include observation reports, anecdotal records, reports of group discussions, collections of students' work, class diaries, logbooks, teacher-made tests, committee reports, class projects, checklists, attitudinal measures, and standardized national tests or assessment inventories. All of these provide evidence or data upon which evaluation is based.

In the final analysis, evaluation is a judgmental act. Your tasks are to (1) formulate clear and precise goals; (2) set appropriate and attainable criteria; (3) gather data about the instructional process that are as accurate and objective as possible; and finally, (4) report the data to students, parents, and administrators in clear, meaningful, and accurate ways. Given such conditions, evaluation fulfills an important role in the teaching-learning process.

"We come now to deal with the problem of vigorous interfaces between educational professionals and pupil's nonsibling, but kin or legally related significant others which reflect strong effective responses directed to perceptions about competency-based evaluations of learning facilitators. Or, as some say, what to do when a parent says you're a lousy teacher." (*Source*: Ford Button. Used with permission.)

INSTRUCTIONAL OBJECTIVES: A TECHNIQUE FOR EVALUATION

It is virtually impossible to evaluate learning in social studies if the instructional goals or objectives are not clearly stated at the outset. Indeed, you might think of objectives and evaluation as opposite sides of the same coin. The more clearly and precisely you state the objectives, the more likely you will be able to obtain precise data on the outcome or results of the instructional process. Using this approach, you can specify objectives in terms of students' performance or behaviors that are readily observable and that can be easily evaluated by a criterion measure of acceptable performance. Thus the name behavioral (or performance) objectives. These are examples of objectives phrased in behavioral terms.

The student is able to:

recall the cardinal directions.

estimate population growth.

form the concept of population density.

Note that the italicized words above are quite specific and indicate well-defined intellectual processes. The processes have been discussed earlier in this text. They indicate clearly what the student is expected to do. You can use a checklist or an observation form to verify that the student achieved the required task.

In contrast, vague or ambiguous words do not provide help for evaluation since they do not identify readily observable learning behaviors. Here are some examples of vague or ambiguous objectives:

To *know* the major rivers and capital cities
To *understand* the growth of large cities
To *appreciate* the importance of transportation routes.

Despite the fact that such words as *know, understand*, and *appreciate* are commonly used as objectives, they give no evidence of a specific outcome that can be easily recognized and used as a basis for objective evaluation.

Developing Instructional Objectives in Social Studies

Stating an objective in behavioral or performance terms means that the objective must tell what the students are doing when they demonstrate their achievement of the objective. Table 16.1 consists of action verbs classified as

The teacher in this photograph is providing this student with constructive feedback in order to enhance her understanding and retention. (*Source*: Terri Malinowski, Northshore School District, Seattle.)

TABLE 16.1. A Sample of Strong Action Verbs

Cognitive Processes	Affective Processes	Social Studies Skills
to recall	to prefer	to construct (a model)
to recite	to choose	to draw (a map)
to describe	to believe in	to interpret (symbols)
to identify	to react positively or	to locate (countries)
to compare	negatively toward	to identify (time zones)
to contrast	to respond to	to measure (distance)
to evaluate	to judge as good or bad	to determine slope (from a
to solve	to approve	contour map)
to apply	to comply with	to translate (color codes)
to observe	to acclaim	to show distortion of
to analyze	to react with pleasure	various map projections

cognitive or affective processes or as social studies skills. Each of these is a recognizable action that you can observe and record on a checklist or an observation record. These action words are combined with appropriate social studies content to complete the objective as shown in Table 16.2.

CRITERIA OF ACCEPTABLE PERFORMANCE

Performance objectives are usually stated in ways such that the demonstrated performance is either evident or it is not. In the checklist shown in Figure 16.1, an individual student's progress is reported in terms of objectives ac-

TABLE 16.2. Combining an Action Verb with Social Studies Content

The student will be able to . . .

recall . . . the names of the continents

compare . . . population distributions

develop the concept of . . . population density

apply . . . the principles of a grid coordinate system to a hypothetical country

estimate . . . population growth

point out . . . areas of greatest distortion on a Mercator projection

explain why . . . windward slopes receive greater precipitation than leeward slopes

judge as good (or bad) . . . a system of land tenure

react with sympathy . . . to evidence of hunger or poverty

be moved to action . . . to improve environmental quality

prefer (or choose) . . . a flood control project over preserving a district as a wilderness area

develop the generalization that . . . people's use of the land in a given region is a function of the attitudes, objectives, and technical skills of the population

As a result of this unit of work on _____ *population* _____ (TOPIC)		
_____ *Jerri Ann* _____ is able to. (STUDENT'S NAME)		Comments
1. Recall the names of the seven continents.	X	
2. Compare the population distribution patterns of New York, Chicago, and Seattle.	X	
3. Develop the concept "population density."		
4. Apply the principles of a grid coordinate system to a hypothetical country.	X	*See attached map completed in class*

FIGURE 16.1   Individual Progress Report.

complished. Note that Jerri Ann has not yet developed the concept *population density*. Rather than grade it with a traditional F, it is simply left blank, indicating that it still must be accomplished.

Here is where the teacher must make several important instructional decisions. Must every student accomplish every objective? If not, then how many and which ones shall constitute a basic or minimal mastery of the goal? Has enough of the important content been learned to provide a basis for future learning? Are some content goals essential prerequisites that cannot be omitted? Generally, teachers set a mastery goal of 80 percent of a lesson's major objectives. This includes all those that are considered minimum essentials. Figure 16.2 shows a class record of goals accomplished. Note that item 1 is marked with an asterisk to indicate that it is an essential. All students have accomplished it.

As result of this unit of work on _____ *population* _____ (TOPIC) the students are able to	Chris	John	Mark	Robert	Connie	Matt	Stuart	Carolyn	Allison	Joey	Jay Dee
* 1. Compare population distribution.	✓	✓	✓	✓	✓	✓	✓	✓	✓	✓	✓
2. Explain the concept of "population density."	✓		✓	✓			✓			✓	
3. Apply principles of the grid coordinate system.	✓			✓		✓		✓			✓

FIGURE 16.2   Class Progress Report.

Given the need to individualize instruction and to provide higher levels of accomplishment for various students, several other approaches to setting criteria measures are possible. The simplest approach is to increase the quantities in the examples given above, for example, nine out of 10 responses correct, 100 percent accuracy, or the same task completed in a shorter time. Such criteria test for greater retention, accuracy, or speed of learning, but the learning task remains essentially the same. There is no *qualitative* increase in the intellectual level of learning or in social studies content goals.

Qualitative increase in the learning level may be accomplished by specifying more complex, sophisticated, and higher-order processes of cognitive or affective learning. We refer you back to the discussion of Bloom's *Taxonomy of Educational Objectives* in Chapter 4. The list of key words given at each of the levels of the *taxonomy* can be used as verbs for specifying instructional objectives at different cognitive levels. Examples of affective processes are listed in Table 16.1.

Here are examples of instructional goals which specify more complex tasks:

Given data from the 1960, 1970, and 1980 censuses, the student will be able to construct a bar graph showing the change in population for the following cities: New York, Cleveland, Chicago, and Pittsburgh. The student will propose several hypotheses that could explain the changes in population.

Students can project an estimate of the 2000 population of the same cities using the same data from the 1960, 1970, and 1980 censuses. Assume that there are no changes in basic demographic trends.

Another approach to setting different levels of performance is to require a more creative approach to the task. For example, the criterion may be to present two or more *different* approaches or solutions to the same problem, rather than to seek a single, convergent solution. To use some of the higher-level thinking processes we discussed in Chapters 3 and 15, students may be asked to provide two or more alternate solutions in a decision-making situation. Each might be equally feasible or might solve the problem, although one might be preferable to the other.

IS THE MINIMUM ALSO THE MAXIMUM?

As an outgrowth of public demands that schools be more accountable for student performance (or the lack of it), many states have established state-wide minimum competency tests in basic skill areas. Passing these tests is often a prerequisite for high school graduation. Many educators have expressed concern that the basic or minimum levels of performance specified will become—by default—the maximum as well. To date, many of the minimum skills specified in social studies areas represent low-level, often trivial goals that will hardly prepare citizens for the rapidly changing world of the twenty-first century. You need to be alert to this danger and to be sure to specify goals that, while tailored to individual differences, stress imagination,

Students need to receive feedback in a variety of situations and settings in order to increase their knowledge and skills in the social studies. (*Source*: Robb Mitchell, Lake Washington School District [Seattle] [first 3 photographs]; Edna Kellman, Seattle Public Schools [last photograph].)

creativity, and higher thought processes. You must challenge students so that (to paraphrase Tennyson), their reach exceeds their grasp, else what are schools for?

METHODS OF EVALUATION

There are many methods of evaluation you may use to assess student performance. They range from informal observation and simple checklists to formally administered standardized tests and national assessment programs. Some of the most commonly used techniques include

Autobiographies	Interviews
Activity records	Log books
Attitudinal measures	National assessment tests
Anecdotal records	Observation records
Behavior journals	Performance charts
Cumulative records	Charts
Class diaries	Questionnaires
Checklists	Semantic differential tests
Committee reports	Sociometric measures
Collections of student work	Standardized tests
Class projects	Teacher-made tests
Group discussions	

In order to provide a more systematic framework for discussing the many techniques listed above, we have chosen to focus our discussion of evaluation strategies around several major dimensions of the social studies. This approach will put the evaluation techniques into an appropriate context and will show how more than one method can be used to gather data on the same goal.

EVALUATING THE RESULTS OF SOCIAL INQUIRY: FACTS, CONCEPTS, GENERALIZATIONS, AND THEORIES

We have placed a heavy emphasis upon the importance of social inquiry and its products (Chapter 3), questioning strategies (Chapter 4), and a variety of specialized social studies skills (Chapter 5). In the following sections we shall suggest a variety of evaluation measures that are both simple and effective for gathering data on student performance in these areas. Notice that we place emphasis upon simplicity and ease of use. Our experience is that when evaluation measures are complex, time-consuming, or difficult to administer, teachers simply will not use them, no matter how much potential data they promise. It is far better to use a variety of information measures on a regular and systematic basis than to rely upon one or two tests during the term.

In Chapter 3 we discussed the products of social inquiry: facts, concepts, generalizations, and theories. You can use a variety of techniques to assess whether students have acquired these important learning products and whether or not they can use them in making reflective decisions. Some of these include

Anecdotal records	Teacher-made tests
Group discussions	Samples of student work
Checklists	Class projects

Anecdotal Records An anecdotal record is a brief, factual record of a student's performance, noting what a student has done but avoiding judgmental inferences. Table 16.3 illustrates a few entries from Manuel's record. The entries are related to learning the concept of historical time. He is in the fifth grade.

This extract from an anecdotal record relates Manuel's progress in developing the notions of order and sequence as parts of the concept of chronological (or historical) time. It has the advantage of providing a detailed record of learning diagnosis and what was done to develop the prerequisite notion of sequence. The obvious disadvantage is that careful reporting, even though brief, does take time to do. Yet the analytic detail in Manuel's case is of far more value than a simple checklist that only shows he has not mastered the concept.

Group Discussion Group discussions are often an important vehicle for having a class formulate generalizations about several samples of data that have been logged into a data retrieval chart for easy study and analysis. See, for example, Table 5.3, "The Political System in Three Nations." Assuming that research groups have filled in the chart with data from the three countries, discussion will no doubt be lively as students compare and contrast political experiences under the three political systems. Using an informal checklist like

TABLE 16.3. Anecdotal Record

Sept. 25 Manuel seems to have trouble with the concept of *historical time* and a sense of chronology.

Sept. 26 Today I worked separately with Manuel. He read a story about Columbus. He could retell most of the important facts in correct sequence.

Oct. 1 Class began to develop a time line of European explorers who came to America. Manuel helped draw in the lines and markers for 100-year intervals.

Oct. 2 Rosalie worked with Manuel to make up a list of explorers. Needed much practice to put them in order. He is still confused and uncertain about how to arrange years in order.

Oct. 4 M. put explorers and dates on 3 × 5″ cards and moved them back and forth on his desk. Success! This worked. He could now arrange them from earliest to latest and vice versa. He now has the idea of sequence. But the notion that 1492 is almost 500 years ago still has no meaning for M.

that shown in Table 16.4, you can evaluate both the *process* of arriving at the generalization and the *validity* of the generalization itself. The students arrived at the following generalizations:

1. In each of the three societies, some individuals and groups are authorized to make decisions that all citizens must obey.
2. The ways in which the three nations determine which groups will make binding political decisions differ.

As is evident from Table 16.4, the criteria for evaluation relate to both the process of forming the generalization and its validity. The teacher listens carefully to the discussion and checks off the items as the discussion goes along or at its end. When students have had some experience with the process of generalizing, they can use the same checklist as a means of self-evaluation. Notice that the criteria refer almost entirely to the data base and the students' use of it, thus helping to make the evaluation as objective as possible, yet keeping the instrument informal.

The same process can be used with simpler content and with younger students. In Chapter 10, for example, we discussed the concept of *role* and how it was developed within the family. In many primary grades, a class studies families in its own community and then studies families in other parts of the world for a cross-cultural comparison. The chart shown in Table 16.4 could easily be modified with simpler language to assess generalizations formed about roles of mothers and fathers in various parts of the world (e.g., our town, Japan, and Nigeria). Table 16.5 shows a modified version for use in primary grades.

Here again, the emphasis is upon the students' development and use of the data about mothers' roles in different cultural settings, but the checklist's language is simplified. The chart could be filled out entirely by the teacher,

TABLE 16.4. Checklist for Student Discussion of a Generalization

Criteria	Yes	No	Comments
1. Are all data accurate?			
2. Are there data from all three samples, U.S., U.K., and U.S.S.R.?			
3. Are comparisons and contrast based upon the data?			
4. Do the data support the generalization?			
5. Is it accurate (true) for all three samples?			
6. Are there obvious exceptions that might disprove it?			
7. Is it stated as a testable statement?			

TABLE 16.5. Generalization Checklist for Primary Grades

Criteria	Yes	No	Comments
1. Do we have information about mothers' roles in all three places?			
2. Are there things that are the same in all places?			
3. Are there things that are different?			
4. Do we have facts to back up our statements?			
5. Are the statements true in all three places?			

or the students could determine whether the criteria had been met through group discussion. Students could enter the check marks with the teacher's help.

Teacher-Made Tests   Teacher-made tests are one of the most widely used forms of evaluation of social science facts, concepts, generalizations, and theories. There are many formats, including true/false (or yes/no) responses, multiple choice, sentence completion (fill in the blanks), and open-ended essays. They are relatively easy to give and to score and most teachers believe them to be impartial or "objective."

There are limitations, however, that must be considered. Good test items require students to think carefully before answering, and they are not easy to construct. Too often, test items deal only with low-level thought processes or with trivial content knowledge. Moreover, the skills needed for taking objective tests are often not the same skills developed in learning the content. Students must learn to "psych" out what the teacher expects in the test items and to work under the pressure of time limits.

Since many of the technical aspects of constructing teacher-made tests are beyond the scope of this book, we shall provide here only a few illustrations of sample test items. Each of the items shown in Table 16.6 is keyed to a social science concept that forms the organizing focus of a unit on water resources. The items were also written at various levels of Bloom's *Taxonomy*, to test a wide range of higher-level thinking abilities.

Hints for Writing Test Items. To help you write test items for teacher-made tests, here are a few hints to keep in mind.

True/False Items

1. T/F items are best used to test knowledge recall or comprehension level knowledge.
2. Use this type only for information that is genuinely true or false. Avoid material that may be open to interpretation.

TABLE 16.6. Sample Test Items Written at Various Levels of Bloom's *Taxonomy*

Taxonomy Level and Concept	Test Item
1. Knowledge (watershed)	A watershed is a a) wet region of land b) building for storing water c) marshy area d) land area that drains into a stream or river or lake
2. Application (landform)	The best name for this group—*mountain, plateau, hill*—is a) region b) landform c) area d) town
3. Application (river system)	People can control the flow of water by a) planting trees and building dams b) building dams and filtering water c) using water meters and planting trees d) filtering water and planting trees
4. Comprehension (landforms)	Which of the following have caused *natural* changes in landforms? a) roads and highways b) glaciers and fast streams c) dynamite and rainfall d) running water and irrigation
5. Comprehension (supply and demand)	As more people draw upon the same water supply, the amount of available water tends to a) increase b) decrease c) remain the same d) evaporate
6. Application (watershed)	Which of the following would you consider when searching for a water supply for a large city? a) the closest stream and pure water b) a natural lake c) pure water d) an abundant supply and pure water
7. Analysis (population)	Population decreases in a community most likely result from a) decline in the number of businesses b) better schools in the community c) better jobs elsewhere d) decline in businesses and better jobs elsewhere
8. Analysis (supply and demand)	Examine the conclusions given below. Using the charts in Figure 16.3, decide which *statement* is the best conclusion. a) City A is a rapidly growing community and does not have enough water for the people. b) City B is entitled to help from the state as it has the greatest need for a new water supply. c) City C is experiencing many problems with water shortage.
9. Analysis (supply and demand)	Choose the statement that explains your conclusion. a) City A is near to us and we have relatives there. If they want more water they should have it.

TABLE 16.6. (*continued*)

Taxonomy Level and Concept	Test Item
	b) The governor lives in City B, and therefore they need help from the state to provide them with a new water supply. c) Many people have moved into City C, and the rainfall has been constantly decreasing. d) All three cities need more water due to growth in population. e) All three cities are experiencing water problems due to decreasing rainfall.

Factory and Fish

A committee has been working on a problem of what to do about a large factory in their town. This factory is polluting the river, and as a result many of the fish in the river have died. Some of the townspeople think the factory should be made to move out of town. Other townspeople feel the factory is more important than the fish. There are many people in town who work there.

Taxonomy Level and Concept	Test Item
10. Evaluation (technology)	What do you think the committee should do? Choose the best solution. a) The factory should be made to move out of the town. b) The factory should be allowed to stay and operate as it is. c) The factory should be allowed to stay if it installs a purifying plant.
11. Evaluation (technology)	Choose the statement below that best explains the solution you chose for question 10. a) The plant should be made to move. If it moves, there are other jobs in other factories for the workers. They will only have to travel a short distance. b) The factory should be allowed to stay. The job is more important than the fish. People who fish can fish in other streams. c) They should install a purifying plant. No matter where the plant moves, it will have to do this, as no one will allow the plant to pollute the river. d) The town should help to pay for the purification plant since many townspeople fish in the river. e) Make the plant move, since we don't want factories dirtying our town. Besides, the more factories, the more people and we might have to build a new school.
12. Synthesis (supply and demand, river systems, watershed, landforms, technology, population)	Suppose that a large city is in need of a new water supply. Briefly describe the factors you would consider in searching for this supply.
13. Synthesis (supply and demand, river systems, watershed, landforms, technology, population)	Suppose you are told by the town council that it thinks your town will not have an adequate water supply in 10 years. Outline a plan to test whether its belief is true or false.

SOURCE: Adapted from Alberta P. Sebolt, "The Construction of a Test for Concept Learning and Identification of the Cognitive Processes Required," *Curriculum Model No. 1: Water Resources* (ERIC Document No. ED 040 892.)

FIGURE 16.3 Rainfall and population graphs for three different cities. Each of thes_ cities has asked the state to help them find a new supply of water. The state says they can help only some of the cities this year.

3. Avoid words like *always*, *sometimes*, or *never*. They tend to confuse or raise suspicions in the students' minds.
4. Keep the sentences short, clear, and positively stated.
5. Avoid negatives such as not, none, or neither-nor.
6. Use yes/no for younger students. This prevents confusion in writing the letters T and F.

Samples:

1. ___T___ Albany is the capital of New York.
2. ___F___ The earth is the center of the universe.
3. ___F___ Chicago is a city on the Gulf of Mexico.

Sentence Completion

1. Fill in the blanks are best used for very specific knowledge recall items.
2. The main statement should contain enough information to give the students an idea of the response sought.
3. Decide what alternative responses you will accept as correct. (Be prepared for surprises from some students!)
4. Decide whether you will penalize for incorrect spelling.

Samples:

1. The city of Japan with the largest population is _____ .
2. _____ wrote the Declaration of Independence.
3. Congress makes our national laws. It is made up of two parts, the House of Representatives and the _____ .

Multiple Choice Items

1. These can be used to test a wide variety of higher-level thought processes. See examples in Table 16.6.
2. Be sure that alternatives represent reasonable choices that will require students to choose carefully among them. Avoid obviously wrong or absurd choices.
3. Don't intentionally try to trick or mislead students with cunningly worded items. Questions should be forthright even if difficult.
4. Avoid items that test obscure trivia.
5. Vary the place of the correct response. Don't establish a pattern that the third response is always the correct one.

See Table 16.6 for samples.

Essay Tests

1. Essays provide the best test of learning at the analysis, synthesis, and evaluation levels.
2. Give clear directions about what is expected, how the theme or topic should be handled, and the maximum length.
3. Prepare a short list of criteria for judging the essay and use it as a basis for grading and for giving feedback to the students on their performance. If necessary, list factual data that must be presented for correct response.
4. If possible, grade the essay blind (i.e., without knowing the student's name) to help increase objectivity.
5. Place a premium on unusually creative responses; encourage independence of thought and judgment; reward provocative and highly original thinking.

See Table 16.6, items 12 and 13, for samples.

In summary, teacher-made tests are good measures for assessing students' learning of facts, concepts, generalizations, and theories. If carefully designed, they can be used to evaluate a wide range of thinking levels. Remember, however, that such tests have as many weaknesses as they do strengths; they are not necessarily superior to the many other informal measures mentioned above. A good checklist, like those shown in Tables 16.4 and 16.5, can produce more useful evaluation data than a number of hastily prepared tests dealing only with factual recall or low-level thinking processes.

EVALUATING THINKING SKILLS

Throughout this book, and particularly in Chapter 5, we have stated that thinking skills are an important component of the social studies curriculum. It is equally important to evaluate whether or not students have developed such skills and how well they are able to use them.

In Chapter 5, we discussed a number of thinking processes including describing, inferring, analyzing, conceptualizing, generalizing, applying generalizations to new situations, and making decisions. Since we are here looking at the *process* of thinking, informal measures are more appropriate for evaluation than formal tests, which are better used to assess the product or outcome of the thinking process. Some informal measures include

Charts	Interviews
Checklists	Observations
Group discussions	Samples of student work
Anecdotal records	Student log books

Describing

The activities suggested on pp. 140–141 all require students to observe some activity and record what they saw. Thus, a list dictated to a teacher by young children or student log books recording what pupils ate in the cafeteria or who did the shopping on Saturday morning become the primary sources of evidence. What is important is the criteria applied to the lists. A checklist might include questions or criteria like

1. Were all events recorded?
2. Did anything unusual happen?
3. Did you notice any kind of pattern of events?
4. Do others agree the record is accurate?
5. Is sufficient detail given to create a mental image?
6. Is vocabulary expressive yet still accurate?

Note that the activities suggested range from observing and counting food choices at lunch to describing characteristics of French Impressionist painting, or the ways women are depicted on TV commercials. Thus, students must learn not only how to describe in objective detail (what and how many), but also how to describe in qualitative terms, using rich and varied vocabulary, yet still retaining accuracy. A checklist developed around the above criteria provides a good measure for evaluating describing skills.

Making Inferences

To make an inference means to draw a conclusion or make a deduction from facts or observations. Here again, informal measures provide good evaluation devices. Building upon the activities mentioned above for describing, you can examine charts or logs with students. You can ask questions to nudge the students into giving an explanation or interpretation of who bought more groceries on Saturday morning, men or women:

How do you explain this situation?
What can you conclude from these facts?
Why might there be more women (or men) shopping at this time?
What might men (or women) be doing at that time?
Could you conclude that women like to shop more than men?
Could you conclude that it is a woman's role to do the grocery shopping on Saturday morning?

The above questions are designed to tease out inferences from the students, and to derive meaning from their observations. For more advanced students the criteria are stated in logical terms:

Are the inferences logically deduced from the data?
Are other conclusions equally plausible? (Many men work on Saturdays, therefore women do the shopping.)
Has the inference gone beyond the data to support it?

In summary, the teacher observes group (or individual) discussions carefully using a checklist based on the above criteria to record evidence of students' ability to make inferences.

Analyzing Information

When students analyze information, they identify its parts and establish logical relationships between the parts and the whole. In teaching the skills of analyzing social science material, we most often want students to separate facts from opinions, assumptions, or conclusions. Another skill is the ability to determine whether facts are presented to support a conclusion or generalization. Lastly, it is important that students be able to analyze materials such as films, posters, slogans, or TV commercials to recognize such forms as stereotypes, propaganda, racism, chauvinism or sabre-rattling.

Checklists offer one of the simplest ways of evaluating students' progress in analyzing information, as shown in Table 16.7.

Teacher-made tests can also be used to evaluate a student's ability to analyze information. For example:

Directions. Read the article "Teddy Roosevelt Urges War with Spain." It appeared in the *New York World* in 1898.

1. The statement that the USS Maine exploded in Havana harbor is a (an):

_____ fact   _____ conclusion
_____ inference   _____ assumption

TABLE 16.7. Checklist for Analyzing Information

Jane is able to:	Yes	No	Comments
1. Identify facts and relate to generalizations.			
2. Distinguish inferences from facts.			
3. Point out unstated assumptions.			
4. Determine whether facts support a conclusion.			
5. Recognize propaganda, bias, and chauvinism.			
6. Identify sarcasm, satire, and irony.			
7. Identify main theme and subtopics.			

2. The statement that all the Cuban people support immediate independence from Spain is a (an):

_____ fact   _____ assumption
_____ conclusion   _____ inference

3. Teddy Roosevelt's statements about American power and might, his claim of sole right to control the Caribbean, and his call for an immediate attack upon Spanish forces are called:

_____ prejudice   _____ sarcasm
_____ jingoism   _____ propaganda

Conceptualizing

The role of concepts in social science inquiry has been discussed at length in Chapter 3, and two strategies for concept formation and concept attainment were presented in Chapter 5. Teacher-made test items for concept learning have already been presented in Table 16.6. Here we are concerned with the skill of conceptualizing. Once again, one of the easiest and most direct sources of evidence regarding students' ability to form or attain concepts is close observation of individuals or small groups while they are directly involved in the process. The checklist shown in Table 16.8 takes its format directly from the elements of the strategy.

If the deductive concept attainment strategy had been used, the teacher would follow the basic strategy shown in Table 5.5 (p. 164). The teacher assesses the students' mastery by asking them to identify examples of the concept from a list of examples and nonexamples of it. The student then defines the concept. For example:

Which of the following are transportation vehicles?

_____   automobile   _____   airplane
_____   bicycle   _____   ship

TABLE 16.8. Checklist for Concept Formation

Julie is able to:	Yes	No	Comments
1. Observe and list data.			
2. Put similar things together in groups.			
3. Identify what characteristics are common in each group.			
4. Rearrange things into other groups if other characteristics seem obvious or more logical.			
5. Give a name or label to the group.			
6. State a definition of the group that correctly applies to things in the group.			

——— bed   ——— helicopter
——— rickshaw   ——— seesaw

The students might define *transportation vehicle* as "a thing you can get on or into that will take you somewhere faster than you could walk there." They might also add, "You can get on a bed or a seesaw but it doesn't take you anywhere." Obviously, the phrasing is that of young children, but the essence of the definition is there.

EVALUATING DECISION-MAKING AND CITIZEN ACTION

In Chapter 15, we developed an extensive rationale and presented a variety of strategies for decision-making and citizen action. We also discussed the skills related to these two areas in Chapter 5. Here we shall present briefly a number of evaluation measures that can be used with these important processes. They include

Charts   Student logs
Checklists   Attitudinal measures
Student diaries   Case study reports
Anecdotal records   Interviews with students

Our model for the decision-making process is presented in Figure 15.4. The schematic drawing in Figure 15.3 shows the concept of a decision-making tree and Table 15.5 shows how a variety of alternative courses of action and their possible consequences might look when put in chart or poster form. Table 16.9 is a chart for evaluating decision-making ability. It

TABLE 16.9. Chart for Evaluating Decision-Making Ability

A. Decision-problem: _____

B. Related knowledge (identify concepts and generalizations): _____

_____

_____

C. Value position (clarification and identification): _____

_____

D. Identifying alternatives: Predicting consequences of each:

_____   _____

_____   _____

_____   _____

_____   _____

E. Ordering alternatives (which is most consistent with value position identified above?):

1. _____

2. _____

3. _____

4. _____

F. Acting (in a way consistent with values, willingness to accept possible consequences of action chosen):

_____

_____

_____

TABLE 16.10. Checklist for Evaluating Decision-Making Skills

Sonya is able to:	Yes	No	Comments
1. Identify related knowledge appropriate to the problem.			
2. Identify and clarify values involved and own position.			
3. List alternative course of action.			
4. Predict possible consequences.			
5. Rank order alternatives consistent with value position.			
6. Choose a course of action consistent with values.			
7. Act upon decision; willing to accept possible consequences.			

provides a means to log in all the essential components of the process and identify what is missing. A checklist such as shown in Table 16.10 records student performance on the process.

EVALUATING CITIZEN ACTION AND PARTICIPATION

As we discussed in Chapter 15, students should have opportunities to follow up decision-making processes with direct involvement in some form of citizen action or participation. The key goal of the social studies program is to help students develop a greater sense of personal, social, and civic efficacy. In short, students should develop strong and positive attitudes that (1) they can make important and worthwhile contributions to dealing with social problems; (2) they can work effectively with others to solve such problems; and (3) when working with others, they can find effective means to influence public policy. Put even more simply, students who have had good experiences with citizen action programs in schools should develop strong beliefs that (1) "I have something worthwhile to say, so I will speak out"; (2) "Together we can get something done about this"; and (3) "My vote counts and we can fight City Hall."

None of the above statements should suggest a naïvely simplistic approach to the problem of citizen participation in government. We are fully aware of the power and importance of money, lobbies, and special interest groups, entrenched bureaucracies, election politics, and political alignments. What we are more concerned about are the pervasive citizen attitudes of *apathy, helplessness,* and *alienation* from the entire political process. Such attitudes are expressed in statements like "What good will it do? Who will listen to me? I can't get any answers at City Hall. My vote won't count. You can't fight City Hall. Politicians control things."

In evaluating the role of citizen participation and action, you must pay close attention to the students' expression of feelings, beliefs, and attitudes about participation in the political process. In evaluating the wide array of activities suggested in Chapter 15, you may use informal devices like

Student diaries	Class logs
Role playing	Anecdotal records
Student interviews	Student reports
Attitudinal measures	

The important point in using the above measures is that you must look for expression of student beliefs or attitudes or create situations, such as role playing or class dramas, in which such attitudes can be expressed.

An attitudinal scale like the one shown in Table 16.11 is a useful device. The scale is designed to measure the strength of attitudes and runs from "strongly agree" through "uncertain" to "strongly disagree." The open-ended

TABLE 16.11. Attitudinal Measure for Citizen Action

Name: Alexandra		Project: Visits to elderly at Peterson House			
Attitude	SA	A	U	D	SD
1. This project was important to me.					
2. I felt free to discuss it in class.					
3. I made some good suggestions in planning the class visits.					
4. The director of the Peterson House was interested and helpful in getting this project started.					
5. Planning with others in the group helped make the plan workable.					
6. I believe we did something useful.					
7. I am willing to get involved in another project like this.					

What I liked best: _____

What I liked least: _____

Things we could do better: _____

_____

questions at the end of the inventory provide further opportunity for students, feedback on the class project and their role in it.

EVALUATING MAP AND GLOBE SKILLS

As we pointed out in Chapter 5, map and globe skills are very important elements in the social studies program. Students must not only know what types of maps are available, but also how to use them, and what limitations they have. But first, a word of caution. For some unexplained reason, many teachers and those citizens involved with back-to-basics groups seem to have placed an inordinate and excessive emphasis upon map and globe skills, particularly the rote memorization of place location—countries, rivers, and capital cities—cardinal directions, and latitude and longitude using antiquated Mercator style maps. Perhaps it is a desire to return to the "good old days" of what they learned in school, or perhaps a belief that this knowledge is fixed, true, and certain and can be tested objectively. Important though map and globe skills are, they are not the entire curriculum, and emphasis upon them should be kept within the perspective of the total social studies curriculum.

A number of the evaluation measures we have already described can be used to evaluate map and globe skills. These include

Teacher-made tests   Checklist
Student-made maps or scale models   Standardized tests

Teacher-Made tests

These are the most common evaluation measures. The several types discussed above and illustrated in Table 16.6 lend themselves well to evaluating map and global skills. Avoid the tendency, however, of having too many knowledge-recall questions, simply because they are so easy to construct.

Student-Made maps

Here is another good source of data for evaluation. You can devise checklists to evaluate a neighborhood map, such as shown in Figure 5.2, using criteria such as these:

1. Are the major streets shown?
2. Are they correctly related to one another?
3. Are major buildings correctly placed and marked with proper symbols?
4. Can students show where they live on the map?
5. Can students mark cardinal directions?

Building Scale Models

All too frequently teachers shy away from class projects such as constructing models of physical features of the land using sand tables, clay, papier-mâché, or other construction materials, or building scale models of a landscape, a mountain range, or a model of a local town. Perhaps these teachers fear the projects will be too messy, take too long to complete, or create too much confusion in an otherwise well-ordered classroom. Too bad! For students (and adults too!) love to "goosh around" in gooey papier-mâché or in soft, wet clay. It appeals to the tactile sense of the fingers and helps to develop a keen sense of height and depth, smooth and rugged, that no set of colors on a topographical map can convey. What a tremendous way to teach scale in three dimensions: build coastlines, indent harbors, create great mountain ranges and smooth out wide flat plains!

Models can be evaluated with a student-developed checklist much like the one below:

1. Is the general contour accurate?
2. Are physical features generally correct in shape, location, and relative size?
3. If a scale of miles or altitude were used, would the model be generally accurate?

Note that the criteria do not emphasize precise accuracy, only a general sense of accuracy and a reasonable attention to scale (in the case of older students). Remember that the goal is to have fun learning about geography, not to become expert cartographers. We certainly wish to encourage this form of learning when evaluating map and globe skills.

EVALUATING TIME AND CHRONOLOGY CONCEPTS AND SKILLS

Time and chronology concepts and skills are among the most difficult in the social studies field, largely because they are abstract, difficult to comprehend, and have few concrete referents in the life experience of students. We provided a number of activities in Chapter 5. Because these skills tend to be abstract, teachers should place more emphasis upon informal measures than formal ones. Too often test items tend to be at the knowledge-recall level only. Some of the evaluation measures that can be used include

Anecdotal records	Class projects (e.g.,
Teacher-made tests	time lines or family
Checklists	genealogy charts)

In Table 16.3 we gave an extract of an anecdotal record and used the concept of chronology to illustrate how it could be used as an evaluation measure. The student's progress in learning the concepts of order and sequence are carefully noted by the teacher. This could be supplemented by a checklist of other specific concepts and skills.

The Family Genealogy Chart

This is another device for teaching the concept of time as it relates to family and social history. Here, chronological time can be extended in meaning from "long, long ago" (or "once upon a time" when reading stories) to so many generations ago. This can also be stated as "how many grandparents ago?" The teacher can ask relevant questions that provide criteria for evaluation using a checklist:

1. Does the chart show several generations?
2. When looking at a family photo of mother, daughter, grandmother and great-grandmother, can students define the concept *generation?*
3. Using the photo mentioned above, can students take the date when each person was born and place it on a time line?
4. Using the time line developed above, can students calculate the average number of years in a generation?
5. Can students correctly place significant national or world events on the family time line?

Criteria such as these provide abundant data to evaluate the growth of the concepts *generation* and *chronology.* They also provide data to evaluate the skills of placing significant social and national events in chronological order and establishing meaningful personal relationships between them.

EVALUATING GROUP SKILLS

Group skills are an essential goal of the social studies program, yet it is surprising how often they are ignored as specific areas for teaching and evaluation. We discussed in Chapter 5 many ways of developing skills for working in groups, including both leadership and group membership (participant) rules. Some useful evaluation measures are:

Teacher observation	Checklists
Student interviews	Autobiographical records
Anecdotal records	Attitudinal measures
Role playing	

Checklists are frequently used for evaluating group skills. The example given in Table 5.4 uses appropriate criteria and emphasizes many of the positive and effective group characteristics shown in Table 5.3. Group membership is equally important and students must learn not only how to lead, but also how to participate effectively when someone else is leading the group. Table 5.5 presents two forms for evaluating group working relationships, particularly in the primary grades.

TABLE 16.12. Self-Evaluation Form for Group Leadership

Name: Neil M.			Role: Leader of Map-Making Group		
	SA	*A*	*U*	*D*	*SD*
1. I enjoy being a leader.					
2. I work easily with others in the group.					
3. I believe the group respects me when I am the leader.					
4. I am willing to let others be in charge of part of the work.					
5. I am willing to listen to suggestions from others.					
6. I am good at keeping the group at a task to complete its work.					
7. I can accept criticism from others without getting upset by it.					
8. I can praise or compliment others for good work.					
9. I can give help or encouragement to those who may need it.					
10. I am able to develop a good group spirit; that WE met OUR goal.					

TABLE 16.13. Self-Evaluation Form for Group Membership

Name: David E.	Role: Member of Map-Making Group				
	SA	A	U	D	SD
1. I can offer suggestions easily.					
2. I help keep the group focused on the task.					
3. I support the leader when he/she is right.					
4. I can work cooperatively with others in the group.					
5. I make positive and constructive criticisms.					
6. I feel good about our group and what it is doing.					
7. I enjoy working with other people in a group, even if I am not the leader.					

Attitudinal measures are another means for evaluating growth in group skills. A self-evaluation measure such as that shown in Table 16.12 can be a useful device to use in conjunction with a student conference to help the student relate his or her own perceptions of group performance to those of the teacher or other members of the group.

The self-evaluation chart in Table 16.11 presents a number of very important leadership criteria that can indicate areas of accomplishment or needed growth. More importantly, it provides a good yardstick for testing a student's own perceptions against those held by members of the group (which may not always be as positive as one's own). Conversely, a student who is trying out a leadership role for the first time may also receive positive feedback and encouragement to help develop a stronger self-concept and a willingness to take a leadership role again.

Since people cannot be leaders in every situation, a similar self-evaluation chart could be developed for group membership or participation skills using some of the characteristics for effective groups shown in Table 5.5. Such a chart is shown in Table 16.13.

EVALUATING WRITING SKILLS

Writing skills are a very important part of the social studies program. While they are principally taught in the language arts, they need to be reinforced in the social studies. In Chapter 5 we discussed four types of writing: (1) summary, (2) synthesis, (3) analytic and critical, and (4) creative. Many activities were described for each type of writing. Some evaluation measures that can be used to assess writing skills include

Essay tests   Committee reports
Samples of student work   Checklists
Scripts for class plays   Imaginary diaries of famous people

Summary Writing

While being able to write accurate summaries is an important skill, it is too often overemphasized. The other three forms mentioned above are often neglected. Criteria for summary writing might include

1. Major points included.
2. Limited in detail.
3. Brief, to the point.
4. Conclusions/recommendations clearly listed.

Synthesis Writing

Synthesizing is an important skill that builds upon summary writing. But a synthesis is not achieved by adding two summaries together with a few linking words or sentences. Students must give evidence of being able to

1. Summarize in their own words two or more sources.
2. Show relationships between ideas or views expressed.
3. Identify points of agreement/disagreement; strengths/weaknesses, pros or cons.
4. Quote directly, or paraphrase longer quotes.
5. List references in a simple manner.

Analytical and Critical Writing

This is a goal most teachers like to aim for, but students get too little actual experience and even less evaluation of it. These skills have been discussed at length in Chapter 5 and evaluation measures for analytic thinking have been suggested in an earlier section of this chapter on thinking skills. Checklists for evaluating student written work should include such criteria as

1. Determining perspective or point of view
2. Separating fact from inference or opinion
3. Identifying bias, propaganda, or stereotypes
4. Relating minor parts to main idea or theme
5. Making judgments about the quality of facts presented, or ideas expressed
6. Making judgments about the overall worth or merit (or lack of it) of a speech, book, play, or report, using some criteria as the basis for critical judgment

Creative Writing

Unlike the other forms of writing discussed above, creative writing gives free rein to a student's creative and expressive talents. While it may involve some summary and some synthesis, these are only vehicles for expressing thoughts and feelings in new and novel ways. The activities suggested on p. 170 provide excellent opportunities for writing expressively and creatively about actual or likely historical events. Checklists for evaluating creative writing might include such criteria as

1. Novelty of approach
2. Imaginative portrayal of events or characters
3. Expressive and varied dialogue
4. New, imaginative solutions to old problems
5. Several solutions, each solving the problem, but in a different and perhaps novel way

SUMMARY

This chapter has presented a variety of techniques for evaluating instruction in social studies. These involve formal as well as informal approaches, with emphasis upon such measures as checklists, performance charts, teacher-made tests, anecdotal records and attitude measures. In each case we stressed the importance of developing relevant criteria and using these as means of assessing student progress toward instructional goals.

We discussed a number of forms of teacher-made tests, such as true/false, sentence completion, multiple choice and essay questions. We identified strengths, weaknesses, most appropriate uses, and gave many examples of each type. In the last section we discussed ways of evaluating each of the social studies skills discussed in Chapter 5. These included thinking skills, map and globe skills, time and chronology skills, group skills and writing skills. Throughout the chapter we made frequent cross-reference to ideas and activities developed in other parts of the book and related evaluation measures to them.

DISCUSSION QUESTIONS AND EXERCISES

1. Examine a curriculum guide from a local school district. How are instructional objectives expressed? If they are not written in behavioral or performance terms, try to rewrite some of them using the techniques presented in the first part of this chapter.
2. Teachers frequently use objective tests such as multiple choice, true/false, completion, or essay tests. What are some of the strengths and weaknesses of each type?
3. We have listed a variety of informal assessment techniques in this chapter,

such as checklists, anecdotal records, and attitudinal scales. What strengths and limitations do such measures have compared to the more formal measures mentioned in Discussion Question 2 above?

4. A group of students is preparing a play about a family in Massachusetts in 1820 that is considering moving westward to Ohio. What criteria and what techniques might you propose to evaluate this play? (Hint: Consider it from the point of view of social studies content, thinking skills, group skills, and creative writing.)

5. Students in the second grade have been studying their local community. The class has decided to make a model of the town on a large table. What criteria and techniques would you use to evaluate this project? Be sure to include group leader/member skills.

6. Demonstrate your understanding of the following key concepts and terms by writing or stating a brief definition for each of them. Give an example of each.

   a. evaluation
   b. behavioral/performance objective
   c. criteria for evaluation
   d. anecdotal record
   e. attitudinal measure
   f. analytical skills
   g. creative writing

FOR FURTHER READING

Beyer, Barry K. *Developing a Thinking Skills Program.* Boston: Allyn & Bacon, 1988.

Beyer, Barry K. *Practical Strategies for the Teaching of Thinking.* Boston: Allyn & Bacon, 1987.

Hunkins, Francis P. *Teaching Thinking Through Effective Questioning.* Needham Heights, MA: Christopher-Gordon Publishers, 1989.

Mehrens, William A., and Irvin J. Lehman. *Using Standardized Tests in Education.* White Plains, NY: Longman, 1986.

Sanders, Norris M. *Classroom Questions: What Kinds?* New York: Harper & Row, 1966.

Worthen, Blaine R., Walter R. Borg, and Karl R. White. *Measurement and Evaluation in the Schools.* White Plains, NY: Longman, 1989.

Index